BLURRING BOUNDARIES

Developing Writers, Researchers and Teachers

A Tribute to William L. Smith

Research and Teaching in Rhetoric and Composition
Michael M. Williamson and Peggy O'Neill, series editors

Basic Writing as a Political Act: Public Conversations About Writing and Literacies
Linda Adler-Kassner & Susanmarie Harrington

Culture Shock and the Practice of Profession: Training the Next Wave in Rhetoric and Composition
Virginia Anderson & Susan Romano

New Worlds, New Words: Exploring Pathways for Writing About and in Electronic Environments
John F. Barber & Dene Grigar (eds.)

The Hope and the Legacy: The Past Present and Future of "Students' Right" to Their Own Language
Patrick Bruch & Richard Marback (eds.)

Market Matters: Applied Rhetoric Studies and Free Market Competition
Locke Carter (ed.)

The Rhetoric and Ideology of Genre: Strategies for Stability and Change
Richard Coe, Lorelei Lingard, & Tatiana Teslenko (eds.)

In Search of Eloquence: Cross-Disciplinary Conversations on the Role of Writing in Undergraduate Education
Cornelius Cosgrove & Nancy Barta-Smith

Teaching/Writing in the Late Age of Print
Jeffrey Galin, Carol Peterson Haviland, & J Paul Johnson (eds.)

Rhetoric in(to) Science Inquiry: Style as Invention in the Pursuit of Knowledge
Heather Graves

Revision Revisited
Alice S. Horning

Multiple Literacies for the 21st Century
Brian Huot, Beth Stroble, & Charles Bazerman (eds.)

Identities Across Text
George H. Jensen

Against the Grain: Essays in Honor of Maxine Hairston
David Jolliffe, Michael Keene, Mary Trachel, & Ralph Voss (eds.)

Classroom Spaces and Writing Instruction
Ed Nagelhout & Carol Rutz

Toward Deprivatized Pedagogy
Becky Nugent & Diane Calhoun Bell

Unexpected Voices
John Rouse & Ed Katz

Directed Self-Placement: Principles and Practices
Dan Royer & Roger Gilles (eds.)

Who Can Afford Critical Consciousness?: Practicing a Pedagogy of Humility
David Seitz

BLURRING BOUNDARIES

Developing Writers, Researchers and Teachers

A Tribute to William L. Smith

edited by

Peggy O'Neill
Loyola College

HAMPTON PRESS, INC.
CRESSKILL, NJ 07626

Printed in the United States of America

Library of Congress Cataloging-in-Publication Data

Blurring boundaries : developing writers, researchers and teachers : a tribute to william l. smith / edited by Peggy O'Neill.
    p. cm. -- (Research and teaching in rhetoric and composition)
    Includes bibliographical references and index.
    ISBN 1-57273-707-7 (casebound) -- ISBN 1-57273-708-5 (perfectbound)
1. English language--Rhetoric--Study and teaching (Higher) 2. Academic writing--Study
    and teaching (Higher) 3. English teachers--Training of. I. O'Neill, Peggy, 1963- II.
    Smith, William, L., 1940-
    PE1404.B5894 2006
    808'.0420711--dc22

                2006033715

Hampton Press, Inc.
23 Broadway
Cresskill, NJ 07626

William L. Smith

CONTENTS

III. BEYOND THE CLASSROOM

THE URGE TO KNOW

A Tribute to Bill Smith

Peggy O'Neill

The idea for this volume began circulating many years ago before I even knew Bill. In 1994, Bill had left the University of Pittsburgh, where he held various positions in the English department; that happened to be the same year I entered graduate school. I began working with Bill via e-mail in fall 1995 as an editorial assistant for the journal *Assessing Writing* while a doctoral student at the University of Louisville. For the first couple of years, our e-mails were primarily focused on journal business. Gradually, Bill became my e-mail mentor—sending me encouragement as I struggled through a statistics course, letting me vent about the injustices of graduate school, responding to my dissertation writing, counseling me through my job search, and advising me about anything else that came up. His support became even more important once I moved into my first tenure-track job in Statesboro, Georgia. His pithy responses brightened my day as I struggled to adjust to life in a small southern town. We discussed topics as diverse as baseball, Web courses, showing dogs, teaching writing, academic politics, southern living, and so much else. All of this occurred through e-mail exchanges. I never met Bill face to face until March 2002—7 years after we met in e-mail—when the National Council of Teachers English (NCTE) spring conference was held in

Portland, Oregon, where Bill had moved after leaving the University of Pittsburgh.

Bill and his wife, Susan, hosted a dinner party for some of us at the conference. Everyone enjoyed themselves that evening; however, for me, it was a very special night. I finally got to meet Bill in person after all of our e-mail exchanges and stories that I had heard about him. My expectations were of course exceeded—Bill was more interesting, enthusiastic, amusing, and smarter than I had experienced in our online connection. That night also clinched my commitment to this volume. Previously, Mike Williamson, Brian Huot, and even Michael Moore had encouraged me to take on the task of editing a volume in tribute to Bill, but I had resisted—I was too busy; I wasn't even one of his real students; I barely "knew" him; I wasn't capable of doing it.

After meeting Bill in person that night, I decided to do the book. I still felt like a fraud because I had never been a student of Bill's nor worked on any research with him. I was even more intimidated by the idea of working with his students. In the end, however, it wasn't about me. It was about Bill and sharing his contributions with others. I wanted other researchers and teachers to understand the difference that one person can make to his or her students and ultimately to the field—through not only his research, but, even more importantly, through his students. In the hectic bureaucratic world of institutional life, folks like Bill are rare, but we all need more academics who are like him. This book is about Bill and his incredible work—not just the typical scholarly work manifested in publications and awards, but about the more important and less recognized work that Bill did as a teacher. For someone like Bill—someone not only committed to research and teaching, but also someone genuinely enthusiastic about both—a collection of work in his honor by his students and colleagues seems the only fitting tribute.

Gathering together the necessary people to bring this idea to fruition has been a challenge—more than I had anticipated. One reason is that Bill worked across education, composition, and linguistics. This meant envisioning a text that could address disparate disciplines and specialties that represented Bill's work and contributions. He did scholarly work in reading, sentence composing, writing assessment, teaching writing, computers and writing, and more. He directed dissertations in schools of education as well as English departments and served on many committees at other institutions. He also worked at several different institutions (e.g., Boston University, University of Georgia, and University of Pittsburgh) and collaborated with faculty and students across institutions (e.g., Carnegie Mellon and Indiana University of Pennsylvania). Besides his teaching and research, Bill was an active member in the profession, attending conferences, and serving on committees for organizations such as NCTE and American Educational Research Association (AERA), and serving as a reviewer or editorial board member for several journals (see Bill's Curriculum Vitae in the appendix for specific details).

After making the decision to go forward with a book, trying to corral Bill's graduate students became the biggest challenge. Most of his students seem to have developed into faculty members in his own image: enthusiastically committed to the profession, their students, and their research with too many commitments all around. In fact, many of Bill's students and former colleagues are very successful, nationally known scholars who get many professional requests and already have lots of commitments. My outsider status made connecting and convincing folks a little more difficult. So I connived with Susan, Bill's wife, and the work began.

Tracking down former students and colleagues and negotiating with their competing interests, schedules, and needs was a formidable task. Most folks I was able to connect with were enthusiastic, and most wanted to be included. The next challenge was figuring out how to be inclusive and make sense of the contributions because his students were spread across disciplines and fields representing a wide range of specialties within English and education. In the end, Bill's own career and interests became the inspiration for the collection's theme—blurring of boundaries. Bill crossed over among disciplines, departments, and institutions. He didn't let institutional or disciplinary boundaries limit his thinking, his ideas, or his students. He transcended traditional boundaries and so did his students. For example, Glynda Hull, whose dissertation Bill directed, received her PhD in English at the University of Pittsburgh and now works in the University of California Berkeley's Graduate School of Education. She also works in a university–community collaboration (which she writes about in her essay in this volume). Glynda is just one example of how Bill's students have stayed true to the spirit of inquiry Bill embodies, regardless of what department, field, or specialty they work in now. In addition to his students, several of the contributors are Bill's former collaborators and colleagues (e.g., Hayes, Koziol, Kirby). Their participation in this volume is a testament to Bill's collegial spirit. Bill envisioned research as a collaborative process as evidenced by the many co-authored works on his Curriculum Vitae, and it was an essential feature of the mentoring he offered students. Many of the contributors who worked directly with Bill, whether as graduate students or colleagues, have carried on this hallmark of Bill's work, submitting co-authored pieces for this collection.

Whether collaborating, or teaching, or researching, Bill's work is united by his "urge to know." No matter what he was focused on—syntax, writing prompts, placement essays, error rates, or teacher education—Bill's zeal for research was contagious, matched only by his commitment to teaching. In fact his research was deeply connected to his teaching, as several students explain in their contributions to this volume (e.g., Sommers, Huot, Moore, Land, and Miller). Bill excelled as a researcher and teacher: He didn't see these as separate endeavors, but rather concurrent ones. Learning, teaching, and researching were intertwined, cross-fertilizing each other. Contributors demonstrate the symbiotic relationship between researching and teaching in their essays (see especially Ruzich, Land, and Latchaw). Bill's commitment to research and teaching extended to his administrative work and service to the profession. Mentoring, research, teaching, and learning were all part of Bill's commitment to education. As he explained to me in an e-mail:

> What it all comes down to is the difference between education and training: One trains dogs, but one does not educate them. One trains others, but one educates one's self. Colleges, especially the undergraduate level, should be places where people can educate themselves (teachers do not do the educating; they create the environment). And education is best accomplished in a mentoring environment. Your work with Brian gave you the opportunity for an education (you worked your butt off and got that education). Brian didn't teach you; you learned from him. The difference is not subtle; it is one who is the agent. I can't "teach" you unless 1) you want to learn and 2) the conditions are right. (January, 27, 2001)

This book is a testament to the opportunities for learning that Bill created.

CONTENTS

The contents of the volume, then, speak across boundaries of disciplines, institutions, methodologies, and genres. Essays address topics of writing assessment, teaching writing, preparing teachers of English, graduate education, electronic technologies, community literacy and professional issues. Contributors write traditional research reports, personal reflections, analyses, as well as blurred genres that combine personal reflection with more traditional academic forms. Likewise, a variety of research approaches are included—teacher-research, textual analysis, case study, survey, and reviews of the research. Some essays are single authored, and many are collaborative. Uniting all of these works and underlying all of Bill's work is the urge to know.

The variety as well as the blurring and transgressions of forms, approaches, and topics represented in the chapters are the perfect tribute to Bill and his career. The chapters are organized by themes in Bill's own work. Part I is devoted to work on writing assessment. It opens with Brian Huot's (chap. 1) review of Bill's contributions to the field through his ground-breaking work on placement. Following are two chapters that review some of this early work and extend it. Michael Moore (chap. 2), who was one of the graduate students working with Bill in the early 1980s, examines the research on essay topics they did and moves forward to the essay topics in the new SAT. Robert Land (chap. 3), who also worked on this research as a graduate student, "tells the story of this ongoing line of inquiry and presents a sort of progress report" on some of the findings. Land reports on a survey of writing teachers and suggests that college-level writing teachers may belong to an entirely different discourse community than K–12 teachers.

These two chapters reveal not just the results of the inquiry Bill led, but also explain the story of that inquiry, which is critical but typically unrecorded. After getting an insider perspective on the research Bill did with his graduate students, chapter 4, "Adding Portfolios to the Placement Process," presents more recent placement research that springboards off Bill's work. Like Bill's work, it was carried out by a professor, Brian Huot, with his graduate students over several years. The longitudinal study uses the placement method Bill developed, which relies on teacher expertise, as a starting point for reading students' secondary portfolios to make decisions about placement into college composition. Concluding this part on writing assessment is Pamela Moss' (chap. 5) exhortation for literacy educators and measurement specialists to join in the theoretical discussions about validity. She urges professionals to stretch beyond their comfort zones to learn more about validity theory and to engage in the professional discussions about what validity offers for teachers, learners, and assessment specialists.

Part II, Research and Teaching, breaks down the boundary between research and teaching as contributors show how these two activities are intertwined. It opens with David Wallace's (chap. 6) chapter on attitude surveys as tools of reflection in writing courses. In reviewing the literature on writing apprehension and large-scale studies that used attitude surveys, Wallace explores the tension between the psychometric theory informing these instruments and more constructivist, postmodern theories that seem at odds with it. He explains how as a classroom teacher he used these surveys as prompts for student reflection about their writing and themselves as writers. Following Wallace's narrative essay is Stuart Green and Amy Orr's (chap. 7) report on research of first-year writing across the curriculum. Their chapter examines the types of writing and the claim structures found in it, as well as the extent of the variation in writing across disciplines. They recommend, among other things, that more dialogue needs to take place across disciplines about the way we use terms such as *analysis* and *argument*, and the way texts are used to configure the world. Chapter 8, by Connie Ruzich, picks up on the way language conveys values and attitudes and takes readers into one undergraduate classroom where students study linguistics. In her exploratory research, Ruzich examines why some students persist in believing language myths, such as the belief that varieties of English that differ from the standard variety are inferior, whereas others are more willing to accept linguists' views, which in this example explains that one variety is not inherently better than another.

Chapter 9 also focuses on undergraduates, but it looks beyond a single classroom. John R. Hayes and his collaborators report on their efforts to develop and test an online writing tutor program that provides instruction and practice for science and engineering students. The rationale for an online tutoring program, which consists of modules focused on topics specific to writing in science and engineering, as well as more general writing concerns, is rooted in judgment training as well as clearly defined pedagogical principles.

Technology is also a major theme in chapter 10, although the focus is different. In "Pedagogical Transformations in a Mythic Age," Joan Latchaw examines the theoretical assumptions about technology in composition studies and the use of courseware in composition classrooms. From here she narrows her focus to a graduate "Cyberseminar in Composition Theory" that convened on three different universities' campuses and was mediated through online communication. After taking into consideration various theoretical perspectives and testing them against daily classroom practice, Latchaw offers a set of "guiding observations to attempt educational reform in the digital age."

Chapter 11 also focuses on graduate-level education—this time in an MAT program. J. Bradley Minnick and Julie Aungst tell the story of one preservice English teacher's "journey—a journey complete with wrong turns and misjudgment—a journey that will take her through her own search to find good pedagogical practices necessary to teach her sixth grade students effective research-narrative writing." In telling Mary's story, Minnick and Aungst use excerpts from Mary's teaching journal, situating it in the literature on teaching writing. Concluding this part is another look at preservice teacher preparation, the Field Center model. Dawn Latta Kirby and Dan Kirby (chap. 12) recount the formation of the University of Georgia's Department of Language Education Field Center and Bill's work in the center. They explain the benefits of the center as well as Bill's insistence on being on site in the public schools. Although many people saw him "as more at home in a doctoral seminar, pursuing esoteric linguistics questions," the authors explain that his "irreverence for mindless school practice and his willingness to engage in heated discussions without rancor made him a favorite among all who participated in his field center." This move beyond the university campus connects to the next section, which turns to issues beyond classroom teaching and research.

Part III, Beyond the Classroom, addresses topics of community and the profession. The contents cover topics that Bill was involved in and cared about: community, graduate education, professionalization, and policy issues. This part opens with a multivocal reflection on Bill as a teacher and mentor orchestrated by Suzanne Miller (chap. 13). In this chapter, Miller gathers together the voices and experiences of several of Bill's former students who describe their experiences with Bill and how he influenced them.

Chapter 14 features one of Bill's doctoral student's from the University of Pittsburgh, Glynda Hull, who, with her colleague Michael Angelo James, writes about a collaboration between the University of California–Berkeley and the local community of West Oakland. In "Geographies of Hope: A Study of Urban Landscapes and a University–Community Collaborative," Hull and James use theories of postmodern geography to examine how a community is identified through its signage, juxtaposing signs erected by outsiders to those created by community members. From this analysis, they move to the multimedia autobiographical stories created by children in the community center and how identity is constructed by these students. As an epilogue, Hull explains how Bill's creation of "spaces for learning" informed her own academic identity.

Professional identity is taken up in chapter 15, "Crossing Over: The Move From Education to Composition," by Russel Durst. In this chapter, Durst starts by explaining his own professional path and then traces the formation of composition studies through a mix of work done by teachers and researchers from schools of education and departments of English. He explains some of the struggle involved in the formation of composition's disciplinary identity emphasizing the influence of those scholars coming out of education. Although he acknowledges the detrimental effects that the social turn had for many professionals and the field as a whole, Durst concludes that composition studies has benefited in many ways from the tension between the empirically oriented work coming from education and the more theoretical, archival, text-based work associated with English studies.

Durst's chapter focuses in on the formation of a disciplinary community, whereas chapter 16 looks more closely at the shaping of a profession. Stephen Koziol takes a historical look at K–12 teacher accreditation and standards over the last several decades. He concludes his review of the history and process of accreditation of English teachers with five observations and five recommendations, ultimately arguing that it is time for the NCTE to step up. Following on Koziol's contribution and concluding the section is an examination of educational policy. In "Evidenced-Based Education Policies: Beyond the Yellow Brick Road," authors Lucretia (Penny) Pence and Linda Jordan Platt (chap. 17) use the story of the *Wizard of Oz* as a framework for "examining the relationship between research and practice in education" and the way that plays out in public policies. They argue for more recognition of the "limits and worth of differing research paradigms," and for the valuing of both personal insight and systematic inquiry, which is what they learned from Bill, who "gave us the tools we needed and allowed us to discover their power."

The volumes end with an afterword by Bill: "Some Thoughts on Successful Mentoring of Future Researchers." Bill shares his advice on "nourishing a better breed of professors." In offering his list of "thou shalts," Bill reflects on the past, but also argues for the future. His essay is quintessential Bill—enthusiastic, frank, and perceptive. His contribution makes a fitting conclusion: His advice for mentors dovetails with the experiences reported by his students and colleagues.

Taken together, the chapters in this volume represent the diversity of work found in Smith's opus, convey a sense of Bill Smith—as teacher, researcher, and mentor—and illustrate the legacy that one person can have on his students and on the field.

THE CALL OF RESEARCH

Nancy Sommers

"How do you know that," Bill Smith would ask, challenging, prodding, but always with good humor and playfulness. He wanted data and evidence, not the fluffy stuff I arrived with—opinions or speculations. He could cite chapter and verse of *Research in Teaching English (RTE)*, and he would send me home before our next meeting to read key articles, most of which had been written by friends or former colleagues at the University of Georgia. I never knew much about Bill, his personal life, or his background, but I knew that he loved research and he loved turning his students into researchers.

That Bill took me as his student and spent so much time reading my tortuous graduate student prose continues to amaze me. I was not a good graduate student. Living a life that was more often unhinged than hinged, with *incomplete* as my most frequent grade, I was not given to showing much respect to authorities, be they professors or parents. In the beginning, I would arrive in Bill's cramped office, wearing my Bohemian clothes and always unprepared and disorganized, and plop down in the chair next to his desk, filling the air with my hastily conceived questions. Bill was gracious and patient, somehow seeing a shape and form—even a future—to these scattered questions. Both of us liked the big, unanswerable questions about language and learning—the ones that pushed us beyond one class-room, one teacher. But in the end, the only good questions to Bill were ones we could research. Over time I found myself in the library, reading those back volumes of *RTE*, prepared to respond to his queries with evidence, not speculation.

When we didn't get together in Bill's office, we found ourselves meeting in empty classrooms, where Bill covered the chalk board diagramming my ideas, drawing arrows between seemingly disconnected thoughts, and showing me, with an infectious glee, why the questions I was asking were worth pursuing. When it came time to write my dissertation, I knew I wanted to research the composing process, but nothing definitive emerged until Bill and I had one of our late-after-noon classroom sessions. Bill drew a long line across the entire chalk board to rep-resent the composing process, dividing it equally into three segments, and label-ing each section: prewriting/writing/rewriting. With a dramatic gesture toward this line, as if we were explorers discovering a new world, he turned to me with this grand invitation: "The Composing Process: Pick your territory." Even now, 25 years later, I can still see that long line spreading back and forth, without begin-ning or end, and I feel the excitement of the open landscape, the unknown terri-tory we had started to call the *composing process*. So little was known then about how students or experienced writers create texts, the moments of putting word after word on paper, and even less was known about the mysterious part of the process we called *rewriting*. It didn't take long for me to select my territory—rewriting—a subject that as a writer both filled me with hope and despair. If rewriting offered us the opportunity to retract our words, something missing from speech, to be saved from the roughness of our early drafts, it also offered an endless series of choices to make our writing (and ourselves) anew. What didn't make sense to me about the linear model of composing was that rewriting came *after* writing, as if it were a further growth of what was already there, almost an afterthought, not a creative, dynamic process, a way of seeing again. If other researchers had staked claims in the prewriting and writing landscape, the territory of rewriting, or revi-sion as I preferred to call it, had been disregarded, wide open, and mine to explore.

I stumbled through this new territory, learning how to interview research subjects, collect primary source data, code and analyze data, and, finally, draw con-clusions and implications. Along the way, I learned how much I loved research, especially case studies, and I discovered a passion for interviewing student writers and their teachers, and collecting my own primary sources. In research I found an academic identity and a scholarly purpose that had eluded me as a graduate stu-dent, one that complemented my love for teaching writing. Bill gave me not only the tools for designing research questions and methods, but also a belief in myself as someone who asked interesting questions and who could claim some part of that unknown territory we called composing.

I'm sure that as a graduate student I didn't sufficiently appreciate Bill's gra-ciousness—how he was always able to find time for me in what must have been an oversubscribed schedule, filled with graduate students clamoring for his attention, in addition to a crowded schedule of teaching and research. It is only now, having turned 50 and having taught undergraduate and graduate students for over two decades, that I marvel at the way Bill always made time for me and welcomed me into his office, be I prepared or unprepared. With time I've grown more appreciative of my own teachers, and I'm keenly aware of how important Bill's gentle, accepting, seemingly easy-going, but rigorously demanding approach helped me find my way and set me on a life-long quest to research and write. So it didn't surprise me 6 years ago, when I first started to dream and sketch out the possibility of conducting a longitudinal study, that I called Bill to ask his advice. He listened, patiently, to my wild, unfocused thoughts about following 400 undergraduates through their college years, and he reminded me that a longitudinal study was not one study, but a series of small studies, encouraging me to figure out what those smaller studies might be. Six years later, having completed my longitudinal study, sitting with over 600 pounds of student writing, 520 hours of transcribed interviews, and countless megabytes of survey data, I'm appreciating the wisdom of Bill's advice as I begin to make sense of my fascinating data.

I once read a definition of a *true gift* as something larger than a possession passed between giver and receiver, but rather something that is kept in motion, moving back and forth between giver and receiver, and outward into the world. As I look back over all these years, appreciating the many ways in which Bill instructed and inspired me, I realize that his true legacy is the way in which he gently pushed me to figure out what mattered to me, leaving me alone to do my own research, confident that he had given me the tools to ponder and pursue the questions that seized my imagination. That Bill took me seriously before I was prepared to take myself seriously is a gift for which I will always be grateful. To this day, Bill's question "How do you know that?" and the follow-up "Why can't you know that?" shape my students, who, in turn, will shape their students, moving back and forth into the world, keeping Bill's gift in motion.

I

WRITING ASSESSMENT

1

STANDING ON HIS SHOULDERS

.

Understanding William L. Smith's Contributions to Writing Assessment

Brian Huot

When I was first asked to be a part of this volume, I learned that I had the option of writing about Bill as a person or his work or about both. Ambitiously, I chose both. Over the years, I have found it more and more difficult to separate the personal from the professional, and I must admit that it was working with Bill that first pushed me to reconsider any separation between the two. Because I was never "officially" Bill's student, I never got to know him well as a person. I was never in one of his classes nor did I, like most of the people in this volume, have the opportunity to work on a research project with him. Most of my interactions with Bill took place in western Pennsylvania, where I was a student and he a professor, although at different schools, or at conferences or over the phone or Net. However, just like all of the people in this volume, I have my stories and memories of Bill. I remember one of the first times I saw Bill. He was sitting in Penny Pence's back-yard with a straw hat on, looking like someone out of a late 19th century French painting. As memorable and important as Bill remains for me as a person, his work continues to have even more importance for me and others who work in writing assessment.

Working on a chapter about writing assessment for a volume that celebrates Bill Smith's dual vision of English education and composition reminds me that my own vision for the study of writing assessment demands that the educational measurement and college writing assessment communities work together (Huot, 2002). Writing this chapter also makes me realize that my vision for a unified field of writing assessment probably depends on Bill's influence to include both areas of study to provide the most nuanced and sophisticated picture for the teaching and learning of writing and, in my case, their assessment.

I met Bill in the summer of 1985. I was a doctoral student in rhetoric and linguistics at Indiana University of Pennsylvania (IUP), and Bill came down from Pittsburgh (about an hour drive away) with a couple of his graduate students to do a panel on what he at that point had thought was a 40% error rate in the Writing Placement Program at the University of Pittsburgh.[1] Little did I realize at the time that I was hearing the beginning of an inquiry that was to change writing assessment during the next two decades. In the mid- to late 1980s, when I first began to study and work in writing assessment, there were two maxims. One, to be valid, an assessment had to be reliable. Two, reliability was something that had to be accomplished through adherence to a set of procedures that allowed readers (really they were called *raters* at the time) to agree on numerical scores for the same papers at a high enough rate to be acceptable according to psychometric principles. It is important to note that holistic scoring in and of itself was never seen as generating high enough reliability to be statistically valid (Breland et al., 1987; Camp, 1993; Cooper, 1984; Godshalk, Swineford, & Coffman, 1966). In a psychometric sense, these studies and Camp and Cooper's discussion of the developmental research for holistic scoring pretty much conclude that multiple measures of student ability, including scores from multiple-choice tests of usage, grammar, and mechanics, produce the most trustworthy scores about student writing ability.

In the late 1980s and early 1990s, the main problem as it had been framed (Schon, 1983) throughout much of the 20th century for writing assessment was to ensure that the same papers received identical or similar scores. Through the years, test designers have employed a continuous array of technologies for educational measurement (Madhaus, 1993, 1994). The solution to the problem of writing assessment has always been to create better and better reliability. Eventually a set of procedures was created that revolves around describing writing quality

---

[1] It is important to note that Bill's inquiry into the accuracy and adequacy of placement scores is an inquiry into the validity of writing assessment, rather than its reliability, which had been the main thrust of research into writing assessment up until that time. In 1994, when I wrote the introduction to *Assessing Writing*, I commented on how, up until the 1990s, work in writing assessment was about establishing the use of direct writing assessment. What I might have easily said is that research had focused primarily on reliability. Bill's work, which I believe signals an entirely new direction into writing assessment, focuses on its validity.

according to a set of categories or score points and then training raters to agree in their scoring. This technological emphasis in addressing the problem of reliability in essay scoring is currently embodied in the machine scoring of student essays that provides unprecedented rates of agreement for multiple readings, even if all the readings aren't provided by human beings. This essay-scoring software can be tailored to the readings of local faculty, so that even if only one or two essays are read by teachers or other humans in a specific location, machine scoring will produce reliable scores for any number of student essays.

Reliability, mainly scoring reliability, had been the main sticking point for writing assessment as we understood it (many people still understand it this way). It is in this context for writing assessment in the mid-1980s that Bill's inquiry, which would document new structures for assessing student writing, began. As Bill conducted one research project after another on the scoring of placement essays at Pitt, he ended up reframing the major problem for writing assessment. When I talk of framing or reframing a specific problem, I'm referring to *frame* in the way Donald Schon (1983) understands and defines it:

> In real-world practice, problems do not present themselves to the practitioner as givens. They must be constructed from the materials of problematic situations which are puzzling, troubling and uncertain. . . . But with this emphasis on problem solving, we ignore problem setting. . . . Problem setting is a process in which interactively, we name the things to which we will attend and frame the context in which we will attend to them. (p. 40)

Instead of addressing the problem of writing assessment as how to get different raters to agree—the way it had been historically set—Bill set the problem as how the identity and experience of the reader within a specific literacy event affects not only the ability of the raters to agree on a particular judgment, but how the position(s) of the reader as a person expert for making certain educational decisions (placement is after all an educational decision) impacts the value and adequacy[2] of the decision based on that judgment. In this way, Bill frames the problem within the context of teachers reading placement essays, resetting the

---

[2]I am consciously repeating Bill's use of the word *adequacy* in his book chapter that delineates his research on writing assessment. Bill wanted to avoid using the word *validity* because of all the baggage the term carries. It should also be noted that a decade or so later, *validity* has been defined in productive ways unavailable at the time Bill made his decisions (Cronbach, 1989; Messick, 1989; Moss, 1992, 1995; Shephard, 1993). Although I certainly understand Bill's decision, working in 2005, I think we should acknowledge as I already have (Huot, 2002) that Bill's work on writing assessment constitutes the finest example I know of validation research in writing assessment, an example that I and others have tried to emulate.

basic problem–solution for writing assessment. Bill's work allowed researchers and theorists in writing assessment to widen their scope of interests beyond just how to get readers to agree, refocusing that attention on how to structure writing assessments in educationally meaningful ways that foster agreement among readers.[3] But I'm getting ahead of the story here, ahead of the influence Bill has had on my personal and professional life and career, and ahead of the impact his work has had in changing the ways we can think about writing assessment.

In 1987, a couple of years after I first met Bill, I had an important conversation with him at the Conference on College Composition and Communication (CCCC) in St. Louis. At that point, I had decided to do a dissertation on writing assessment. Mike Williamson (my dissertation director) knew Bill, had introduced me to him and asked him, if he would be willing to read my dissertation.[4] At this point, I was still designing my study. Although I don't remember the details, I do remember Bill listening intently to my description of my project as we walked around the conference, ultimately telling me that I had two projects and that I should pick one of them to do. We were going down on one of those multifloor escalators found in conference centers and hotels, and I had to look up to Bill as we talked. When he told me to choose, I asked him, "Can I do that?" He smiled down at me, looking as amused as if I had asked him whether grass was green, saying in a flat, matter-of-fact voice, "It's your dissertation."

I can't recall how many times over the last 15 years or so I've told some version of that story to a graduate student who was struggling to balance her scholarly interests with pressure from a specific program, program director, or potential dissertation director or committee member or some other outside pressure(s) to do a certain kind of work or conduct a specific study. Bill's words made me realize that all worthwhile scholarly endeavors begin with a personal urge to know something, and this commitment to a specific inquiry can only be sustained if it has real importance to the individual. This is an important lesson to learn and one that is not always apparent to the student who climbs the academic ladder, completing assignments about which she may have little or no interest. At that moment, Bill's words were a powerful mandate for me to realize that writing my dissertation didn't have to be school all over again and that school didn't have to be separate from me as a person. Realizing that I could and should choose what to work on changed my attitude from that of a student fulfilling requirements to that of a colleague among colleagues, a researcher with his own agenda. I can only

---

[3]In case the reader hasn't noticed, I use the word *rater* to refer to psychometrically supported procedures and *reader* to refer to those procedures based on the context of reading and evaluating in a specific context for a particular educational purpose.

[4]Unfortunately, at that time, IUP did not have a policy that allowed Bill to serve officially as a committee member. My mention of him in the acknowledgments is the only connection I knew about until Peggy told me Bill listed me on his c.v. among the graduate students with whom he had worked.

hope that Bill's words continue to inspire students even in some small fashion, given their profound impact on me.

Once I had completed a draft of my dissertation about a year later, I sent copies to all of my official committee members and to Bill. He, of course, responded first. In the years during which I've coedited *Assessing Writing* and the *Journal of Writing Assessment*, we were always pleasantly surprised at the immediate, thoughtful responses Bill gave to the manuscripts we sent him. When Bill called me that morning in 1988 to tell me what he thought of my dissertation, of the study I had designed, conducted, and written up, I remember sitting in my office in the writing center at the University of Northern Iowa and feeling that on some important level I had finished my work as a doctoral student. I knew I would have to defend my dissertation for real with my official committee who would eventually sign off on my work. But even before I knew the way my real committee would respond, I knew Bill was right when he told me I was done as a student. He was excited, his voice clipped and quick, talking animatedly about the different parts of the study. Bill had much to say about the implications of my study, which used protocol analysis to find out what raters consider when reading student writing in holistic scoring sessions. Later I would realize that he followed my lead and collected protocols from his own readers as part of his ongoing inquiry into placement reading. He also advised me to revise (which I did) my literature review for *Review of Educational Research*, a journal I hadn't heard of before then.[5] I officially defended my dissertation in May, receiving good input from the members of my committee, especially my director, Mike. I remember, however, Mike saying after the defense that, because Bill had already responded favorably, there was little doubt my official committee would concur.

In 1989, Bill, Mike, and I presented a roundtable at CCCC in Seattle. I don't remember exactly what the roundtable was about or what Mike and I presented on (it could be looked up). I do remember that it was then that Bill first began to share the stunning results of his ongoing inquiry that began with an unfounded suspicion that there was a 40% error rate in placement at Pitt. At this point, Bill began to research the ways in which the reading and decision making can be structured for writing assessment. After the session, I remember Mike Williamson mentioning how unnerving it felt to be sitting between two very excited people on the panel. When Bill shared results that he was able to get readers to agree with each other at a higher rate than holistically trained readers by having readers make a decision about which they were expert, at that instant I knew that what he had found could not be explained within the beliefs and assumptions of the theoretical basis for holistic scoring or any other psychometric measures for evaluating writing.

---

[5] A journal from the educational community—working on a manuscript for *Review of Educational Research* (at Bill's suggestion)—was one of my first introductions to the educational research community.

HOLISTIC SCORING

In 1990, I attended and participated in my first American Educational Research Association (AERA) conference in Boston. Bill had been instrumental in getting me there, proposing a panel for him, Mike Williamson, and me. A couple of hours before we presented, we were all up in Bill's room talking writing assessment. It was one of those conversations that had a strong impact on my thinking. I don't remember most of it—I wish it had been recorded. I remember Bill saying that it was a mistake to think that indirect approaches to writing assessment, like multiple-choice tests or machine-scored essays, and direct approaches, like holistic scoring, were products of two different schools of thought because ultimately they had been developed by the same group of people with a similar goal in mind—to produce reliable writing assessments. The other thing I remember Bill saying was that holistic scoring assumed that student writing ability would distribute into all possible scoring categories, whereas in scoring for placement it could be possible to have an empty cell or category, because student preparation for first-year writing can vary over time. For example, we recently mainstreamed first-year writing at the University of Louisville after smaller and smaller numbers of students were being placed in perquisite writing courses (Edgington, Tucker, Ware, & Huot, 2005). In effect, the category for which we screened student writing ability ceased to be relevant to a necessary number of students, and the class (the category) ceased to exist.

Although some in college writing assessment (White, 1993; Yancey, 1999) have portrayed teachers taking an active role in determining the design and structure of holistic scoring, in truth holistic scoring was developed primarily by researchers at the Educational Testing Service. However, when the College Board discontinued the use of essay exams in 1942, strident and vociferous protest from English teachers forced the Board to initiate a 1-hour English Composition Examination in 1943 (Fuess, 1967; Palmer, 1960). Certainly English teachers had a role as advocates for writing assessment procedures that actually involved students writing and teachers reading that writing, and it's pretty clear that without this advocacy the measurement community, which ultimately developed holistic scoring, would not have felt the same need or urgency to create reliable direct writing assessment procedures.

To understand the paradigmatic shift that Bill's work in writing assessment ultimately signaled, I begin by outlining the beliefs and assumptions that drive holistic scoring to contrast the driving theoretical assumptions with the new assessments Bill created and whose creation fostered and supported a range of new writing assessments (Harrington, 1998; Haswell, 2001; Lowe & Huot, 1997). The purpose of holistic scoring procedures is to create a structured reading environment in which individual teachers and/or raters can assign the same scores to the same papers. Normally, the emphasis in holistic scoring is on providing necessary training through the reading of anchor papers and discussions of how certain papers meet the scoring guidelines or rubrics' definition of each score point. Once readers can agree in training sessions, they are allowed to read real papers while supervisory staff monitor individuals' ability to agree with other readers.

HOLISTIC SCORING BELIEFS AND ASSUMPTIONS

- Agreement is the most important and troublesome issue in assessing student writing.
- Student writing can be categorized and labeled numerically.
- Raters can be trained to agree on what scores papers should receive.
- A reliable scoring session is good writing assessment.

In truth, I could go on about the theoretical assumptions that inform holistic scoring, but these four should demonstrate the paradigmatic differences between holistic scoring and the kinds of scoring procedures Bill's research made possible.

One of the biggest differences between holistic scoring and the procedures Bill developed at Pitt in the late 1980s is that the former requires that a rater give a student paper a numerical score. This score is then combined into a sum score of the two raters and compared to a cut score for a decision about placement. In holistic scoring, raters code their decisions about student writing into a number and then the scores are aggregated and re- or decoded into the appropriate decision. Clearly, holistic scoring for placement or in any other situation in which a decision is to be made for a specific student requires a level of abstraction in coding the decision numerically as well as a level of labor that codes and then recodes what teachers think about a student's ability to succeed in one or another class.

If we look at the research on the way that teachers read student writing for placement (Huot, 1993; Pula & Huot, 1993; Smith, 1993), these levels of abstraction and labor appear multiplied and unnecessary, because the evidence from all three studies seems to indicate that raters first think about what course students should enter and then look for the appropriate number on the holistic scoring guideline that is then recoded into a placement decision. Holistic scoring depends on a theory of scoring that uses numerical representation of data (a rater's decision) to make an educational decision. Bill's research demonstrated that readers can reliably evaluate student writing for placement and make a straightforward decision about what class best suits a specific student without the unnecessary coding and recoding of that decision.

BEYOND HOLISTIC SCORING

Unlike holistic scoring and the beliefs and assumptions that undergird its use and development, Bill's system for placement reading at Pitt was based on a search for accuracy and adequacy—for the validity of the procedures, rather than for their reliability. Unlike holistic scoring, in Bill's system, readers make a decision rather than score a specific piece of writing. In this way, we can say that holistic scoring is based on theories about scoring, whereas Bill's system is based on theories of reading and language use. Whether we go back a couple of decades to Michael Halliday's (1978) germinal work, *Language as Social Semiotic,* or look more recently at James Gee's (1999) *An Introduction to Discourse Analysis,* language theorists are united in determining that context is crucial for making meaning from any language or literacy event. For Halliday, "Any account of language which fails to build in the situation as an essential ingredient is likely to be artificial and unrewarding" (p. 29). He goes on to say that, "*All* language functions in contexts of situations and is relatable to those contexts" (p. 32). Gee's ideas about context are similar: "The context of an utterance (oral or written) is everything in the material, mental, personal, interactional, social, institutional, cultural and historical situation in which the utterance was made . . . " (p. 54).

Up until Bill's work, the emphasis in writing assessment was to decontextualize (creating a context of its own) the assessment situation; raters read within a prescribed set of criteria so they could agree with each other at an acceptable level. Along with linguists' emphasis on context in making meaning with the written and spoken word, literary scholars since Holland, (1975), Iser (1978), and Fish (1980) and a host of others have asserted the importance of context and the positions and individual situations that various readers bring with them to make meaning and value out of specific texts. Bill's findings that certain readers who had experience and expertise with specific students from particular classes can be supported by a theory of reading that recognizes the variable meanings available in certain texts and contexts (e.g., Gee, 1999; Halliday, 1978; Hernstein-Smith, 1988).

Within a theory of reading and meaning-making dependent on context, structuring placement reading within the realm of specific courses and particular teachers makes great sense. A placement decision based on a general rubric calibrated according to numerical guidelines makes much less sense. Bill's research isolates the problem for writing assessment as the setting of an appropriate context within which teachers can read student writing and make informed decisions about students. His structure focuses reading for placement around a specific context, honoring that some readers are better able to make certain decisions than others. His procedures are easily supported and explained through what we now know about reading theoretically and in the research about reading.

Ideally, without focusing on agreement at all, Bill's procedures promote agreement among different readers at a higher rate than in holistic scoring sessions that train raters to agree. In other words, the variation in agreement found in various studies throughout the 20th century (see Godshalk, Swineford, & Coffman, 1966) was not because teachers inherently disagree on writing quality or are unable to create a particular consensus of what students need to be doing at specific junctures in writing instruction. As Bill demonstrates in his research, the problem with most of the developmental research on holistic scoring and/or direct writing assessment is that context was never an important factor. For example, in the most famous study on reliability conducted by Diederich, French, and Carlton (1961), 55 readers read over 300 essays, and 90% of the essays received seven or more scores on a 9-point scoring guideline. However, these readers who came from a variety of professions received no context for the scores they were giving.

In some ways, the research on reliability in writing assessment is a good example of the importance of context in reading and meaning-making. Without context, readers cannot agree about the relative merit of specific pieces of writing and more important, the decisions to be made on behalf of that writing. It seems safe to say, then, that although traditional direct writing assessment procedures are based on a theory of scoring, of how to produce the most reliable scores for specific pieces of writing,[6] Bill's procedures rest theoretically on an understanding of reading and the importance of context to meaning and decision making. For Bill, not all variation in reading is bad; looking beyond a psychometric explanation for writing assessment, his procedures are based on the fact that in different situations and for different purposes different readers read different texts in different ways. Bill uses the variation in reading to build procedures that are accurate, and consistent, and still variable. What's crucial in Bill's model is the creation of a familiar and robust situation in which the reader (the teacher for a specific class) makes a decision for which she is expert and is supplied context based on her reading of a specific student.

Bill (Smith, 1992, 1993) and Peggy O'Neill (2003) have both written about the difference in the kind and nature of the decisions being made, in which the reader considers the student and not just the writing. The context created for the reader allows her the opportunity to make a richer decision that considers the whole student in her development as a writer, rather than just looking at a specific text according to prescribed criteria the rater may or may not have had any say in articulating.

Before going any further, let me describe briefly what procedures Bill developed, so as to be friendly to readers not familiar with Bill's work in writing assessment and provide a clear point of reference for the list of beliefs and assumptions I display later. Bill used pairs of readers for each of the classes students could possibly be placed into. A reader who first read a student's paper had one

---

[6]It should be noted that, in addition to scoring procedures, reliability can also depend on the way writing prompts are constructed (Hoetker, 1982; Murphy & Ruth, 1993; Ruth & Murphy, 1988).

decision to make: Does this student belong in my class? If the reader thought yes, then the paper was given to the other reader for that specific course. If the reader thought no, then she would give the paper to the reader she thought would be most expert for making this decision. In this way, a student was placed when two readers for a specific course thought she belonged there. Readers were chosen for specific courses based on their most pervasive and recent teaching experiences. Most of the papers were routed without incident, although Bill did identify "tweeners" that produced cross-readings. But these were few, and Bill has had a lot to say about them (although at this point it's really outside the purview of this discussion).

ASSUMPTIONS AND BELIEFS
OF BILL'S PROCEDURES

- Placement reading should produce decisions not scores.
- Placement decisions are best made course by course.
- Placement decisions are best made by the teacher for the course.
- There is no need for rubrics or training.
- Procedures should promote validity and reliability.

In 1992, I heard Bill talk at the CCCs about his placement program. I remember him being very guarded about looking at his results at Pitt out of the context of a specific institution and the specialized group of people who give a place its identity. Of course from the moment I'd first heard about Bill's work, I wanted to implement a placement system based on his research. So, I asked him that day during the session if he were saying these procedures were not viable somewhere else. He said he thought they could be replicated elsewhere, but that institutional and other contexts would affect whatever could be done elsewhere. At IUPUI, my first tenure-track job, I was hired to direct the placement program. Although I planned on revising what were holistic procedures at the time, I only stayed 1 year. Harrington (1998) did eventually revise placement at IUPUI based essentially on Bill's ideas, although she used infused technology into a system that serves a large contingent faculty and a commuter student body.

I eventually did get my chance to experiment with Bill's ideas for placement a few years later at the University of Louisville (U of L). A couple of education professors and the director of admissions came to the composition director, who asked me if I would like to become involved in a project through which high school seniors could use their state-mandated writing portfolios as a way to place into their college writing courses. To encourage students to submit their portfolios for placement, we offered students the possibility of placing directly into English 102, an option not otherwise available. In our first year, we read around 50 portfolios from five feeder schools in the Louisville area. Within 2 years, any student in the state of Kentucky was eligible to submit a portfolio. For 5 years, over 10% of incoming students submitted a portfolio for placement (see Hester, O'Neill, Neal, Edgington, & Huot, Chapter 4, this volume). Overall, we continued to place students in first-year writing classes for 7 years based on our reading of their portfolios. We quit the practice in the fall of 2002 when we mainstreamed first-year writing and placement procedures were no longer necessary.

In 2002, we replaced the CLEP exam with a portfolio. Kentucky high school students can still use their portfolios if they wish to be exempt from the written communication requirement at U of L. Over the 7 years we used portfolios for placement, we streamlined the process and managed to make portfolios a viable placement option. We published the first 3 years of our results in *The Kentucky English Bulletin* (Lowe & Huot, 1997) and presented the first 5 years of the project at AERA in 2000 (Hester, Huot, Neal, O'Neill, 2000). Chapter 4 in this volume describes in some detail the ways we revised our methods over the years, and the research we undertook to make sure that students were being placed accurately and adequately, as well as maintaining acceptable rates of instrument reliability. In the 2001–2002 academic year, we also adapted Bill's procedures to read single-sample essays when the composition program became responsible for placement. All of these experiences document that the procedures developed by Bill can be used to make reliable and valid decisions at other institutions.

THE IMPORTANCE OF BILL'S RESEARCH

The last CCCC I've attended with Bill was in 1994 in Nashville. It was Bill's last CCC before he moved to Oregon and his current position(s) at Oregon Health Services University. We went to hear Haswell's (1994) presentation about the placement procedures he had devised at Washington State. Unlike the procedures Bill had developed, Haswell's procedures involved only a single reading of 60% of the student essays, with the remaining 40% being read a second time. After the presentation, Bill and I talked. He told me he thought that if he were staying in the placement business, he would experiment with what Haswell had accomplished, using only one reader for as many student papers as possible. In the several years we read portfolios for placement, one of the changes we made was to have all the papers read initially by readers who were expert for the most heavily enrolled course. Unlike Haswell, however, we kept Bill's structure for having the initial (English 101) reader pass the portfolio on to the reader expert for a particular course. In this way, we no longer had to read each sample twice, and we still retained the theoretical and research basis of Bill's research.

There have been so many site-based, locally controlled placement systems devised over the past several years that they are no longer news. In a survey of placement programs in the early 1990s, only 19% of the 1,100 respondents indicated using a nonnumerical scale (Huot, 1994). My guess would be that a current survey would show a huge jump in the number of institutions whose placement procedures do not rest on scoring student writing according to numerical guidelines. Clearly, Bill's work has had an important impact on the ways in which students are being placed into first-year writing courses. Although it is important to note that directed self-placement has really revised the ways in which we can think of placement procedures. As Michael Neal and I (2003) urge in our response to a volume on directed self-placement, more validation work like that undertaken by Bill needs to be completed before we can be knowledgeable enough about directed self-placement to know how and why it works.

In his germinal essay on writing assessment and reliability, Williamson (1994) draws on Lord, Novick, and Torgerson's work in the 1960s and 1950s in education to frame the problem for writing assessment: "The greater the reliability of an assessment procedure, the less interesting a description it provides of writing" (p. 163). In other words, we can have reliable procedures with questionable validity or valid procedures with questionable reliability. Such a state of affairs causes both Yancey (1999) and Camp (1993) to talk about balancing reliability with validity, so that neither concept drives writing assessment to the detriment of the other because the two concepts are in tension and opposition to each other. Camp refers to the need to strike a compromise between the two—a compromise Bill's work makes unnecessary for placement.

This traditional tension between reliability and validity in educational measurement in general and in writing assessment in particular disappears within Bill's research on writing assessment. The same procedures that ensure the accurate and adequate placement decisions—that is, having the teachers who are expert for the course also make the determination—supply a higher rate of reliability than what Bill was able to achieve using holistic scoring. There is no need to balance reliability or validity because, within an understanding of the way experts read texts about which they are able to make important and accurate decisions, reliability and validity work together within the context of teachers making decisions reliably and accurately. Both Moss (1994) and Williamson (1994) argue that we should treat reliability as a component of construct validity. Bill's research in writing demonstrates that reliability and validity can be complementary within a structure that recognizes the expertise of teachers and a theoretical understanding of the way we people read. Radway's (1989) study of the ways important decisions are made by Book of the Month Club employees outlines the ways in which certain readers are expert for making certain kinds of decisions about texts, decisions in a business context that can often mean the difference between making and losing money.

Unfortunately, Bill's work and the great number of locally controlled writing assessment procedures are mostly geared toward placement or other site-based decision making. Holistic scoring is still probably the best option for the large-scale reading of student writing, although the recent advent of the writing portions for the SAT and ACT college entrance tests are also being marketed for placement and could threaten the inroads made in site-based placement procedures (White, 2005). For me, the greatest impact of Bill's work lies in his ability to create assessment based on theories of reading and teaching. In addition, Bill's work supplies the finest model of validation for writing assessment currently available. It can only be hoped that all of us who work in writing assessment follow his lead in carefully examining every aspect of writing assessment procedures and their impact on student learning.

As far as Bill and me personally, I've enjoyed seeing him again in San Francisco (2003) and Pittsburgh (2005) at the NCTE Convention and getting his reaction to this essay. He sits on the editorial board for *The Journal of Writing Assessment*, which I edit, and he is still a quick and thorough reviewer. I'm still telling my students stories about Bill and passing on his wisdom. Of course, everyone who works in writing assessment, whether they know it or not, is standing on his shoulders.

REFERENCES

Breland, H., Camp, R., Jones, R. J., Morris, M. M., & Rock, D. A. (1987). *Assessing writing skill* (Research Monograph No. 11). New York: College Entrance Examination Board.

Camp, R. (1993). Changing the model for the direct assessment of writing. In M. M. Williamson & B. Huot (Eds.), *Validating holistic scoring for writing assessment: Theoretical and empirical foundations* (pp. 45–78). Cresskill, NJ: Hampton.

Cooper, P. (1984). *The assessment of writing ability: A review of research.* Princeton, NJ: Educational Testing Service (GREEB No. 82–15).

Cronbach, L. J. (1989). Construct validation after thirty years. In R. L. Linn (Ed.), *Intelligence, measurement, theory and public policy: Proceedings of a symposium in Honor of L. G. Humphreys* (pp. 147–171. Urbana and Chicago: University of Illinois Press.

Diederich, P., French, J., & Carlton, S. (1961). *Factors in judgment of writing* quality. Princeton, NJ: Educational Testing Service. Research Bulletin No. 61–15.

Edgington, A., Tucker, M., Ware, K., & Huot, B. (2005). The road to mainstreaming: One program's successful but cautionary tale. In S. J. McGee & C. Handa (Eds.), *Discord and direction: The postmodern WPA.* Logan: Utah State University Press.

Fish, S. (1980). *Is there a text in this class? The authority of interpretive communities.* Cambridge: Cambridge University Press.

Fuess, C. (1967). *The college board: Its first fifty years.* New York: College Entrance Examination Board.

Gee, J. P. (1999). *An introduction to discourse analysis: Theory and method.* London: Routledge.

Godshalk, F. I., Swineford, F., & Coffman, W. E. (1966). *The measurement of writing ability.* Princeton, NJ: Educational Testing Service (CEEB RM No. 6).

Halliday, M. A. K. (1978). *Language as social semiotic.* Baltimore: Edward Arnold.

Harrington, S. (1998). New visions of authority in placement test rating. *WPA: Writing Program Administration, 22,* 53–84.

Haswell, R. H. (Ed.). (2001). *Beyond outcomes: Assessment and instruction within a university writing program.* Westport, CT: Ablex.

Hester, V., Huot, B., Neal, M., & O'Neill, P. (2000). *Reporting on the results and implications of a six-year pilot program using portfolios to place students in first-year college composition.* New Orleans: American Educational Research Association.

Hoetker, J. (1982). Essay examination topics and students' writing. *College Composition and Communication, 33,* 377–392.

Holland, N. N. (1975). *5 readers reading.* New Haven, CT: Yale University Press.

Huot, B. (1993). The influence of holistic scoring on reading and rating student essays. In M.M. Williamson & B. Huot (Eds.), *Validating holistic scoring for writing assessment: Theoretical and empirical foundations* (pp. 206–236). Cresskill, NJ: Hampton Press.

Huot, B. (1994). A survey of college and university writing placement practices. *WPA: Writing Program Administration, 17*(3), 49–67.

Huot, B. (2002) *(Re) articulating writing assessment for teaching and learning.* Logan, UT: Utah State University Press.

Iser, W. (1978). *The act of reading: A theory of aesthetic response.* Baltimore, MD: The John Hopkins University Press.

Lowe, T. J., & Huot, B. (1997). Using KIRIS writing portfolios to place students in first-year composition at the University of Louisville. *Kentucky English Bulletin, 46*(2), 46–64.

Madaus, G. (1993). A national testing system: Manna from above? An historical/technological perspective. *Educational Measurement, 11,* 9–26.

Madaus, G. (1994). A technological and historical consideration of equity issues associated with proposals to change the nation's testing policy. *Harvard Educational Review, 64*(1), 76–95.

Messick, S. (1989). Meaning and values in test validation: The science and ethics of assessment. *Educational Researcher, 18*(2), 5–12.

Moss, P. A. (1992). Shifting conceptions of validity in educational measurement: Implications for performance assessment. *Review of Educational Research, 62*(3), 229–258.

Moss, P. A. (1994). Can there be validity without reliability? *Educational Researcher, 23*(4), 5–12.

Murphy, S., & Ruth, L. (1993). The field testing of writing prompts reconsidered. In M. M. Williamson & B. Huot (Eds.), *Validating holistic scoring for writing assessment: Theoretical and empirical foundations* (pp. 266–302). Cresskill, NJ: Hampton Press.

Neal, M., & Huot, B. (2003). Responding to directed self-placement. In D. Royer & R. Gilles (Eds.), *Directed self-placement: Principles and practices* (pp. 243–255). Cresskill, NJ: Hampton Press.

O'Neill, P. (2003). Moving beyond holistic scoring through validity inquiry. *Journal of Writing Assessment, 1,* 47–65.

Palmer, O. (1960). Sixty years of English testing. *College Board, 42,* 8–14.

Pula, J. J., & Huot, B. (1993). A model of background influences on holistic raters. In M. M. Williamson & B. Huot (Eds.), *Validating holistic scoring for writing assessment: Theoretical and empirical foundations* (pp. 237–265). Cresskill, NJ: Hampton Press.

Radway, J. A. (1989). The book of the month club and the general reader: The uses of serious fiction. In C. N. Davidson (Ed.), *Reading in America: Literature and social history* (pp. 254–289). Baltimore: The John's Hopkins University Press.

Ruth, L., & Murphy, S. (1988). *Designing writing tasks for the assessment of writing.* Norwood, NJ: Ablex.

Schon, D. (1983). *The reflective practitioner.* New York: Basic Books.

Shephard, L. A. (1993). Evaluating test validity. *Review of Educational Research in Education, 19,* 405–450.

Smith, W. L. (1992). The importance of teacher knowledge in college composition placement testing. In J. R. Hayes, R. E. Young, M. L. Matchett, M. McCaffrey, C. Cochran, & T. Hajduk (Eds.), *Reading empirical research studies: The rhetoric of research* (pp. 289–316). Hillsdale, NJ: Erlbaum.

Smith, W. L. (1993). Assessing the reliability and adequacy of using holistic scoring of essays as a college composition placement program technique. In M. M. Williamson & B. Huot (Eds.), *Validating holistic scoring for writing assessment: Theoretical and empirical foundations* (pp. 142–205). Cresskill, NJ: Hampton Press.

White E. M. (1993). Holistic scoring: Past triumphs and future challenges. In M. M. Williamson & B. Huot, (Eds.), *Validating holistic scoring for writing assessment: Theoretical and empirical foundations* (pp. 79–108). Cresskill, NJ: Hampton Press.

White, E. M. (2005). The misuse of writing assessment for political purposes. *The Journal of Writing Assessment, 2,* 21-35.

Williamson, M.M. (1994). The worship of efficiency: Untangling theoretical and practical considerations in writing assessment. *Assessing Writing, 1,* 147–174.

Yancey, K. B. (1999). Looking back as we look forward: Historicizing writing assessment. *College Composition and Communication, 50,* 483–503.

2

SOME ADDITIONAL EFFECTS OF VARYING THE STRUCTURE OF A TOPIC ON COLLEGE STUDENTS' WRITING

Michael Moore

We hand out the paper, and they write. There is nothing evil in this. . . .

—Phillip Lopate (1978, p. 148)

THE TOPIC OF THE TOPIC

The impetus for the Topic Structure study was for a group of seven graduate students at the University of Pittsburgh to learn to do research in composition. This was a noted departure from the usual postsecondary liberal arts and education model, where one learns about research, works through possible areas of interest in various graduate courses, and then ultimately chooses an original project as a dissertation. Bill's approach more closely followed a science research model, where one learned research by working with researchers.

Our group discussed a number of topics in an attempt to find our own research niche. Influencing the search for the topic of the topic study was a plethora of recent composition studies, and because we were seven graduate students either of Bill Smith's or working with Bill, we were reading extensively in the field. Although the "topic structure" study was published in 1985, we began the research in 1983 on quiet Friday afternoons by first discussing our own jobs of teaching writing. Bill was the director of the Writing Workshop at the University of Pittsburgh; Glynda (who was further ahead than most of us and working on her dissertation), Carolyn, Don, and Linda were teaching assistants and doctoral students in English; Connie was a masters student and ready to leave for graduate work at the University of Pennsylvania; and Bob and I were high school English teachers and doctoral students in education. It was to Bill's credit that so many doctoral students were interested in composition coming from traditional English literature backgrounds. Part of this was due to Bill's enthusiasm, but another part was due to the exponential growth of composition as a cutting-edge area of study. Composition, however, was still the step-child in English departments and the way potential college English professors proved themselves eventually worthy to teach literature. To Pitt's credit, however, composition was never treated as poorly as we found it to be treated elsewhere. Bill, however, defied the norm of English department professors; he was a fusion of linguistics (which had "cousin" status), rhetoric (which had "grandfather" status), psychology (second cousin status) and composition.

For many of us, Bill was the first real interdisciplinarian we had ever met. His interests were wide ranging and encompassed not only work in composition, linguistics, and rhetoric, but also education, literacy, cognitive psychology and foreign languages. At this time, Bill was building his own computer (remember, this is 1983), was experimenting (along with Glynda) with invisible ink writing projects, and constantly playing around with grammar for both English and Chinese. Most of us had known Bill for about a year, and all of us had taken Bill's "Teaching of Composition" course and were overwhelmed at the "new" scholarship rapidly filling the "new" journals. Also, a couple hundred yards up the road from the fifth floor of Pitt's Cathedral of Learning, Linda Flower and John Hayes were further legitimizing composition at Carnegie Mellon University (CMU) by examining how students might be taught to move from writer- to reader-based prose using problem-solving processes. It was not unusual to find occasional CMU students visiting our classes, and Pitt students taking courses at CMU was highly encouraged. (These cultural exchanges were highly encouraged by all the faculty in the program, but particularly by Bill. Bill was known for paying the travel expenses for visiting scholars who classes were particularly interested in meeting. One of Bill's classes was particularly interested in meeting Stephen North shortly after his book, *The Making of Knowledge in Composition: Portrait of an Emerging Field* [1987] was published. Bill paid for Dr. North to fly to Pittsburgh and meet with Bill's graduate writing seminar students.)

We were also influenced by the numerous studies emerging on writing process but particularly the aspect of process, that examined underlying linguistic features that influenced how student writing was evaluated. Thus, we knew we were all interested in doing research that examined freshmen composition that would have a carryover to teaching high school writing. Our first choice of research topic for discussion was to do research on student voice in writing. We discussed this as an area where little had been done, and we thought that a study examining voice might serve to define what was meant by voice and perhaps serve to provide a research variable for observing and distinguishing voice in student writing. An alternate topic was also discussed concerning error in student writing and whether different topics produced varying productions of error. The argument was that such research might influence the development of placement essay topics for placing college students into appropriate freshman writing courses. The University of Pittsburgh was using placement essays written during summer freshmen orientation/writing placement testing to determine whether students should be placed into an Advanced Writing course, General Writing course, or Basic Reading and Writing course. Faculty and teaching assistants holistically evaluated these essays. Discussion ranged back and forth over the potential of each topic.

We split into teams to examine more closely voice and topic structure. The group reporting on voice found several possible research areas. First, Diederich's (1974) scale served our efforts, because voice was part of her analytic six-part rating scale. Because the scale had been in use for some time, an examination of voice as a variable for student placement held potential. Bill was also aware of research that would soon be published (see *New Directions in Composition Research*, 1984), where voice was being discussed by such writers as Ken Macrorie, Peter Elbow, and Donald Murray. At the time, voice, referred to the ways students either engaged or distanced themselves from a topic. "Voice" could be authentic or inauthentic depending on the contexts. Also influencing us on this topic was the engaging research of Kroll (1978) on audience awareness. Voice was thought to play a key role in how students responded to various audience prompts. Kroll was also a close friend of Bill's and a sometime visitor to our group. He also served on doctoral committees for Bill's students. Although, in retrospect, and clearly too early for any of us to articulate, we were fumbling with the notions of "modernist" public schooling and "reader response" expectations.

The group reporting on topic structure noted the immediate effect such a study might have on essay topics chosen for placement purposes. This was an area of interest to writing process researchers, audience awareness researchers, revision researchers, and assessment researchers. Glynda was working on error in her dissertation, and we were all interested in how error affected raters of placement essays. Error was held by many as an oversimplified concept that adversely affected carefully defined analytic scales that were used to train evaluators. (A by-product of the topic structure study Moore and Dunham,[1984] actually looked at this question.) Writing prompts had been viewed in light of the Britton et al. (1975) work, in that expressive writing was the place to start because it is nearer to talk than transactional writing, which was the writing of the world of work, and poetic, which was a "glimpse into a lifetime of feeling" (p. 83).

Britton provided a different approach to mode from the traditional four categories of narration, description, exposition, and argument. This particular aspect of topic structure research was receiving considerable examination from researchers. As mentioned, numerous mandated minimal competency exams had recently been initiated around the country (Hoetker, 1982), and placement admissions essay tests were becoming the norm at many universities. Testing companies seemed more concerned with holistic evaluation and rater reliability than what was influencing holistic evaluation. Thrown into this mix was how modes of discourse influenced student holistic evaluation. Although many believed that when students produced writing in the argumentation mode that their writing was syntactically more mature, Hoetker (1982) reported that this was not necessarily the case. Actually, students tended to use more than one mode on various topics sometimes even in the same paragraph (Stratta & Dixon, 1982) or failed to produce writing in the expected mode (Emig, 1971; Pianko, 1979).

Thus, topic structure for student writing was rife for examination. Our own experiences as writing teachers was that topics—how they were structured and their cognitive demands on students—affected the writing that students produced. Although we could have structured a study along these lines, this group reasoned that most writing prompts were expressive by nature and relied on general knowledge that each student should possess. If a traditional topic asked students to write about their summer vacations, the expressive nature of the topic allowed for students to theoretically "think" in the language of talk. Britton et al. (1975) called this, "writing close to the self, carrying forward the informal presuppositions of informal talk and revealing as much about the writer as about his matter" (p. 141).

What might happen as we move from expressive to transactional writing where the emphasis becomes more expository? What if all the students had gone to the same place for their summer vacations and you asked that they all wrote about one aspect—for instance, a particular ride at Disney World? This would involve knowledge of the ride, but still allow for an expressive element. What would happen if students had to write about three rides, describe each, and recommend one? How does this affect the Britton et al. continuum? (My notes from that time suggest that we did discuss this.) As this second group spoke, it became clear that that the topic structure project held the most potential mainly because this area allowed us to focus on error, fluency, and holistic ratings. We quickly decided to focus our efforts in this direction.

Although we decided to focus on topic structure, we must have briefly outlined a dozen other studies on wide-ranging subject. This was how Bill was different from any other teacher I had ever met. Bill made every subject sound interesting, fun, and important. We never seemed pressed for time. It was like we had all evening for these discussions. Graph paper was a staple at all our sessions, and we could quickly fill whole tablets imagining the results of these various hypothetical studies. I personally wanted to do every one of the proposed studies we discussed, whether it was voice, topic, or any of a number of studies that always seemed to begin, "What if . . . ." This was a lesson I learned as both a teacher and researcher.

Enthusiasm is "catching" when you are interested in everything, and Bill was literally interested in everything in every field. There were roads not taken, but not until we had wandered down the path far enough to know where each one led. To Bill, everything is interesting. I pass this along to my preservice teachers, student teachers, and practicing teachers regularly. Find what it is about what you are teaching that is personally interesting to you. Stay with every topic until you find it . . . the point where you want to go on even when you don't have to. I guarantee them that if they find why a subject is personally interesting, their students will not be far behind.

Unbeknown to us, the topic of the topic was a hot topic. Brosell (1983) was testing topics varying in "information load." Kahn and Johannessen (1982) had actually preceded our thinking by testing a topic that asked students to write about an event that happened to them or someone they knew and then, on the basis of this, to write on what one might conclude about the person from the event. Greenberg (1981) had experimented with topics that had high or low cognitive demands. Hillocks, (1986), however, summarized this research on topic structure writing as yielding "no significant differences." He went on to write, "For instructional purposes, however, the variations in topics examined here provide little of promise, despite the widespread belief in the importance of selecting the 'right' topics" (p. 173). Hillocks' book, I imagine, was in press at the time of the publication of the Smith et al. (1985) study. He also missed Kinzer and Murphy (1982) and their analysis of topic-related variables. Kinzer and Murphy are adamant that "topic effects are reflected in student responses and and influence holistic scores" (p. 119). Our results support Kinzer and Murphy when they write (Murphy & Ruth, 1993), "If multiple topics are to be used, all the topics must make comparable demands; otherwise the students within the same administrative unit are, in effect, taking different tests" (p. 276). Although we did not look at the topic demands, our results are consistent with Kinzer and Murphy (1982). Whatever the demands are, different demands produce different results at least in regards to word production, assessed quality, and some error.

BILL'S ROLE AS GROUP MENTOR

At this stage—the problem-posing stage of the project—Bill provided the setting, the peanuts, of course, and the sense that this widely disparate group could work together and contribute to the growing body of composition research. I had first met Bill a year and a half before in a graduate education class taught by Anthony Petrosky. Glynda and I were both in this class, and Bill was a guest lecturer who talked about composition research, especially the writing workshop aspect. Bill ended his lecture by inviting anyone in the class to work with him on various research projects that he was conducting.

Bill was in the English department, and I was a graduate student in reading education. Still, no professor had ever made such an offer. Bill also offered a sense of wonder and enthusiasm about his work. Both were foreign to me in higher education. I took a course from Bill soon after, and he challenged my notion of research and general assumptions of higher education. I asked Bill to direct my dissertation, ignoring the politics of an English department professor chairing a reading education dissertation. (Bob Land did the same thing.) By then I had learned that there was no subject Bill was not interested in. Bill's response to my asking him to chair my dissertation committee was typical of Bill and atypical of my experience with academics. Bill refused; that is, until I had worked with him for a year on something else. Topic structure was something else (see Suzanne Miller's chapter in this volume for a more complete account).

In The *Courage to Teach*, Palmer (1998) examines mentoring from a unique perspective. Palmer poses the question of what was it about "you" at this time and situation that allowed "you" to be mentored? I find this question better than the one about how your mentor influenced "you." At this time, I had no interest in becoming a college teacher. Quite frankly, universities could not pay me as much as I was making as a high school English teacher. Bill offered the gift of time. He always had time for any of us in our group. He offered his own unique view of the world that fused so much together. But most important, I was ready to be mentored by someone who had a passionate love of learning. This was not something to be embarrassed by. Yet in western Pennsylvania steel culture, this was not something one aspired to.

At the inception of this project, several of us were in a seminar on writing that Bill conducted. We examined a pair of different research articles each week and critiqued them. Now, looking back through old copies of *Research in the Teaching of English, College Composition and Communication and College English*, I can see that the topic structure study followed a research line that started with Janet Emig (1971), went to Nold and Freeman (1977), to Crowhurst (1980) to Bridwell (1980) and to Brossell (1983). Thus, we were learning how to read and becoming knowledgeable about the field of composition research. Bill's role in our Friday afternoon gatherings was as devil's advocate. Bill challenged our thinking at every turn. Bill's "What if . . ." questions were maddening. I never thought we would come up with the research questions and topics we used because at every turn Bill was "What iffing . . ." different topics and different possible responses. He seemed to know everyone in the writing research community and often would invite us to "call them up and ask them" if we had a question or comment on the research influencing us.

Once we finally settled on a procedure, meetings were pure business. Getting essays written, read, and scored consumed us for months. When we finally started to look at the results (carefully graphed for us by Bill), the real "What iffing . . ." started. I credit Bill with shaping all our thinking at this point. We were no longer looking at a published article in a journal; we were looking at our own research and attempting to make sense of it. None of my statistics or research courses prepared me for this.

Finally, we had talked enough. I don't remember exactly how the article came to be written or who contributed what to the writing. It suddenly appeared and was gone. In the meantime, we continued to work on the college database. We also conducted our study, with smaller numbers, at my high school. Bill and I took a small sample of the college essays, had them typed, and the surface-level error corrected. We had these rated again by a different set of raters and compared the results to the original ratings. We found that raters tended to rate the errorless essays much lower, confirming a suspicion that error played a larger role than it should have. We both knew we should have followed this pilot study with a larger scale study using all the original essays, but by then, I was leaving Pittsburgh and had started a different line of research.

Bill's role as mentor is, from his perspective, a life-long obligation. Although over 20 years have passed since our study and 22 years since my dissertation, Bill continues to read anything I send him as thoroughly as he reads everything. Although he infrequently attends conferences, he still makes time at those conferences he does attend to meet and discuss research. These meetings involve many cocktail napkins, and because I usually always carry graph paper (my homage to Bill), we quickly fill these, too.

A couple of years after leaving the University of Pittsburgh and moving to Georgia, I had the opportunity to bring Bill to Georgia to visit our school as part of a campus life-enrichment grant. Bill stayed with me for 5 days. There were a number of results from this visit. First, those who came to hear Bill learned the latest research on holistic evaluation of student writing and essay placement testing. The University System of Georgia had a minimum competency rising junior essay test that was holistically evaluated, as well as a developmental studies program where underprepared students had to both pass the course and a final essay. Needless to say, Bill's observations and his take on the state's system proved unsettling to some in attendance and gratifying to many. Second, in true Bill fashion, he helped all three of my children with their homework in *every* subject (something I never mastered), he helped my wife with her master's thesis by suggesting a change in the design of her study, and he helped me design my next three studies. Although I had moved away from composition and even writing research and into the areas of problem finding and teacher planning, Bill brought back to me the sense of fun and a level of excitement in doing new research.

A few years later, I hit an impasse in my research line. I was looking at problem finding/creativity and teacher planning. At Bill's insistence, I began to teach myself how to do qualitative research. He pointed out that the variables I was researching were too limiting. We kept going back to the question of "What do teachers actually really do?" This meant that I needed to begin observing teachers to find new variables to study. Although I am simplifying and summarizing to make a point, the point is that the research question is the most important decision one makes as a researcher, and the methods for investigating the questions do not come from the researcher's background, but from the question. Neither of us was trained to do qualitative research. Pitt did not have a qualitative class, and it was only briefly mentioned in our research sequence. Qualitative research was certainly not in Bill's training. But to Bill, research is research. To help me, he became interested in qualitative research. The studies he helped me design did the trick. Also, as qualitative research started to burgeon in the 1970s, I knew it would-n't be long before graduate students brought their studies to Bill. I think a bibliography of all the studies Bill has consulted on would make a head-spinning volume of its own.

SOME EFFECTS OF VARYING THE STRUCTURE OF A TOPIC ON COLLEGE STUDENTS WRITING

Briefly, we found that the structure of the topic does appear to make a difference in student writing in quality of the written product, fluency or words produced, and in total error produced. Topic Structure 1 (TS1), an open or expressive prompt (see Smith's Curriculum Vitae, this volume), is best to be used to distinguish advanced writers from average and poor writers. To really distinguish poor writers, use TS3, which has students reading and responding to three different perspectives on the same topic. TS2 produced the fewest errors and the least fluency, but seemed the least accurate for placement purposes. TS1 produced the most fluency and error. The article makes the point that the different topic structures should be used for different purposes. Interestingly, we replicated the study using high school students in two different grades (Moore & Dunham, 1984) with similar results. Bill led us through involved discussions of the results that culminated in several proposals to national conferences. The research database was used for a number of other studies (Moore, 1984a, 1984b, 1984c, 1984d; Dunham & Moore, 1984; Moore & Dunham, 1984). Further, as part of Bill's mentoring process, he took us through preparations for these presentations as thorough and grueling as only he could make them. No one in our audiences at these meetings asked us any questions that we hadn't already anticipated in several different forms and variations. If there were more prepared graduate students than us, I would have been greatly surprised.

In reviewing the research for this chapter, I was immediately struck by how much composition research dominated the journals in the 1980s. The research reported was decidedly positivistic. Composition research dominated *Research in the Teaching of English, College Composition and Communication, College English,* and even the *English Journal.* An annotated bibliography of research by Marshall and Durst (1985) noted 116 citations of writing/composition research. A recent review by Brown et al. (2002) revealed 10.

THE TOPIC OF THE TOPIC LATELY

From The New SAT (2003), Although research will determine exactly what kind of writing assignment to include on the test, we suspect the assignment will be persuasive in nature and will ask the student to take a position on an issue and support it with reasons and evidence from his or her reading, experience, or observation. (p. 1)

Sample essay prompt from The New SAT: Directions: Consider carefully the following excerpt and the assignment below it. Then plan and write an essay that explains your ideas as persuasively as possible. Keep in mind that the support you provide—both reasons and examples—will make your view convincing to the reader

Appreciation of music, paintings, books, and movies doesn't make us into better people. In fact, it may actually worsen us, diminishing our ability to respond to actual situations and making it more difficult to identify with the real world. As one scholar said, "the voice in the poem may come to sound louder, more urgent, more real than the voice in the street outside."

Adapted from George Steiner "To Civilize our Gentlemen" (1965).
In Language and Silence: Essays on Language, Literature, and the Inhuman. 1970.

Assignment: What is your view of the idea that enjoying music, painting, and other forms of art does not improve people, but instead makes them less able to relate to real life? In an essay, support your position by discussing an example (or examples) from literature, the arts, science and technology, current events, or your own experience or observation.

The SAT Web site cites a number of recent studies conducted by their own psychometricians. Studies were conducted on timing conditions (Camaro, 2003), forecasting predictive validity (Kobrin n. d.) and reliability (Breland, Kobota, Nickerson, Trapani, & Walker, 2004). Only one of these attends to the topic of the topic. Breland et al. (2004)) refer to Hoetker, Brossell, and Ash (1981), an article that preceded ours by 4 years, who said that the more language used in the prompt, the harder it is for students to get beyond the language and discover their own thoughts and ideas. In our article, we wrote, "Thus it seems that the TS (topic structure) used should be chosen only after considering the purpose of the essay exam" (p. 79). According to the general criteria for scoring the new SAT (The New SAT, 2004), readers must consider "rewarding what is done well," "Ignore the quality of handwriting," "Not judge an essay by its length," and "understand that grammar is not an overriding factor in determining an essay score" (p. 2). Although quoted material is provided in the New SAT essay prompt, writers do not have to summarize or interpret the quotation (although I suspect that many might infer that they should).

After reviewing the criteria for scoring, the NEW SAT's purpose is to separate advanced writers from general and poor writers. The New SAT sample prompt and the prompts used in the Breland et al. (2004) study are probably closer to our TS2, although all elements of our TS1 are represented in TS2 and TS3. One focus of the Breland et al. study was to determine whether there was any difference moving from a general prompt to a persuasive prompt. The College Board appears to assume that, despite the evidence (Stratta & Dixon, 1982), persuasive writing will generate the best writing from students. However, it is more likely that writers will produce narrative/expressive products (Crowhurst, 1980; Nold & Freeman, 1977). Also, despite evidence, the College Board assumes that, by telling readers not to focus on length, however, the topics studied and proposed by the New SAT should distinguish in terms of quality the advanced writers from general ability writers.

The NEW SAT topic should also separate advanced writers from others due to its implied high cognitive demand. Hoetker (1982) wrote, "the more language and information students are given the more difficult it seems to be for them to get beyond the language of the topic to discover what they themselves might have to say…" (p. 387). If I were a writer asked to write on this topic, under time constraints, knowing that the quality of my writing might make a difference in the quality of institution I attend next year, I think I would have much to consider with this topic before I could begin to write. Into this mix I must consider my audience (readers for these essays must teach or have taught in the last 5 years a high school or college level course that required writing). I imagine that most writers will picture their high school English teachers as their target audience. Although it would be much easier to agree with the quoted material and argue that music, painting, and other forms of art do not improve people, I know that my audience certainly would not approve. Should I cover as many art forms as possible in making my point? Or only a couple? Should I really use my own experience and skill or observation? I think advanced writers would stay away from expressing personal perspective, and I suspect that poorer writers will see personal perspective as a way out of the topic, especially if they are not up on their art forms. Finally, I have to wonder that if other parts of the country are using different prompts, or when I take the SAT again and have a different prompt, would I do better, or, more important, would raters think I did better?

A FINAL COMMENT

In 1982, James Hoetker wrote in his review of the literature on topic variables that this area is rife for investigation. Until research is clear, we should be careful about topics and look critically at those offered for various purposes.

Investigating the effects of topic variations on student writing performance is going to involve researchers in all sorts of perplexing difficulties. It will demand a better understanding of reading processes involved, the development of new methods for scaling essay quality and essay characteristics, and perhaps the invention of new methodologies. In the course of such studies, though, we should learn a good deal not only about topics, but about reading and writing. (pp. .387-388)

Although, research focusing on understanding essay quality and especially holistic evaluation has continued, Hoetker's call for more research on topic variation (especially as it relates to large-scale testing) has gone unheeded. We know little more than we knew when we began our project in 1983. Six years later, Ruth and Murphy (1988) state, "Up to now, deciding when a topic is good has typically been more intuitive than objective" (p. 1). Because universities that currently require placement essays of new students will likely examine whether the new SAT provides this information accurately, it is more important than ever to question the demands of different writing tasks and the different profile of the student writer that each provides. Of course, results from research on topic structure, mode of discourse, assessment, or audience doesn't necessarily mean that those who design large-scale assessments will pay any more attention than they already have.

When I left the University of Pittsburgh, moving from high school teaching to college teaching, Bill threw a going-away party for me. Our research group gathered for its final time (at least its final time with me involved), and I was presented with a going-away present from Bill and the group that I still cherish. On a blue Georgia Southern sweatshirt, prominently featured across the chest in black letters is "**TS3 Y'all.**" I can imagine Bill pondering which topic structure to enshrine on the sweatshirt. *"Should I tell Michael that his opinion and experiences are valid by using TS1? Should I limit his fluency and quality by invoking TS2? Or should I tell him that the cognitive demands from now on increase, and that quality only becomes distinguishable as his ability increases?"* I suspect that Bill, ever the teacher and mentor, chose **TS3** to remind me how complex things would become from now on. To Bill, however, I bequeath **TS1** . . . keep telling us like it is.

REFERENCES

Breland, H., Kobota, M., Nickerson, K., Trapani, C., & Walker, M. (2004). *New SAT writing prompt study: Analyses of group impact and reliability* (Research Report #2004-1 ETS RR-04-03). Princeton, NJ: Educational Testing Service.

Bridwell, L. (1980). Revising strategies of twelfth-grade students' transactional writing. *Research in the Teaching of English, 14*, 197–222.

Britton, J., Burgess, T., Martin, N., McLeod, A., & Rosen, H. (1975). *The development of writing abilities* (pp. 11-18). London: Macmillan.

Brosell, G. (1983). Rhetorical specifications in essay examination topics. *College English, 45*, 165–173.

Brown, D., Beavis, C., Kalman, J., Stinson, A. D., & Whiting, M.E. (2002). Annotated bibliography of research in the teaching of English. *Research in the Teaching of English, 36*(4), 531–541.

Camara, W. J. (2003). Comparing essays written under different timing conditions (Research report #RS-08). Princeton, NJ: Educational Testing Service.

Collegeboard.com, Inc. (2004). *The New SAT.* Retrieved August 26, 2004, from http://www.collegeboard.com/about/newsat/writing/essay.html.

Crowhurst, M. (1980). Syntactic complexity and teachers' quality ratings of narration and arguments. *Research in the Teaching of English, 14*, 223–231.

Diederich, P. B. (1974). *Measuring growth in English.* Urbana, IL: National Council of Teachers of English.

Dunham, D. E., & Moore, M. T. (1984, January). *Assessing the content variable of a commonly known topic.* Paper presented at the New York State English Conference Seminar on Research in Language, SUNY, Buffalo.

Emig, J. (1971). *The composing processes of twelfth graders.* Urbana, IL: National Council of Teachers of English.

Greenberg, K. L. (1981). The effects of variations in essay questions on the writing performance of college freshmen. *Dissertation Abstracts International, 42*, 685-A.

Hillocks, G. (1986). *Research on written composition: New directions for teaching.* Urbana, IL: National Council of Teachers of English.

Hoetker, J. (1982). Essay examination topics and students' writing. *College Composition and Communication, 33*, 377–392.

Hoetker, J., Brossell, G., & Ash, B. (1981). *Creating essay examination topics.* Unpublished manuscript, Florida State University, Tallahassee.

Kahn, E. A., & Johannessen, L. R. (1982). *Does the assignment make a difference? Four variations of a writing task and their effects on student performance.* Unpublished manuscript.

Kinzer, C., & Murphy, S. (1982). The effects of assessment prompt and response variables on holistic score: A pilot study and validation of an analysis technique. In J. R. Gray & L. P. Ruth (Eds.), *Properties of writing tasks: A study of alternative procedures for holistic writing assessment*, (pp. 132–214). Berkeley University of California, Graduate School of Education, Bay Area Writing Project. (ERIC ED230576).

Kobrin, J. L. (n.d.). *Forecasting the predictive validity of the new SAT 1 Writing Section.* Retrieved July 22, 2004, from http://www.collegeboard.com/about/newsat/writing/essay.html

Kroll, B. M. (1978). Cognitive egocentrism and the problem of audience awareness in written discourse. *Research in the Teaching of English, 12*, 269–281.

Lopate, P. (1978). Helping young children start to write. In C. R. Cooper & L. O'Dell (Eds.), *Research on composing: Points of departure* (pp. 135–149). Urbana. IL: NCTE .

Marshall, J. D., & Durst, R. K. (1985). Annotated bibliography of research in the teaching of English. *Research in the Teaching of English, 19*(2), 183–204.

Moore, M. T. (1984a). *Bridging the gap between high school and college: Altering the high school sequence to facilitate college teaching in writing.* Paper presented at the 13th Conference on Teaching the English Language Arts annual meeting, Athens, GA.

Moore, M. T. (1984b). *Critical reading skills in the high school/college reading class and critical writing skills in the high school/college writing class.* Paper presented at the 14th Annual Conference on Teaching the English Language Arts, Athens, GA.

Moore, M. T. (1984c, April). *Bridging the gap between high school and college: Altering the high school sequence to facilitate college teaching in writing.* Paper presented at the 13th Conference on Teaching the English Language Arts annual meeting, Athens, GA.

Moore, M. T., & Dunham, D. E. (1984, April). *Assessing the content variable of a commonly known topic: A new look at holistic ratings.* Paper presented at the American Educational Research Association annual meeting, New Orleans.

Moore, M. T. (1984d). *The structure of the topic: Implications for teachers and curriculum.* Paper presented at the Conference on College Composition and Communication annual meeting, New York.

Murphy, S., & Ruth, L. (1993). The field-testing of writing prompt reconsidered. In M. W. Williamson & B. A. Huot (Eds.), *Validating holistic scoring for writing assessment: Theoretical and empirical foundations* (pp. 266-302). Cresskill, NJ: Hampton Press.

Nold, E., & Freeman, S., (1977). An analysis of readers' responses to essays. *Research in the Teaching of English, 11,* 164–174.

North, S. M. (1987). *The making of knowledge in composition: Portrait of an emerging field.* Upper Montclair, NJ: Boynton/Cook.

Palmer, P. J. (1998). *The courage to teach.* San Francisco, CA: Jossey-Bass.

Pianko, S. (1979). A description of composing processes of college freshmen writers. *Research in the Teaching of English, 13,* 5–22.

Ruth, L., & Murphy, S. (1988). *Designing writing tasks for the assessment of writing.* Norwood, NJ: Ablex.

Smith, W. L., Hull, G. A., Land, R. E., Moore, M. T., Ball, C., Dunham, D. E., Hickey, L. S., & Ruzich, C. W. (1985). Some effects of varying the structure of the topic on college students' writing. *Written Communication, 2*(1), 73–89.

Stratta, L., & Dixon, J. (1982). *Teaching and assessing argument.* Southampton, England: Southern Regional Examinations Board.

3

WHAT TEACHERS VALUE IN STUDENT WRITING

The Story of a Research Journey

Robert E. Land

FELLOW TRAVELERS

It is a fine September evening in Pittsburgh in the early 1980s. There are about a dozen of us seated around a seminar table in Forbes Quadrangle.[1] We are an eclectic group: a freeway flier composition teacher, who never seems to stop grading her papers; a precocious undergraduate, who seems a little *too* eager to impress; a full-time doctoral student who can say hello in 17 languages; and an assortment of tired classroom teachers taking an elective to finish up their master's degrees. One of the tired teachers, I am listening to the discussion as best I can, hearing bits and pieces. The man at the head of the seminar table sports an Abe Lincoln

---

[1] "FQ," as we called it, now "Wesley Posvar Hall," is a complex of seminar rooms and lecture halls and the home of the school of education. It was built on the site of the stadium where the Pirates beat the Yankees in the 1960 World Series. On the first floor, home plate is still preserved under glass. The room we occupied that fall hovered about 40 feet over the spot where Bill Mazeroski played second base, the same position Bill Smith played, although I doubt if the connection ever occurred to him.

beard and wears a brown suede coat, jeans, and cowboy boots. He says, "Research is science, but every really good research study tells a story." He says, "I am here to seduce you into becoming a researcher." He has my attention. I change—almost over night—from a somewhat aimless teacher and course taker to a committed doctoral student. I become part of a group of researchers who work closely together and closely with Bill. We conduct studies together, travel to conferences together, present papers together, and even today many of us still stay in touch. Even today, when I write, I find myself asking, "What would they think? What would Bill think?

It has been more than 20 years since those "halcyon days," as Bill called them, but everything I have done professionally is deeply connected with the experiences I had with that group under Bill's mentorship. One of the most influential moments of that experience was a time Bill showed me a book case along one wall of that wonderfully asymmetric corner office in the gothic Cathedral of Learning. The book case was filled with three-ring binders labeled "Research Project 1," Research Project 2," and so on. How I wanted an office with shelves of binders like those!

FIRST STEPS

This chapter on what teachers value in student writing has its origins in one of those research binders, the "topic structure" study (Smith et al., 1985). In that study, we (Bill and his "legion of graduate students," as the editor of *Written Communications* called us) examined the effect of providing lots of text, limited text, or no text on fluency, quality, and syntactic complexity of lower, medium, and higher ability college students' placement test essays. We found, among other things, that topic structure made a difference in writing quality. Of particular interest to me at the time, given my job as a dropout prevention English teacher, was that "weaker" writers performed better on the text-abundant topic structure than on the text-free, personal experience topic structure. The implication was that colleges could create additional barriers for my at-risk students by using a placement test with a topic structure that placed them at a disadvantage, the personal experience structure, which so many writing experts, then and now, seem to think is the easiest to write to. My continued inquiry into external factors affecting students' writing scores now fills several three-ring binders. I propose to tell the story of this ongoing line of inquiry and present a sort of progress report on some of the more interesting findings to date.

At the time we were conducting the topic structure study, high levels of interrater reliability seemed inarguably desirable. After all, disagreements were error, and an aim of experimental research was to increase statistical power by reducing error in our measurement instruments. We managed to count errors, and words, T-units, and clauses accurately, so, we reasoned, we should be able to correctly identify an essay's proper location on a 4-point scoring continuum. But we had frequent disagreements; like countless scorers before and since, we tried to "norm ourselves into conformity." In our discussions, we frequently anchored our score justifications in our professional experiences as teachers. Our group included teachers of basic, advanced, and ESL college writing as well as teachers of middle- and high school English, and each of us could make fairly compelling arguments for our deviant scores, from our disparate perspectives. We began to understand that reasonable people might disagree for good reasons.

As we gained more experience looking at disagreements, some members of the group began calling papers that received widely disparate scores—say a 1 and a 4 on a 4-point scale—"Archies" and papers that seemed to get split scores from multiple scorers—say a 2 and a 3 on a 4-point scale—"Crackers."[2] Archies seemed to be characterized by rhetorical or stylistic extremes that either charmed or annoyed the reader. Crackers seemed to be papers that looked like the writing of a student in the midpoint of someone's course. In both cases of consistent disagreement, we tended to be reading and rating the writer, not the text.[3]

CROSSING LINGUISTIC BORDERS

My interest in teachers' differences in evaluating student writing increased when I started my first post-PhD job supervising teachers of college writing. That composition program employed a diverse group of graduate students, including international students studying comparative literature, MFA students writing fiction and poetry, and traditional English doctoral students acquiring literary critical postures and stances. Few had ever taught anything and most were assigned to teach courses they had never even taken themselves. As one Teaching Assistant (TA) put it after his first year of teaching, "I can't believe they gave *me* the chalk!" As an added challenge, our campus was experiencing a dramatic increase in the number of students who were speakers of English as a second (third, fourth . . .) language, and all of these students were required to complete regular composition classes. With as many as 150 sections of writing offered each term, getting inexperienced teachers to grade consistently seemed like a good idea. Sure, reasonable people may disagree for good reasons. But I was not willing to defend too

---

[2]It has been alleged that these names referred to the sites of two CCCC conferences where some of these ideas were to be presented—St. Louis and Atlanta. I think "edgy" and "iffy" might be better descriptors. In later published work, Smith refers to "crackers" as "tweeners" and both categories of disagreement and "microsplits" and "macrosplits" (Smith, 1993).

[3]Barritt, Stock, and Clark (1986) published an important article that also reported the influences of reader background and the tendency to rate the writer on placement essay score disagreements.

vigorously that idea to hundreds of undergraduates complaining that their friends were getting better grades on similar essays (sometimes the same essay) from other T.A.s. Besides, I was not certain that our newly minted composition teachers knew enough to be considered "reasonable people."

Our efforts to create a consistent "interpretative community" were moderately successful; however, as seemingly random variations in paper grading diminished, certain set patterns of grading differences became more visible. In particular, I noticed that grades given to English learner (E2) undergraduates tended to vary according to the first-language status of their T.A. It seemed that T.A.s whose first language was English (E1s) gave consistently lower grades than did E2 T.A.s. Grades given to E1 students seemed consistent across graders. Because all E2 students were mainstreamed after a sequence of up to four quarters of ESL classes, a typical lower division course enrolled substantial numbers of E2 students, often more than half the class.[4] Additionally, E2 T.A.s covered roughly a dozen sections of composition each quarter. Thus, the apparent difference in evaluative standards had a potentially large cumulative effect.

In keeping with the Bill Smith tradition at Pittsburgh, I started my own research group to investigate the E1/E2 grading interaction. We conducted an experimental study (Land & Whitley, 1986, 1989) which demonstrated that four E2 teachers were significantly more likely than four E1 teachers to give higher holistic scores to 20 essays (10 narrative and 10 expository) written by E2 writers. We found no significant differences in scores given to 20 essays written by E1 students.[5]

Over the next several years, as the students entering my university became increasingly linguistically diverse, faculty across the campus, predictably, began to complain of a "writing crisis." A campus-wide writing improvement taskforce was formed. Early meetings were filled with almost cloying unity and good will: "Writing is important." "Writing is good." "Students' must write well." "We want good writing." "Writing Yes, Yes, Yes!"

Then we started revealing to each other what we meant by *good writing*. The chair of the taskforce, a brilliant computer scientist, gave a talk to the faculty one evening where he used essays written by undergraduates to show that inaccurate, illogical, and ungrammatical work was being accepted by teachers in the composition program. He went on to lament that these teachers' written comments were so cursory and careless when his dissertation chair, a Nobel Prize Winner, was able to find time to provide extensive, detailed, written responses to his dissertation draft. His view was that good writing is a grammatically correct presentation of facts.

---

[4]By the early 1990s, well over half of our undergraduates were native speakers of languages other than English, although most were able out pass out of our ESL sequence.

[5]Nor were there significant differences related to whether essays were narrative or expository. Teachers' justifications for their holistic scores showed that E1 readers pointed to organization—as much as error—as a problem with many of the E2 students' essays. E2 teachers did not see organization as a problem. Moreover, cohesion analyses of the 20 E1 and 20 E2 essays showed that the E2 essays were significantly longer, more syntactically complex, and had far more remote cohesive ties.

Although some of us wondered aloud at our chair's reasoning, one taskforce member representing the ESL program said she agreed, at least that grammar was not given sufficient focus. Her perspective was that English learners need direct, systematic instruction in grammar; they do not just learn it through experience. The campus-writing director was more concerned with thesis-driven essays and arguable claims. Then (and increasingly these days) deeply influenced by thinkers such as Rohman and Wlecke (1964), I was, *sub rosa*, attached to the idea that the real point of writing was self-discovery. Our differences bared, the love-in was over, and the taskforce's mission was doomed. As one member put it when the report finally came out, "After the gestation period of an elephant, the taskforce gave birth to a mouse"—a little-read, largely ignored report.

A NEW ROAD MAP

About this time, Fulkerson (1990) published "Composition Theory in the Eighties," which presented what seemed to be a compelling theoretical explanation for patterns of disagreement among readers with different backgrounds. Paraphrased and simplified, Fulkerson's notion is that writing teachers tend to be oriented toward one of four distinct axiologies (or general value orientations): "Formalist" "mimetic," "expressivist," and "rhetorical" axiologies privilege, respectively, the text, external reality, the writer, and the reader. A formalist values correctness at the sentence level, perhaps a particular style of sentence, and maybe a certain paragraph structure or even the five-paragraph essay. A mimeticist emphasizes accurate, plentiful information, logic, and perhaps models of argumentation. An expressivist is oriented toward sincerity, originality, authentic voice, and personal experience. Rhetoricists are concerned with effectiveness, persuasiveness, audience awareness, and instrumentality. Although all four are necessary components of an adequate philosophy of good writing, individuals tend to emphasize one over another.

Fulkerson's descriptions of these value systems aligned well with statements I heard over the years from individuals who disagreed over the "right" score to give an essay and over what constituted good writing in general. The thought occurred to me that one could develop an instrument to detect these tendencies, similar to one of the personality or learning styles inventories. Anyone who had to score essays or serve on a writing improvement taskforce would be required to take my survey, and their orientations would be unmasked, saving everyone endless hours of debate and frustration.

You're not stupid. You're just a formalist with a mimeticist overlay. I, on the other hand, am a rhetoricist with expressivist undertones. Of course we disagree!

I tried an experiment (Land, 1993) where I reduced each axiology to a simplistic statement and made a simple survey. I administered the survey to an informal sample of 5 to 10 faculty from each of the four camps: the composition specialists supervising the writing program, T.A.s teaching in the writing program, content faculty, and ESL faculty. Undergraduates in required composition classes were surveyed as well. Based on the average rank given by each group, composition specialists valued rhetoric, graduate student composition T.A.s and undergraduate students in their classes privileged the expressivist view, content area faculty were mimeticists, and ESL instructors were strongly oriented to the formalist axiology. The results affirm Fulkerson's claim that the rhetorical axiology had taken hold among compositionists, but it was clear that other stakeholders held other views. Although my mentor would conclude that these disagreements were predictable because each group belonged to a course-specific discourse community (Smith, 1993), the unwillingness of various camps to acknowledge the legitimacy of one another's differences bothered me then and still does.

A Brief Survey of Teachers' Beliefs About "Good" Writing

Rank each of the definitions below from "1" (*relatively most important*) to "4" (*relatively least important*) according to your expectations of the writing your students do in your classes. If those expectations vary according to class level, or the kind of writing you are working on at a particular time, please give a response that reflects a kind of midpoint or most common expectation, rather than an ultimate or a hoped for but rarely realized goal. Remember that scoring a particular definition as *relatively most important* does not mean that it alone is a sufficient goal or that the other definitions are not necessary to a complete definition of *good writing*.

Definitions:

- Formalist: Good writing shows mastery of the conventions of standard Written English.
- Mimetic: Good writing accurately reports and/or explains reality.
- Expressivist: Good writing reveals discovery and expression of ideas and/or feelings.
- Rhetorical: Good writing effects change in a reader's beliefs and/or actions.

Given my goals for my students, good writing is (Rank from "1" to "4" as noted earlier):

_____ Formalist
_____ Mimetic
_____ Expressivist
_____ Rhetorical

NEW TERRITORY, SAME ITINERARY

Eventually, I left the college composition Scylla for the national research center Charybdis, but the issue of disagreement among readers of student writing followed me. One of my tasks at the research center was to help develop writing assessments for a large urban school district. We piloted the assessments at Grades 3, 7, and 9. To validate the assessments, we held scoring sessions where teachers from appropriate grade levels were trained with "anchor" papers. Although I held out the "reasonable people disagree" theory, and pointed with enthusiasm to Moss' (1994) recently published article on the possibility of validity without reliability, most of the team still focused on the need for exact agreement among readers. Achieving such agreement led to increasingly coercive calibration sessions. Readers of the third-grade essays were especially targeted for group-think lessons.

As it turned out, about half of the teachers who were recruited to score the third-grade essays were certified bilingual educators (Spanish/English). After training, these teachers read and scored 265 essays on a 4-point scale. Overall the rate of exact agreement was just over 50%, but where the reader pair included one regular classroom teacher and one bilingual teacher, exact agreement was only about 30%, with the bilingual teacher giving the lower score twice as often as the teacher with no bilingual certification. Because most of the essays were written by students who were English learners or speakers of "nonstandard" English dialects, I concluded (Land, 1999) that we were observing a phenomenon similar to the one I saw among college ESL teachers: a bias toward the formalist axiology among teachers who were trained and responsible to teach students standard English and/or a bias away from the formalist perspective by teachers with generalist responsibilities and training. The implication was that we could—consciously or unconsciously—raise or lower the overall average score on a set of essays by excluding or including readers whose axiologies would lead them to give systematically higher or lower scores. This implication echoed for me the topic structure study that I worked on with Bill's group many years earlier.

THE PRESENT SURVEY

Although my present career as a professor of reading and English education has caused me to concentrate on issues related to scripted, synthetic-phonics-based reading instruction, I have continued to work on a survey based on Fulkerson's theory. With a graduate student, Tonya Leija, I reviewed the literature on writing assessment and interviewed a wide array of teachers to find as many statements as we could about what constituted good writing. Using Fulkerson's four axiolo-

Writing Assessment Survey

Today's Date: __ / __ / __ /; Undergraduate Major: _____ ; Highest Degree: _____ ;
Home (First) Language(s) Spoken: You _____ , Your Students: _____ ;
Subject(s)/Grade(s) Taught: _____ / _____ ; Years Teaching: Current Level _____ ,
Total _____ ; Weekly Hours: Teaching _____ ; Teaching Writing _____ ; Having Students Write
in Class _____ .

Directions: The following statements were developed from a review of literature and from interviews with teachers who have varying views on what they look for when evaluating student writing. Please read each item carefully. Think about what you value and stress in the writing you expect from students and circle the number from 1 (strongly disagree) to 6 (strongly agree) that indicates your view on the statement. Please feel free to write comments in blank areas of this survey. No results will be associated with any individual or institution.

1=Strongly disagree; 2=Disagree; 3=Mildly disagree; 4= Mildly agree; 5=Agree; 6= Strongly agree

Item	Reference	Statement	Rating
1	R03,6	I prefer student writing that persuades people to believe or do something.	1 2 3 4 5 6
2	E05,34	A good piece of student writing gives examples from the writer's life.	1 2 3 4 5 6
3	F09,43	Good student writing must have correct grammar and mechanics.	1 2 3 4 5 6
4	R25,11	Good student writing has clear ideas supported by strong evidence.	1 2 3 4 5 6
5	F21,93	I prefer student writing to be well structured.	1 2 3 4 5 6
6	M09,27	The main purpose of student writing is to inform the reader.	1 2 3 4 5 6
7	R09,32	I like student writing that acknowledges opposing viewpoints.	1 2 3 4 5 6
8	M04,16	The main purpose of student writing is to show knowledge of a topic.	1 2 3 4 5 6
9	F22,94	Good student writing has sentences and paragraphs that flow well.	1 2 3 4 5 6
10	E20,83	Eloquent student writing reveals a passion for a topic.	1 2 3 4 5 6
11	M15,58	Good student writing accurately reports information.	1 2 3 4 5 6
12	E23,92	I like to read writing that reveals students' feelings.	1 2 3 4 5 6
13	M24,96	An outstanding piece of student writing is truthful.	1 2 3 4 5 6
14	R11,36	I especially look for an awareness of audience in student writing.	1 2 3 4 5 6
15	E17,78	I prefer to read student writing that vividly reflects the writer's emotions.	1 2 3 4 5 6
16	F06,31	Good student writing must use correct sentence structure.	1 2 3 4 5 6

Scoring: Add your ratings for each set of four items as follows:
Items: 3, 5, 9, and 16 = _____ (Formalist Score)
Items: 6, 8, 11, and 13 = _____ (Mimetic Score)
Items: 2, 10, 12, and 15 = _____ (Expressivist Score)
Items: 1, 4, 7, and 14 = _____ (Rhetorical Score)

gies, we independently sorted these statements into categories. Where we both agreed on the fit of a particular statement within a category, we kept it. For example, we easily agreed that the statement "The main purpose of writing is to express one's thoughts" fits into the expressivist category. However, we had to negotiate to fit "Eloquent writers stir their audience" into the rhetorical category.[6] Together, we selected 25 statements for each category and developed a 100-item survey instrument using a random numbers table to mix up the order of presentation of the questions. We administered this instrument to a fairly evenly distributed sample of K–12 teachers and received 142 valid responses. Although we had fewer responses than we wanted, we proceeded with confirmatory factor analysis, winnowing the instrument to 16 items by retaining the four with the highest factor loadings on each theoretical axiology. The four factors explained 60% of the variance in scores, with the formalist axiology most dominant, followed in order by expressivist, mimetic, and rhetorical. We randomized the surviving items and added some preliminary background questions. The current iteration of the survey is presented here.

The reference column on the survey indicates the original classification of the statement ("F" for formalist, "E" for expressive, "M" for mimetic, and "R" for rhetorical), the statement's order within the category on the original 100-item survey, and its overall order in that survey. For example, Item 10, "Eloquent student writing reveals a passion for a topic," was the 20th expressivist item and the 83rd overall on the original 100-item survey.

Some items that seemed certain to be included did not survive the factor analysis. For example, we were convinced that "Students must write in grammatically correct, standard English" and "Students must learn to write as a means of self-expression and discovery" would be the principal items on the formalist and expressivist subscales, respectively. As it turned out, "I prefer student writing to be well structured" and "I like writing that reveals students' feelings" were the strongest items in those subscales. Some items, as one might expect, tend to overlap categories. For example, "Good student writing has clear ideas supported by strong evidence" loads almost as highly on the formalist factor as the rhetorical factor. Perhaps this is not surprising given respondents' apparent preference for well-structured writing. Table 3.1 shows the orthogonal score weights for each of the 16 Writing Assessment Survey items.

One of my hopes was to use the Writing Assessment Survey to predict how teachers with differing axiologies would score student essays that exhibited some prominent features, say a strongly expressive essay with substantial grammatical errors. The idea was that readers who scored high on the formalist scale would probably give the essay a lower score than those who score high on the expressivist scale. Although we had some success in this area (Land, Leija, & Kwan, 2000),

---

[6]Neither statement survived factor analysis.

definitive research would require a larger sample of essays and scorers and perhaps a more accurate instrument for identifying axiologies. I have, however, continued to use the Writing Assessment Survey in workshops and classes as a way to approach the discussion of theories that underlie our instructional practices. Teachers complete the survey, sum their responses on the items within each category, and chart the results on "box and whisker plots" that represent the distribution of scores gathered so far (see Fig. 3.1).

A repeated measures ANOVA on all 416 responses shows a significant main effect for axiology ($F = 73.4$, $df\ 3/415$, $p < .0001$). Scheffe post hoc analyses show significant differences between all pairs except "rhetorical and expressivist" ($p < .001$).

TABLE 3.1. Orthogonal Score Weights for 16 Writing Assessment Survey Items

Item	Reference	Factor			
		Formalist	Expressivist	Mimetic	Rhetorical
1	R03,6	-.089	-.030	-.014	**.388**
2	E05,34	-.104	**.269**	-.043	.181
3	F09,43	**.272**	-.116	.072	-.012
4	R25,11	.089	-.061	.059	**.203**
5	F21,93	**.316**	.039	-.093	-.071
6	M09,27	-.052	-.044	**.328**	.072
7	R09,32	.020	-.062	-.141	**.399**
8	M04,16	-.095	-.036	**.253**	.182
9	F22,94	**.310**	.095	-.035	-.175
10	E20,83	.102	**.260**	-.082	-.107
11	M15,58	.028	-.046	**.363**	-.092
12	E23,92	-.014	**.321**	.028	-.142
13	M24,96	-.027	-.002	**.469**	-.272
14	R11,36	-.064	.168	-.161	**.316**
15	E17,78	-.099	**.313**	.018	-.024
16	F06,31	**.294**	-.116	-.039	.075

Note. Analysis is based on 142 responses to a 100-item survey.
Boldface type indicates weights for the four items in each subscale or factor.

FIGURE 3.1. Box plots for four axiologies based on 416 K–college teachers' responses to the Writing Assessment Survey. Each column presents a "box and whisker" plot. For each plot, 50% of the scores fall inside the box—25% above and 25% below. Half fall above or below the "waistband," which indicates the median. A score above or below a whisker, the T-shaped lines extending from the boxes, would be in the top or bottom 10% of all scores. Compare your response to those of 416 K–college teachers by plotting your score in the appropriate column.

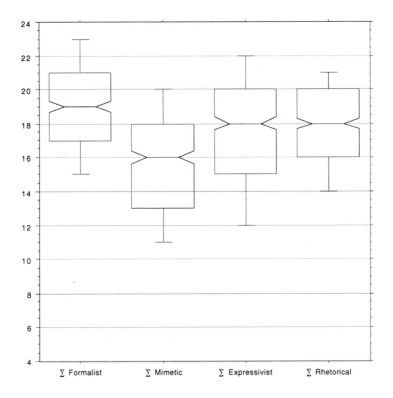

THE TOPOGRAPHY OF WHAT TEACHERS
VALUE IN STUDENT WRITING

One notable result is that teachers seemed more likely to endorse than reject all of the statements about good writing, giving them upper half scores (4 = *Mildly agree*, 5=*Agree*, 6 = *Strongly agree*) more often than lower half scores (1 = *Strongly disagree*, 2 = *Disagree*, 3 = *Mildly disagree*). One would expect an average cumulative score of

14 if scores were evenly split across the scale, but the overall mean was 17.4. This tendency of teachers to endorse all four axiologies is consistent with Fulkerson's claim that all are necessary components of a coherent theory of good writing, even though individuals tend to privilege one over the others.

As the plots and Scheffe contrasts show, the formalist axiology is endorsed significantly more positively than the other three. This seems to contradict Fulkerson's (1990) statement that "the widely held position today is the rhetorical axiology" (p. 411). Perhaps the formalist perspective merely reflects the reasonable response of teachers to reality. Most of those surveyed teach in the greater Los Angeles area, one of the most linguistically diverse regions in the world. As noted earlier, there appears to be a tendency for teachers who feel responsible for teaching standard English to have formalist leanings. It is also possible that the recent, dramatic shift toward easily quantifiable, standardized outcomes and scripted, formulaic instruction might signal an era very different from the rhetoricentric one Fulkerson identified over a decade earlier.

Still, among the sample of 29 college writing teachers represented in the data, the average cumulative rhetorical score is 20.3, significantly higher (Scheffe $p < .05$) than the scores for K–2, 3–5, 6–9, or 9–12 teachers. Also affirming Fulkerson's assertions that the expressivist axiology has largely disappeared from college composition theory is the college teachers' score of 15.1 on the expressivist subscale. This score is significantly lower (Scheffe $p < .01$) than the average for any other subgroup on the expressivist axiology (see Table 3.2).

TABLE 3.2. Mean and [Median] Cumulative Scores by Teaching Assignment and Writing Axiology

Teaching Level, Assignment, and Average Years Experience (n)	Axiology			
	Formalist	Mimetic	Expressivist	Rhetorical
K-2, Primary, 5.7 (n = 46)	18.2 [18.0]	**16.8** [17.0]	19.5 [19.0]	17.3 [17.5]
3-5, Elementary, 5.4 (n = 39)	18.1 [18.0]	*14.5* [15.0]	**19.6 [20.0]**	17.5 [17.0]
6-8, Middle Content, 5.0 (n = 51)	*18.0* [18.0]	15.9 [16.0]	16.9 [17.0]	*17.2* [17.0]
6-8, Middle English, 6.5 (n = 26)	19.0 [18.9]	15.9 [16.0]	18.6 [18.6]	17.6 [18.0]
9-12, High Content, 4.3 (n = 63)	18.6 [19.0]	15.9 [16.0]	17.1 [17.0]	17.3 [18.0]
9-12, High English, 6.4 (n = 48)	19.2 [19.0]	15.3 [16.0]	17.6 [18.0]	17.8 [18.0]
College Writing, 12.4 (n = 29)	**20.7 [21.0]**	16.1 [16.0]	*15.2* [15.0]	**20.3 [20.0]**
Overall (N = 416)	18.8 [19.0]	15.7 [16.0]	17.5 [18.0]	17.8 [18.0]

Note: For each axiology, there are 4 survey items scored 1 to 6 (low to high), yielding a possible range of 4 to 24. Average scores would equal cumulative score divided by 4. Low scores are in italics; high scores are in bold. Content teachers may teach any subject(s) other than English (e.g., physical education, physics, music, mathematics, etc.). Overall N includes all responses where one or more variables such as "Teaching Level" are missing.

Fulkerson (1990) also states that "strict mimetic axiology has never been common in writing courses" (p. 413), and this would seem to be confirmed by the survey results, which show responses on this scale to be significantly lower than each of the other three (Scheffe $p > .0001$). Only about 5% (19) of the 369 respondents gave the highest cumulative score to the mimetic axiology. However, middle-school content teachers placed a relatively high value on the mimetic axiology, and of the small subgroup of 11 secondary and college science teachers, 5 (45%) gave it their highest score. Additionally, the mimetic subscale provides one of the more puzzling results. As Table 3.2 shows, the highest endorsement on this scale was given by K–2 teachers (16.8) and the lowest (14.3) by teachers in Grades 3–5— a difference that approaches significance (Scheffe $p < .08$). The result is even more perplexing given that these two groups of teachers had the highest expressivist scores. Primary (K–2) teachers, it seems, hold an expressivist/ mimetic axiology perhaps because their concept of privileging the writer is to reward the writer's attention to external reality. Indeed, we do see frequent use of assignments calling for recall of real objects or events at that level. A typical language experience lesson at that level (cf. Hawley, Land, & Frank, 2001), for example, would require that a child first experience and then recall and verbally describe an object as the teacher transcribes the words. Perhaps this seemingly odd pairing of axiologies is really just the way smart teachers understand children at this early developmental level. The more expressivist/formalist perspective of the elementary (Grades 3–5) teachers may have to do with the increasing use of writers' workshop approaches coupled with the increasing demands of standardized testing in the schools where most of the respondents teach. Overall, the pattern from kindergarten through college shows a steadily rising emphasis on formalism (see Fig. 3.2), a pattern mirrored in the longitudinal research of Casey and Hemenway (2001).

Subgroup scores of the 238 primary, elementary, middle-, and high school English teachers, and college writing teachers present other interesting patterns. As Fig. 3.2 shows, both formalist and rhetorical beliefs appear to increase slightly across K–12 grades and jump dramatically at the college level. Expressivist beliefs decline more steadily, but most dramatically at the college level. Mimeticism appears flat, but enjoys pockets of favor, as noted earlier. Overall, the results show a trend among teachers of writing across grades away from concerns of the writer and toward a focus on the text. External reality is given small attention, and audience may still be looking for the privilege it deserves outside higher education.

Perhaps the most striking result is the significant difference between college writing teachers and all other teachers on all but the mimetic axiology. In general, the leap in the rhetorical axiology suggests that we may be missing an important instructional focus at the secondary level, and perhaps lower levels as well. In California, at least, writing assessments call for persuasive writing as early as Grade 7 and literary analysis as early as Grade 4 (Jago, 2003). Similarly, college-level instructors may be too dismissive of the expressivist perspective, needing to recall Bitzer's (1968) notion of exigency as the source of a writer's motivation to become a rhetor in the first place.

FIGURE 3.2. Scores on the Writing Assessment Survey on four axiologies for five sub-groups: primary (KH–2), Elementary (3–5) teachers, middle school (6–8), high school (9–12) English teachers, and college writing teachers. Note. As in Table 3.2, for each axiology there are four survey items scored 1–6 (low to high), yielding a possible range of 4 to 24. Average scores would equal cumulative score divided by 4.

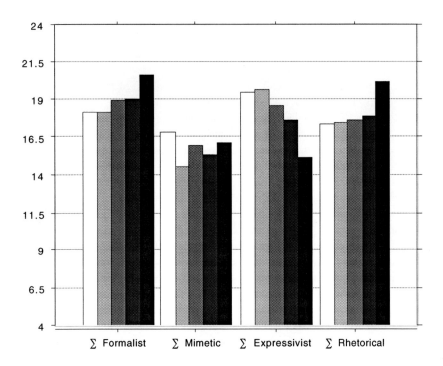

More specifically, the results suggest that college-level writing teachers may belong to an entirely different discourse community than K–12 teachers. Indeed, the college writing teachers and K–12 teachers differ substantially in the three areas that Pula and Huot (1993) identify as important components of extended discourse community: personal background, professional training, and work experience. Compared with K–12, teachers in this group are significantly less likely to be speakers of English as a second language [20% vs. 63%, chi-square df (1 = 19.7), $p > .0001$], significantly less likely to have a background in teacher education [7% vs. 100%; chi-square $df(1, 94.3)$, $p > .0001$), and significantly more experienced than K–12 teachers [12. 5 vs. 5.1 years; $t = 6.7$, 304 df, $p < .0001$). K–5 teachers are also different from other groups in the area of professional training in that they are far less likely to be English majors [22% vs. 74%, chi-square df. (1 = 15.6), $p < .0001$). There are probably many other major differences not documented in the survey.

CONCLUSIONS AT THIS JUNCTURE

As researchers and teachers, most of our conversations about evaluating student writing treat disagreement as something to be eliminated, the "serpent to be stamped out of the garden" (p. 98), as White (1993) puts it. Ever-more detailed standards-based scoring rubrics and unquestioned, coercive training sessions for essay scorers stand as testimony to this too-often-unexamined quest for conformity. Yet as readers of literature and of the world, we are well aware of, tolerate, and even invite inconsistencies and deep differences in interpretation. As Blau (2003) notes, we even wrangle in public life over even legal contracts, the product of hundreds of years of attempts to get agreement on the meaning of written words. If contracts are the legitimate subject of disagreement, how much more so students essays, which are, developmentally speaking, fragments of a works in progress? Again, as White puts it, ". . . we do not have a true score, even in theory" (p. 98).

We need, I would argue, a writing assessment philosophy that places much more emphasis on the diverse, subjective expertise of informed, wild (as opposed to trained) classroom teachers than on conformed, objective, scorers. "A foolish consistency," as Ralph Waldo Emerson (1841/1981) put it, "is the hobgoblin of little minds" (p. 145). Or as Erickson (1968) concludes, " . . . the courage of one's diversity is a sign of wholeness in individuals and in civilizations" (p. 90). As Smith (1993) demonstrated, some student papers receive split scores consistently. What seems like error is really a reliable measurement of the complexity of human performance.

Similarly, teachers appear to have consistent views within—but not necessarily across—various interpretative communities. It seems reasonable that teachers *do* disagree for good reason about what constitutes good writing. If we begin by honoring differing perspectives, we might even work toward a wiser, more complex consistency, one where the rhetoricist/formalist college teachers and the expressivist/mimeticist K–2 teachers stand to learn something valuable from one another about what makes writing good.

REFERENCES

Barritt, L., Stock, P. L., & Clark, F. (1986). Researching practice: Evaluating assessment essays. *College Composition and Communication, 37*(3), 315–327.

Bitzer, L. (1968). The rhetorical situation. *Philosophy and Rhetoric, 1*, 1–14.

Blau, S. (2003, July 14). *Helping students read difficult texts.* Paper presented at the Central Los Angeles Writing Project Summer Institute, California State University, Los Angeles.

Casey, M., & Hemenway, S. I. (2001). Structure and freedom: Achieving a balanced writing curriculum. *English Journal, 90* (6), 68–75.

Emerson, R. W. (1981). Self reliance. In C. Bode & M. Cowley (Eds.), *The Portable Emerson* (p. 145). New York: Penguin. (Original work published 1841)

Erickson, E. H. (1968) *Identity: Youth and crisis.* New York: W.W. Norton.

Fulkerson, R. (1990). Composition theory in the eighties: Axiological consensus and paradigmatic diversity. *College Composition and Communication, 41*(4), 409–429.

Hawley, C., Land, R. E., & Frank, C. (2001). Rapid sight word acquisition using the language experience approach. *The California Reader, 43*(4), 11–17.

Jago, C. (2003, December). *Sandra Cisneros: Teaching literary terminology in context.* Paper presented at the University of California at Irvine Writing Project annual conference for Teachers, Irvine, CA.

Land, R. E. (1992, March). *Student, content faculty, ESL faculty, and writing faculty priorities for writing instruction: When stakeholders disagree.* Paper presented at the national conference of Teachers of English to Speakers of Other Languages, Vancouver, British Columbia.

Land, R. E. (1999, April). *Sources of systematic bias in teachers' evaluations of written performance assessments.* Paper presented at the annual National Council of Measurement in Education at the American Educational Research Association Conference, Montreal.

Land, R. E., Leija, T., & Kwan, J. (2000, August 4). *What makes writing good? Reflecting on our beliefs and practices.* Paper presented at the Fourth International Conference for Global Conversations on Language and Literacy, Utrecht, The Netherlands.

Land, R. E., & Whitley, C. (1986, March). *Interaction of writer's and rater's native language background on holistic quality ratings.* Paper presented at the Conference on College Composition and Communication, New Orleans.

Land, R. E., & Whitley, C. (1989). Evaluating second language essays in regular composition classes: Toward a pluralistic U.S. rhetoric. In D. M. Johnson & D. H. Roen (Eds.), *Richness in writing: Empowering ESL students* (pp. 285–293). New York: Longman. (Reprinted in: V. Zamal & R. Spack (Eds.), *Teaching and learning across languages and cultures* (pp. 135–144). London: Lawrence Erlbaum Associates, 1998.)

Pula, J. J., & Huot, B. A. (1993). A model of background influences on holistic raters. In M. M. Williamson & B. A. Huot (Eds.), *Validating holistic scoring for writing assessment: Theoretical and empirical foundations.* Cresskill, NJ: Hampton Press.

Moss, P. (1994). Can there be validity without reliability? *Educational Researcher, 23*(2), 5–12.

Rohman, D. G., & Wlecke, A. (1964). *Pre-writing: the construction and application of models for concept formation in writing* (U.S. Office of Education Cooperative Research Project No. 2174). East Lansing: Michigan State University Press.

Smith, W. L. (1993). Assessing the reliability and adequacy of holistic scoring of essays as a college composition placement technique. In M. M. Williamson & B. A. Huot (Eds.), *Validating holistic scoring for writing assessment: Theoretical and empirical foundations.* Cresskill, NJ: Hampton Press.

Smith, W. L., Hull, G., Land, R., Moore, M., Ball, C., Dunham, D., Hickey, L., & Ruzich, C. (1985). Some effects of varying the structure of a topic on college students' writing. *Written Communications, 2,* 73–89.

White, E. M. (1993). Holistic scoring: Past triumphs, future challenges. In M. M. Williamson & B. A. Huot (Eds.), *Validating holistic scoring for writing assessment: Theoretical and empirical foundations,* Cresskill, NJ: Hampton Press.

4

ADDING PORTFOLIOS TO THE PLACEMENT PROCESS

A Longitudinal Perspective

Vicki Hester

Peggy O'Neill

Michael Neal

Anthony Edgington

Brian Huot

The placement of students into a writing program's first-year composition sequence continues to be a concern of writing program administrators and an issue in writing assessment theory and practice as evidenced by discussions of national listservs and recent publications.[1] Traditionally, placement procedures have included the use of standardized college entrance scores; multiple-choice tests of grammar, mechanics, and usage (locally designed and scored or purchased from a testing company); holistically scored, timed, impromptu essay exams; and combinations of these methods (Huot, 1994). These placement procedures have been challenged and revised over the last 15 years, most notably through the use

---

[1]See, for example, the WPA-L archives at http://lists.asu.edu/archives/wpa-1.html and chapters in books such as *The Writing Program Administrator's Resource* (Brown & Enos, 2002).

of portfolios, revisions of holistic scoring, and directed-self placement.[2] We begin by reviewing these placement practices before describing our study.

Using portfolios for placement in, or exemption from, the first-year writing curriculum has been tried by a variety of programs across the country. Although the specific contents, process for compilation, and scoring procedures vary across institutions, portfolios typically contain multiple samples of student writing in a variety of genres and an introductory memo or reflective essay. Sometimes process work is included, and sometimes an impromptu essay is included. Regardless of the differences in specific details, supporters of this approach claim benefits of using portfolios for placement for a variety of stakeholders, including the writing program. For example, the University of Michigan's English Composition Board, which instituted a placement portfolio process in 1992, believed that "students would perceive the portfolio as a more valid assessment tool"; it would "encourage the growth of stronger ties between composition teachers at Michigan and high school teachers around the state," and it "would help promote a teaching culture within the framework of required writing courses" (Willard-Traub et al., 1999, p. 43). Borrowman (1999) made similar arguments in favor of the University of Arizona portfolio placement system, explaining that the portfolio provides "a more valid and reliable measure of student writing ability than either a timed essay exam or a multiple choice test" (p. 7). Proponents of Miami University's portfolio also claimed that the "portfolio becomes a form of assessment that, unlike the multiple-choice examination or the impromptu essay, itself stimulates learning and in this way models the education process at its best—a process in which assessment is inseparable from learning" (Daiker, Sommers, & Stygall, 1996, p. 259). In short, advocates argue that placement portfolios bring teaching and assessment together in ways that improve assessment (Huot, 2002).

For the most part, however, portfolio-based placement has merely changed the sample of student writing used, maintaining the same scoring procedures used by most single-sample placement tests—namely, holistic scoring. The Miami portfolios were "read holistically by at least two English instructors and given a single comprehensive score on a six-point scale" (Beck et al., 1998, p. 116). The Arizona portfolio system also used a 6-point scoring rubric; although, it is more detailed than the Miami scale. The reading of the portfolios is based on the holistic model, with anchor portfolios and "controlled sessions" as advocated by White (Borrowman, 1999) and two independent readers and other logistical characteristics typical of large-scale holistic scoring sessions. Michigan experimented with their scoring procedures (Willard-Traub et al., 1999) using a variety of different

---

[2]See the following for more information on recent placement practices: Lowe and Huot (1997), Borrowman (1999), Decker, Cooper, and Harrington (1993), Sommers, Black, Daiker, and Stygall (1993), Smith (1993), Haswell and Wyche-Smith (1994), Royer and Gilles (1998, 2003), and Blakesley (2002).

rubrics and guides, settling on a descriptive guide but still depending on interrater reliability and extensive reader training associated with holistic scoring.

Although the portfolio systems changed the writing sample used for making the decisions, other programs were doing more work on changing the process for evaluating the student sample. While directing placement at the University of Pittsburgh, Smith (1993) devised a system that relied on teaching expertise. Instead of using holistic scoring, he had expert teachers (who were thoroughly familiar with the curriculum, program, and population) place students into appropriate classes. Rather than scoring essays and then creating cut scores that determined the course students would take, Smith bypassed the extraneous steps of calculating scores to determine placement and simply had students placed directly into a course. Simply put, teachers made decisions about students, not texts. Smith also discovered he did not need elaborate training and norming sessions but found that teaching experience was a more effective method of reader calibration. However, his procedures still included having each essay read by two independent readers with a third blind reading if the first two readers did not agree, much as in holistic scoring. His approach grew out of extensive research into the reliability of readings going beyond a simple interrater reliability coefficient (O'Neill, 2003; Smith, 1993, 1992).

Another challenge to holistic scoring came out of Washington State University and the work of Haswell and Wyche-Smith (1994), who also developed a system that relied on teaching expertise. They had one experienced teacher initially read all the placement essays because most of the students would be placed into Composition I, the first semester of composition that fulfills the university writing requirement. Those placed into the regular first-semester course were not read a second time. Only those who the first reader felt might belong in a developmental or advanced course were re-read by a more experienced teacher and/or administrator. Again, as in Smith's procedures, Haswell and Wyche-Smith collected data and used their experience as researchers and composition specialists to revise and refine the placement process.

The latest method of placement embraced by many composition programs for its efficiency—directed-self-placement (DSP)—requires no writing sample, no testing, no scoring, and no external decision making. The writing program provides more detailed information about the courses available to entering students, provides them with prompts about their reading and writing experiences, and is available for consultation with individual students. The students then select the course they think best suits them. The rationale for this approach, explains Royer and Gilles (1998), is rooted in John Dewey's (1938) democratic and pragmatist philosophy of education, particularly Dewey's notion of instrumentalism. The responsibility of selecting the appropriate course rests with the student writer and "relies on honest student inquiry and interactive participation" (Royer & Gilles, 1998, p. 69). The model Royer and Gilles promoted, based on their program at Grand Valley State University, had composition specialists guiding incoming students through the self-selection process in a presentational mode to large cohorts of students during orientation. Students primarily reflected on their experiences and could consult with a composition instructor if they desired. Students did not get any specific feedback from the composition program on their writing, nor were they asked to provide any writing to the program because DSP does not include student-generated texts as part of the placement procedures. Students rely on their previous experience and descriptions of the college writing curricula. Only after students have already selected a course and after the start of the semester is their writing examined. Other programs have adopted—and adapted—Royer and Gilles' model to fit their particular institutional contexts although the underlying principle is that the student, not the writing program, has the responsibility to select the most appropriate writing course (Blakesley, 2002; Royer & Gilles, 2003).

Procedures for DSP, as is the case for portfolio placements and impromptu essay exams, have grown out of local contexts because placement, as many writing assessment scholars explain, is a contextual decision influenced by the student population, the institution, the writing faculty, the curriculum, and the available resources. Writing assessments function within complex social systems. Because teachers and administrators make important educational decisions based on the results of assessments, the actions surrounding the assessment will necessarily influence multiple stakeholders as well as the environments in which the assessments function (Smith, 1998). Although local conditions such as funding and time constraints must be considered, it is also important for procedures to be theoretically informed with results validated through ongoing, systematic inquiry. Placement directors conducted pilot studies and collected data over several years in their quest to design effective placement procedures (Daiker, Sommers, & Stygall, 1996; Haswell, 2001; Smith, 1993; Willard-Traub et al., 1999). They situated the writing tasks, evaluation tasks, and procedures within the local context, including theories about literacy, as well as the larger field's research and literature on writing assessment.

In the pilot project that we report here, we follow their lead by including aspects of all of these recent placement trends—portfolios, revisions of holistic scoring, and DSP—as we designed placement procedures that addressed our local context at the University of Louisville. Moreover, we conducted ongoing validation research as we refined the pilot placement process. This chapter, then, reports not only on the procedures we used, but, more important, on how the ongoing validation inquiry led us to refine procedures and rethink our understanding of what we were doing. The implications of this program and our approach go beyond the use of specific procedures to answer the call for developing methods to validate emerging, alternative assessment procedures and open up the possibility of creating models for others wishing to use portfolios and other locally based writing assessment procedures (Moss, 1998).

What follows focuses on the procedures we used for placement and validating placement, the results of our study regarding the accuracy of the placement decisions, the satisfaction of teachers and students with placement, and the implications of such a program and its validation for the study of writing program administration and assessment. In presenting the procedures and results, we develop a validation argument that links together theories about the teaching and assessment of writing with evidence about accurate placement, teacher satisfaction, student success, and benefits for those students who might otherwise be required to enroll in basic writing courses. Overall, we aim to establish not only the viability, but also a high degree of validity for the methods we used and to model the kinds of procedures local stakeholders who design and develop site-based alternative writing assessment procedures can use to build convincing validity arguments for local and national audiences.

THEORETICAL RATIONALES

Validity

Validity is the essential issue in assessment, with reliability contributing to the validity, but not sufficient to make a validity claim. Messick (1989), Cronbach (1988), and other psychometric theorists argue that validity must be considered as a unified construct, although they acknowledge the various dimensions that contribute to a validity argument. As Messick (1989) explains, validity arguments must consider a balance of the following elements: a theoretical rationale, empirical evidence to support its accuracy and appropriateness, and an intentional examination of social consequences resultant from the assessment decisions. Each of these categories includes information that is relevant in determining the overall degree of validity. Messick's definition of *validity* includes both theoretical and empirical support for the "adequacy and appropriateness" of the assessment. Shepard (1993) notes a dual role of validating assessments: "Every test use involves inferences or interpretation; therefore, all validation requires the combination of logical argument and empirical evidence needed to support those inferences" (p. 406). Although some studies focus on evidence for the accuracy of an assessment, they may overlook the theoretical justification and rationale for their uses of writing assessments. So much of writing assessment is data driven—for the purposes of grading students, defending or promoting a department or program, or other practical concerns within the educational arena—without necessary attention given to theories of composing and language. Assessments should be designed so they are theorized prior to their application and systematically analyzed on interpretation and decision making.

Another significant measure within a validity argument is the empirical evidence gathered to support the accuracy of decisions made based on results from the assessment process. Haswell (1998) argues that a validity argument should be based on a multimodal analysis of the assessment. In his model, he suggests four rationales for multiple inquiry: (a) a pragmatic examination of utility, (b) a multiperspective analysis to achieve critical distance, (c) crosschecking or triangulation, and (d) consistent probing. Quantitative evidence includes, among other measures, reliability. Rather than being a necessary although insufficient, measure, instead reliability is one quantifiable measure that can be used to argue for the degree of validity of an assessment. So, the measure remains viable to the extent to which consistency between interchangeable measures is theoretically supported by the assessment system. Indeed, low consistency measures among readers, results collected over a period of time, or any other consistency measure could be (but does not necessarily have to be) included as part of the larger argument as to the degree of validity. As Williamson (1994) points out, reliability may or may not be an important measure within a validity argument:

> Therefore, the properties of a test that establish its reliability do not necessarily contribute to its validity. . . . Thus, comparatively high reliability is neither a necessary nor a sufficient condition for establishing the validity of a measure. It is one aspect of a test that has to be weighed in conjunction with many other aspects of the validity of that test. (p. 162)

In addition, each instance of consistency would have to be supported in terms of its relevance to the system. In each instance, the evidence (quantitative as well as qualitative) must work within a larger theoretical framework for the argument. Validation is required for every use of an assessment, according to validity scholars (Cherry & Meyer, 1993; Cronbach, 1988; Messick, 1989; Moss, 1994, 1998; Shepard, 1993). In short, validation of writing assessments must include both theoretical and empirical evidence to support the uses of the results.

Placement

An essential component of developing a localized placement assessment examines the local context and needs as well as the underlying assumptions about language, literacy, and testing of the local community. Zebroski (1994) argues that teaching theory and practice cannot be separated: All teaching practices are necessarily theoretical regardless of whether those theories are ever articulated. Likewise, all assessment practices, instruments, and decisions are necessarily theoretical and carry with them assumptions about testing and learning, regardless of whether these are made explicit. As such, assessors need to articulate the theories and assumptions regarding assessments and compare them to the assumptions and theories that underlie the variety of available assessment instruments and practices. In terms of placement assessment, we identified the following principles as guidelines for the way that we would approach our pilot portfolio placement assessment.

First, assessment is a powerful discourse and a discourse of power. Placement, like any other form of assessment, directly impacts the education of students and influences—whether directly or indirectly—the local curriculum. Often placement can be viewed as the institution or writing program enacting its power on the student in the student's interest, with the student having little say in the decision. Directed self-placement is interesting because in a DSP system the institution acknowledges its power and the potential impact on students. Consequently, the institution grants students the power to select the course that best suits their individual needs in relationship to the course offerings. However, students do not have experience with or direct knowledge of the curriculum in which they are placing themselves. In addition, it is unclear how informed students are about their own writing ability in relationship to this curriculum. In other words, students have the authority to choose but do not necessarily have the experience and expertise that the faculty have in terms of the curriculum (as well as college in general because the students are typically entering college for the first time).[3]

The second assumption we made is that placement assessment is determined by the local context; therefore, it should be designed and implemented in institutionally specific ways. This means that factors such as faculty, finances, time constraints, student demographics, and curriculum need to be considered. Typically, institutions offer a number of first-year writing courses for a variety of reasons, and those courses reflect local issues and needs. For example, Smith (1993) explains the theoretical orientation of Pitt's writing program and the way specific courses were designed to address specific needs and abilities. Because of the distinct difference between each institution's curriculum, students, and environment, one institution should neither replicate nor import a placement assessment, but should base placement procedures on local needs and conditions, taking into account the local knowledge, expertise, and needs unique to each institution.

A third assumption about placement, related to the prior two, is that institutions make placement decisions about students, not texts. Holistic scoring focuses on the text not the student, yet it is the student who is placed, not the text. The decision about the student may have far-reaching educational and personal outcomes. Clearly, students placed into either the honor's or remedial tracks will experience the consequences of the placement. Depending on the context of the local institution, placing students into remedial writing might prohibit them from advancing toward graduation or require them to take courses from the university without receiving college credit, but at the same financial cost as other college courses. Likewise, under-prepared students placed into regular first-year writing courses may not do as well as they need to do, so those students end up paying to retake courses because of withdrawal or failure. Even if the students pass, they may not have positive academic experiences and individual weaknesses may not be adequately addressed. Students' sense of self may also suffer because so much of what they decide about their literacy and learning comes from classroom expe-

---

[3]See O'Neill and Schendel (1999) for a more thorough critique.

riences and other assessments. If a program has differentiated courses, and if placements are not accurate—that is, students are not put in the most education-ally appropriate class—consequences affect the individual students, but they also ripple out from the individual to affect classes, instructors, and programs.

This leads to another assumption that needs to be acknowledged when creat-ing writing assessments: Writing is a far more complex and interconnected activi-ty than any trait listing could ever represent (Cherry & Witte, 1998). Theoretically informed writing programs have built their curricula around the belief that writ-ing is a complex, meaning-making activity that cannot be learned through a regi-ment of discreet, isolated skills, but rather is developed through a variety of inter-connected literacy activities. The theoretical influence of the curriculum should also be a guiding principle in the placement system. Developing a trait rubric that focuses on individually defined skills could hinder the reader in the decision and distract from the larger decision being made about the student because placement readers retro-fit the rubric to their decision (Pula & Huot, 1993).

Defining *writing* as a complex, contextual, meaning-making activity leads to another guiding assumption: Multiple writing samples, in multiple genres, written over time allow for a more informed decision about a writer's abilities. This posi-tion means that using standardized tests (i.e., Compass, ACT, or SAT scores) or timed impromptu writing samples cannot be theoretically justified for making placement decisions because these tests assume writing is acontextual, transfer-able, and defined by isolated skills. However, portfolios, which allow for several writing samples in different genres and produced over time, provide a method for sampling students' writing abilities and experiences that are theoretically consis-tent with this understanding of writing.

Based on these assumptions about testing, placement, and writing, we devel-oped a pilot placement system that uses portfolios to place students into the first-year writing curriculum. We refined and collected data about the system and the students for the 7 years it ran. Over this time, we made modifications and changes to the system and data-collection methods in response to changing local condi-tions as well as the findings from our ongoing research. In what follows, we out-line the procedures we developed and explain our rationales for them, specifical-ly in terms of the local context.

PILOT PORTFOLIO PLACEMENT PROCEDURES

Local Context

Placement assumes, as we mentioned earlier, a differentiated curriculum with dif-ferent courses designed to meet different student needs. At the University of Louisville, (U of L) as at many large, public state universities that are not highly selective, students were admitted with a variety of writing experiences and abilities. The following is a brief overview of the available courses for first-year composition students at U of L when the portfolio pilot started until the 2001–2002 academic year:

- ENG 098—first in the developmental sequence, noncredit
- ENG 099—second in the developmental sequence, noncredit
- ENG 101—first required course in sequence (3 credits), focuses on writing processes and developing as a writer
- ENG 102—second required course in sequence (3 credits), focuses on academic writing
- ENG 105—honors, one-semester course (3 credits), satisfies the first-year composition requirement
- ESL sequences—ENG 098 B 102, follows same descriptions as above, but designed to meet needs of ESL students, both from immigrant and international student populations

Although each course had its own goals and expectations, they shared a basic theoretical orientation that approached writing as a complex meaning-making process that focuses on invention, drafting, and revising. Students are provided with guided practice in a range of literacy activities, such as critical reading of essays, peer review workshops, review of student samples, evaluation of sources, and writing multiparagraph essays, depending on the particular course. Instructors were mostly graduate students and nontenure-track lecturers (although in the latter years of the program, tenured faculty also taught first-year writing courses). There was no common book or syllabus for the courses, and many instructors organized their courses around a theme, and many used portfolios for teaching and assessing. In the noncredit courses, student portfolios were used to determine whether students were ready to enter the credit-bearing sequence of courses.

Because portfolio placement was a pilot and participation was not only voluntary but also limited to Kentucky high school graduates,[4] the traditional placement at U of L continued concurrently with this pilot. Traditional placement relied on ACT scores and an impromptu essay test. If a student's verbal ACT score was less than 18, the student took a timed, impromptu essay test that placed him or her into English 098, 099, 101, or one of the ESL sequences. If a student's verbal ACT score was 18 or greater, the student would take 101 and would not take the timed essay test.[5] To be placed into 105 under the traditional placement

---

[4]Students not graduating from a Kentucky public school could compile a portfolio on their own and submit it, although few students did.

[5]ACT verbal score was raised to 20 during the last 2 years of the pilot.

system, a student needed a composite ACT score of 26 or higher. (Though this placement was part of the general honors program and not specific to composition, and though the composition program had no input into the honors course, the composition program staffed the course and determined the curriculum.) The traditional system had no mechanism for placing students directly into English 102, the second course of the requirement. In addition, the writing program did not administer or score the impromptu essay; instead, the developmental studies program, which taught English 098 and English 099 (as well as other developmental, noncredit courses in math and study skills), handled the placements. This program was not part of the College of Arts and Sciences, but functioned separate from the normal academic structure as part of student services.

Although the traditional placement relied on ACT scores and impromptu testing, all students graduating from Kentucky public schools—which was University of Louisville's primary constituency—were required to produce a writing portfolio during their senior year of high school as part of the Kentucky Instructional Results Information System (KIRIS), the accountability index calculated as part of Kentucky Education Reform Act (KERA). The portfolios were submitted to the district departments of education, where they were stored. They were scored yearly by Kentucky educators (see Callahan, 1997, 1999, for more on this). The KIRIS portfolios, which typically students produced as part of their senior English class, contained seven selections:

1. A table of contents
2. A letter to the reviewer
3. A personal narrative, memoir, vignette, or personal essay
4. A short story, poem, or play
5. Three expository pieces (two from content areas outside of English or Language Arts) that predict an outcome; defend a position; analyze or evaluate a situation, person, place, or thing; solve a problem; explain a process or concept; draw a conclusion; and/or create a model.[6]

Brian Huot, a composition scholar in U of L's English department who became the director of the composition program in 1996, envisioned the KIRIS portfolio pilot project as a way to achieve many outcomes:

• Use a portfolio of writing produced as part of classroom instruction, which was more theoretically aligned with the composition program's approach to teaching, to place students;

---

[6]When CATS was first implemented in 1999, one less expository piece was required for the state-mandated student writing portfolio.

- Develop a theoretical and empirical argument for placement procedures;
- Foster connections between the composition program and secondary educators;
- Make the connection between high school writing and college
  composition explicit for students;
- Involve the composition program in the placement process; and
- Foster connections between the developmental studies writing
  program and the composition program.

After securing funds and permissions from U of L and local education officials, we began by inviting students from five Louisville area high schools. By the
third year, all students graduating from a Kentucky public school were eligible to
participate. We sent letters to each student explaining the portfolio placement
program and requesting permission slips, which we needed for the school districts
to release the portfolios. To ensure that contents had not been altered, we did not
accept portfolios mailed to us by students, but only those portfolios sent to us by
the school districts. Besides, we wanted to foster connections with the local districts, so going through them facilitated this, whereas dealing with students individually would not. After collecting permission slips, we then forwarded them to
their respective superintendents or school counselors, who copied the portfolios at
the semester's end and mailed them to us in late May or early June. Working out
the intricacies of the notification and permission process took a few years as we
learned more about the state and local bureaucracies.

Pilot Placement Procedures

Although the placement project used the same portfolios as the state assessment,
it did not rely on the portfolio scores given by the state or the state's rubric because
those scores—Novice, Apprentice, Proficient, Distinguished—did not match up
with the composition program's curriculum. Not only did the rubric not match
our curriculum, but the state's purposes for the assessment were not consistent
with our purposes. We also rejected conventional holistic procedures because of
the extra steps involved in coding and decoding raters' decisions into numbers and
then back into classes. This seemed especially ineffective given research findings
using talk-aloud protocols and interviews of readers, which indicate that raters in
a placement context often make direct decisions about placement and then code
them into numbers on a scoring rubric (Huot, 1993; Pula & Huot, 1993; Smith,
1993).

Instead of using holistic scoring, we adopted and revamped a method used by
Smith (1992, 1993) in which teachers make more accurate and cost-efficient placement decisions for their own courses without the need for scoring guidelines,
quantification, or rater training. In lieu of rubrics or numerical guidelines, we

selected readers according to the courses they most often and most recently taught (Lowe & Huot, 1997). The readers made a single decision about whether students would enter the class for which they were reading.

Over the 6 years, we modified some aspects of Smith's system to allow for more placement decisions on initial readings. We began by first selecting local placement readers who had most recently taught the courses for which they were reading. We assumed that local readers have the most current knowledge about a particular course, so they can make the most appropriate decisions about student placement. As Pula and Huot (1993) noted, "teaching experience helps raters make an assessment of teachability" and "placement rating is best carried out by those who teach the courses into which they are placing students" (p. 260). Rather than trying to calibrate readers to a holistic scoring rubric that is then applied to a placement decision at the local institution, it was more efficient and effective to get readers who have been calibrated to a local curriculum through years of teaching specific courses within the local system because, as Smith (1993) pointed out, this method is "more powerful than any training sessions" (p. 175).

Although Smith's system was the basis for the initial reading procedures, we eventually varied it. Traditional placement procedures, including Smith's model, require at least two readers; if there is disagreement, a third reader would break the tie. Based on the data we collected, our experience with the system, and our knowledge of the curriculum, we decided that two readers are needed only when the portfolio indicates that a student is not ready for placement into the first semester of composition, English 101. In these cases, which were a small percentage of the larger group, each portfolio would be read by two readers, and maybe a third, before a decision was made for a developmental English course, English 102 (the second semester of composition) or even English 101. Although we did not rely on Haswell and Wyche-Smith (1994), we ended up with a similar reading procedure as the one they describe.

Besides the number of readers, we had to decide how portfolios would be read. Typically, placement reading of impromptu essays involves a single quick read leading to a single overall judgment. Readers form an overall impression and are not evaluating various features of the essay separately to come to the overall score. The portfolios, however, included several different samples, of different types of writing, which potentially showcase different strengths and weaknesses. Readers were encouraged to adapt the holistic reading of single sample essays to portfolios, reading straight through the portfolio to come to an overall impression and judgment.

In place of holistic procedures, rubrics, or numerical guidelines, we assembled experienced readers who had most recently taught the composition courses for which they were reading (Smith, 1992, 1993). Although the actual processes and procedures varied across the years, we finally settled on a basic process. English 101 readers were the first to review each portfolio answering one question only: "Does this student belong in 101?" If yes, we placed the student into 101 with a single read (Haswell & Wyche-Smith, 1994). If not, the reader considered another question: "Is this student not yet ready for 101 or has the student already achieved the goals of 101?" Depending on the answer to this question, the reader passed the portfolio to another reader for a higher or lower course, whichever they felt would be most appropriate.

Because most student portfolios placed into 101 courses, the 101 readers began a day or so earlier than the other readers. For the majority of the portfolios, 101 readers were the sole readers. When the other readers began, we did not tell them that 101 readers had placed the portfolios in their stacks because that could influence their reading (Smith, 1993). As far as they knew, all of their readings were first readings, and like all first readers, they answered only one question: "Does this student belong in the course for which I am reading?" If the second reader did not "see" a student in his or her class, the scoring leader read the portfolio in consultation with the two raters to make a consensus decision on where to place the student (Lowe & Huot, 1997).

Readers on average spent 15 minutes reading and making decisions about each portfolio. After all portfolios were rated, the placement coordinator sent letters to students according to their placement. Students whose ACT scores and portfolio ratings placed them in the same course received a letter explaining the placements and course sequences. Students who received portfolio ratings that were different from the ratings they received from the traditional placement received letters explaining the U of L course sequence and were told that the choice was theirs to make. In other words, students placed into English 101 by the portfolio placement and English 105 by their ACT scores were told they could choose between English 101 and 105. Students whose ACT score indicated they could go directly into 101, but whose portfolio reading indicated 099, could decide which course they thought was best for them. In other words, students were given a choice (much like with DSP) about where they entered the curriculum.

Validation Inquiry Procedures

While we worked on refining the procedures for placement, we were simultaneously conducting validity inquiry, which includes both theoretical and empirical evidence as Messick (1989) argued. Theoretical rationales, which we acknowledged earlier, need to be coupled with empirical data to determine whether students were being adequately placed into the composition curriculum. But, as Smith (1992, 1993) articulated, there is no single method of determining the adequacy of placement. Multiple data sources need to be collected and then triangulated to determine whether students are in the most appropriate course. Smith explained that final grades are influenced by too many factors (e.g., effort and attendance) to be used alone to justify student placements made at the start of the semester. Likewise, looking at the number of students moved to a different course after the first day was also inaccurate because of the reluctance of teachers to move both strong and weak students. He found that teacher perception about the students' placement, if done at appropriate times in the semester, was the most accurate measure of adequacy of placement, but the error rate was still too high. Smith (1993) concluded that only by using all of these data sources could he determine the adequacy of students' placements.

To address the validity of the placement results—that is, the adequacy of placement—we collected various types of data over the 6 years, including the following:

- Comparison of traditional placement results with the portfolio results
- Comparison of grades of students who took the traditional placement and the portfolio placements
- Surveys of instructors about adequacy of placement
- Surveys of students about the adequacy of course (as well as other issues)

Results of our validity inquiry (reported later) are drawn from multiple sources, including data about student success in writing courses, teacher surveys concerning their satisfaction with student placement, student perceptions of their placement, and the results of a study into the procedures' reliability.

RESULTS AND DISCUSSION

Table 4.1 reports the placements of students who participated in the Portfolio Placement Program from 1994 to 2000. On average, 65% of the students placed into the regular first-semester course as would be expected; however, there is a wide range for this placement from year to year. On average, 25% of the students placed into a developmental course, but again there is a wide range spanning from a high of 39% to a low of 4%. The average placement into the second semester course, English 102, was 10%, with a low of 7% and a high of 19%. Because the pool of students varies from year to year and the curriculum stays more stable, we expected placement rates in courses to vary from year-to-year. Although the portfolio placement may first appear to place a large percentage of students into developmental writing, over the same time period, 32% of students placed higher using portfolio placement than the timed writing test (see Table 4.2). In comparison, through 1997, about 56% of all incoming students were eligible for English 101 based on the traditional placement methods, so the portfolio method did place a higher percentage of students into English 101. In addition, the portfolio placement allowed students to place directly into English 102, which was not possible given the traditional methods. However, students participating in the portfolio placement were self-selected and not necessarily representative of the larger population of incoming students.

TABLE 4.1. Distribution of Portfolio Placements into First-Year Writing Courses

	Developmental	English 101	English 102	TOTALS
1994	19 (38%)	26 (52%)	5 (10%)	50
1995	15 (17%	57 (64%)	17 (19%)	89
1996	64 (39%)	89 (54%)	12 (7%)	165
1997	120 (35%)	192 (57%)	27 (8%)	339
1998	51 (17%)	222 (74%)	28 (9%)	301
1999	85 (26%)	214 (65%)	31 (9%)	330
2000	14 (4%)	283 (88%)	24 (7%)	321
AVERAGES	**53 (25%)**	**155 (65%)**	**21 (10%)**	**185**

TABLE 4.2. Portfolio Placement Comparisons to Timed Writing Test

	Placed Higher	Placed Same	Placed Lower	Totals
1994	4 (33%)	8 (67%)	0	12
1995	14 (58%)	8 (34%)	2 (8%)	24
1996	22 (40%)	27 (49%)	6 (11%)	55
1997	15 (22%)	40 (58%)	14 (20%)	69
1998	25 (26%)	33 (35%)	11 (12%)	69
1999	10 (24%)	21 (51%)	10 (24%)	41
2000	2 (18%)	5 (45%)	4 (36%)	11
Averages	**32%**	**48%**	**16%**	**40**

By 2000, the final year of the study, the developmental placement of a mere 4% represented the lowest percentage recommended for developmental English in the 7-year history of the study. Also down—but only slightly—was the placement for English 102. The mainstream placement, English 101, achieved its highest placement percentage in 2000 compared with the other years of the study—88% as compared with 7-year average of 65%. However, with only eleven students participating in both the timed writing and the portfolio assessment, the numbers are considerably less meaningful.

The number of students participating in both assessments continues to drop because U of L gave students more decision-making power in placement decisions. In 2000, if students scored below an 18 on the ACT-V, U of L gave them *options* to participate in one, the other, or both assessments (timed writing and portfolio placement). Perhaps a more meaningful calculation in 2000 is the comparison between our portfolio placement and the traditional timed writing placement. In 2000, of the total number of portfolios assessed, 96% of the students were placed into English 101 or higher, with only 4% placed into developmental English courses. On the timed writing tests in the summer of 2000, 59% of all entering students (248 of 422) scored at the English 101 level, with 41% (174 of 422) placed into developmental English. These numbers demonstrate the greater propensity of timed writing tests toward developmental English placement as compared with portfolio placement.

Significant changes in U of L's policies for admissions and developmental education programs also contributed to the results. In 1997, the president of U of L announced that the university would stop offering remedial classes and admission standards would increase. Consequently, the traditional placement methods and the pool of entering students gradually changed, which influenced the number of students placed into developmental writing courses as is most obvious in 2000. For example, in Fall 1998, 35 sections of developmental writing were offered; in Fall 1999, 32 sections were offered, and in Fall 2000, only 8 sections were offered. By Fall 2002, developmental writing was no longer an option, and students who may have been placed into a developmental course were mainstreamed into English 101. (For more information on this change, see Edgington, Tucker, Ware, & Huot, 2005.)

The disparity between higher and lower placements is not as noticeable in the average comparison of ACT-V to portfolio placement as timed writing test differences (see Table 4.3). However, in 2000, the numbers indicate the highest level of mainstream placement, the lowest level of lower placement by portfolios, and the highest (tied with 1998) level of placement higher by portfolios. The specific data available for this analysis are more limited due to the change in testing policy from the university. Previous to 1998, U of L *required* students scoring lower than an 18 on the ACT-V to take the timed writing test, but by 1998 the timed writing test became optional if the students submitted a writing portfolio. In most cases, students scoring below 18 took the timed test, submitted a portfolio, or participated in both assessments.

TABLE 4.3. Portfolio Placement Comparisons to ACT Verbal Placement

	Placed Higher	Placed the Same	Placed Lower	Totals
1998	65 (22%)	173 (57%)	63 (21%)	301
1999	46 (14%)	189 (59%)	85 (27%)	320
2000	71 (22%)	228 (71%)	20 (6%)	319
Averages	61 (19%)	197 (62%)	56 (18%)	313

Adequacy of Placement

Placement "success," or what Smith (1993) called "adequacy of placement," can be measured with a variety of indicators. We collected the following data, each partial indicators of placement success: (a) student grade in enrolled course, (b) instructor surveys, and (c) student surveys. Students who participated in portfolio placement tended toward slightly higher success rates as indicated by final grades in most years (see Table 4.4). However, these numbers do not distinguish between students who followed the suggested placement and those who did not.

In addition to looking at final course grades, teachers were asked to indicate their perceptions of the adequacy of all students placed in their first-year composition courses during fall semesters. Students participating in the portfolio placement were not identified. These surveys, conducted after Week 2 and before midterm, were intended to ascertain the teachers' perceptions of the appropriateness of the students' placements, not the students' actual performance. In the beginning of the study, teachers, using a letter code (A–E), indicated their perception of each student's preparedness for the class by writing in the appropriate letter next to the students' names on the class roster. Instructors informed us of the confusion of the letters, which in a teacher's frame of reference represented grades for many of the faculty. In response, we changed the rating system to a simpler check—a plus or minus system. In addition to the conflation between grade and rating, the high and low ends of the 5-point scale were rarely used. The 3-point scale communicates the same information and makes the process clearer for instructors. Because we had modified this process over the years to get better (more reliable) feedback from the instructors, representing the results for each year is cumbersome and not useful. However, year-to-year results consistently indicate that instructors thought placements were adequate for the majority of students, with more students identified as writing above rather than below expectations.

Besides polling instructors, starting in 1997, we also surveyed all first-year composition students during the fall semester. The surveys, which students completed anonymously during class halfway to one third of the way through the semester, asked about several issues besides their perceptions of the appropriateness of the placement (e.g., demographic information, knowledge of the portfolio placement option, and influence of the placement option on the students' efforts in compiling the portfolio). However, for our purposes here, we only report the results of the students' perceptions of their placement (more information from the student surveys are offered later). On average, students who submitted their KIRIS portfolios were more satisfied with their placements than those who were placed by traditional means, although there were variations in degree from year to year. The 1999 results, however, do not fit this pattern (see Table 4.5). The survey data were difficult to interpret because they did not discern whether students chose the placement recommended by the portfolio reading. In other words, students who submitted their portfolios could have selected the course recommended by the traditional placement method instead of the portfolio or vice versa. Although there are definite limits to the data, the consistently higher satisfaction for their current course by those who participated in the pilot study leads us to conclude that allowing students to make a choice increases their satisfaction with the course.

TABLE 4.4. Student Grades in Composition Course Completed

Year	GRADE DISTRIBUTION				
	A	B	C	D	F*
1994					
Portfolio Placement	45%	38%	10%	0	7%
N = 29**					
Current Placement	27%	36%	19%	3%	15%
N = 2,419					
1995					
Portfolio Placement	40%	33%	13%	4%	9%
N = 75					
Current Placement	30%	32%	18%	3%	17%
N =2413					
1996					
Portfolio Placement	35%	42%	16%	.7%	6%
N = 135					
Current Placement	35%	29%	17%	4%	15%
N = 2383					
1998*					
Portfolio Placement	46%	32%	11%	2%	9%
N = 235					
Current Placement	40%	28%	14%	3%	15%
N = 2436					
1999					
Portfolio Placement	47%	28%	15%	3%	7%
N = 234					
Current Placement	40%	29%	15%	3%	10%
N = 2618					
2000					
Portfolio Placement	45%	32%	14%	2%	7%
N = 255					
Current Placement	40%	30%	13%	3%	13%
N = 2,689					

*Incomplete and audit grades not included.
**Totals for grade distribution and follow-up are based on number of students who actually enrolled in a first-year course during the fall semester after the portfolio reading. Some students may not have enrolled in the university or in a composition course.
***Grade distribution information was not available for 1997.

TABLE 4.5. Student Survey Responses

Do you think your current writing course is appropriate for your ability?

	Too Difficult	Too Easy	Just Right
1997			
Portfolio	3.1% (8)	13.8% (36)	83.1% (216)
Nonportfolio	3.2% (28)	15.4% (136)	81.5% (721)
1998			
Portfolio	2.5% (5)	9.6% (19)	88.9% (174)
Nonportfolio	3.5% (26)	14.1% (104)	82.4% (608)
1999			
Portfolio	4.0% (9)	13.2% (30)	82.8% (188)
Nonportfolio	2.6% (16)	10.9% (68)	86.5% (539)
2000			
Portfolio	1.9% (3)	12.4% (20)	85.7% (138)
Nonportfolio	3.3% (15)	9.1% (42)	79.7% (886)

Reliability

Calculating interrater reliability, as well as other types of reliability, for the portfolio readings caused some problems for several reasons. Unlike an impromptu test where all students are basically writing in response to the same prompt and individual texts do not necessarily stand out, portfolios have more distinct characteristics that differentiate them from each other. The individuality of portfolios, coupled with the small number of portfolios and the small pool of readers, made typical reliability checks more difficult. Mixing in portfolios that had already been placed to determine whether they would be placed the same on a second read or by a separate reader was not always feasible because we may have had only one reader reading for that course, or because the readers read so few portfolios that they could remember having placed it already, which would interfere with their decision making.

However, once there were enough portfolios in the pool to make it feasible, we did mix in some portfolios from previous years to discover how they would be placed the second time around. Although, again, depending on the selections in the portfolio and the choices in content made by the writer, it was not always easy to make sure they did not stand out. In 1998, when we felt that there were enough portfolios to reread portfolios blindly to check for reliability, 33 portfolios were selected from previous years and mixed in with the 301 portfolios submitted for placement. Of these 33, 70% (23) received the exact same placement with no need for discussion, and 30% (10) received different placements. Interestingly, nine of these were higher than the original placement; the ACT scores of six of these indicated the higher placement. Five of these students had opted for the higher placement than the one recommended by the portfolio readers, all of whom passed their course. In 1999, 40 portfolios were randomly chosen from the 1998 pool and mixed in with the 1999 portfolios. However, only 60% received the same placement as in the previous year. But when looking at reliability within the same year—that is, readings of portfolios by a second reader during the same year—there was an agreement of 87%. In 2000, 20 portfolios from 1999 were reread and 65% received the same placement. Although we did not consistently achieve the 70% agreement rate considered acceptable in holistic scoring, we felt confident that our readings were acceptable.

The incoming population and the curricular expectations were gradually changing over the span of the study. Reading procedures and selection of readers were also modified over the years. For example, although we began with the idea that expert instructors in one course that they most recently taught would be selected to read for that particular course, as Smith (1992, 1993) did, staffing at U of L was different so that many instructors taught more than one course during the spring semester. In 1999, changes were recommended in the selection of readers so that readers with expertise in a variety of courses were preferred over those expert in one course. But perhaps what we saw as most important in looking at the issue of reliability was the fact that the portfolio placement decisions were essentially suggestions: Students made the decision about which course to enroll in based on a variety of information. Eventually, we realized that the portfolios allowed the students to get direct feedback from the U of L writing program based on work that they did during their high school careers, but this feedback worked in concert with other information—ACT scores and impromptu essay exam results (if they took it). Students ultimately were able to decide where they wanted to enter the writing curriculum, so in essence, they were doing self-placement but with more information, including feedback from instructors.

Student Feedback

As noted earlier, we surveyed all students in first-year composition courses during the fall semester to gather more information about the portfolio placement and the KIRIS portfolio. Although much of that information was demographic, the 14-question survey also included questions aimed at getting feedback from students to help us refine the program. For example, students who graduated from a Kentucky high school (and therefore had been required to compile a KIRIS portfolio) but did not participate in the portfolio placement option consistently reported that they did not know about this option (see Table 4.6). Although there is an increase each year in those responding yes, the majority of students reported that they did not know about the program. Most of these students also reported that they would have considered participating in the placement program if they had known about it. According to this feedback, we needed to do a better job

TABLE 4.6. Survey Responses for Students Not Participating in Pilot Study

Did you know you could use your KIRIS Portfolio for placement into first-year composition?

	Yes	No
1997	27.5% (233)	72.5% (615)
1998	28.9% (209)	71.1% (513)
1999	31.1% (191)	68.9% (423)
2000	34.6% (160)	65.4% (303)

of getting the word out to high school teachers and students. To help publicize the portfolio option, some of us presented at Kentucky Council of Teachers of English annual conferences on this project and even wrote about it in the *Kentucky English Bulletin* (Lowe & Huot, 1997). But because the project was only a pilot, funding was budgeted for it on a yearly basis and we were never entirely sure that the project would be funded from year to year.

We also asked students who submitted their portfolios if this decision influenced their portfolio work. Table 4.7 summarizes the results to this question. A significant number of students responded that knowing they were going to submit the portfolio for placement did influence their portfolio writing. Again, this information is limited because it does not provide information about how it influenced them or why it did not influence others, but we believe it is significant because it indicates the potential for more cross-institutional connections between high schools and colleges. In fact, the portfolio project did facilitate more connections between the writing program and local high schools. For example, local high school English teachers had one of the coordinators of the portfolio placement project conduct inservice workshops in 1996 about writing expectations for first-year students entering U of L. However, one of the limitations in developing more connections with the local high schools was the staffing of the writing pro-

TABLE 4.7. Responses from Students Participating in the Portfolio Project

If you used your KIRIS portfolio for placement, did this influence your writing in your portfolio?

	Yes	No
1997	35% (89)	65% (165)
1998	42.1% (82)	57.9% (113)
1999	41.4% (94)	58.6% (133)
2000	37.6% (59)	62.4% (98)

gram. Because the first-year courses were overwhelmingly taught by graduate students and part-time adjuncts, there was consistent turnover in college writing instructors undermining efforts to establish ongoing relationships. Similarly, asking contingent faculty to put in the extra time and commitment to work with the high schools was difficult given their compensation and the university's lack of commitment to them and the program.

We also asked all students who graduated from Kentucky high schools if they felt that working on their KIRIS portfolio helped to prepare them for their first-year writing course (Table 4.8). Although most students reported that they felt the portfolio was helpful, more students who participated in the pilot project responded positively. In 1997 and 1998, there was not a large gap between those who participated and those who did not, but in 2000, there was a wider gap. As with other data, we do not have enough detailed information to draw firm conclusions, but the consistently positive response to this question indicates that students felt that working on their high school portfolio helped prepare them for expectations of college composition.

Besides asking about the general helpfulness of the portfolio in preparing them for college composition, we asked students whether their first-year composition course used portfolios and, if so, whether their experience with the KIRIS portfolio helped them (Table 4.9). In asking this question, we were trying to determine whether the previous experience with portfolios, although they were associated with state-mandated assessments and accountability systems, was beneficial to students because most composition instructors used a course portfolio. These portfolios, which instructors designed and defined with no program-wide require-

TABLE 4.8. Students Response to Helpfulness of KIRIS Portfolio

Do you feel that preparing your KIRIS portfolio readied you for your first-year writing course?

	Yes	No
1997		
Portfolio	55.7% (142)	44.3% (113)
Nonportfolio	51.4% (418)	48.6% (396)
1998		
Portfolio	53.8% (105)	46.2% (90)
Nonportfolio	50.1% (341)	49.9% (340)
1999		
Portfolio	67.0% (148)	33.0% (73)
Nonportfolio	53.6% (314)	46.4% (272)
2000		
Portfolio	68.8% (110)	31.3% (50)
Nonportfolio	52.2.% (228)	47.8% (209)

TABLE 4.9. Student Feedback on Value of KIRIS Portfolio to College Portfolio

If your current first-year composition course uses portfolios, how valuable was the experience with the KIRIS writing portfolio for your college portfolio?

	Very Valuable	Somewhat Valuable	Not Valuable At All	Damaging
1997				
Portfolio	21.8% (52)	56.7% (135)	18.5% (44)	2.9% (7)
Nonportfolio	18.1% (135)	52.8% (394)	24.5% (183)	4.6% (34)
1998				
Portfolio	24.7% (43)	46.6% (81)	22.4% (39)	6.3% (11)
Nonportfolio	14.6% (88)	53.8% (325)	25.8% (156)	5.8% (35)
1999				
Portfolio	31.1% (66)	44.3% (94)	19.3% (41)	5.2% (11)
Nonportfolio	19.2% (106)	49.4% (273)	23.9% (132)	7.6% (42)
2000				
Portfolio	24.7% (36)	54.1% (79)	17.1% (25)	4.1% (6)
Nonportfolio	16.9% (68)	56.5% (227)	22.4% (90)	4.2% (42)

ment or rubric, were very different than ones mandated by the Kentucky Department of Education for the KIRIS system. Most students reported that they found the experience with the KIRIS portfolio valuable but a substantial number found it not valuable at all or even damaging. Again, these responses indicated a place where the college and high school faculty could make a connection so that students could make a better transition from one writing context to another.

The idea of using the high school required portfolio for placement sparked an exchange of information between the U of L writing program and the high schools. Although some of this was overt (e.g., explicit sharing of information, such as doing a workshop on college writing expectations or participating in the KCTE), others were more indirect. By reading the portfolios, asking questions of students beyond the appropriateness of their course, the portfolio placement project encouraged connections between the high school writing programs and the college one. However, unlike most other placement systems (such as Miami's and Michigan's), the college writing program was positioned to learn from the high school—information was flowing from the secondary schools and teachers to the college instead of from the university to the high school teachers and students. This information flow is unusual in placements; typically the college hands down the requirements and information and it is up to the high schools and incoming students to comply.

Costs

Because this was a pilot project, we were given a separate budget that was supposed to cover all expenses, including copying and postage for mailings to students inviting them to participate, a coordinator to administer the program, and money for readers. In 1997, readers were paid $14 per hour and it cost $3.86 per portfolio for the placement (excluding the logistical expenses). In 1998, expenses were slightly higher: Readers were paid $15 per hour and 55 more portfolios were received and 33 more were added to the reading for a reliability check. Overall, excluding the expenses for logistics and oversight (which were directly related to the project's pilot status), the cost of reading the portfolios remained between $3.15 and $3.80 per portfolio, an affordable cost given the rich benefits this offered to students and the writing program.

CONCLUSIONS AND IMPLICATIONS

The pilot portfolio placement study ended in 2000. In Fall 2002, the remedial writing courses were discontinued in favor of mainstreaming students into the regular first-year writing program and the standard courses so that placement was no longer an option for most students. Although the portfolio placement project was not directly responsible for this change, it did contribute (along with a study in mainstreaming conducted earlier) to the decision to mainstream all students accepted into the university into the regular first-year composition course. Other factors, such as a changing profile for the entering student class, a changing university mission, and a reorganization of developmental studies at the university level, also contributed to the policy change. However, the data we collected over the 7 years of the study provided some confidence that students who may initially be categorized as basic writers can be successful in the regular composition classroom.[7]

Although the pilot portfolio placement project ended because of the changing needs and context at U of L, we consider the project a success because we developed a viable alternative placement system that provided valid results and encouraged more connections between college and high school writing. Although a local, contextually specific placement system should not be adopted wholesale into another university, the system can be used by other writing assessment scholars and practitioners as a model for designing, implementing, and validating a placement system, much as Smith's (1993) work at Pittsburgh did for us. In fact, it

---

[7]See Edgington et al. (2005) for more information on the mainstreaming at U of L.

is this aspect of our research that is most valuable to others. The methods, experiences, and results contribute to the growing research-based literature on writing assessment and placement, demonstrating how a program can use research not only to develop new procedures, but also to validate the results as it learns more about its program and students. Huot's (1994, 2002) emerging theory of writing assessment acknowledges both the intellectual and practical aspects of writing assessment. He argues against the positivist approach to assessment that informs holistic scoring and for assessment that is theoretically consistent with language and literacy learning. Huot (2002) outlines the principals necessary for a new theory and practice of writing assessment that is consistent with theories of language and literacy as well as validity; he calls for methods that are site-based, locally controlled, context sensitive, rhetorically based, and accessible to all stakeholders. The pilot portfolio project attempted to enact all of these principles as it developed.

Although our overall project was a success—we were able to demonstrate that using the KIRIS portfolios for placement was both viable and valid—there were some limitations to our study. We realize that over the 7 years, our sample was self-selected and not random, compromising in some ways the generalizability of the results. However, the academic profile of this population was not unlike that of the larger incoming class. We also recognize that the constant flux in the personnel involved in the study may have influenced the year-to-year placement sessions and data gathering. Although the director of the composition program remained consistent from 1996 to 2000, the portfolio placement coordinator changed almost yearly. In addition, the overreliance on part-time lecturers and graduate teaching assistants (both MA and PhD students) meant that there was a constant flux in the pool of instructors who were the potential portfolio readers. This fluid labor pool made other parts of the placement program more difficult. For example, one of the rich benefits of the program was its potential to foster high school–university connections; although there were improvements in this area, it was difficult to sustain connections and efforts when graduate students—most of whom were not actually part of the local community—would move on in their careers and away from the area.

Finally, because this was not an experimental study, we could not control all the variables; instead, we were constantly dealing with the realities of working within a changing institution—the university mission, admissions standards, personnel, funding, and program structures were just some of the contextual factors that changed during the time the study was conducted and that influenced the writing program and, by necessity, placement. Of course, these are the same challenges faced by programs all over the country. Like them, we adapted to the changes but did so in ways that were consistent with the theoretical frameworks we had identified.

Despite these limitations, the portfolio placement project contributes to the literature on writing assessment, specifically portfolio placement. Some writing assessment scholars have debated the efficacy of using portfolios for placement

(White, 1995) whereas others have heralded portfolio placement as an important way to showcase teaching and learning (Borrowman, 1999; Black, Daiker, Sommers, & Stygall, 1994; Willard-Traub et al., 1999). Our study reports the implications for not only the debate surrounding the use of portfolios, but for the way we think about portfolio placement. Our study also answers an objection to the early portfolio placement programs at Miami and Michigan—that these programs require more resources and institutional support than necessary or possible for most programs and writing program administrators. By using a more efficient scoring system, readers placed students at a cost not unlike that associated with holistic scoring, making portfolio placement feasible for most institutions now using single-sample, traditional methods.

A more important feature of the U of L portfolio placement system that distinguishes it from others is the way it fostered interest in curricula and pedagogy between high school and college writing instructors. Although many other portfolio placement programs, such as those at Arizona, Michigan, and Miami, claimed this same benefit, the U of L program inverted the typical hierarchical design in which the university designs a portfolio (with or without consultation with feeder high school teachers) and hands it down to the high school teachers and incoming students. U of L took the high school portfolio and used it for its own needs, designing the placement system around the work that was done as part of the regular high school curriculum. This is a substantial change in the way university–high school collaborations typically work. Instead of telling high school teachers what it needed or wanted, U of L adapted the placement system to the high school requirements, but it was able to do so in ways that were not detrimental to the integrity and autonomy of the college program, the high school program, or students and teachers. The effects of this placement procedure on the relationship between college and high school English teachers is especially important given the nature of emerging forms of validity that considers the consequences of the assessment on teaching and learning.

The procedures introduced into this pilot placement system are designed specifically for the local context at U of L. We are not suggesting the wholesale reproduction of our assessment into other contexts; rather, we suggest using our methods more as a model of a process to be adapted to other local contexts. In other words, placement administrators need to outline their own underlying theories and assumptions about language, literacy, and learning. Also important in adapting this model is to consider the local factors that influence placement, such as the college composition curriculum, first-year student populations, composition teaching cohorts, feeder schools, resources, and expertise. Conducting ongoing validity inquiry is another essential component of developing a placement system because that allows placement administrators to collect systematic data about the system, which are then used to help refine not only the placement process, but also other aspects of the program. Again, validity remains one of the most important aspects of an assessment, with reliability contributing to validity but not in itself sufficient to make a validity claim. According to Cronbach (1988), validity "must link concepts, evidence, social and personal consequences and values" (p. 4). Messick (1989) argued that validity uses "integrated evaluative judgment," supported by empirical evidence and theoretical rationales, "to support the adequacy and appropriateness of inferences and actions based on test scores and modes of assessment" (p. 5). In other words, validity arguments must include a theoretical rationale, empirical evidence to support its accuracy and appropriateness, and an examination of social consequences that result from the assessment decisions (Messick, 1989).

When individuals in charge of placement consider the more complex definition of validity by first articulating underlying theoretical assumptions about language, literacy, and learning, they begin to make decisions about assessment procedures—which ones to adopt and which ones to adapt. Throughout the 7 years of this project, we learned that an ongoing validation inquiry leads to the refinement of the assessment. As placement coordinators link together theories of teaching and assessment of writing, they not only improve and validate the assessment, but improve teacher and student satisfaction. As our study also shows, readers placed students into higher level courses for all years, student grades reflected a higher success than students placed by traditional means, and student and teacher satisfaction rates were high. Again, at U of L, traditional writing tests had a greater propensity to place students into developmental English, yet our data show these same students do very well when mainstreamed. Our project developed a validation argument that linked together theories about teaching and assessing writing with evidence that portfolio placement is a viable and valid method for placement. Overall, we produced both viability and validity arguments for our methods as well as a placement model for local site-based alternative writing assessment procedures, a model that can be used to build validity arguments tailored for context-specific situations. It is our hope that, by adopting and adapting our methods, others will join us in answering Moss' (1998) call for developing methods to validate emerging, alternative assessment procedures.

POSTSCRIPT

Vicki, Peggy, Michael and Tony

Over the last decade, the four of us, at various times, worked on this project as doctoral students of Brian's at the University of Louisville. Although none of us knew Bill directly during this time, and, in fact, we had all started our doctoral studies after Bill's move to Oregon, we directly benefited from his work through Brian.

The work we did on the portfolio placement system was inspired by Bill in two ways. First, as Brian explained in chapter 1, Bill's breakthrough placement system at the University of Pitt and his ongoing research about it influenced Brian's conception of our assessment procedures and continued research. Second, Bill's approach to graduate education and collaboration, modeled what Brian enacted as our graduate professor and mentor. We went through graduate school hearing stories about Bill (e.g., the famous escalator story that Brian recalls in chap. 1, or about how Bill required all his graduate students to collaborate with him) from Brian and reading Bill's assessment work.

Some of us even had our own cryptic, first-hand experiences with Bill, who was the most favored reviewer for the *Assessing Writing* journal that Brian co-edited and some of us worked on. Because Bill had a profound impact on Brian, he also greatly influenced our own graduate education, although he had already left Pitt and stopped his overt participation in composition.

REFERENCES

Beck, A., Dautermann, J., Miller, C., Murray, K., & Powell, P. R. (1998). *The best of Miami University's portfolios 1997*. Miami, OH: Department of English, Miami University.

Black, L., Daiker, D. A., Sommers, J., & Stygall, G. (1994). *New directions in portfolio assessment: Reflective practice, critical theory, & large-scale scoring*. Portsmouth, NH: Boynton/Cook, Heinemann.

Blakesley, D. (2002). Directed self-placement in the university. *WPA: Writing Program Administration, 25*, 9–39.

Borrowman, S. (1999). The trinity of portfolio placement: Validity, reliability, and curriculum reform. *WPA: Writing Program Administration, 1/(2)*, 7–27.

Brown, S. C., & Enos, T. (Eds.). (2002). *The writing program administrator's resource: A guide to reflective institutional practice*. Mahwah, NJ: Lawrence Erlbaum Associates.

Callahan, S. (1997). Tests worth taking? Using portfolios for accountability in Kentucky. *Research in the Teaching of English, 31*, 295–336.

Callahan, S. (1999). All done with the best of intentions: One Kentucky high school after six years of state portfolio tests. *Assessing Writing, 6*, 5–40.

Cherry, R. S., & Meyer, P. (1933). Reliability issues in holistic assessment. In M. M. Williamson & B. A. Huot (Eds.), *Validating holistic scoring for writing assessment: Theoretical and empirical foundations* (pp. 109-141). Cresskill, NJ: Hampton Press.

Cherry, R. S., & Witte, S. P. (1998). Direct assessments of writing: Substance and romance. *Assessing Writing, 5*, 71–88.

Cronbach, L. J. (1988). Five perspectives on validity argument. In H. Wainer (Ed.), *Test validity* (pp. 3–17). Hillside, NJ: Lawrence Erlbaum Associates.

Daiker, D. A., Sommers, J., & Stygall, G. (1996). The pedagogical implications of a college placement program. In E. M. White, W. D. Lutz, & S. Kamusikiri (Eds.), *Assessment of writing: Politics, policies, practice* (pp. 257–270). New York: Modern Language Association.

Decker, E., Cooper, G., & Harrington, S. (1993). Crossing institutional boundaries: Developing an entrance portfolio assessment to improve writing instruction. *Journal of Teaching Writing, 12*, 83–104.

Dewey, J. (1938). The pattern of inquiry. In *Logic: The theory of inquiry*. New York: Holt.

Edgington, A., Tucker, M., Ware, K., & Huot, B. (2005). The road to mainstreaming: One program's successful but cautionary tale. In S. J. McGee & C. Handa (Eds.), *Discord and direction: The postmodern writing program administrator* (pp. 72-88). Logan: Utah State Press.

Haswell, R. (1998). Multiple inquiries in the validation of writing tests. *Assessing Writing, 5,* 89–109.

Haswell, R. H. (Ed.). (2001). *Beyond outcomes: Assessment and instruction within a university writing program.* Westport, CT: Ablex.

Haswell, R., & Wyche-Smith, S. (1994). Adventuring into writing assessment. *College Composition and Communication, 45,* 220–236.

Huot, B. A. (1993). The influence of holistic scoring procedures on reading and rating student essays. In M. M. Williamson & B. A. Huot (Eds.), *Validating holistic scoring for writing assessment: Theoretical and empirical foundations* (pp. 206–236). Cresskill, NJ: Hampton Press.

Huot, B. (1994). A survey of college and university writing placement practices. *WPA: Writing Program Administration, 17,* 49–65.

Huot, B. (2002). *(Re)articulating writing assessment for teaching and learning.* Logan: Utah State University Press.

Lowe, T. J., & Huot, B. (1997). Using KIRIS writing portfolios to place students in first year composition at the University of Louisville. *Kentucky English Bulletin, 20,* 47–64.

Messick, S. (1989). Meaning and value in test validation: The science and ethics of assessment. *Educational Researcher, 18*(2), 5–11.

Moss, P. A. (1994). Can there be validity without reliability? *Educational Researcher, 23*(2), 5–12.

Moss, P. A. (1998). Response: Testing the test of the test. *Assessing Writing, 5,* 111–122.

O'Neill, P. (2003). Moving beyond holistic scoring through validity inquiry. *Journal of Writing Assessment, 1,* 47–65.

O'Neill, P., & Schendel, E. (1999). Exploring the theories and consequences of self-assessment through ethical inquiry. *Assessing Writing, 6,* 199–227.

Pula, J. J., & Huot, B. A. (1993). A model of background influences on holistic raters. In M. M. Williamson & B. A. Huot (Eds.), *Validating holistic scoring for writing assessment: Theoretical and empirical foundations* (pp. 237–265). Cresskill, NJ: Hampton Press.

Royer, D., & Gilles, R. (1998). Directed self-placement: An attitude of orientation. *College Composition and Communication, 50,* 54–70.

Royer, D., & Gilles, R. (Eds.). (2003). *Directed self-placement: Principles and practices.* Cresskill, NJ: Hampton Press.

Shepard, L. A. (1993). Evaluating test validity. *Review of Research in Education, 19,* 405–450.

Smith, W. L. (1992). The importance of teacher knowledge in college composition placement testing. In R. J. Hayes (Ed.), *Reading empirical research studies: The rhetoric of research.* (pp. 289–316). Norwood, NJ: Ablex.

Smith, W. L. (1993). Assessing the reliability and adequacy of placement using holistic scoring of essays as a college composition placement test. In M. M. Williamson & B. A. Huot (Eds.), *Validating holistic scoring for writing assessment: Theoretical and empirical foundations* (pp. 142–205). Cresskill, NJ: Hampton Press.

Smith, W. L. (1998). Introduction to Special Issue. *Assessing Writing, 5,* 3–6.

Sommers, J., Black, L., Daiker, D. D., & Stygall, G. (1993). The challenges of rating portfolios: What WPAs can expect. *WPA: Writing Program Administration, 17,* 7–29.

White, E. M. (1995). Apologia for the timed impromptu essay test. *College Composition & Communication, 46,* 30-45.

Willard-Traub, M., Decker, E., Reed, R., & Johnston, J. (1999). The development of large-
    scale portfolio placement assessment at the University of Michigan: 1992–1998.
    Assessing Writing, 6, 41–84.
Williamson, M. M. (1994). The worship of efficiency: Untangling theoretical and practical
    considerations in writing assessment. *Assessing Writing, 1,* 147–174.
Zebroski, J. (1994). *Thinking through theory: Vygotskian perspectives on the teaching of writing.*
    Portsmouth, NH: Boynton/Cook.

5

JOINING THE DIALOGUE ON VALIDITY THEORY IN EDUCATIONAL RESEARCH

Pamela A. Moss

Over the years, I have become increasingly aware of how few of us in the educational research community have contributed to the literature on validity theory. By validity theory, I mean scholarship that considers, explicitly and critically, the epistemological and ethical principles underlying judgments of quality. I use the word *explicitly* with the recognition that validity theory is implicit in any act of research and thus, in a sense, we are all always writing about validity theory. However, only a handful of us take the seemingly bold step of explicitly offering an elaboration, critique, or alternative perspective on validity theory. This is not surprising; texts on research methods frequently do little to invite such dialogue. In my field of educational measurement, for instance, authors of documents like measurement text books or the *Standards for Educational and Psychological Testing* typically assert that, "Validity is . . . ," "Reliability is . . . ," "Test developers and users should . . ." as if these issues were nonproblematic and uncontested. (I have written my own share of such assertions.) Although well intended to provide clear guidance, such language promotes an uncritical acceptance of existing validity theory and an understanding of validity research as simply applying—albeit sometimes with great creativity and sophistication—universal standards to concrete situations.

As a graduate student, I was fortunate in having mentors (among them Nancy Cole and Bill Smith) who encouraged me not only to read more deeply, but to think with them in a generative way about validity theory. That was a transformative experience for me. I came to understand that validity theory was socially constructed, that it reflected an evolving and frequently contested set of perspectives, and that I could play a role in contributing to that dialogue.

In this chapter honoring the mentorship of Bill Smith, I would like to suggest that all of us who work within the field of educational research have a role that we can play in the dialogue on validity theory and to argue, moreover, that we all have a responsibility to participate in the dialogue within our own research communities in critical and generative ways. First, I would share what I think it means to prepare to do research in validity theory, and then I offer some more concrete suggestions for what I think are productive directions for research and writing. I use my experience in my own field of educational assessment or measurement—a field that has both contributed to and benefited from the work of composition and writing assessment researchers—as the work of Bill Smith and many of his students attests. I invite readers from other fields to think analogically about how this case might inform their preparation to participate in important dialogues about the epistemological and ethical moorings of their own research communities.

PREPARING TO JOIN THE DIALOGUE: THE CASE OF EDUCATIONAL MEASUREMENT

First, I believe preparation to join the validity dialogue in educational measurement or assessment means understanding the evolution of validity theory within the field, including the range of issues that have been and now are under debate (e.g., Angoff, 1988; Cronbach, 1988, 1989; Kane, 1992, 2004; Messick, 1989; Mislevy, 1994, 2003; Moss, 1992, 1995, 1998; Shepard, 1993). This also includes understanding something of the philosophy of social science from which these theories and practices have evolved. Equally important, it means reading beyond the field to see how validity theory and practice are undertaken in other disciplines. That kind of contrast highlights theories and practices we might take for granted and opens them to critique and possible evolution (as illustrated more fully later).

We measurement theorists are often criticized by theorists working outside our tradition for being somewhat monological in our ways of studying the world. French sociologist Pierre Bourdieu (Bourdieu & Wacquant, 1992) offers his students the following critique of "the famous metholodogy courses" in American universities:

It is revealing that entire "schools" or research traditions should develop around one technique of data collection and analysis.... We find monomaniacs of log-linear modeling, of discourse analysis, of participant observation, of open-ended or in-depth interviewing, or of ethnographic description. Rigid adherence to this or that one method of data collection will define membership in a "school." ... And the fact of combining discourse analysis with ethnographic description will be hailed as a breakthrough and a daring challenge to methodological monotheism. We would need to carry out a similar critique in the case of techniques of statistical analysis.... Here again, monotheism reigns supreme. Yet the most rudimentary sociology of sociology teaches us that methodological indictments are too often no more than a disguised way of making a virtue out of necessity, of feigning to dismiss, to ignore in an active way, what one is ignorant of in fact. (p. 226)

The long and the short of it is, social research is something much too serious and too difficult for us to allow ourselves to mistake scientific rigidity ... for scientific rigor, and thus to deprive ourselves of this or that resource available in the full panoply of intellection traditions. (p. 227)

Although I might argue that Bourdieu has overstated his case or prefer that his criticism were a bit more gracious, I find it instructive nevertheless. As I try to translate it into our context and my tone, I imagine something like the following: When you think of the various purposes to which tests are put, (e.g., certification, placement, selection, admission, accountability, etc.), we have a broad responsibility to help the communities we study and serve make sound judgments, and yet the range of professionally sanctioned tools we have available to us for meeting those responsibilities is narrow. Consider a secondary school like Central Park East (e.g., Meier, 1995), where certification for graduation looks something like a dissertation exam and accountability is served through public discussion of standards as they are applied to the work of members of that community. In that case, it becomes clear that we in educational measurement have only limited resources to offer that community to help it strengthen and document the validity or soundness of its decisions.

As a profession, ultimately, we need to be as prepared to help Central Park East as we are to help the school that uses the state-wide assessment to serve the same purposes of accountability and certification. We need to be prepared to learn from that contrast. Otherwise, we may find ourselves increasingly obsolete or, worse, standing in the way of productive evolution in the way educators think about accountability. Along with Bourdieu, I do not mean to reject any discipline specific theories and practices, but rather simply to locate them in a broader field of possibilities.

Alternative Conceptions of Validity

For instance, let me give you an example of possible variations in validity theory that become visible when we consider contrasts across research traditions. One of the validity issues that has become increasingly salient for me is the role of those who are researched (the people we study) in the research process. Consider our conventional ways of representing validity theory in educational measurement—generalized definitions, descriptions or processes, categories of validity evidence, issues, or standards. If you look at the definitions of those categories, as they are characterized, for instance, in the *Standards for Educational and Psychological Testing* or in the work of some of our major theorists, you will see that the role of the researched remains largely invisible, taken for granted, perhaps. If I were setting up a "straw man" argument, I might characterize the role of the researched in educational measurement as "providing data," "responding to our questions," or "doing what they're told as we observe them," but that sort of polemic is not my intent. Rather, my intent is simply to highlight taken-for-granted practices, explore their consequences, in light of alternatives, and make a newly self-conscious decision about their value.

If you look across approaches to validity theory in alternative research traditions—ethnographic, hermeneutic, critical, postmodern, and so on—you will not only see explicit attention to this issue, but a wide range of validity criteria associated with different roles for the subjects of our research. Validity criteria include whether (a) the meanings reported and interpreted are consistent with what the subjects of the research (or the assessed) intended, (b) the interpretations can be justified to the researched rather than imposed on them, (c) the understandings and awareness of the researched evolve as a result of participating in the research process, and (d) the researched have the power to construct and represent their own interpretations in the research process. For any of us who have ever had the experience of being researched ourselves, of having our meanings represented in others' terms, then the significance of these categories may become more apparent. Perhaps one analogous experience many of us share is seeing our work cited by someone else or having our work evaluated by a colleague or mentor. Does the other's interpretation fit with what we intended? Is it taken out of context? Does it misrepresent and dismiss without understanding the details of our argument? These are epistemological issues—related to the soundness of the interpretation as much as they are ethical and political issues related to who has the right to represent whom.

Now, one might argue that there is nothing in our conventional categories of validity in educational measurement that precludes alternative roles for the researched. But the point is that neither do our conventional categories illuminate alternative roles for the researched as validity criteria nor raise the issue as something that needs to be considered and resolved. Bernstein (1976) speaks to this issue:

> If we get away from the obsession of setting up and shooting down impossi-
> bility arguments—as I believe we should—then the objections raised by more
> sophisticated critics . . . can be seen as questioning present and prevailing

emphases, concerns, and problems. Intellectual orientations . . . lend weight to a sense of what are the important issues, the fruitful lines of research to pursue, the proper way of putting the issues. The most important and interesting challenges to any dominant orientation are those which force us to question the implicit and explicit emphases, that make us self-conscious not only of what is included in the foreground, but excluded or relegated to the background as unimportant, illegitimate, or impractical. (p. 41)

Preparing to do research in validity theory means being willing and able to raise these kinds of questions about even the most venerable concepts of our profession. None of this is intended to overturn conventional notions of validity theory. Rather, my point is simply that it be considered one possibility among a range of possibilities—fully appropriate for some purposes and less appropriate for others.

Some Productive Directions for Research in Validity Theory

At this point, I would like to offer some more concrete suggestions about fruitful directions for research in validity theory. I invite readers to consider three general possibilities—admittedly idiosyncratic and far from exhaustive—each of which encourages critical reflection on our theories and practices by drawing on the strengths of alternative research traditions.

Evaluating One Method or Inquiry in Terms of Another In his benchmark chapter on validity theory, Messick, (1989) suggested a "Singerian mode of inquiry," where one method of inquiry is evaluated in terms of another to highlight the assumptions and values underlying each. Elsewhere, I have illustrated that concept with plans for comparing two different methods of portfolio evaluation—one based in psychometrics and one in interpretive research traditions, most particularly hermeneutics (Moss, 1996). Here the contrast is between two quite different means of constructing interpretations about teaching competence. As another example, I might cite Mislevy's (1994) contrast between legal and psychometric modes of reasoning, which suggests new strategies for serving the validation purposes that more conventional practices, such as generalizability studies, serve. Messick's Singerian inquiry is an extremely powerful concept—one that has tremendous potential for pushing educational measurement, and any field in educational research, forward. It serves both critical and generative functions by simultaneously encouraging us to consider alternative methodologies and illuminating our own taken-for-granted practices for critique.

A Role for Consequences in Validity Theory A second fruitful area involves the study of consequences in the context of assessment. The relationship between validity and consequences remains a matter of considerable theoretical debate within our profession (see, e.g., Moss, 1995, 1998, for an overview). Should consequences be considered an aspect of validity at all? If yes, how should the concept be related? Are inappropriate consequences relevant to validity only if they can be traced to a source of construct underrepresentation or construct-irrelevant variance? Could negative consequences associated with an otherwise valid interpretation call the validity of the test use into question? If yes, does that mean we have expanded the focus of validity from an assessment-based interpretation to the entire system of which the assessment is a part? What are the consequences—scientific, economic, political—to the profession and communities we serve by making these different choices?

A related set of questions focus on how best to study consequences of assessment use. Although we have a great deal of experience and methodological advice available to us for studying the validity of interpretations, we have much less experience and fewer theoretical resources for studying the consequences of assessment use. Our history, in quantitative, experimental traditions of social science, has encouraged us to try to control contextual factors—to eliminate construct-irrelevant sources of variance—rather than to understand the ways in which these factors naturally interact within the phenomenon we are studying.

Bryk and Hermanson (1993) criticize models of educational reform that rely on generalizations about the relationships between processes and outcomes for underpresenting the complexity of schools. "Schools [they argue] are places where personal meaning and human intentionality matter" (p. 457). Theories of reform should reflect a view of schools where interaction among individuals is fundamental and reform requires "changing the values and tacit understandings that ground these interactions." Following Bryk and Hermanson's suggestions, case studies of the contexts in which assessments are used can highlight the ways in which results are interpreted in local contexts and how the community is in turn transformed by those interpretations (e.g., Davis & Felknow, 1994; Mehan, 1993; Smith et al., 1994). Researchers informed by interpretive traditions of social science have much to offer us in that regard.

A Role for Cases in Validity Theory. Another fruitful area for research is in developing cases of validity research both to illustrate validity theory and to critique it. Here I suggest and point to examples of three genres of cases that might inform validity theory: (a) cases as reflected in reviews of (or plans for) a program of validity research, (b) cases as empirically based descriptions of the actual practices of working scientists, and (c) cases as critical analyses that locate our theories and practices in the sociohistorical-political contexts in which they are developed and used.

As I suggested earlier, articulations of validity theory in measurement typically offer generalized definitions, processes, and categories of evidence, criteria, or aspects to be considered. Although these categories are invariably illustrated with real or hypothetical examples of practice, the examples are typically brief and intended to represent a single category of evidence or aspect of validity research. A number of concerns have been raised about this approach to representing validity theory. Each of these concerns points to the value of cases—albeit cases that reflect somewhat different genres.

One concern is that these brief and decontextualized examples of validity theory do not adequately represent the programmatic nature of validity research. Responding to concerns like this, Kane (1992) and Shepard (1993) moved toward more contextualized ways of thinking about validity theory by considering the assumptions, inferences, or questions necessary to support a particular interpretation and use. Shepard's (1993) treatment of cases moves further beyond a priori decisions about appropriate criteria to an explicit consideration of the contingencies represented in actual programs of research.

A second concern is that generalized methodological characterizations may actually undermine sound practice. Kaplan (1964), who distinguishes between reconstructed logic and logic in use, argues that the reconstructed logic can constrain practice by failing to illuminate practices that do not fit and encouraging conformity and "premature closure" on alternative possibilities. Building on Kuhn's conception of exemplars, Mishler (1990) suggests replacing "the storybook image of science" with an empirically based description of the "actual practices of working scientists," which are typically marked, he says "by uncertainty, controversy and ad hoc pragmatic procedures." These descriptions should be accompanied by "a context-based explication . . . of how observations are transformed into data and findings, and how interpretations are grounded" (pp. 423, 435). In this way, candidate exemplars are created for members of the scientific community to evaluate for guiding their own practice.

Some social theorists would push us even further in exploiting the role that cases can play in validity theory. Bourdieu and Wacquant (1992), for instance, wants us to trace the genesis and consequences of the problems, concepts, categories, and taxonomies we use (such as gender, achievement, poverty, profession, etc.). As an example, he criticizes one American methodologist for his arbitrary operational definition of *homelessness*—not so much because it is wrong or off base, but more because it is inadequately problematized in terms of its historical evolution and consequences.

> This effort to pass off a socially arbitrary definition of "homelessness" as grounded in "scientific" considerations is . . . notable for its blindness to its own presuppositions. . . . Instead of showing how different definitions produce populations of different sizes, compositions and trajectories and of analyzing the political and scientific interests involved . . . , [this researcher] is content to assert . . . his definition tailored to existing data and preconceptions. . . . It ends up yielding a "fairly narrow definition" which basically borrows and ratifies that of state bureaucracies whose interest in normalizing and minimizing the phenomenon is amply documented. . . . (pp. 244–245)

Citations by Bourdieu (1984), Foucault (1984), and Hanson (1993) provide examples of this sort of case. Within educational measurement, there have already been moves toward this kind of critical reflection. Consider Shepard's (1991) study of psychometricians' beliefs about learning, Crooks' (1988) review of the multidimensional impact of testing on students, or Madaus' (1994) analysis of the consequences of measurement technology for our conceptions of education.

CONCLUDING COMMENTS

Although my example of how one might contribute to the dialogue on validity theory has focused on the field of educational measurement, the underlying principles are, I believe, relevant to any social science research discourse, including literacy or composition research. These include: reading beyond our field, whatever it might be, to challenge the theories and practices we take for granted; examining cases of actual research practice not just to illustrate our validity principles, but to challenge them; inviting and participating in studies of our research practices by scholars from outside the field (and vice versa); and considering collaboratively the consequences of our research practice for those we study and serve. Hoy and McCarthy (1994) suggests that this kind of work "makes us aware of the problems we did not know we had. Once we discover these problems, we may well become motivated to unlearn patterns of thought and action that have become second nature" (p. 164). Bill Smith inspired his students to engage in this sort of generative work.

I am not suggesting that researchers should abandon the strengths of their fields. I am suggesting that we each begin to educate ourselves about alternatives and expand who we consider our teachers, colleagues, collaborators, and critics to be. One of my favorite authors, Bernstein (1992), suggests that this kind of pluralistic dialogue is the responsibility of participants in any vital substantive tradition.

REFERENCES

Angoff, W. H. (1988). Validity: An evolving concept. In H. Wainer & H. Braun (Eds.), *Test validity* (pp. 19-32). Hillsdale, NJ: Lawrence Erlbaum Associates.

Bernstein, R. J. (1976). *The restructuring of social and political theory.* Philadelphia: University of Pennsylvania Press.

Bernstein, R. J. (1992). *The new constellation: The ethical-political horizons of modernity/post-modernity.* Cambridge: MIT Press.

Bourdieu, P. (1984). *Homo academicus.* Stanford: Stanford University Press.

Bourdieu, P., & Wacquant, L. J. D. (1992). *An invitation to reflexive sociology.* Chicago: University of Chicago Press.

Bryk, A. S., & Hermanson, K. M. (1993). Educational indicator systems: Observations on their structure, interpretation, and use. *Review of Research in Education, 19,* 451–484.

Cronbach, L. J. (1988). Five perspectives on validity argument. In H. Wainer (Ed.), *Test validity.* Hillsdale, NJ: Lawrence Erlbaum Associates.

Cronbach, L. J. (1989). Construct validation after thirty years. In R. L. Linn (Ed.), *Intelligence: Measurement, theory and public policy* (pp. 147–171). Urbana: University of Illinois Press.

Crooks, T. J., (1988). The impact of classroom evaluation practices on students. *Review of Educational Research, 85*(4), 438-481.

Davis, A., & Felknow, C. (1994, April). *Graduation by exhibition: The effects of high stakes portfolio assessment on curriculum and instruction in one high school.* Paper presented at the annual meeting of the American Educational Research Association, New Orleans.

Foucault, M. (1984). The means of correct training. In P. Rabinow (Ed.), *The Foucault reader* (pp. 188–206). New York: Pantheon.

Hanson, F. A. (1993). *Testing testing: Social consequences of the examined life.* Berkeley: University of California Press.

Hoy, D. C., & McCarthy, T. (1994). *Critical theory.* Oxford: Blackwell.

Kane, M. (1992). An argument-based approach to validity. *Psychological Bulletin, 112,* 527–535.

Kane, M. (2004). Certification testing as an illustration of argument-based validation. *Measurement: Interdisciplinary Research and Perspectives, 2*(3), 135-170.

Madaus, G. F. (1994). A technological and historical consideration of equity issues associated with proposals to change the nation's testing policy. *Harvard Educational Review, 64*(1), 76–95.

Mehan, H. (1993). Beneath the skin and between the ears: A case study in the politics of representation. In S. Chaiklin & J. Lave (Eds.), *Understanding practice: Perspectives on activity and context* (pp. 241–268). Cambridge: Cambridge University Press.

Meier, D. (1995). *The power of their ideas: Lessons for America from a small school in Harlem.* Boston, MA: Beacon.

Messick, S. (1989). Validity. In *Educational measurement* (3rd ed.). Washington, DC: The American Council on Education and the National Council on Measurement in Education.

Mishler, E. G. (1990). Validation in inquiry-guided research: The role of exemplars in narrative studies. *Harvard Educational Review, 60*(4), 415–442.

Mislevy, R. J. (1994). Evidence and inference in educational assessment. *Psychometrika, 59*(4), 439–483.

Mislevy, R. J. (2003). On the structure of educational assessments. *Measurement: Interdisciplinary Research and Perspectives, 1*(1), 3–62.

Moss, P. A. (1992). Shifting conceptions of validity in educational measurement: Implications for performance assessment. *Review of Educational Research, 62*(3), 229–258.

Moss, P. A. (1995). Themes and variations in validity theory. *Educational Measurement: Issues and Practice, 14*(2), 5–13.

Moss, P. A. (1996). Enlarging the dialogue in educational measurement: Voices from interpretive research traditions. *Educational Researcher, 25*(1), 20-28, 43.

Moss, P. A. (1998). The role of consequences in validity theory. *Educational Measurement: Issues and Practice, 17*(2), 5–12.

Shepard, L. A. (1991). Psychometricians beliefs about learning. *Educational Researcher, 20*(7), 15–22.

Shepard, L. A. (1993). Evaluating test validity. *Review of Research in Education, 19*, 405–450.

Smith, M. L., Noble, A. J., Cabay, M., Heinecke, W., Junker, M. S., & Saffron, Y. (1994). *What happens when the test mandate changes? Results of a multiple case study* (CSE Technical Report 380). Los Angeles, CA: University of California, National Center for Research on Evaluation, Standards, and Student Testing.

II

RESEARCH AND TEACHING

6

NOBODY LAPS ME TWICE

Attitude Surveys as Tools for Reflection

David L. Wallace

I passed Sam about halfway into my 17-lap, 3.1-mile run around the track in the university's fitness center. I had noticed him running as I stretched before I ran. He moved along at a good pace, and the dampness of his shirt suggested that he had been at it a while. I had been gaining a little on Sam each lap, and I must admit that I was pleased I could catch and pass a runner almost 20 years my junior. I slowly gained on Sam again during the second half of my run, and at the beginning of Lap 17—the end in sight—I picked up my pace a little and passed him for the second time. Down the last straightaway I even sprinted a bit, lengthening my stride, pumping my arms a bit harder. I was feeling pretty good about my run when I heard feet pounding hard behind me and then beside me. I turned to see Sam flying past me, and for a few seconds I chased him, pushing even harder, but then relaxed, slackened my pace, and smiled to myself. "Of course he has to win."

We are in the stretching area now, and we have managed to say hello to each other, although we are both doubled over, hands on our thighs, trying to catch our breathe. "That was some sprint you made at the end," I wheezed out. Sam looked up, holding my eyes directly with his, and said, "Nobody laps me twice." I smiled. When we finally straightened up and shook hands to say goodbye, I noticed that Sam was almost my height now, a couple inches taller than he had been 2 years ago when he walked into my honors composition course, a 16-year-old college prodigy bursting with confidence and ready with a firm answer for every query I posed.

As I walked down to the locker room, I could remember three things about Sam's performance in my course: (a) His papers were full of sweeping claims that he was sure he could support, and he did not hide his frustration well when I and the members of his writing group poked holes in his arguments; (b) Sam had bullied the other three students in his writing group when they argued that the draft of their group project, which he had insisted that he compose alone, failed to address several issues that they saw as important—he was not happy with me for giving the project an A-, rather than an A; and (c) the writing attitude surveys that Sam took at the beginning and end of the course indicated that his writing apprehension increased significantly during the course, even though the scores for most of his classmates decreased.

Back in my office, I dug through my files searching for the final exam Sam had written about the changes in his attitudes about writing and class talk during the course. I had given the students their pre- and postsurvey scores for six different attitude factors. In their final ungraded writing assignment, I asked them to comment on their change in scores (or lack thereof) for each category, discussing whether they agreed or disagreed with the change scores and about why they felt their attitudes about writing and classroom talk did or did not change.

In the front of the folder for Sam's class was a sheet summarizing the pre- and postchanges in the students' scores. Overall, the class' attitudes had moved in the directions that made sense to me. The biggest gain (+2.5 points on average) was in their belief that collaboration with others was useful for their own writing. I was not surprised by this result because I had seen how much the students helped each other in their peer review groups and because they showed up during my office hours, drafts in hand. The next biggest gain was a .675-point average increase in their desire for active student involvement in class discussions, which pleased me because I had worked hard to move myself out of the center of the class and make room for them to explore issues that were important to them. The next largest effect—a .600-point gain in the desire for teacher control of class talk and content—disappointed but did not surprise me because I had been aware throughout the course that there was a contingent of students who were frustrated that I couldn't or wouldn't tell them exactly what they needed to do to get an A.

Taken together, the students also gained over a half a point (.575) in their belief that writing ability was learnable. Again, I was pleased with this gain, but a quick scan of the students' scores revealed that the result was much more bipolar than it first appeared. Students who got good grades or felt they improved their writing posted 2-, 3- and 4-point gains, whereas students who got lower grades (usually Bs and B-s) posted lower scores, which reflected, I suspect, feeling like they could not compete with their peers for the first time in their academic careers.

The smallest two average effects were for changes in the students' writing apprehension and the usefulness they saw in group work. The students' attitudes about group work declined a bit (-.300), with some students posting small gains and some small losses. Again, this did not surprise me because nearly all the students had reported in their individual evaluations of their group projects that they had always led group projects in high school and were either relieved to have motivated peers to work with or frustrated (like Sam's group) that they could not always get their way. For writing apprehension, there was a small overall loss (-.325), which pleased me because I had hoped that the course would make my students more comfortable with writing. But again, for a handful of students, the effect seemed entirely the opposite: Their writing apprehension increased.

As I scanned the students' individual scores, I saw that Sam's 4-point gain in writing apprehension was the largest in the class, and I began flipping back through the stack of papers to find his final reflection. After 2 years and a couple hundred more students, I could not remember exactly what Sam had written, but my hypothesis was that this rise in his writing apprehension was good because it meant he ended the course less overly confident than he began it—that his sense of self-efficacy as a writer was more realistic, less inflated. The story I found in his reflection journal was much more interesting.

Sam had been particularly thorough in his analysis. He had sorted the questions for each factor (they were mixed up on the form) so that he could compare his scores for each question on the pre- and postsurveys to explore in more detail what the changes in his scores meant. To my surprise, he saw his rise in writing apprehension as a fairly minor change, which he attributed to the fact that he had discovered that he could not watch TV while doing the writing for my class as he did with his other homework and he could not adequately argue his points in response to controversial readings because "I suffer from not being about to write (or sometimes speak, even) as fast as my brain may be formulating a rebuttal to the sample reading." He saw a smaller decrease (2 points) in his desire for teacher control as much more significant (and he is likely right given that he started on the low end of this factor and dropped even lower). He said that he now "despised teacher control over what students believe even more [than at the beginning of the semester]" because "students, at least at the collegiate level, can virtually instruct themselves." I liked this pedagogical role that Sam was constructing; in fact, he articulated what I was trying to do in the course better than I had at that point:

> The teacher can just serve to keep them on the best course if they should stray. The definition of the term "best" is not the opinion of the teacher, rather it means that if the students begin to walk down the road towards problems, the teacher simply reminds them of where they are heading.

But there was yet more. Sam ended his analysis with a discussion of the 9-point positive change in his collaboration score. He had begun the course with the lowest score for the usefulness of collaboration for one's own writing factor and ended by posting the largest gain of anyone in the class for any factor. He cited interactions with me and his physics instructor as pivotal events in this change. He described an interaction in one of our conferences (which I could only vaguely remember), in which I explained that trying to prove something as absolutely true is a very hard task. He said, "I had been living my entire life on the basis of pure absolutes everywhere. You, however, made me realize that only rarely is anything absolute. This definitely made my paper better." Apparently, I worked in an unwitting tag-team with Sam's physics teacher, who nailed this point home to Sam when he shared the following quote in class:

> What everybody echoes, or in silences passes by, as truth today may turn out to be falsehood tomorrow, mere smoke of opinion, which some had trusted for a cloud that might sprinkle fertilizing rain.

As I read on, I was delighted to see that this new attitude did not just extend to authority figures. Rather, Sam now saw his peers as an important part of his learning process as well:

> I guess that learning to look to others for help is just one of those parts of growing up. I hate admitting that I am stuck, but sometimes, someone else possesses the answer that could send me on my way to better and brighter places. Often times, a simple answer from a friend, looking at the problem from a different perspective, is all that I need to improve everything I do.

I have not seen Sam since that day we raced each other, and I am sure he has long since graduated. But I still feel a sense of accomplishment when I look back on his case—a sense that I won with this kid, that the choices I made about the writing challenges I gave him, the way I conducted the class, and the opportunities I gave Sam to reflect on how my course and his first semester in college had changed him all made an important difference. I also recognize that I have learned a lot from Sam and other students who have taken up the challenge to reflect on what caused the changes they saw in their attitudes about writing and classroom interaction. I am not so vain as to take all the credit for Sam's new understandings; clearly—for good or ill—much of what Sam learned was due to the spirit that drove him to run past me and then tell me, "Nobody laps me twice."

Psychometric Methods Meet Feminist Research Theory With a Postmodern Twist

I began this chapter with Sam's story because it illustrates what it meant for me to bring together the psychometric tradition of building survey tools that attempt to identify and measure underlying psychological constructs with feminist critiques of traditional empirical research methods that call for the researched to have a larger role in the research process. One of my goals in this chapter is to illustrate that these two intellectual traditions need not be seen as diametrically opposed to one another. More specifically, I want to sort out what is sensible in the psychometric tradition that I and a number of other researchers have attempted to harness in the service of better understanding the effects of writing instruction on students. An equally important goal is to explore what it means to apply feminist principles to the development, application, and interpretation of such research tools and concepts.

Obviously in a single chapter I cannot possibly recount the development of either of these two important research traditions, nor do I have the time or space to expose and explore all of the historical and continuing conflicts between them. In fact, the only way I can see to mix this strange methodological cocktail is to begin with a postmodern twist, to accept from the outset that trying to establish Truth is the wrong goal, and to recognize that examining what is being valued in the search for knowledge is an integral part of those processes. However, I do not mean to embrace deconstruction as the new master method because I understand the fears and frustrations that my students express when I assign them critical theory readings, which they see as carrying deconstruction so far that it loses connection with the lived experiences of people and becomes an exercise in showing the author's cleverness. Instead, deconstruction needs to work as a tool—in this case, to raise questions about how these survey instruments came to be and about how they abstract from human experience.

To create a substantive deconstruction of the psychometric tradition of survey research about writing, I use a basic feminist research principle articulated by Harding (1987), who argues that the best feminist analysis:

> insists that the inquirer her/himself be placed in the same critical plane as the overt subject matter. . . . That is, the class, race, culture, and gender assumptions, beliefs, and behaviors of the researcher her/himself must be placed within the frame of the picture that she/he attempts to paint. (p. 9)

Harding is clear that applying this principle requires more than simply beginning each research report with a disclaimer or rambling soul-searching reverie. Instead, she argues that the researcher must appear to us "not as an invisible, anonymous voice of authority, but as a real, historical individual with concrete, specific desires and interests" (p. 9). In addition to Harding's insistence that researchers explicitly give up their claim to an objective stance, her principle of putting the researcher in the same plane as the research also calls, I believe, for researchers to consider the extent to which they have invited (or failed to invite) research participants to actively engage in various aspects of their research projects. As the following review illustrates, the major developments in writing attitude survey research have proceeded without any explicit attention to Harding's feminist research principle and the corollary that I have drawn from it.

The primary genesis of work in writing pedagogy about students' attitudes can be dated to a pair of articles by John A. Daly and Michael D. Miller that appeared in 1975 in the same issue of *Research in the Teaching of English*. The first article (Daly & Miller, 1975a) reported the development of the survey tool beginning with the premise that something called *writing apprehension* existed, could be measured, and had predictive value in understanding students' experiences with writing instruction (much like the well-documented phenomenon of speech apprehension). The second article (Daly & Miller, 1975b) reported the results of a study that tested seven hypotheses about the relationships between writing apprehension and such factors as SAT verbal scores, sex, success expectations in writing courses, and students' willingness to take advanced writing courses.

Two things strike me as particularly important in Daly and Miller's account of the genesis of the construct of writing apprehension. First, as they briefly set up their argument in the introduction to their initial article, they refer to the experiences of writing teachers, a brief appeal to lived experience: "Most teachers of composition have recognized in their classes students who seem to be unduly apprehensive about writing" (1975a, p. 242). However, in the body of the first article, it is the psychometric procedure that establishes a believable and reliable tool for measuring the phenomenon that gives the construct of writing apprehension status as researchable. Daly and Miller presume that the procedure of testing and culling possible questions with a factor analysis and successful checks of the split-half and test–retest reliability of the resulting items is sufficient evidence to establish the construct. For example, they argue that a .99 correlation between a 26-question version of the form and a 20-question version indicates that the two versions "were essentially measuring the same construct" (p. 247).

As I reread these articles more than 25 years after they were written, it seems clear that Daly and Miller's approach to research as well as their presumptions about the roles of researchers, teachers, and students in pedagogical research projects are ripe for feminist critique. The reports of their research are written in the usual author-evacuated style of the times in which Daly and Miller do not represent themselves as having any particular motivation for conducting this study. They do not even identify themselves as writing teachers concerned about these problems. Also, there remains a great gulf fixed between researchers and the researched in their reports of their research. In the first 1975 article, writing teachers appear briefly in the introduction and then disappear entirely until the discussion section, and students appear only as aggregate bodies (164 students at the University of West Virginia take the 63-item version that is culled down through the factor analysis, and another 174 take the culled version as well as a second survey about their jobs and majors). As was the case with most empirical writing research of this era, writing students and teachers were passive participants who did what the researchers asked of them, whose attitudes and behaviors were characterized by researchers who used a variety of empirical methods to approximate Truth. In this case, the Truth approximated was that a psychological construct called *writing apprehension* existed, was measurable, and, at least in terms of writing instruction, was bad in high doses.

This view of writing apprehension as a stable psychological construct remains largely unchallenged through a decade of research that explored connections between writing apprehension and issues such as writing competence and other self-efficacy beliefs (see Daly, 1985 for a review of this research). For my purposes, the next significant development in our understanding of writing apprehension comes in Daly's (1985) chapter in the highly influential *When a Writer Can't Write*, edited by Mike Rose. In his reflection on more than 10 years of research on writing apprehension, Daly moves slightly away from the notion of writing apprehension as a unitary, universal phenomenon when he makes a distinction between dispositional attitudes, which "endure in a relatively consistent fashion over time and across situations" (p. 65), and situational attitudes, which vary according to immediate circumstances. He describes writing apprehension as a "relatively enduring" (p. 44) dispositional attitude that is "relatively independent of other personality dimensions" (p. 50) and concludes that "the construct is both measurable and valid" (p. 74).

What I find interesting in Daly's review of writing apprehension research are the competing notions that, from a psychometric perspective, writing apprehension must be an independent construct that applies across situations and, from a pedagogical perspective, it must be seen as amendable to change in certain situations or there would be no use in identifying high- or low- apprehensive writers. Further, it is clear that, at least in this 1985 research report, Daly does not see students (or others who take the writing apprehension survey) as having any significant insights to contribute as we hear not a single word from any of the students involved in the many studies he summarizes, and further neither students nor teachers are described as active participants in sorting out such knotty problems as what distinguishes among situations: "*Investigators* can contrast situation A with situation B, seeking differences between the two" (p. 71; italics added). In Daly's 1985 understanding of writing apprehension, researchers remain the question askers, data interpreters, and problem setters, and students' roles are largely limited to filling out forms.

My point here is that in the mid-1980s, Daly and the field of rhetoric and composition at large were beginning to see that research needed not only to search out large, empirically measurable effects, but also to examine the kinds of circumstances that create those effects and to tease out smaller patterns of differences in people's experiences with writing that can lead to success or, as the cases in Rose's book illustrate, the inability to write at all. In this instance, Daly clearly recognizes the infinite possibilities involved in defining the differences in situational contexts in meaningful ways. However, instead of considering that student participants may provide important information about how a given situation works for them, Daly chooses a limited set of eight factors about which he believed researchers should collect data and make judgments.

The next important step in the development of the writing attitude surveys that I report in this chapter was Palmquist and Young's (1992) survey questions (see the Belief That Writing Ability as Learnable Factor in Fig. 6.1) that measure the extent to which students buy into the romantic notion that writing ability is a gift and cannot be learned. In addition, the factor analyses that they proposed also allowed them to confirm that a much shortened version of the Daly/Miller writing apprehension survey was a distinctively different factor from their new giftedness factor. (NOTE: Palmquist and Young's belief that writing is a *gift* factor was later renamed belief that writing is *learnable*, and I follow this change in my references to their work.)

Two things seem important in Palmquist and Young's treatment of writing ability. First, although they take pains to create statistically independent measures, they see students' attitudes as interrelated in practice. Indeed, about the writing-ability-as-learnable (Writing as Learnable) factor they present, they conclude: "the notion of giftedness appears to make an important, though largely unacknowledged, contribution to a constellation of expectations, attitudes, and beliefs that influence the ways in which students approach writing" (p. 159). Second, students remain largely passive in the research process. For example, in explaining a difference between students' and writing teachers' perceptions of the difficulty of writing various genres, Palmquist and Young speculate that students might "have been thinking along the lines of the five-paragraph essay" (p. 153), but have no data other than the marks the students made on survey forms to speak from. The most active role Palmquist and Young give to students appears in their conclusion, where they discuss pedagogical applications. They make the sensible point that their study suggests that "teachers must remember that their students come to them freighted with rhetorical lore, not all of which is sound, and some of which may well impede their ability to learn and write better" (p. 162). In short, Palmquist and Young provide a new tool for better understanding the complex ways that students' attitudes about writing intertwine. However, the flow information remains one- way: Researchers provide tools and insights for teachers, who in turn can attempt to correct the false lore that students bring with them. There is no sense in this research that students may have significant contributions to make in the research process.

The trend of researchers seeing writing apprehension and the belief that writing is learnable rather than a gift as part of a larger set of students' self efficacy beliefs continues in Charney, Newman, and Palmquist's (1995) study. The authors used Palmquist and Young's survey tools, together with a survey tool developed by Newman that examines students' epistemological styles (i.e., absolutist, relativist, and evaluativist positions). Surveying a group of 446 students enrolled in first- and third-year college writing courses, Charney and her colleagues found evidence of connections between epistemological styles and attitudes toward writing in that, "Students with less absolutist or more evaluativist epistemological styles have more positive attitudes toward writing" (p. 323). However, as in the other studies I have reviewed, there is not a word from students

FIGURE 6.1. Survey Questions by Group

Writing Apprehension (6)

+   I avoid writing.
-   Discussing writing with others is an enjoyable experience.
-   I enjoy writing.
-   Writing is a lot of fun.
+   I'm no good at writing.
-   I waste a lot of time when I write because I don't know what I want to say.

Belief That Writing Ability Is Learnable (4)

+   Good teachers can help me become a better writer.
-   Good writers are born not made.
+   Some people have said, "Writing can be learned but it can't be taught." I believe writing can be learned.
+   I believe writing can be taught.

Usefulness of Collaboration (5)

+   When I have a writing assignment, I like to talk to someone about it before I write.
+   People can give me useful advice about what I'm going to write.
+   When I have a problem writing, I like to bounce ideas off other people.
+   Telling a friend about my ideas for writing helps me write better.
-   It's a waste of time to talk with other students about my writing.

Student Involvement in Class Discussion (4)

+   I feel comfortable asking questions when I don't understand something.
+   I feel comfortable contributing to class discussion.
+   I feel comfortable voicing complaints about a class to the teacher.
+   I enjoy participating in class discussions.

Teacher Control of Class Talk and Content (5)

+   A teacher's primary job is to present information to students.
+   Good teachers retain complete control of the content of a course.
+   Even when teachers want students to "come to their own conclusions," they should still indicate which answers are best.
+   Teachers should always control class discussion.
+   A teacher's main responsibility is to make sure that he or she covers all the course material.

Usefulness of Group Work (3)

+   Working in small groups with other students is an effective way of learning.
-   I'd rather figure something out for myself than work with others in a group to figure it out.
-   When students are paired or grouped in class activities, it's like the blind leading the blind.

in their report of this study. Much like Daly and Miller, Charney and her colleagues invoke a teacherly frame at the beginning of their article: "Every writing teacher knows the frustrations of having students who decline opportunities to revise their papers, who avoid conferences and peer review sessions, who persist in unsophisticated rhetorical strategies even after instruction, who just don't seem to try to improve their writing skills" (pp. 298–299). But again in the body of the methods, analyses, and results, teachers and students are not actors in any sense. Students' participation is limited to filling out an 83-item survey and deciding whether to release their SAT verbal scores.

The survey instrument that I report in this chapter extends the work just reviewed by adding survey measures for four more attitudes relevant to writing instruction: the usefulness of collaboration for one's own writing (Collaboration), desire for active student involvement in class discussion (Student Involvement), desire for teacher control of class talk and tasks (Teacher Control), and the usefulness of group work (Group Work). Indeed, I began the process of developing these survey instruments by assuming that large-scale surveys and psychometric statistical procedures (mainly factor analyses) could help me sort out sets of questions to reliably distinguish between different attitudes, although I assumed these measures would also be incomplete descriptions of the ways in which students' beliefs about themselves and their experiences with writing affect their ability to learn to write better. I diverged from the previous tradition, in that I include as part of my research design giving students back the tools I've developed so they can participate in the analysis of the results and have some voice in reporting those results.

The survey instrument (see Fig. 6.2) is probably best seen as two separate, but related, surveys. One part of the survey examines students' attitudes about writing using a short writing apprehension measure, Palmquist and Young's Writing as Learnable questions, and a new set of questions about how useful students see collaboration with others for their writing. The other part of the survey examines three attitudes about preferences for classroom discourse (Student Involvement, Teacher Control, Group Work). Both surveys were developed as assessment tools for larger research projects.

The writing attitude survey was developed as an assessment tool for the Making Thinking Visible Project at Carnegie Mellon University (see Flower, Wallace, Norris, and Burnett, 1994, for a report of this project). The premise of the larger project was to explore the usefulness of Collaborative Planning—of asking students to plan together in pairs or groups using the Blackboard Planner, a simple heuristic device developed by Linda Flower from her previous planning research. The purpose of the project was not to establish Collaborative Planning as an effective pedagogical technique using traditional educational experiments. Instead, the project invited elementary, high school, and college writing teachers to experiment with Collaborative Planning and to engage in individually designed teacher-research projects, in which they invited their students to reflect on their experiences using collaborative planning using a variety of methods.

FIGURE 6.2. Writing Attitude Survey

Name _____

Respond to the following statements about writing by **circling** the appropriate letter(s) to indicate how strongly you agree or disagree that the statement applies to you. There are no right or wrong answers; answer honestly in terms of your own writing experiences in school.

SA=Strongly Agree, **A**=Agree, **D**=Disagree, **SD**=Strongly Disagree

---

Writing Attitude Survey

1.	SA A D SD	I avoid writing.
2.	SA A D SD	When I have a writing assignment, I like to talk to someone about it before I write.
3.	SA A D SD	Discussing writing with others is an enjoyable experience.
4.	SA A D SD	People can give me useful advice about what I'm going to write.
5.	SA A D SD	I enjoy writing.
6.	SA A D SD	I waste a lot of time when I write because I don't know what I want to say.
7.	SA A D SD	When I have a problem writing, I like to bounce ideas off other people.
8.	SA A D SD	Writing is a lot of fun.
9.	SA A D SD	Telling a friend about my ideas for writing helps me write better.
10.	SA A D SD	I'm no good at writing.
11.	SA A D SD	It's a waste of time to talk with other students about my writing.
12.	SA A D SD	Good teachers can help me become a better writer.
13.	SA A D SD	Good writers are born not made.
14.	SA A D SD	Some people have said, "Writing can be learned but it can't be taught." I believe writing can be learned.
15.	SA A D SD	I believe writing can be taught.

Classroom Style Preferences Survey

1.	SA A D SD	Working in small groups with other students is an effective way of learning.
2.	SA A D SD	A teacher's primary job is to present information to students.
3.	SA A D SD	I feel comfortable asking questions when I don't understand something.
4.	SA A D SD	I'd rather figure something out for myself than work with others in a group to figure it out.
5.	SA A D SD	Good teachers retain complete control of the content of a course.
6.	SA A D SD	I feel comfortable contributing to class discussion.

7.   SA A D SD   When students are paired or grouped in class activities, it's like the blind leading the blind.

8.   SA A D SD   Even when teachers want students to "come to their own conclusions," they should still indicate which answers are best.

9.   SA A D SD   I feel comfortable voicing complaints about a class to the teacher.

10. SA A D SD   Teachers should always control class discussion.

11. SA A D SD   A teacher's main responsibility is to make sure that he or she covers all the course material.

12. SA A D SD   I enjoy participating in class discussions.

As a member of the project team, one of my jobs was to develop an attitude survey that we could use as an assessment tool for the project. Following the procedure laid out in Daly and Miller (1975a), I got a group of the project teachers together to brainstorm possible questions for three factors: usefulness of planning (Planning), sense of control over one's writing (Control), and Collaboration. Next, I constructed a survey with the most promising of the new questions, the short Writing Apprehension survey, and the Writing as Learnable survey from Palmquist and Young. Then I conducted a factor analysis with the survey results of 249 first-year college students to discover which of the five proposed factors hung together in practice. The factor analysis grouped three sets of questions together (again using the standards set by Daly & Miller): the five questions from the shortened Writing Apprehension survey plus one of the Control questions, the four Palmquist and Miller questions for Writing as Learnable, and five collaboration questions. The questions we had intended to measure attitudes about Planning and Control failed to group in any coherent way.[1]

The survey examining students' attitudes about classroom discourse was developed in a similar fashion as part of a research project examining how teachers create (and fail to create) mutuality in knowledge making with students. I conducted this study with my colleague Helen Rothschild Ewald when I was teaching at Iowa State University (see Wallace & Ewald, 2000, for a report of the larger project). In the larger project, Helen and I observed and tape recorded meetings of each others' classes, conducted case studies with students from each others' classes, and analyzed discourse patterns in the transcripts of our class sessions. At the beginning of the project, we brainstormed a set of possible survey questions and then asked the students in our classes not only to fill out the surveys (we chose

---

[1]Split-half reliability using Cronbach's alpha procedure was .64 for Writing Apprehension, .58 for Writing as Learnable, and .74 for Collaboration. The alpha value for Writing as Learnable is lower than what most researchers would accept as reliable. However, I chose to keep the measure in the survey because Palmquist and Young reported a much higher alpha level for the same questions and because the factor analysis clearly identified these questions as different from the Writing Apprehension and Collaboration factors.

case study participants from each others' classes based on the results of the surveys), but also to comment on the questions. After refining the questions, I gave the survey to 383 students enrolled in 18 sections of first-year composition or junior-level business and technical writing courses at Iowa State and conducted a factor analysis. The three constructs we intended to measure with the questions— Student Involvement, Teacher Control, and Group Work—emerged clearly, although only about half of the questions for each construct were grouped together consistently by the factor analysis (see Fig. 6.1 for a list of the questions that loaded consistently as factors).[2]

For several years after I completed the second factor analysis, I collected data from several groups of students using a form that included the six constructs identified in the two factor analyses. My initial purpose in collecting these data was to follow Daly and Miller's example and establish the validity of these survey instruments by correlating them with other established measures (e.g., ACT-English scores and course grades) as well as look for patterns of difference by groups (e.g., gender, admissions status [honors or regular], and race) and to look for differences in students' scores at the beginning of writing courses and their scores at the end. I found some interesting results asking these kinds of questions.

For example, Sam was 1 of 111 students enrolled in one honors section, two entry-level sections, and two second-level sections of first-year composition in a study that I conducted at Iowa State. When I examined the pre- and postsurvey results for this group, several interesting patterns emerged. There was a consistent and statistically significant increase (+.675) for the Student Involvement factor across all five sections, as well as a statistically significant decrease in writing apprehension (-.315). These results pleased the other two teachers and me (the other teachers taught two sections each) because we had designed our courses to try and get students more actively involved in their own learning and because we hoped our courses would help our students become more comfortable with writing. However, these generalized results gloss over some important differences: The writing apprehension decrease was largely due to big average declines in just one section of the entry-level course and one section of the second-level course (each taught by different teachers). There was no statistically significant difference in the students' pre/post scores for the Collaboration and Group Work factors. However, as noted earlier, the students in my honors section posted a whopping 2.5-point increase in their collaboration scores; a closer look at the Group Work results revealed a statistically significant interaction effect, where men started with a higher belief in the usefulness of group work than women, but ending the semester with lower beliefs and women had the opposite experience.

My point here is that analyzing the survey trends was useful because it allowed the three of us teachers to see some patterns of difference that probably would

---

[2]Split-half reliability using Cronbach's alpha procedure was .66 for Group Work, .76 for Student Involvement, and .65 for Teacher Control.

have been invisible to us without comparing the survey results across our classes. However, those results were not the end game; in fact, the statistical results raised more questions for us than they answered. Why did my honors students post such a high gain for Collaboration? Why did each of the other two teachers have one class that greatly reduced its writing apprehension and one that stayed more or less the same? Why did women in our courses seem to find group work more beneficial than men? The good news for us was that we were not just limited to our own imperfect recollections of our courses for seeking answers to these questions. In a sense, our students became our post hoc partners in seeking answers to these questions because we could read what they had written about their scores and the experiences they saw as relevant to their change or lack of change in their attitudes.

Listening to Students: Using Attitude Surveys as an Inquiry Tool

The more I conducted these large-scale survey analyses, the more I became dissatisfied with them because the patterns that I saw when I ran correlations, *t-* tests, ANOVAs, and multiple regression analyses did not show enough of the picture. I still believe that there is value in looking at the kinds of large trends that statistics can describe. For example, if most of the students in a writing program end up feeling much more apprehensive about their writing than they did when they began the program, then the program needs to take a serious look at why that is occurring. However, the more I read insights of students like Sam, the more I began to wonder about my preconceived notion that my or others' teaching would or should always result in lower writing apprehension, a greater belief that writing is learnable and collaboration and group work are useful, as well as the belief that student involvement in class discussion should always go up and desire for teacher control to always go down.

In recent years, I have used pre- and postsurveys in my own writing classes as a tool to examine not only classwide patterns of change, but also to understand better what my teaching choices meant to individual students. It is this use of the survey form by individual teachers to examine their own classes that I most highly recommend to readers of this chapter. To that end, I have included the profile form (Fig. 6.3) that I use to report my students' pre- and postsurvey scores back to them as well as the instructions for preparing for and writing the final reflection (Fig. 6.4) to help the students understand how usual or unusual the changes in their scores are.

The procedure I most often use is simply to have the student fill out the survey at the beginning of the course. I score it and record their initial scores along with the range of those scores on the pre- side of the profile sheet. Sometimes I give these results to the students and ask them to write a journal entry about their results, addressing such issues as: Are they surprised by any of their scores? Do they agree or disagree with their scores? What experiences do they see as impor-

FIGURE 6.3. Profile Sheet

Profile Sheet for _____

GENERAL ATTITUDES ABOUT WRITING

WRITING APPREHENSION—*High* scores indicate general discomfort with writing or talking about writing. Usually, people with high writing apprehension scores tend to avoid writing whenever possible. *Lower* scores indicate more comfort with writing.

"Before" score: _____ (6 to 24)   "After" score: _____ (6 to 24)

_____   _____

BELIEF THAT WRITING ABILITY IS LEARNABLE—*Low* scores reflect the belief that people are either born with the ability to write or they aren't. *High* scores indicate the belief that writing can be learned and that it can be taught.

"Before" score: _____ (4 to 16)   "After" score: _____ (4 to 16)

_____   _____

USEFULNESS OF COLLABORATION FOR ONE'S OWN WRITING—A *high* score indicates that a person finds talking with others about his or her writing helpful. A *low* score indicates that a person would prefer to work alone on his or her writing.

"Before" score: _____ (5 to 20)   "After" score: _____ (5 to 20)

_____   _____

ATTITUDES ABOUT CLASSROOM TALK

STUDENT INVOLVEMENT—A *high* score indicates that a person enjoys participating actively in class discussion. A *low* score indicates that a person would rather not talk much in class.

"Before" score: _____ (4 to 16)   "After" score: _____ (4 to 16)

_____   _____

TEACHER CONTROL OF CLASS TALK AND CONTENT—*High* scores generally indicate a preference for teachers who strictly control class discussion, ensuring that content is covered sufficiently. *Lower* scores suggest that a person is comfortable with teachers who allow students to explore topics in class discussion even at the risk that students might not know what the teacher thinks the "right answers" are.

"Before" score: _____ (5 to 20)   "After" score: _____ (5 to 20)

_____   _____

USEFULNESS OF GROUP WORK—A *high* score indicates that a person finds group work (including collaborative projects) a good way to learn. A *low* score indicates that a person tends to find working with other students a waste of time.

"Before" score: _____ (3 to 12)   "After" score: _____ (3 to 12)

_____   _____

FIGURE 6.4 Instructions for Final

Scoring Your "After" Survey

1. Score all the positively oriented questions: SA=4, A=3, D=2, SD=1 (A&D=2.5; none circled=1).

   Writing Attitude Survey   Classroom Style Preferences Survey
   Questions: #1, 2, 4, 6, 7, 9, 10, 12, 14, 15   Questions: #1, 2, 3, 5, 6, 8, 9, 10, 11, 12

2. Score all the negatively oriented questions: SA=1, A=2, D=3, SD=4 (A&D=2.5; none circled=1).

   Writing Attitude Survey   Classroom Style Preferences Survey
   Questions: #3, 5, 8, 11, 13   Questions: #4 & 7

3. Calculate your score for each of the attitude factors in the surveys. Simply add your scores for each of the question sets listed below and record your scores on your profile sheet.

Writing Attitude Survey   *Classroom Style Preferences Survey*

Writing Apprehension   Student Involvement
   Questions: #1, 3, 5, 6, 8, 10   Questions: #3, 6, 9, 12

Belief That Writing Is Learnable   Teacher Control
   Questions: #12, 13, 14, 15   Questions: #2, 5, 8, 10, 11

Usefulness of Collaboration   Usefulness of Group Work
   Questions: #2, 4, 7, 9, 11   Questions: #1, 4, 7

Preparing to Write the Final

1. Complete your new profile sheet by transferring your "before" score for each factor and the range to the spaces provided and by writing your "after" score in the space provided. Then find the range for your change score (after minus before) for each factor using the list below. Record those ranges below each after score. The change ranges are based on previous research with 111 students enrolled in regular and honors composition courses.

Writing Apprehension (-0.462)   Student Involvement (+0.771)
   extremely large +   6.5 or higher   extremely large +   6.5 or higher
   very large+   4.5 to 6   very large+   4.5 to 6
   large +   3 to 4   large +   3 to 4
   average   1.5 to -2.5   average   -1 to 2.5
   large -   -3 to -5   large -   -1.5 to -3
   very large -   -5.5 to -7   very large -   -3.5 to -4.5
   extremely large -   -7.5 or lower   extremely large -   -5 or lower

Writing as Learnable (+0.014)   Teacher Control (+0.009)
   extremely large +   5 or higher   extremely large +   6 or higher
   very large+   3.5 to 4.5   very large+   4 to 5.5
   large +   2 to 3   large +   2.5 to 3.5
   average   -1.5 to 1.5   average   -2 to 2

FIGURE 6.4 Instructions for Final. (continued)

large -	-2 to -2.5	large -	-2.5 to -3.5
very large -	-3 to -4	very large -	-4 to -5.5
extremely large -	-4.5 or lower	extremely large -	-6 or lower

Usefulness of Collaboration (+0.419)		Usefulness of Group Work (-0.059)	
extremely large +	8.5 or higher	extremely large +	4.5 or higher
very large+	6 to 8	very large+	3.5 to 4
large +	3.5 to 5.5	large +	2 to 3
average	-2 to 3	average	-1.5 to 1.5
large -	-2.5 to -4.5	large -	-2 to -3
very large -	-5 to -7	very large -	-3.5 to -4.5
extremely large -	-7.5 or lower	extremely large -	-5 or lower

2. Examine the change in each score and the relative size of the change (remember that most of your change scores are likely to be average by definition). Mark whether you agree or disagree with the direction and size of the change for each factor.

3. Re-read the journal that you wrote at the beginning of the semester.

4. Make notes on the profile sheet about what things you think caused your attitude changes (or lack of them) during this semester. Be as specific as possible.

5. Rest. DON'T WRITE OUT YOUR ANSWER BEFORE CLASS!

Writing the Final

Write me a lengthy journal entry about how your attitudes changed or did not change throughout the course. I'd like you to comment (at least briefly) on each of the six factors, but you may want to focus on those that you find most interesting. Be as specific as possible about why you think your attitudes did or did not change.

Remember that surveys are not perfect. Feel free to disagree with your survey results. Also remember that there are no right answers. The surveys are descriptive tools; they do not say what should happen to your attitudes. Finally, having "average" scores does not mean that you are an average person; it just means that your scores tend to be like other people's scores.

When you finish writing, turn in all of the before and after surveys, journals, profile sheets, and any other notes you made with your new journal entry on top.

Evaluating the Final

The final will count as a triple journal (the equivalent of journals 11, 12, & 13). I will look over your preparation to see that you put some thought into preparing, and I will read your journal to see that you addressed the issues I asked you to address (see the first paragraph in the writing the final section). Be honest; I want to know what you really think.

tant to forming these attitudes? During the last week of class, I have them take the survey again and have them score it with me in class. We then fill in the second side of the profile sheet, recording their change scores and examining the ranges to give them some sense of how usual or unusual such a change score is. I ask the students to prepare some notes about their scores (do they agree/disagree, are they surprised, what things happened during the semester to change or reinforce their scores) to prepare for the final. During the final exam period, they write a long journal entry about the change or lack of change in their scores, which I read but grade only for completeness.

I have learned several things about making this process work. First, the procedure can be formative: It can affect what students believe about themselves as writers and students. I always emphasize that students can disagree with their scores because I found that some students look on scores as if they simply must be true. Second, I have learned that students often need help in interpreting their scores. Because of the law of averages, most students have average original or change scores. Because, in early versions of this assignment, so many students wrote that the most important thing they learned from the survey was that they "were average," I now emphasize that average scores simply mean scores that are similar to others' scores, and that they should look on the survey as a tool for reflection, not an absolute indication of their personal value. Third, I have learned that I am often wrong about my students' attitudes—that the quiet kid in the back who I was never able to drawn out in class discussions saw himself as actively participating in class discussion even though he never said a word. I find that this kind of information is often more detailed than what I get in the course evaluation and more useful because it is not anonymous, and because I can think about what the course and its activities meant for a particular student.

ACKNOWLEDGMENTS

Research reported in this chapter was supported in part by a grant from the Center for the Study of Writing and Literacy at Berkeley and Carnegie Mellon.

REFERENCES

Charney, D., Newman, J. H., & Palmquist, M. (1995). I'm just no good at writing: Epistemological style and attitudes toward writing. *Written Communication, 12*(3), 298–329.

Daly, J. A. (1985). Writing apprehension. In M. Rose (Ed.), *When a writer can't write: Studies in writer's block and other composing-process problems* (pp. 43–82). New York: Guilford.

Daly, J. A., & Miller, M. D. (1975a). The empirical development of an instrument to measure writing apprehension. *Research in the Teaching of English, 9,* 242–249.

Daly, J. A., & Miller, M. D. (1975b). Further studies in writing apprehension: SAT scores, success expectations, willingness to take advanced course and sex differences. *Research in the Teaching of English, 9,* 250–256.

Flower, L., Wallace, D. L., Norris, L., & Burnett, R. E. (1994). *Making thinking visible: Collaborative planning and classroom inquiry.* Urbana, IL: National Council of Teachers of English.

Harding, S. (1987). Introduction: Is there a feminist method? In S. Harding (Ed.), *Feminism and methodology: Social science issues* (pp. 1–14). Bloomington: Indiana University Press.

Palmquist, M., & Young, R. (1992). The notion of giftedness and student expectations about writing. *Written Communication, 9*(1), 137–168.

Rose, M. (Ed.). (1985). *When a writer can't write: Studies in writer's block and other composing-process problems.* New York: Guilford.

Wallace, D. L., & Ewald, H. R. (2000). *Mutuality in the rhetoric and composition classroom.* Carbondale: Southern Illinois University Press.

7

FIRST-YEAR COLLEGE STUDENTS WRITING ACROSS THE DISCIPLINES

Stuart Greene

Amy J. Orr

Part of a 4-year longitudinal study, this investigation examines the kinds of writing 30 students completed during their first year of college in their composition classes and in all of their classes across disciplines. Based on analyses of students' texts, the assignments students received, their instructors' written comments, and interviews with both students and their instructors, we addressed the following questions: (a) What types of writing did students complete? (b) What types of claim structures are present in student papers? and (c) Were there differences between the types of writing students produced in their composition classes and the writing completed in other courses? To help us contextualize the results, we also explore various factors that may influence how and what students write.

As studies show, the literate practices of reading and writing "are at the heart of study and learning in higher education; these are the central ways in which students learn new subjects and develop their knowledge about new areas of study" (Lea, 1999, p. 111). Yet the tendency has been to place the burden of writing and teaching writing on first-year composition programs (Dias, Freedman, Medway, &

Pare, 1999). This is in large part due to the perception that writing is a general set of skills that can be learned once. Such an assumption is what Rose (1989) called the "myth of transcience," recognizing that knowledge about writing cannot be reduced to a single course on composition (see also Carroll, 2002; Petraglia, 1995). With the emergence of the writing-across-the-curriculum movement in the United States and England (for reviews, see Ackerman, 1993; Ochsner & Fowler, 2004), however, writing has begun to play an increasingly important role across disciplines as a means of fostering student learning about both a given subject matter and the acceptable conventions of academic discourse (McLeod, Miraglia, Soven, & Thaiss, 2001).

A number of studies have offered contextualized views of writing and writing tasks in different disciplines (e.g., Chiseri-Strater, 1991; Clark & Doheny-Farina, 1990; Freedman, 1994; Greene, 2001; Herrington, 1988; Herrington & Curtis, 2000; Nelson, 1990, 1995; Sternglass, 1997). In each case, the writing students produce reflects the complexity of thought that underscores the "collision of discourses" (Durst, 1999) that students confront in writing across fields. Students learn to adopt specific dispositions of mind, interpreting and critiquing what they read in developing their own writing. These studies have provided valuable detail for explaining what is involved in becoming acculturated to the practices of reading, writing, and thinking within the culture of a discipline.

However, research in writing has tended to focus on a limited number of case studies. As a consequence, those involved in the study and teaching of writing have lost sight of the bigger picture of how we are preparing writers, the kinds of writing produced, and the functions of writing in composition courses and across disciplines (cf. Dias, Freedman, Medway, & Pare, 1999). Both Sternglass's (1997) and Carroll's (2002) longitudinal studies of students' development as writers are notable exceptions that underscore the importance of understanding individual growth and development over time.

Carroll's investigation of 20 undergraduates through 4 years of study suggests that students are generally asked to complete the complex "literacy tasks" of "synthesizing, analyzing, and responding critically to new information" (p. 9). It would appear that students across disciplines are given opportunities to practice a variety of both general and specific types of writing, albeit with the purpose of conveying the extant knowledge of a field (Geisler, 1994; see also Anson, 1988). Indeed, current theory supports the view that a curriculum in writing should provide students with a wide range of experiences in writing, sequenced in such a way as to move "from narrative and summary writing to analysis, argument, and theory, from self-examination to investigation of a wider frame of reference" (Durst, 1999, p. 15; see also Britton, Burgess, Martin, McLeod, & Rosen, 1975; Moffett, 1968). The assumption here is that students learn to write by focusing on what they know best (their experience) and then complete relatively simple tasks as summary before engaging in such tasks as synthesis that require complex, higher order thinking. In each case, the task, purpose, and materials involved distinguish one type of task from another. The developmental view posited here seems to inform such recent reports on higher education as the Boyer Commission report (1998; see also Crosson, 1999), which have specified the kinds of tasks that students should complete as undergraduates: that students should practice the skills of inquiry, analysis, evaluation, synthesis, and critical thinking in what they both read and write.

However, as Anson (1988) observed, disciplines can vary significantly in how they define certain kinds of tasks. For example, informational writing can include knowledge that a writer already has (e.g., a review of the literature) or it can convey original findings. Moreover, he points out, the way instructors present a task is informed by their own belief systems about how specific types of writing function. Thus, the following questions remain: How might we characterize what students actually write? If disciplines differ in the way they define a particular type of writing, what constitutes an analysis, explanation, or argument? What distinguishes these types of writing in the context of a first-year composition class from the ways they are construed across disciplines? How does writing function in composition classes and across disciplines?

Addressing questions about what students write in first-year composition and across disciplines with a sample of 30 students can enable us to identify some of the critical features and purposes of writing at the college level, how this writing might vary, and what instructors understand as the functions writing might serve in their courses. In turn, we can begin to make visible what often remains hidden: the problems students face in meeting the demands of writing requirements across disciplines where the nature, functions, and purposes for writing vary. We can also address the level at which we should be thinking of writing and writing practices in higher education—not simply as skills and effectiveness, but "high level reading, research, and critical analysis" that will enable students to become reflective, intelligent writers (Carroll, 2002, p. xiv; see also Jones, Turner, & Street, 1999, p. xvi).

As researchers and teachers, we also wish to enter a conversation about the pedagogical challenges many of us face: not only how we are preparing writers, but how we can make the sort of changes that exploit more fully the potential ways writing can be used as a tool to support a wide range of possibilities that fulfill the conventions of academic inquiry and thinking. Assignments are a critical pedagogical tool in fostering learning. If we are to make writing a more positive experience for students, we need to understand more fully what they are writing and where they might be struggling.

THEORETICAL BACKGROUND

To understand the kinds of writing that students produce in school, we bring together theories derived from rhetoric, cognition, literacy, and activity theory in framing writing as the result of both cognitive and social processes. For example, our focus on text structure in student writing finds its source in cognitively driven theories of reading and writing. These theories have helped identify those processes of organizing, selecting, and connecting information characterizing the ways both readers and writers shape meaning (for reviews, see Greene & Ackerman, 1995; Paxton, 1999; Spivey, 1996; see also Flower, 1994). When students read and write, they invoke knowledge about discourse, their beliefs about writing in school, and their knowledge about a given topic or problem. Moreover, studies have suggested that as writers perform such different tasks as writing a report, a comparison, an analytical essay, or solving a problem, they build different representations of meaning because these tasks appear to invite people to approach information differently. Therefore, one could predict that different transformations of meaning would result because these tasks appear to require different methods of reorganization and a different basis for selecting information from sources (Spivey, 1996).

As studies show, texts reveal the issues students choose to focus on, their ways of categorizing experience, and the principles of selection students use. Coe (1994) argues that "texts are artifacts and as such we can try to infer the functions [of writing], to resurrect strategies implicit in structures and to relate them to the context" (pp. 160–161). For example, Young and Leinhardt (1998) found that students' texts embody many specific decisions and actions that individual writers make, reflecting principles of explanation, evaluation, and argumentation. These are the strategies that the centuries-long tradition of rhetoric has foregrounded, particularly in helping speakers and writers determine what is at issue in order to open up inquiry, test possible lines of argument and counterargument, and establish both the timeliness and relevance of their argument. Of particular importance is how writers identify the issues about which they write as questions of fact, definition, or causality (Fahnestock & Secor, 1996) and the claims they make in taking a position. As forms of social action, texts are viewed as genres—purposeful, situated, and repeated social responses to rhetorical situations (Miller, 1984; see also Berkenkotter & Huckin, 1994).

To adopt a rhetorical view of composing, we have sought to account for what students write, the function of students' writing, and students' understanding of who they believe will respond to their text. To function well in a genre, theorists have pointed out that writers need situated or genre knowledge, grounded in both the activities (e.g., tools, methods, interpretive frameworks) and situations (e.g., purpose, audience, occasion) in which a text is produced (Johns, 2002; Lave & Wenger, 1991). This knowledge (i.e., cognition) is distributed in culturally organized practices.

Moreover, Dias and his colleagues (1999) underscore the intertextual nature of written genres when they explain that texts embody the experiences of writers within a community of practice. These experiences manifest themselves on each occasion of writing and are "inherent in the reiteration of the genre: textual regularities of form and category, habit of information collection and archival practices, patterns of writing and reading" (p. 31; see also Bakhtin, 1986). But literate practice is never neutral; instead, the genres and models of literacy we learn determine the norms, expectations, and roles that define what is legitimate and what is not (cf. Jones, Turner, & Street, 1999; Street, 1984).

With Anderson, Reder, and Simon (1996), we argue that it is an exaggeration to claim that all knowledge is specific to the situation in which the task is performed and that more general knowledge cannot be applied to other situations. How tightly learning will be bound to context "depends on the kind of knowledge being acquired" (p. 6). Moreover, despite their focus on describing what is involved in producing different types of writing, researchers studying the connections between reading and writing have not helped educators understand what students are writing across disciplines. Thus, we have sought to understand the types of writing students complete during their first year, the claim structures involved, and the extent to which writing may vary across disciplines. We also attempt to contextualize the process by understanding the factors that influence how and what students write. In doing so, we address the broad question of whether students are completing the types of writing expected of them.

METHOD

Participants

To answer the questions motivating this study, we collected all writing from 2 cohorts of students at a private research institution in the midwest. In all, 30 students agreed to participate. The 30 participants are a representative sample of first-year students who on average score in the 80th percentile on such standardized tests as the ACT and SAT. Eighty-percent of all first-year students rank within the top 10% of their high school graduation class. These 30 students were originally part of a larger group of 50 students chosen at random by computer through the office of First Year of Studies. The initial sample of 50 students was stratified by gender and the college in which they were enrolled. The final sample of students consists of 16 women and 14 men enrolled in the five colleges at the university: Architecture, Engineering, Science, Arts and Letters, and Business. Participants were enrolled in over 20 departments and over 30 different courses.

Of the 30 students, 2 were chosen as case examples for the purposes of this chapter. One student, Christian, is enrolled in the College of Science and is taking courses in preparation for medical school. He is also minoring in a program in the College of Arts and Letters, "Science, Technology, and Values." The second student, Megan, came to the university expecting to major in psychology, but has decided to major in both English and Art History. (The students' names are pseudonyms.) These students' writing illustrates the range of writing that students completed during their first year of college, representing a cross-section of the types of papers students wrote. In fact, results of our analysis indicate that the types of writing Christian and Megan produced during their first year reflect the overall mean for all 30 students. However, we recognize that these two students cannot be truly representative of all students in this research because of the complex socioeconomic factors that influence how we are to understand gender, race, and class. In turn, this fact limits our ability to make claims that necessarily apply to other students at other institutions.

Data-Collection Procedure

The 30 students were told that the study focused on writing in the different classes they would be taking during the 4 years of their college experience; therefore, they were being asked to turn in copies of all of the writing they did each semester, together with the written assignments for each piece of writing and their instructors' written comments. The students were also requested to keep a log recording the title of the assignment, the class for which it was assigned, and the length in pages of the assignment. Overall, 689 papers were collected during the first year of college from the two cohorts.

Data Analysis Procedure

To classify the kinds of writing students produced, we first read each paper from one student's corpus of writing (46 papers) at the end of the first year, developed our categories with definitions and illustrations, and then refined these categories in reading additional student writing. Reading of students' writing was motivated by the question, What is this paper an instance of? We also consulted writing assignments when they were available to guide us in our reading of students' essays and faculty's written comments when they were available. However, assignments often contained such generic terms as *Write an essay of 3 to 5 pages*, and not all faculty provided written comments other than a check mark or grade. Interviews with students also provided some information about the kind of writing they had produced. For the purposes of achieving reliability, we taught two raters to identify the type of text and claim structure of a given student's essays.

Three separate analyses of students' essays were conducted to answer the first three questions motivating this study—the types of writing students produced, the claim structures present in students' writing, and the differences between the type of writing students produced in their writing classes and in their other courses.

Text Types. Our first approach to understanding the type of writing students completed was to read students' papers with two questions in mind: What is the student writing about? Is the writer making any sort of claim? Each student essay was read and analyzed to pinpoint the underlying logic or frame informing a given essay. As in Haswell (1986), the method consisted of identifying "the one logically coherent arrangement of ideas that embraces the largest number of words in the main body of the essay" (p. 403; see also Greene, 1994; Meyer, 1975, 1985). To identify the "one logically coherent arrangement of ideas," we examined the topical structure (e.g., Witte, 1983) of students' essays, focusing on the topics of each sentence. This entailed answering two questions: What is the topic of this sentence (i.e., its content)? What function does this topic sentence play? We chose the terms *narrate, explain, argue,* and *interpret* in classifying the text structure of students' essays. These are terms that grew out of our analysis of students' essays and focus on features of students' texts. These terms are also discussed and analyzed by writing researchers (e.g., Macken-Horarik, 2002). Here students' purposes are realized through what Bhatia (2002) identified as a "rhetorical value" expressed by typical "lexical-grammatical features," as opposed to a more specific genre that is "grounded in a specific rhetorical situation" (pp. 280–281).

Following Paltridge (2002), we classified student writing as text types according to their function or purpose, readership, nature of task, claim structure, and mode of categorizing experience. In doing so, we embrace the view that writing in academic settings is constituted by a set of practices and texts that are mutually informing. By this we mean that (a) there is a dynamic interplay between texts and their social contexts (e.g., Freedman & Adam, 2000), where genres are typified responses to situations that writers socially construct (Miller, 1984); (b) texts are influenced by a history of communicating that precedes the present moment (Bakhtin, 1986); and (c) texts have the potential to reshape the social and material environments in which they are produced (e.g., Bazerman & Paradis, 1991).

We include in the following the definitions of four text types we identified in our reading of student essays; illustrations are taken from the writing collected from 30 students. As in all examples, we have not changed or corrected students' writing. We have italicized the topics of sentences that guided our decisions; further, we have annotated illustrations to make clear how we arrived at our decisions.

The first category is *narrative.* In composing a narrative, a writer rarely makes a claim. The focus of the essay is on the writer, who refers to personal experience and develops the essay using a chronological structure. We can see that the topical structure (in italics) focuses on the writer when she reflects on her memories, impressions, and recollections, not information itself, which is the case with an explanation.

> As I reflect upon my K–12 years, the things *I remember* clearly are not the endless hours of taking notes and taking tests, but of particular impressions I was left with concerning the teachers and administrative staff to which I was exposed. More specifically, *I vividly recall* such things as effective and ineffective teaching styles and professional and nonprofessional teacher behavior. *I remember* those educators who perfected the art of teaching, but at the same time *I*

can't seem to forget the ones who fell short of fulfilling the educational standards of teachings. *These memories* are the reason I am guaranteed to enter the teaching profession with a thorough list of good and bad teaching methods.

The second category is *explanation*. Unlike narrative, which foregrounds a writer's state of mind or emotion, an explanation focuses on information that writers glean from what they read or another writer's position. Explanations are typically framed by an interpretive claim ("There have been several opinions about it" [the question of the nature of reality]), as opposed to an evaluative claim ("The author is mistaken"). Explanations include summaries of what another author has read and may include comparisons between two or more authors.

The following instance illustrates one student's explanation, actually a summary of another writer's views. The topical structure of the first two paragraphs of her essay—"Berkeley feels," "Berkeley's views," "He claims," "He defines"—focuses on the writer whose ideas the student summarizes. If and when the student writer includes an evaluation, it is not the student's own, but the criticism posed by another writer.

The student summarizes accepted positions and then addresses the theory about which she has been asked to write.

The question of the nature of the reality of objects in the world is one that has been asked by philosophers for hundreds of years. *There have been several opinions about it. Some philosophers,* like Locke, feel that the perception of the qualities of objects in one's mind is not actually correct. *The properties* that are perceived are considered secondary qualities, which are not inherently in objects. Rather, *objects* only have primary qualities that are inherently in them. *All other qualities,* which are the secondary qualities, are subject to individual minds. *Other philosophers* contradict these ideas, though. *The early eighteenth century philosopher,* Berkeley, for instance, has an opposing viewpoint that is in direct response to Locke's theory. *Berkeley feels* that all matter is real, and that the qualities perceived in matter actually are the correct qualities, meaning that they are inherently in matter. *He explains* this opinion by stating that there is no such thing as mind independent matter.

The writer summarizes Berkeley's theory and what the philosopher claims, defines, and thinks.

Berkeley's views on the nature of the reality of matter are relatively straightforward and simple. Because *he claims* that everything is in the mind, his views are sometimes called subjective idealism. *He claims* that they are the only possible explanation for the nature of the world that do not have any amount of skepticism in them. In his Dialogues between Hylas and Philonous, which he uses to explain his position, *Berkeley defines* a skeptic as "one who doubted of everything or who denies the reality and truth of things" (Berkeley, p. 191).

The third type of text is an *argument*, in which the focus is on the writer's own position and is developed with evidence from experience, observation, other texts, or experimentation. Writing an argument can entail explaining a problem or issue at some length before the writer actually makes a claim. This often includes an explanation of what the student has read. However, in the case of an argument, an explanation is used to develop a claim of fact (e.g., something is or is not the case), cause, consequence, or definition. (This is in contrast to an explanation, in which writers stop short of making an evaluation of their own.) Moreover, an argument is supported by evidence (i.e., good reasons) to illustrate that a case could be made to support the writer's assertion. The addition of reasons distinguishes an explanation from an argument. The writer's claim can appear at the beginning or end of the essay.

The student provides historical background.	Throughout the development of the Mexican Revolution, many rebel leaders emerged and then disappeared into the chaos of political upheaval. Emiliano Zapata and Francisco Madero, however, emerged as two figures that would remain in the public eye. By the end of 1911, Madero had managed a successful revolt against Porfino Dfaz and had become president. During Madero's presidency, from November 1911 until February 1913, Madero had to reckon with the leader of the revolutionaries in southern Mexico, Emiliano Zapata. Despite several attempts during his reign, Madero was unable to
The writer makes an evaluative claim.	reach a compromise with Zapata. *Considering various factors, it is inconceivable that Madero and Zapata could have ever reached a solution to their differences. The disparities between these two men's views* of the revolution and the way in which they promoted their causes leads one to believe that Madero and Zapata could not have agreed. In addition, in examining the stages of each of their revolutions, *it is unlikely that they would have been able to unite.*
Historical background helps set the stage for further statement of the argument.	Madero first entered the political scene as the leader of the Anti-Reelectionist Party in Mexico City. His goals, as leader of the Anti-Reelectionist Party, were strictly political—to obtain "a real vote and no boss rule" (pp.

54–55). Since the beginning of his revolutionary campaigns, Madero was uninterested in bringing his ideas and forces into Morelos. Madero focused on cities as the center of military attacks and did not want to broaden his revolution for fear of wasting money and resources. (pp. 67–69).

....

Further statement of the student's claim.

Even if Zapata had been more involved in the politicking that was going on, or was willing to join forces with the political revolutionaries, it is still unlikely that a compromise would have been successful. Between 1911 and 1913, Zapata and Madero were at different stages of their respective revolutions. Madero achieved power in Mexico very quickly, with the help of many of the nation's revolutionary factions, but he had not created a solid base for his regime. Dfaz's supporters remained in their positions even though their leader had left (class notes, 2/1, pp. 90-91). *Madero's regime was divided and it had not proven itself*

The writer makes a final evaluation.

politically yet. It was too early for Zapata to join a party that had not fulfilled any of its promises to him.

Finally, an *interpretation* is a close analysis of language in a literary text (fiction, drama, poetry) that explains the possible meaning of such literary devices as metaphors, images, and point of view. It is a close reading of what Fahnestock and Secor (1996) identified as "understanding the available means of persuasion" (p. 77) in a literary text. Thus, the question motivating a student is one that touches on matters of process—in this case, how authors create a particular effect through language, as well as matters of definition and value.

The student begins with an interpretive claim about the "concept of duality."

The concept of duality is used frequently throughout the novel Wuthering Heights. This concept is especially illustrated through Bronte's use of language. It is through her diction that she is able to manipulate the reader's point of view in regards to the events occurring throughout the novel. The effects of her use of language in regards to point of view is best illustrated early in the novel in relation to descriptions of setting, direct quotes from the characters, and the name choices for all involved.

The student then provides an illus-

Bronte's exploitation of diction is first introduced through the way in which she describes the two contrasting tration of the way the author uses language to distinguish two different worlds in the novel.

worlds present in her novel. For instance, the book begins with Lockwood's impressions of the first of the two worlds, Wuthering Heights. Throughout his description, Bronte utilizes phrases such as "grotesque carvings of crumbling griffins and shameless little boys" to depict the atmosphere of this house. She also goes on to describe the dog of the house as a wolfish villain, the jugs as towering on a vast dresser, the chairs as high-backed, black, and primitive, and its external environment as being characterized by mud and heath. *Common to all of these depictions is her use of short usually single syllable words that are all of a cacophonous nature.* The majority of the words chosen also hold negative connotations. Due to Bronte's choice of language, the reader develops, from the very outset of the book, an opinion of Wuthering Heights as being a harsh, dark, and simple environment.

Claim Structure. In addition to classifying text type, we also categorized student writing by claim structure. Following Herrington (1988), we analyzed claim statements as *interpretive* or *evaluative* (see also Greene, 2001; cf. Toulmin, Rieke, & Janik, 1984). An interpretive statement offers a response to a what or how question. What happened? Is this the case or not? How would you describe . . . ? These are questions that respond to matters of fact and matters of process, respectively (Fahnestock & Secor, 1996). Here, for example, a participating student describes how an argument works: "To begin with, the neurological dependency argument [based on Descartes] is based mainly on the concepts embodied in modern neuroscience." An evaluative claim responds to matters of value in justifying one's conclusion, such as the following example taken from a different student: "Descartes continually defended his method in an attempt to prove his critics wrong. Although admittedly controversial, Descartes' response to the Cartesian Circle objection proves very strong and certainly puts to rest any qualms concerning the validity of his argument." An evaluative claim may also take the form of a statement about causes or consequences, deriving from questions of fact, definition, or consequence (Cicero, 1949; cf. Fahnestock & Secor, 1996) when the writer offers reasons for making the claim (Crosswhite, 1996).

Coding. Each paper was coded on the factors mentioned previously. The majority of the variables are categorical (nominal), and were therefore assigned random numbers for the statistical analyses. Overall, variables coded in this manner include claim structure, text type, course (first-year writing course vs. other), and course instructor.

Interrater Reliability. For reliability purposes, each paper was coded by at least two investigators. Coding information from the two individuals was compared and required to match before a final code was established. In over 85% of the cases, the two coders had identical coding information. In those cases where there was disagreement, a third investigator was asked to examine the paper. Final coding was established only when two investigators were in agreement.

As a further check on reliability, two individuals not connected to the study were trained to use this coding scheme. These outside readers practiced analyzing student papers on 15% of the total sample of student writing collected for this study. In those cases where there was disagreement with the coding done by the investigators, discussion focused on the nature of those disagreements in order to bring about agreement. These raters then analyzed student papers on a different set of student writing collected for the study, again analyzing 15% of the total sample. There was 81% agreement between the coding done by the two outside raters and the coding done by the investigators.

Statistical Procedures. The statistical procedures used varied by the nature of the question being explored. The unit of analysis was a student's paper. To explore text type, claim structure, and functions of writing in the classroom (based on interviews with faculty), frequency tables were examined. Frequencies were determined for all papers in general, as well as separately for papers written in the first-year writing course and those written in other disciplines. In addition, frequencies were run separately by the year in which the paper was written. To explore whether there are statistically significant differences between the types and claim structures of papers written in the first-year writing course versus other disciplines, chi-square statistics were calculated.

RESULTS

The analyses were aimed at answering three main questions: (a) What types of writing did students complete? (b) What types of claim structures are present in student papers? and (c) Were there differences between the types of writing students produced in their composition classes and the writing completed in other courses?

Text Types

Table 7.1 presents the frequencies for the types of papers students wrote in Year 1 of the study. The majority of papers consisted of explanation (73%). Only 12% of papers could be categorized as arguments. Students were unlikely to write narratives (9%) or interpretations (4%).

TABLE 7.1. Types of Papers Completed by the Students

Text Type	Frequency
Explanation	506 (73%)
Argument	82 (12%)
Narrative	59 (9%)
Interpretation	25 (4%)
Other	20 (2%)
Total	**692**

Types of Claim Structure

The frequencies reveal that 71% of papers written contained interpretive claim structures, whereas only 28% contained evaluative structures (see Table 7.2). This finding is consistent with the types of papers students wrote. Given that students wrote primarily explanatory papers, we would expect that their claims would be more interpretive than evaluative. Moreover, the emphasis on explanatory writing reflects the pragmatic purposes of disciplinary classes in students' first year—to learn a specific body of information and some of the interpretive strategies in a given field for analyzing and developing an argument. Students learning new information in a new field cannot be expected to know what is relevant or what is at issue, much less be prepared to take a stance. One percent of students' papers did not contain an identifiable claim structure. This was especially true in personal narratives and lab reports.

TABLE 7.2. Claim Structures of Papers Completed by the Students

Claim Structure	Frequency
Total number of interpretive papers	492 (71%)
Total number of evaluative papers	193 (28%)
Unidentifiable claim structure	4 (1%)
Total	**689**

First-Year Writing Courses Versus Courses Across Other Disciplines

A Pearson chi-square test indicated that there was a statistically significant differ-ence between the types of papers written in first-year composition courses and those written in other disciplines ($X^2 = 81.67$, $df = 5$, $p < .001$). Table 7.3 presents the frequencies for text type by course type. Although papers written in both types of courses are predominantly explanations, the extent differs greatly. Forty-three percent of papers written in composition courses are explanations, whereas 79% of papers written for other disciplines are of this type. Papers written in compo-sition courses were over four times more likely than those in other disciplines to be argument papers and three times more likely to be narratives. However, stu-dents are not writing interpretive essays in composition courses.

There is also a statistically significant difference between the two types of courses with regard to claim structure ($X^2 = 23.32$, $df = 2$, $p < .001$). As Table 7.4 shows, whereas the largest number of papers for both types of courses contain an

TABLE 7.3. Types of Papers Written for First Year Composition vs. Other Courses

Text Type	First-Year Composition	Other Disciplines
Explanation	40 (43%)	466 (78%)
Argument	32 (35%)	50 (8%)
Narrative	19 (21%)	40 (7%)
Interpretation	0	25 (4%)
Other	1 (1%)	15 (3%)
Total	**92**	**596**

TABLE 7.4. Claim Structures of Papers Written for First-Year Composition versus Other Courses

Text Type	First-Year Composition	Other Disciplines
Interpretive	47 (51%)	445 (75%)
Evaluative	45 (49%)	148 (25%)
Unidentifiable claim structure	0	4 (1%)
Total	**92**	**597**

interpretive claim structure, the extent varies significantly by course type. Interpretive claims are 1.5 times as likely to be found in papers written in courses other than first-year writing, whereas evaluative claims are twice as likely to be found in papers written by students in first-year writing courses.

Factors Influencing How and What Students Write

Overall, writing courses ask for argument papers and evaluative claims. Classes in other disciplines are more likely to ask for explanations and interpretive claims. If we assume that argument and evaluation are more complex types of writing requiring greater sophistication, then we conclude that this higher level writing taught in first-year composition is not carried across the curriculum.

Interviews with faculty enabled us to explore factors that may influence how and what students write. One factor is the type of assignments they receive. If professors do not assign papers that require the use of argument and evaluative claim structures, students will be unlikely to write them. By asking professors to describe the function of writing in their classrooms, we can begin to understand the types of papers they may be assigning. To gain insight into the functions of writing within a given classroom, interviews were conducted with a sample of 35 instructors. These were instructors who assigned and, in most cases, responded to the writing of at least 1 or more of the 30 students' writing completed during their first year of college. Instructors were asked such general questions as, "What function did writing serve in your course?" (see Smith's Curriculum Vitae (CV), this volume for a complete list of questions). The second part of the interview focused on students' writing—in particular, the type of paper he or she had asked the student to write (cf. Prior, Hawisher, Gruber, & MacLaughlin, 1997).

A second factor that may influence what students write is the social context in which they write (students' prior assumptions about writing and commitments to specific issues). To explore this factor, brief interviews were conducted with each student at the end of each semester of the first year. We gathered such information as students' intended majors, their approach to writing a given paper, and their understanding of what type of paper they believed they were writing: What did students think the assignment asked them to do? Who was their audience for this paper? (see CV for the complete protocol for interviewing students in their first year). Follow-up interviews were conducted with the two students chosen as case examples to understand whether students were beginning to forge connections among the different papers they were writing across disciplines (see CV for the complete protocol for interviewing case study students).

Function of Writing. All of the professors interviewed, including those teaching writing, indicated that writing served multiple functions in their classrooms. When asked the particular functions served by writing, a variety of responses were given (see Table 7.5). The majority use writing to support thinking (71%),

TABLE 7.5. Percentage of Professors Indicating That Writing Served the Listed Functions

Function of Writing	Percentage of Professors
Support discussion	36%
Support reading	50%
Assess content knowledge	36%
Testing	21%
Support thinking	71%
Support learning	29%
Learning disciplinary conventions	36%
Learning general writing conventions	57%
Personal growth/development	14%

and over half (57%) use writing to teach general writing conventions. These two goals may not be as mutually exclusive as they might first appear. For example, one professor wanted his students to learn the format of an engineering report by asking them to write up their study of what he called a *launch project*. He also encouraged his students to understand how they arrived at the correct mathematical formula as evidence that the softball they launched would hit their intended target. In turn, he wanted them to speculate about those factors that might affect their calculations. Fifty percent of the professors use writing to support reading completed by the students. Writing is used by approximately one third of the professors to support classroom discussions (36%), assess content knowledge (36%), teach disciplinary conventions (36%), and support student learning (29%). Less than one quarter of the professors used writing for the purpose of testing (21%) or to foster personal growth or development (14%).

The Social Context in Which Students Write: Two Case Examples. In what follows, we provide specific examples of writing from our two case examples, Christian and Megan. Examples of their writing enable us to probe more deeply into the type of writing students completed in composition and across disciplines. Our aim is to unpack what it means to write explanatory and argumentative papers or to organize writing around interpretative and evaluative claims. What we find is that students' prior assumptions about writing and commitments to specific issues (e.g., ethical action, social justice, or poverty) are powerful influences that determine how and what they write (cf. Herrington & Curtis, 2000; Sternglass, 1997)—at times more so than the assignments they are given.

Christian. Interested in both science and religion, Christian is majoring in Biology and taking courses in an interdisciplinary minor, "Science, Technology, and Values." In his first year, 13 of the 17 papers (76%) he wrote were explanatory. He wrote three argumentative essays in his first year—two in first-year composition and one in a discipline-specific writing course in economics.

Writing in First-Year Composition. Because we compare the types of papers written in composition with papers written in all other classes, it is important to understand something about the composition course. The aims of the composition course that Christian and 17 other participants completed during their first year are consistent across the 80 sections offered each year. Specifically, the aims of first-year composition are "to introduce students to the skills of writing and reasoning that have become accepted conventions in university courses across the curriculum" (course syllabus). Essentially, this course is a course in rhetoric: Rhetoric provides a way to think about writing and speaking as part of a conversation, a conversation that aims to bring forth both understanding and, perhaps, agreement. Like any university-level course, the composition class is organized around a theme, a set of readings relevant to that theme, and a set of issues around which students can develop their essays. Thus, students practice writing papers that require them to read closely, to develop an interpretation of what they have read, and to tailor their writing for the needs of their peer readers and their teacher. These are readers who expect that writers will teach them something in what they discuss, analyze, and argue in their essays.

To emphasize writing as a process of both composing and rewriting, instructors in the writing program defer grading students' writing until the end of the semester when students submit a final portfolio. This portfolio includes all drafts that a given student has written, comments that both peers and the instructor have provided during the semester, and students' reflective memos, describing their understanding of the extent to which their drafts fulfilled their goals as writers. Writing a reflective memo enables students to take a broad view of their development over time, chart the course of their progress, take more responsibility for their learning, and demonstrate in their own terms what they know and can do.

In Christian's composition class, the theme focused on education and included essays written by bell hooks, who considers race and class in schools; E. D. Hirsch, who centers his argument on fostering common culture and history through what he calls *cultural literacy*, and Mary Louise Pratt, who emphasizes what she calls a *contact zone* in teaching students to honor and respect difference. However, students were not required to write specifically about these authors in their essays, and Christian pursued his interests in motivation ("A Fugitive Seeking Refuge in the Willows"), the potential value of school vouchers ("The Saving Grace of School Vouchers"), and school violence ("Touch Me and I'll Sue"). For the first essay, he was simply asked to write an argument on an educational topic using his personal experience; for the second essay, he was expected to incorporate the views of published writers in developing an argument; and for the third, his instructor asked students to write an argument based on original research.

Original research could entail using focus groups, a survey, interviews, or the archives in a library to address the writer's research question.

Although all three papers in first-year composition required Christian to write an argument, only the latter two were classified by both the raters and teacher as *arguments*. In writing his first essay for college, based on personal experience, he tells of the monotonous routine of going to school, describing the conditions that might be more motivating for students. More than taking a position and using evidence to support his argument, Christian tends toward explaining his experiences in school—something he recognized after writing the paper. In his introduction, which follows, he frames what he believes is the problem—that routine can "strip one's vigor for life"—and provides an interpretive claim: "The way in which individuals go about achieving ways to recuperate from the rigors of school life vary; however, those who find a successful way to recuperate inevitably excel in their respective educational experiences."

> The unbearable monotony associated with life's rigorous routines can drive any individual searching for a peaceful place of relaxation and rejuvenation. This drive to find a little space of peace and quiet in the world can cause an individual to fall upon unconventional methods to achieve his or her ideal goal of rest and relaxation. The high school educational system [where I live] provides one example in which daily routines can strip one's vigor for life, sending any individual that attends in search of his or her own utopia amongst life's craziness. The way in which individuals go about achieving ways to recuperate from the rigors of school life vary; however, those who find a successful way to recuperate inevitably excel in their respective educational experiences.

Christian then describes the required courses he and others take, questioning whether educators achieve their goal of encouraging a liberal education.

Despite setting up the possibility for developing an argument ("Getting the most from an educational experience depends on an individual's ability to set the fugitive free"), Christian does not follow through on this claim, instead describing the value of extracurricular activities, E. D. Hirsch's conceptions of academic success, and the value of block scheduling. That he does not follow through on developing this argument may not be surprising in a first paper in which Christian is coming to terms with what he has read and what he thinks. Moreover, the assignment is broad—"Write an argument based on an educational topic"—and requires that he use personal experience, something he was unaccustomed to doing in his writing.

In composing his second paper, Christian writes an argument about vouchers, making an evaluative claim that he feels quite confident about, in large part, because he has read widely in this area. That he was able to base his argument on what he has read is consistent with his experiences on his debate team in high school. That experience taught him to read as much as possible to ensure that he covers all angles and will not be surprised by a counterargument. With that experience in mind, he establishes in his introduction the claim that, "The necessary creation of a national school voucher program would enable individuals of lower economic standing to be given the same opportunities as those who can afford a private education." In turn, he offers as a first piece of evidence the inequities in school funding that Jonathon Kozol details in *Savage Inequalities*:

> A number of studies have shown the deficiencies within today's inner-city school systems. One only needs to look at Jonathan Kozol's book, *Savage Inequalities*, to see an accurate depiction of the shortfalls suppressing children's education in many of today's major American cities. Kozol points at extremely low graduation rates, low-test scores, overcrowded classrooms, and teacher inadequacies as few of the many indicators depicting the poor public education that is being given to some of the brightest minds in our country. (51–77)

Christian cites 11 different sources to support his contention that vouchers will be the saving grace of the minority and poor students attending urban schools, that "Instituting a national school voucher program would be a great asset in the fight against the poor public education that millions of children are forced to suffice with." He also anticipates the possible counterargument to his position as a way to further support his position. In the following, he observes that others may argue that publicly funded vouchers may be used by families to send their children to parochial schools:

> One of the biggest arguments against such a system revolves around the fact that government money is being directly siphoned to private schools. The major opponents to the school voucher program include the National Education Association and the American Civil Liberties Union. Both organizations stand opposed to the notion of school vouchers on the grounds that government money would be going directly to private schools, many of which have a religious affiliation, and therefore the government is benefiting and promoting certain religions groups (Gilberti). Such governmental action is prohibited by the "separation of church and state" clause of the United Sates Constitution.

Acknowledging this possibility, he turns to legal studies and points to further evidence to support his argument: "The litigation director of the Institute for Justice, Clint Bolick, gravely disagrees with the notion that school voucher programs are in violation of the constitution." He then asserts that, "Arguments against school vouchers should focus less on what is written in the constitution and more on the success of each student. In certain areas of the country, students who have the ability to attend a private institution inevitably have greater opportunity for success in education."

Christian leaves readers with questions that focus on his insistence on creating equity, appealing to readers' sense of justice: "Why is it that certain children have a greater educational advantage than others? Whatever happened to the clause in the constitution that states, 'All men are created equal?' Is not the current educational system limiting the equality of education available to different students whose parents are of different economic classes?"

In his third and final paper in first-year composition, Christian develops an argument focusing on the need to stem the proliferation of violence in schools, an argument based on extensive library research: He cites 21 different sources and a survey of 98 undergraduates at the university he attends. For him, the issue is clear:

> Teachers have lost control in many classroom settings. Acts of school violence are becoming more pronounced in current newspaper headlines. In the wake of this crisis, the teachers of the United States need to take a deep breath and ask, what feasible disciplinary methods can and must be implemented to ensure classroom tranquility and violence-free environments in which students can learn?

In supporting a return to harsher discipline, Christian explains at some length the prevalence of violence in schools in leading up to his claim. For example, findings from Christian's survey of 98 undergraduates reinforce his point that implementation of public policies "are a vital step toward giving more power back to the teachers and administrators" and eliminating the possibilities for "frivolous lawsuits." After several pages, he returns to his initial claim that, "It is clearly evident that action needs to be taken at the national level to amend the injustices in the current educational system, and restore power back into the hands of teachers and administrators." Citing a number of studies, he concludes that, "Corporal punishment works," although he also recognizes the importance of teachers establishing "rapport with students," developing "mutual respect," and "avoiding power struggles." However, he argues that the key is to "enforce effective classroom policy."

Writing Across Disciplines. The arguments that Christian wrote in first-year composition represent a departure from the kind of writing that he did in his other classes during his first year. Typically, he wrote papers in which he was asked to explain what he observed, either in the experiments he conducted in his chemistry lab or in an introductory course in anthropology, which fulfilled a general education requirement ("How do you think an anthropologist from Mars would describe life in college?" or "Select a religious or an athletic competition to observe as an example of a ritual"). These are the types of assignments that enable students to learn disciplinary methods of inquiry—in this case, to adopt the perspective of a participant observer in anthropology, to write up a report in biology ("The effect of light intensity on relative growth rates and interspecific competition between *Lemma minor* and *Salvina spp*"), or to conduct experiments in chemistry.

For example, Christian sets up his lab report in chemistry in the following way, demonstrating through precise explanation his understanding of how to conduct an experiment and follow the appropriate procedures:

> **Purpose:** Electrophilic molecules readily add to nucleophilic centers of molecules. The double bonds in alkenes act as nucleophilic centers, and electrophiles such as bromine and chlorine add to these carbon-carbon double bonds-often yielding cyclic intermediates. These intermediates often react with other electrophilic molecules present allowing the formation of a saturated product. In this experiment, N-bromosuccinamide will be reacted with butadiene sulfone to yield succinimide and an enantiomer which will be isolated. An isolation method will be chosen that will most efficiently separate the enantiomer (mp $_{190-191}$oC), based on its physical properties.
>
> **Experimental Procedure:** Add 150–200 mg of butadiene sulfone to a 10 mL Erlenmeyer flask. Add a weight of N-bromosuccinimide equivalent to the number of moles present in the initial butadiene sulfone. Then add 5 mL of water and heat with a sand bath, occasionally swirling for 10–15 minutes. During the heating period, be sure to verify the presence of a carbon-carbon double bond in the butadiene sulfone by use of the aqueous $KmnO_4$ test.
>
> Devise a procedure for isolating the product—see pre-lab questions and consult your T.A. Next, recrystallize the sample from a minimum amount of water and find the melting point. Weigh the product, calculate the percent yield, and submit the product in a properly labeled vial. Add I mL of a 2% Br_2/H_20 solution to two test tubes. Then add 4 drops of cyclohexene to the first test tube. Place a stopper in the tube and shake. Observe and record any changes. Repeat this process with the second test tube using 4 drops of hexane instead of cyclohexene.

The explanations Christian provides serve a number of different purposes. In this excerpt, Christian explains the compounds he used and *why* the loss of one compound was as prominent as it was. He also draws conclusions about the ways to isolate a compound in the type of experiment he conducted. With a more nuanced understanding of our classification system, we might say that embedded within the activity of explanation are the varied actions—referencing previous research, explaining complex chemical processes and experimental procedures, and relating the results of a study.

In his economics class, a discipline-specific writing course, Christian wrote five papers, which, according to Christian, required students to demonstrate their understanding of a specific concept in economics. They could do so by examining two Third World countries of students' own choice. However, students were not expected to take a position (e.g., "Write a 6 to 8-page paper on the burden of foreign debt in the two countries you have chosen to focus on for the semester" or "Write a paper on poverty in the two countries you are studying").

All students at the university are required to take a writing course in a discipline during their first year. These courses share a dual aim: to teach students the "ways of knowing in a given discipline," and to teach students some basic principles of writing. The only requirement is that students produce at least 25 pages of writing and be given the opportunity to rewrite at least one essay during the term. Christian chose to focus on Zimbabwe and Tanzania in three of the five papers he wrote, explaining in an interview with one of the researchers that he planned to work in a medical mission in Tanzania. He said he chose Zimbabwe because it was easy to get information. During the term, he wrote about poverty, the burden of foreign debt, and medicine in Tanzania and Zimbabwe. In two additional papers, he wrote about the North American Free Trade Agreement (NAFTA) and a comparison of the International Money Fund (IMF) and the World Bank.

Although Christian explained that he did not set out to write an argument in any of these essays, he found himself doing so while writing his paper on the IMF and the World Bank. What he wrote was based on 17 different published sources, again reflecting the kind of thoroughness that he said characterized his approach to preparing for a debate in high school. In his introduction, Christian organizes what he writes around an interpretive claim, suggesting that by, "Taking a closer look at the history of both the World Bank and the IMF, their questionable policies in low-developed countries, and possible solutions to current deficiencies within each organization, will provide greater insight into the impact that these organizations have on the rest of the world as well as the future effect each organization will have in reducing poverty and increasing development." The following introduction provides some context for understanding this statement.

> Both institutions have a long history of lending, and their respective goals have been modified over the years. Today, many skeptics and critics are raising serious questions about the lackluster impact that both organizations have had on reducing poverty and increasing development throughout the world. Taking a closer look at the history of both the World Bank and the IMF, their questionable policies in low-developed countries, and possible solutions to current deficiencies within each organization, will provide greater insight into the impact that these organizations have on the rest of the world as well as the future effect each organization will have in reducing poverty and increasing development.

While he frames his essay as an exploration of the World Bank and the IMF, Christian provides the groundwork for an argument in which he elaborates on the "questionable policies" and "current deficiencies" he mentions. Following this assertion, he explains when and where the World Bank was founded, the extent to which the World Bank expanded, and how the World Bank raises money. He then turns his attention to the IMF. Specifically, he explains that the IMF is "another lending organization" with far-reaching "financial capabilities."

After concluding that both the World Bank and IMF have "noticeable and well-documented faults," he lists some of these faults and describes the conditions of countries where policies devised by the World Bank and IMF were implemented. Indeed, much of the eight pages he wrote constitute explanations of the Banks' work and how their policies have fallen short. But Christian also makes two evaluative claims toward the end of the comparison he draws—that "Many detrimental policies and practices associated with the institutional loans have hurt borrowing countries more than they have helped" and "The need for reforming the World Bank is essential."

> Both the World Bank and the IMF were created with noble intentions of helping other countries attain and sustain economic stability. Over 55 years later, a review of the history of both organizations shows that neither was able to promote economic growth and development in borrowing countries as originally intended. Many detrimental policies and practices associated with the institutional loans have hurt borrowing countries more than they have helped. A look at what went wrong, as well as current problems associated with the World Bank and the IMF, will show the dire need for reform.

Ultimately, Christian argues that these two organizations did not fulfill their expressed purposes. In drawing this conclusion, he offers an evaluation ("their implementation and affects were far from satisfactory"); he then proposes a possible solution to a problem. His instructor's only comment, aside from "A," was that Christian might have acknowledged the borrowing countries' responsibilities to explain the failures Christian describes.

That Christian wrote an argument is in keeping with many students' tendencies in writing to stray from the assignments teachers give their students. In fact, a number of researchers (e.g., Greene, 1994) have argued that the assignment is not an accurate predictor of what students will actually write. Students often rely on what is familiar. Here Christian not only demonstrates his understanding of a key concept in economics, but uses many more sources than he was asked to include in order to develop an argument. Both his style of debate and argument, learned in high school and first-year composition, appear significant, influencing the strategies he uses to write.

Megan. Majoring in both English and Art History, Megan wrote 14 papers in her first year in philosophy, a disciplinary writing course in literature, and environmental science, 64% of which were classified as explanatory papers, 21% as arguments, and 14% as interpretations.

Megan wrote papers classified as explanations in philosophy and environmental science. In contrast, she had more opportunities in her writing class in literature to take a position. Again, all students are required to take a writing course in a discipline during their first year. The only requirement is that students produce at least 25 pages of writing and be given the opportunity to rewrite at least one essay during the term. Interestingly, Megan "tested out" of first-year composition despite having little experience writing essays in high school. Instead, as she pointed out in her interview, she had taken creative writing courses. She also wrote a term paper in high school. This meant learning how to keep note cards from the sources of information she collected in the library, cite her sources properly in what she wrote, and construct a bibliography. Such an approach to research is typical in high schools and many first-year composition programs. However, this is not true of the composition course Christian took. He was taught to use print and electronic resources to support an argument; he also learned such strategies for conducting original research as developing his own archive of information based on primary sources of information (e.g., newspaper articles).

Writing Across disciplines. In her literature-based writing class, entitled "Art Caressing Art," Megan was asked to evaluate two of the films her class watched ("My Life in Pink" and "Run Lola Run") and explore and discuss a number of concepts and themes in the poetry, plays, and stories she read. In all, she wrote five essays, three of which were identified as arguments; these were the only argumentative papers she wrote during her first year—a time when she was learning critical reading and writing strategies in literature and the unfamiliar content of both philosophy and environmental science. The remaining two essays, which she wrote in her literature class, were classified as *literary interpretations.*

Typical of the argumentative pieces Megan wrote was an essay in response to the assignment to "Discuss how Baudelaire's poetry explores the plight of the poet." This entailed comparing two of the poet's works and making a claim about how Baudelaire represents the role of the poet in the world. It also meant that students would have to use evidence from the poet's writing to support that argument. In keeping with her professor's expectations, she begins her essay by setting forth her purpose in the following introduction, stating in an evaluative claim that "the two poems' portrayals of the poet's struggles" are not just different, but "appear contradictory:"

> In both "The Albatross" and "Beauty," Charles Baudelaire chooses to explore the plight of the poet. Interestingly, despite their common author, the two poems' portrayals of the poet's struggles appear contradictory. While "The Albatross" seems to give a somewhat sympathetic glimpse into the exile of the poet—his incompatibility with others and his awkwardness in the ordinary world, "Beauty" takes what appears to be a less forgiving stance concerning the futile efforts of the deceived poet. In my paper, I will discuss how both

pieces depict the poet's struggles, and, as I've mentioned, demonstrate how the portrayals differ.

In turn, Megan provides a close reading or explanation of both poems to underscore the two perceptions of the poet she has identified in her introduction: as "shunned by society" among those different from him, on the one hand, and as "deluded, lured into a life of endless devotion," on the other hand.

> In "The Albatross," Baudelaire suggests that the poet's atypical thoughts and ways of life distance him, perhaps physically, but more importantly, socially, from those around him. Because he operates differently from the other people, he seems to exist in a world of his own. Baudelaire implies this social incompatibility at the beginning of the poem, when he describes an albatross being tormented by a heartless group of sailors. The poem "Beauty" seems to portray the poet in a rather different light. Written from the perspective of Beauty herself, the poet is now described as enthralled and hypnotized by her charms, yet unable to ever comprehend her.

To support these claims, Megan cites lines from the poems on 15 occasions.

Megan used interpretive claims for the remainder of her papers in literature, philosophy, and environmental science. Her philosophy class provides an example. In her introductory philosophy class, she was asked in a series of seven essays to demonstrate her understanding of a wide range of philosophical arguments. Specifically, she was asked to define justice in Plato's *Republic*, explain the function of the allegory of the cave in the *Republic*, explain the source of Descartes' doubts in *Meditations*, provide a counterargument to Descartes' proof concerning the existence of God, explain the argument concerning mind and body in *Sixth Meditation*, describe happiness in Augustine's *The Confessions*, and, finally, examine the relationship between good and evil in Nietzsche's *On the Genealogy of Morality*. Each of these essays, approximately 300 words, in contrast to the 500 to 700 word essays she wrote in her literature class, were identified as explanations. We take as an illustration the essay she wrote on the source of doubt in Descartes' *Meditations* as a typical example of the kind of writing she completed in philosophy. In this example, Meagan questions why Descartes takes doubt as his starting point for inquiry and then sets out to answer her question, "Why?" In her introduction, she claims that, "Although there are several factors that led him [Descartes] to question his outlook on life, I believe the most pivotal is his concern that God is an all-powerful joker who manipulates Descartes to sense what is not real." Megan writes:

> Doubt is frightening. To challenge the beliefs that one once considered to be inevitable truth, can leave him feeling confused and bewildered. This, however, is *exactly* what Descartes does in his First Meditations. He chooses to abol-

ish everything that he once believed, and start from scratch. My question is, "Why?" Although there are several factors that led him to question his outlook on life, I believe the most pivotal is his concern that God is an all-powerful joker who manipulates Descartes to sense what is not real.

Here she makes an interpretive claim that sets up her explanation of "several factors" that contribute to Descartes' starting point and his "pivotal concern." What follows is Megan's close reading of Descartes' *Meditations* in an effort to explain the source of Descartes' doubt, citing the text on three occasions and responding to the text with her own illustrations as a means of elaborating on Descartes' observations. However, as her instructor observed, she stops short of actually making an argument supported by evidence from the text that determines why her view is justified.

> Descartes' streak of doubt begins with his observation that, "the senses are sometimes deceptive; and it is a mark of prudence never to place our complete trust in those who have deceived us even once." (14) For example, one may look into the distance at a tree that appears very large, but upon approaching, they realize that it is much closer and smaller than they had believed. If one can be mistaken so easily, how do we know that other things we see, hear, or feel are accurate?

In concluding her explanation of Descartes' source of doubt, she underscores this latter point for two reasons based on her impressions and some speculation:

> First of all, it is the pondering of the nature of God that lights the path for Descartes' second meditation. He assumes that God is manipulating all of his senses, and, given the premises, he is searching for what may still be held as true. Secondly, of the three possible sources of doubt, the last is the most severe, for when one's 5 senses are deceived, one usually corrects them upon closer speculation. When one is in a terribly truthful dream, one eventually wakes up. But, where does the escape come from, with a mighty and twisted God? The ignorance could be eternal.

Ultimately, one could observe that Megan advances an argument through her judgment and this is true. Still the major portion of her essay is explanation.

In her first year, Megan wrote a number of explanatory papers organized around interpretive claims. She conveyed to her professors that she understood the way images and themes worked in the literature she studied, and that she could understand a complex philosophical argument, identifying both its strengths and weaknesses and offering counterexamples to support her own positions. It was also clear from her professor's comments in a course on the environment that she had grasped some important principles underlying ecosystem changes that occur with increased volcanic activity.

IMPLICATIONS

Before suggesting the implications of our analyses of student writing, we return to the questions motivating this study: (a) What types of writing did students complete? (b) What types of claim structures are present in student papers? and (c) Were there differences between the types of writing students produced in their composition classes and the writing completed in other courses?

What Students Write and the Claims They Make

Across disciplines, students wrote more explanation papers than arguments. Consistent with this type of writing, students' essays included more interpretive claims than evaluative claims. We also found that students had more opportunities to write argumentative papers in their composition classes than they did across disciplines, which was expected because the composition class is a course on argument. The overall findings are in keeping with others studies (e.g., Geisler, 1994; Greene, 2001): Students typically write about extant knowledge in a field, in large part, because of the pragmatic goals of disciplinary classes—to become familiar with the content and issues that are salient in a given field. They rarely have occasions to develop positions from which they might take a stance. This finding counters the often-stated goal that undergraduate education should challenge students to analyze, synthesize, and evaluate information through inquiry and investigation—that these skills, in contrast to the absorption of information, represent the hallmark of a liberal education (e.g., Boyer Commission, 1998).

Factors That Influence Student Writing

Writing Assignments. For various reasons, professors may not be assigning papers that require students to synthesize and evaluate information. As the analyses indicate, professors have different views about the functions of writing in their courses. Other factors, not explored here, may also come into play. For example, professors face several constraints on their time. In research institutions, they must commit a significant portion of their time to publishing. This does not leave much time for responding to students' papers.

Student-Level Factors. For Bakhtin (1986), language is always oriented toward what he calls the *addressee*, a social audience that comprises the values and motives within human activity. As he observes, "Both the composition and, particularly, the style of utterance [e.g., text] depend on those to whom the utterance is addressed, how the speaker (or writer) senses and imagines his addressees, and the force of their effect on the utterance" (p. 95). Within the evaluative climate of the classroom, the teacher's authority as an evaluator looms large. If instructors place check marks next to different pieces of information—as they often did in our study—then it is possible that students will see this kind of notation stressing the reproduction of information, even if the instructor also stresses the importance of argument. Students may also transform seemingly complex tasks into trivial exercises when they wait until the last minute or when their goals for completing an assignment are to simply "get it done."

The assignments teachers give students are based on tacit knowledge about how writing assignments accomplish an unstated set of goals in a particular discipline (Selfe, 1997). A number of studies (Chiseri-Strater, 1991; Nelson, 1995) have shed light on the ways students negotiate the literacy practices of academic settings and transform academic work in the complex social systems of the classroom, particularly the evaluative climate of the classroom. For example, students rely on the kind of feedback they receive from their instructors, balancing their own goals as writers with the expectations they feel readers bring in a reciprocal relationship between writer and reader. Megan's experiences as a first-year student underscore this point: "I want to progress and its kind of hard to do that if I don't have comments. Even if, I feel like this is great but . . . I would appreciate more critical comments or if its something that stands out, they could tell me this is really good." As studies show, students rely on comments as cues to what they are expected to do in their writing. In smaller liberal arts colleges, professors may have a higher course load, and responding to a large number of students' papers may seem daunting.

In their writing, Christian and Megan forge relationships with their readers; their writing reflects different social purposes (i.e., to interpret or evaluate) and new ways of understanding, interpreting, and organizing knowledge. In turn, the claims they make and the social purposes their writing serves influence the bases on which they select information, structure knowledge, and make connective inferences. Applicable to their writing is Dias and his colleagues' (1999) description of much academic writing as epistemic. By *epistemic* they mean that writing fulfills a social motive in school that "supports thinking, planning, knowing, and learning" (p. 11). In this way, what students write fulfills a sociocultural purpose that is sanctioned by a discipline's ways of constructing knowledge. Not surprisingly, students are not expected to contribute new knowledge to a discipline, especially in their first year.

The Role of First-Year Composition

The question that this study raises and that others (e.g., Carroll, 2002; Petraglia, 1995) have addressed at some length is, What role should a course in first-year composition play? This question is especially important if the type of writing students complete in first-year composition is considerably different from the types of writing they produce across disciplines. A number of theorists and practitioners in composition studies have argued that discipline-specific writing courses provide a more coherent alternative to the space that general writing skills classes currently occupy (e.g., Petraglia, 1995; Russell, 1995). The argument goes something like this: Writing is shaped fundamentally by its sociocultural context; because genres are responses to context, they cannot be learned out of context (Dias, Freedman, Medway, & Pare, 1999). Therefore, writing is better taught in the disciplines as situated practice. Similarly, Petraglia (1998) argued that "writers rely on situation-specific knowledge in producing texts" (p. 4), questioning the assumption that students can be taught to communicate effectively irrespective of actual situations or that students can learn to acquire writing skills that transcend any particular content or context.

However, such a view ignores the value of first-year composition in students' undergraduate education. Such a course provides students with a transition from writing in high school to college, where students must try to understand conventions for both writing and inquiry that remain tacit in content-based classes. In fact, writing courses serve as a beginning point in students' experiences as writers, not the end. As Carroll (2002) observes, "students will spend years developing new ways of writing" (p. 122). For example, Christian clearly used his prior experiences in debate to argue a position in his composition class, but he also gained some advantage in taking composition because he learned what was expected in college-level writing. In an interview with one of the researchers after completing his first year, Christian explained that he did not actually receive any explicit instruction from his "debate instructor, so it was kind of sink or swim, learn as you go, hear feedback from the judges over the course of every week for four years." Reflecting on the value of his composition class, he said he "learned how to put into paper very early on an oral way of presenting argument to a written way." In turn, what he learned was, again, a starting point because he recognized that "each different area or academic endeavor has their own little nuances in writing."

In contrast to Christian, Megan did not take a composition course; instead, the one course in writing she completed focused on writing literary analyses of poetry and film. Relying more on her impressions of what was expected than any cues that her professor provided, she explained in an interview that the goal of writing short-response papers was "to make sure that you come up with somewhat of an intelligent angle." For longer papers, she continued, "you kind of find out where people agree and disagree. What the hot topics are, you know? Then I start reading and thinking, and okay this is what this person thinks. What do I think? What do I think about this argument? I try to find what's controversial. Where do people disagree and I try to put my opinion in there and develop something from that so its similar in those ways." Like Christian, she also recognized that writing across disciplines is fairly "nuanced," but found her approach to writing succeeded, whether she wrote papers in philosophy, literature, or art history. Although one could argue that Megan was not disadvantaged when she placed out of a required composition class, Megan could have benefited from guided instruction as a means of easing the transition from writing in one context to another and helping her articulate more well-defined strategies for writing. These strategies can be both procedural—what do I do?—and conditional—why might one approach work better than another?

Teaching Writing Across Disciplines

In the end, it is important to recognize and teach the kinds of discourse practices in different communities that influence the strategies that writers use and those that students need to learn. As Johns (1997) asserted, different "communities use written discourses that enable members to keep in touch with each other, carry on discussions, explore controversies, and advance their aims" (p. 56). If different kinds of writing represent "the values, needs, and practices of the community that produces them," then it is not enough to teach genres (p. 56; cf. Berkenkotter & Huckin, 1994) or even offer models (e.g., Freedman & Adam, 2000). Instead, writing needs to be taught as a practice that embodies these values and needs. After all, communities are negotiated and interpreted in rich networks of people, materials, and signs, constituted by contradiction, multivoicedness, and history, neither located in a specific physical setting or concrete entity (Prior, 1998).

Moreover, research on written composition has taught educators the importance of exposing students to as wide a range of writing, audiences, and purposes as possible in an effort to ensure that they are prepared to write across disciplines. These occasions provide them with flexibility and versatility in deciding what is expected of them and how to proceed to fulfilling a given task (Beaufort, 1999). The strategies they learn include analyzing, evaluation, and inquiring, which students should carry forward across the disciplines during their 4 years of college. Thus, we would argue that students should be encouraged to "explore the wide range of written communicative opportunities: language as exploration, as speculation, as interpretation, as imagination, and most of all, as expression of unarticulated thoughts" (Chiseri-Strater, 1991, p. 161; see also Geisler, 1994; Herrington & Curtis, 2000). Unfortunately, we find that, despite the range of functions instructors across disciplines feel writing can serve in the first year, writing assignments appear to fulfill a narrow band of purposes—at least if we use the Boyer Commission report (1998) as a yardstick for what undergraduate training might entail.

More than changing practice at any one institution, these results can encourage dialogue about the ways in which we use such codified terms as *analysis* or *argument* and the ways in which texts serve as a means for configuring the world. Of course, the examples we provide are specific to this study and the context in which students wrote. Therefore, we cannot claim that students' writing in this study represents what students in other contexts can and must write. Instead, readers must judge whether the profiles we present approximate what they see in their own classrooms (cf. Carroll, 2002). Our hope is increased faculty involvement in and responsibility for student writing that will move writing instruction, not just writing, more toward the mainstream in undergraduate education. Such involvement has the potential to teach faculty the extent to which their values about writing converge (and diverge). This is especially important for faculty in composition to understand in developing curricula in students' first year. In keeping with the Boyer Commission report (1998), we see the wisdom of giving students ample opportunities to write with multiple purposes and with multiple readers.

ACKNOWLEDGMENTS

We would like to thank Barbara Walvoord for her valuable comments on an earlier version of this chapter. We also wish to extend our gratitude to Badia Ahad, Cecilia Lucero, Sarah Popek, and Christine Venter for their assistance throughout the process of collecting and analyzing students' papers. Of course, the generosity of both students and faculty made this study possible.

Stuart Greene would also like to add a word of gratitude to Bill Smith, a mentor and life-long friend. Bill is a generous mentor whom I have tried to emulate over the years—someone whose door is always open and who puts aside his own work to help others. I am still trying to reach the bar that he set so high as a friend, mentor, and scholar.

Through the way he taught, Bill Smith has over the years influenced my commitment to working with first-year students. This chapter reflects that commitment. At least implicitly, he has helped me shape the argument I make for the value of first-year composition within the university and its focus on academic literacies. Moreover, Bill taught me a number of things about research—to be vigilant in my analyses, to let the data "speak," and to answer the ponderous question, "So what?" From my dissertation on, I have used multiple lenses through which to understand student writing. This has entailed bringing together ethnographic observations with protocol analysis, case study research, and the type of textual analysis presented here. I owe Bill a lot for helping me see the intelligence of the students I study in developing theories of authorship and sociocognitive theory.

REFERENCES

Ackerman, J. (1993). The promise of writing to learn. *Written Communication, 10,* 334–370.
Anderson, J., Reder, L., & Simon, H. (1996). Situated learning and education. *Educational Researcher, 25,* 5–11.
Anson, C. (1988). A multidimensional mode of writing. In D. Jolliffe (Ed.), *Writing in academic disciplines* (pp. 1–33). Norwood, NJ: Ablex.

Bakhtin, M. (1986). *Speech genres* (Vern W. McGee, Trans.). Austin: University of Texas Press.

Bazerman, C., & Paradis, J. (Eds.). (1991). *Textual dynamics of the professions: Historical and contemporary studies of writing in professional communities.* Madison: University of Wisconsin Press.

Beaufort, A. (1999). *Writing in the real world: Making the transition from school to work.* New York: Teachers College Press.

Berkenkotter, C., & Huckin, T. (1994). *Genre knowledge in disciplinary communication.* Mahwah, NJ: Lawrence Erlbaum Associates.

Bhatia, V. J. (1997). Genre-mixing in academic introductions. *English for Special Purposes, 16,* 181–195.

Bhatia, V. J. (2002). Applied genre analysis: Analytical advances and pedagogical procedures. In A. Johns (Ed.), *Genre in the classroom: Multiple perspectives* (pp. 279–283). Mahwah, NJ: Lawrence Erlbaum Associates.

Boyer Commission on Educating Undergraduates in the Research University. (1998). *Reinventing undergraduate education: A blueprint for America's research universities.* New York: State University of New York at Stony Brook.

Britton, J., Burgess, T., Martin, N., McLeod, A., & Rosen, H. (1975). *The development of writing abilities.* London: Macmillan.

Carroll, L. (2002). *Rehearsing new roles: How college students develop as writers.* Carbondale, IL: Southern Illinois University Press.

Chiseri-Strater, E. (1991). *Academic literacies: The public and private discourse of university students.* Portsmouth, NH: Boynton/Cook Publishers, Heinemann.

Cicero, M. (1949). *De inventione* [The invention] (H. M. Hubbell, Trans.). Cambridge, MA: Harvard University Press.

Clark, G., & Doheny-Farina, S. (1990). Public discourse and personal expression: A case study of theory-building. *Written Communication, 7,* 456–481.

Coe, R. (1994). Teaching genres as process. In A. Freedman & P. Medway (Eds.), *Learning and teaching genre* (pp. 157–169). Portsmouth, NH: Heinemann.

Crosson, F. (1999, November). *The content of a liberal education.* Paper presented at the annual meeting of Phi Beta Kappa, Hunter College, New York.

Crosswhite, J. (1996). *The rhetoric of reason: Writing and the attractions of argument.* Madison, WI: University of Wisconsin Press.

Dias, P., Freedman, A., Medway, P., & Pare, A. (1999). *Worlds apart: Acting and writing in academic and workplace contexts.* Hillsdale, NJ: Lawrence Erlbaum Associates.

Durst, R. (1999). *Collision course: Conflict, negotiation, and learning in college composition.* Urbana, IL: National Council of Teachers of English.

Fahnestock, J., & Secor, M. (1996). The rhetoric of literary criticism. In C. Bazerman & J. Paradis (Eds.), *Textual dynamics of the professions: Historical and contemporary studies of writing in professional communities* (pp. 76–96). Madison: University of Wisconsin Press.

Flower, L. (1994). *The construction of negotiated meaning: A social cognitive theory of writing.* Carbondale, IL: Southern Illinois University Press.

Freedman, A. (1994). "Do as I say": The relationship between teaching and learning new genres. In A. Freedman & P. Medway (Eds.), *Genre and the new rhetoric* (pp. 191-210). London: Taylor & Francis.

Freedman, A., & Adam, C. (2000). Write where you are: Situating learning to write in university and workplace settings. In P. Dias & A. Pare (Eds.), *Transitions: Writing in academic and workplace settings* (pp. 31-60). Cresskill, NJ: Hampton.

Geisler, C. (1994). *Academic literacy and the nature of expertise. Reading, writing, and knowing in academic philosophy.* Mahwah, NJ: Lawrence Erlbaum Associates.

Greene, S. (1994). Students as authors in the study of history. In G. Leinhardt, I. Beck, & K. Stainton (Eds.), *Teaching and learning in history* (pp. 133–168). Mahwah, NJ: Lawrence Erlbaum Associates.

Greene, S. (2001). The question of authenticity: Teaching writing in a first-year college history of science class. *Research in the Teaching of English, 35,* 525–569.

Greene, S., & Ackerman, J. (1995). Expanding the constructivist metaphor: A rhetorical perspective on literacy research and practice. *Review of Educational Research, 65,* 383–420.

Haswell, R. (1986). The organization of impromptu essays. *College Composition and Communication, 37,* 402–415.

Herrington, A. (1988). Teaching, writing, and learning: A naturalistic study of writing in an undergraduate literature course. In D. Jolliffe (Ed.), *Writing in academic disciplines* (pp. 133-166). Norwood, NY: Ablex.

Herrington, A., & Curtis, M. (2000). *Persons in process: Four stories of writing and personal development* (pp. 133-166). Urbana, IL: National Council of Teachers of English.

Johns, A. (1997). *Text, role, and context: Developing academic literacies.* Cambridge: Cambridge University Press.

Johns, A. (Ed.). (2002). *Genre in the classroom: Multiple perspectives.* Mahwah, NJ: Lawrence Erlbaum Associates.

Jones, C., Turner, J., & Street, B. (Eds.). (1999). *Students writing in the university: Cultural and epistemological issues.* Philadelphia & Amsterdam: John Benjamins Publishing Company.

Lave, J., & Wenger, E. (1991). *Situated learning. Legitimate peripheral participation.* Cambridge, England: Cambridge University Press.

Lea, M. (1999). Academic literacies and learning in higher education: Constructing knowledge through texts and experience. In C. Jones, J. Turner, & B. Street (Eds.), *Students writing in the university: Cultural and epistemological issues* (pp. 103–124). Philadelphia & Amsterdam: John Benjamins Publishing Company.

Macken-Horarik, M. (2002). "Something to shoot for": A systemic functional approach to teaching genre in secondary school science. In A. Johns (Ed.), *Genre in the classroom: Multiple perspectives* (pp. 17–42). Mahwah, NJ: Lawrence Erlbaum Associates.

McLeod, S., Miraglia, E., Soven, M., & Thaiss, C. (2001). *WAC for the new millennium: Strategies for continuing writing-across-the-curriculum programs.* Urbana, IL: National Council of Teachers of English.

Meyer, B. (1975). *The organization of prose and its effects on memory.* Amsterdam: North Holland Publishing Company.

Meyer, B. (1985). Prose analysis: Purposes, procedures, and problems. In B. Britton & J. Black (Eds.), *Understanding expository text* (pp. 11–64). Mahwah, NJ: Lawrence Erlbaum Associates.

Miller, C. (1984). Genre as social action. *Quarterly Journal of Speech, 70,* 151-167.

Moffett, J. (1968). *Teaching the universe of discourse.* Boston: Houghton-Mifflin.

Nelson, J. (1990). This was an easy assignment: Examining how students interpret academic writing tasks. *Research in the Teaching of English, 24,* 362–396.

Nelson, J. (1995). Reading classrooms as texts. *College Composition and Communication, 46,* 411–429.

Ochsner, R., & Fowler, J. (2004). Playing devil's advocate: Evaluating the literature of the WAC/WID movement. *Review of Educational Research, 74,* 117–140.

Paltridge, B. (2002). Genre, text type, and the English for academic purposes (EAP) classroom. In A. Johns (Ed.), *Genre in the classroom: Multiple perspectives* (pp. 73–90). Mahwah, NJ: Lawrence Erlbaum Associates.

Paxton, R. (1999). A deafening silence: History textbooks and the students who read them. *Review of Educational Research, 69*, 315–339.

Petraglia, J. (Ed.). (1995). *Reconceiving writing, rethinking writing instruction.* Mahwah, NJ: Lawrence Erlbaum Associates.

Petraglia, J. (Ed.). (1998). *Reality by design: The rhetoric and technology of authenticity in education.* Mahwah, NJ: Lawrence Erlbaum Associates.

Prior, P. (1998). *Writing disciplinarity: A sociohistoric account of literate activity in the academy.* Mahwah, NJ: Lawrence Erlbaum Associates.

Prior, P., Hawisher, G., Gruber, S., & MacLaughlin, N. (1997). In K. Yancey & B. Huot (Eds.), *Assessing writing across the curriculum* (pp. 185–216). Greenwich, CT: Ablex.

Rose, M. (1989). *Lives on the boundary.* New York: Penguin.

Russell, D. (1995). Activity and writing instruction. In J. Petraglia (Ed.), *Reconceiving writing, rethinking writing instruction* (pp. 51–77). Mahwah, NJ: Lawrence Erlbaum Associates.

Selfe, C. (1997). Contextual evaluation in WAC programs: Theory, issues, and strategies for teachers. In K. Yancey & B. Huot (Eds.), *Assessing writing across the curriculum.* Greenwich, CT: Ablex.

Spivey, N. (1996). *The constructivist metaphor: Reading, writing, and the making of meaning.* New York: Academic Press.

Sternglass, M. (1997). *Time to know them: A longitudinal study of writing and learning at the college level.* Mahwah, NJ: Lawrence Erlbaum Associates.

Street, B. (1984). *Literacy in theory and practice.* New York: Cambridge University Press.

Toulmin, S., Rieke, R., & Janik, A. (1984). *An introduction to reasoning* (2nd ed.). New York: Macmillan.

Witte, S. (1983). Topical structure and writing quality. Some possible text-based explanations of readers' judgements of students' writing. *Visible Language, 17*, 177-205.

Young, K. M., & Leinhardt, G. (1998). Writing from primary documents: A way of knowing in history. *Written Communication, 15*, 25–68.

8

STANDARD ENGLISH NEEDS TAUGHT N'AT

Students' Attitudes Toward Language and Linguistics

Constance M. Ruzich

In 1974, the Conference on College Composition and Communication (CCCC) adopted as policy a resolution and position statement affirming and defending "Students' Right to Their Own Language" (published in a special College Composition and Communication (*CCC*) issue in fall 1974). The position statement asserted that, "All English teachers should, as a minimum, know the principles of modern linguistics, and something about the nature of the English language in its social and cultural context" ("Students' Right," 1974, p. 15) and optimistically declared that with this knowledge, "changing attitudes toward dialect variations does not seem an unreasonable goal, for today's students will be tomorrow's employers" (p. 14). It is now almost 30 years later. For the last 7 years, I have been teaching a required introductory linguistics course for communications and education majors at a small private university outside Pittsburgh, Pennsylvania. In my experience, the process of changing attitudes toward dialect variation is far more difficult and complex than the CCCC position statement anticipated. A few semesters ago, after 8 weeks of interactive instruction and exploration of concepts and issues related to linguistics, dialects, and language issues, one of my students turned in a prospectus for a research paper on the local Pittsburgh dialect (Pittsburghese) and offered the following explanation of his interest in the subject:

> I live on the North Side. We speak a totally different type of English language. We speak Pittsburghese. As far back as I can remember, I have been speaking this dialect. In most aspects of my life, it has not hindered anything, but now that I am growing and maturing as a future businessman and communication major, I feel it is now time to grow out of this dialect curse.

To be fair, the student does not exactly label the regional Pittsburgh dialect as substandard (a real no-no for linguists); he merely labels the dialect as a curse. But why, after 8 weeks of instruction in linguistics, was this student still viewing his own dialect in such negative terms? Why was he not more willing to affirm his own right to his own language? In this chapter, I revisit the 1974 language resolution and attempt to understand some of the difficulties that students encounter in the study of linguistics and the application of that knowledge to current language issues and policies.

The 1974 position statement acknowledged that,

> The human use of language is not a simple phenomenon: sophisticated research in linguistics and sociology has demonstrated incontrovertibly that many long held and passionately cherished notions about language are misleading at best, and often completely erroneous. . . . Nor is the linguistic information that is available very widely disseminated. The training of most English teachers has concentrated on the appreciation and analysis of literature, rather than on an understanding of the nature of language, and many teachers are, in consequence, forced to take a position on an aspect of their discipline about which they have little real information. And if teachers are often uniformed, or misinformed, on the subject of language, the general public is even more ignorant. Lack of reliable information, however, seldom prevents people for discussing language questions with an air of absolute authority. ("Students' Right," p. 1)

Margalit Fox, writing for the *New York Times Magazine* in the fall 1999, echoes the CCCC statement in suggesting that, nearly 25 years later, policy decisions and discussions about language are largely shaped by language myths or *folk-linguistic beliefs* as they are termed by Niedzielski and Preston (2000). Fox's (1999) article, like the CCCC's statement, specifically identifies several of the most widely held, mythic beliefs about language: A single, standard variety of English exists; other varieties are substandard and inferior; and the encouragement of multiple languages and dialects is a threat to national unity. Fox argues that, although these beliefs are "advanced by educators, lawmakers and members of the news media" and "inform public discourse and public policy" (p. 40), they are all myths that do not bear up under the scrutiny of linguists or those who study languages and the way they work.

What happens, however, when mythic folk beliefs come into contact with researched linguistic approaches to language? The CCCC statement suggests that attitudes can be changed, and that, provided with knowledge of linguistic theory and research, teachers and students can begin to bring more informed perspectives to the public discourse on language issues. Using my own class as a small case study, I have attempted to investigate this assumption. During the 1999 fall semester, I surveyed students in an introductory linguistic course about their own language practices and their attitudes and beliefs about language. Many of my students (approximately 18 of the 28 surveyed in the course) identified themselves as speakers of what is known locally as Pittsburghese.

Pittsburghese is a dialect that is characterized by what has been described as *relaxed* vowels (the local football team is the *Stillers*, and *down* rhymes with *on*), a local vocabulary (a rubberband is called a *gumband*, and bologna is known as *jumbo*), and some syntactic differences from Standard English (most notably, omission of *to be* after the verbs *need* and *want*, as in "The car needs washed," or "He wants taken seriously"). In local newspaper and magazine articles on Pittsburghese, the dialect has been described as giving "a certain amount of romance" to the area and marking its speakers as "colorful and unique" (Zallon-Conway, 1998, pp. C1, C6). It may be significant to also note that the expert quoted in the article who describes the dialect as romantic is also identified as having "a master's degree in English and speak[ing] with proper diction," whereas the speaker who terms the dialect "colorful and unique" is also identified as teaching the college course, "How to Lose Your Pittsburgh Accent, N'at" (p. C1). The article quotes Scott Paulsen, a co-host of one of Pittsburgh's most popular morning radio shows, as a supporter of the Western Pennsylvania dialect: "Our language is kind of our badge. . . . I think it's important to remember where you're from, and it's important to be proud of it" (Zallon-Conway, 1998, p. C6), while also noting that Paulsen's radio partner, Jim Krenn, "hides his Pittsburgh accent under a professional radio voice" (p. C6).

Frequently, the Pittsburgh dialect is noted for having a social stigma attached to it (Kloman, 1992). In an article published in *Pittsburgh* magazine, the owner of a Pittsburgh consulting firm is quoted as asserting that, "the Pittsburgh slang is a definite liability" in business, and some features "tend to make us sound rather parochial and uneducated" (Kloman, 1992, p. 43). Connelly, an expert on the Pittsburgh job market and author of *Find a Job in Pittsburgh* adds, "A Pittsburgh accent can sound very comfortable and familiar to someone you're greeting across the desk. A Pittsburgh accent can also indicate that you're dumb as a box of rocks, and if it communicates that, it's detrimental to you" (Kloman, 1992, p. 43). Perceptions of the dialect are intertwined with attitudes toward social class: "Pittsburgh is viewed as a blue-collar town, so the accent is viewed as a blue-collar accent" (Kloman, 1992, p. 43).

For many of my students, then, their language practices and their attitudes about language are set against this backdrop: They identify themselves with a city that claims a proud working-class heritage, and many of them speak the local dialect that is identified with that heritage. Yet they have made the socioeconomic decision to attend a business-focused university because they aspire to professions outside the working class; they hope for careers in public relations, communications, media, and education. As part of their career preparation, all communications and secondary education majors in communications and English are required to take an introductory linguistics course.

At the start of the required course, students spend the first full week of class exploring definitions of language and grammar, comparing popular ideas about these concepts with the ways in which linguists define and use the terms. Students read and discuss an article by Harvey Daniels (1998), "Nine Ideas About Language," in which, according to the editors' introduction to the essay, Daniels "dispels a number of myths about language that are all too prevalent among Americans" (p. 43). Daniels' article explicitly identifies and then contradicts folk beliefs about language, explaining that "Everyone speaks a dialect" (p. 47), "A standard dialect is not *inherently* superior to any other dialect of the same language" (although it may have considerable social, political, and economic consequences because of others' perceptions of the dialect), all dialects are equally "logical" and "rule governed" (p. 48), "Value judgments about different languages or dialects are matters of taste" (p. 56), and, finally, that "Language change is normal" (p. 52).

In the week of class discussions following the reading of Daniels' essay, there were several heated discussions about the relative merits of various dialects. Students identified dialects to which they reacted negatively (the West Virginia dialect and the Southern dialect were frequently used as examples) and dialects to which they reacted positively (the British dialect was most often mentioned). There were mixed perceptions about Pittsburghese: Students from outside the Pittsburgh area were quick to denigrate the dialect as confusing and backward, whereas students from Western Pennsylvania were mixed in their assessments of the dialect. Myron Cope, the local color commentator for the Pittsburgh Steelers, was a lightening rod for this discussion: Some students pointed to him as an example of colorful language and local pride, whereas others labeled him as the most irritating man they had ever heard.

As moderator of these discussions, I pointed students back to our text, reminding them of Daniels' claims that everyone speaks a dialect, that no dialects are inherently superior, that value judgments about language and dialects are matters of taste, and that all dialects are equally rule governed. I invited them to explore dialects and attitudes toward dialects within contexts, not simply evaluating good or bad, but good for whom, for what, and in what settings.

By the eighth week of the course, students had read and applied knowledge about linguistic approaches to language as they related to the study of phonology, morphology, syntax, and child language acquisition; they were beginning to study the history of the English language. At this point in the course, in the week after midterm, students were asked to submit a research prospectus describing an area of interest they wished to investigate on their own. It was at this point that one student, "Jeremy," submitted a proposal indicating his interest in researching the Pittsburgh dialect. Although in class we had repeatedly read and discussed descriptive studies of dialects as well as sociolinguistic examinations of dialects and attitudes related to them, Jeremy's proposed research was not situated in either of these contexts. Instead, he explained his interest in the subject as follows:

> The main reason that I am interested in researching this topic is I recently became involved with a family from Chicago, Illinois and they joked and teased me about my accent and dialect and I have since become aware of it and now catch myself speaking as they said, "horribly." Certain words that we Pittsburghers say incorrectly are Dahntahn instead of Downtown, Gumband instead of Rubber Band, Shauer instead of Shower. I understand that these words are all pronounced incorrectly by myself and my fellow Pittsburgh neighbors, but why? . . . I will figure out the reasons behind these misinterpretations . . . and hopefully I will learn to develop my language structure more properly and learn to speak more effectively.

I approved Jeremy's plan for research, but also reminded him to review linguists' beliefs about dialects (everyone speaks a dialect, none is inherently superior, all are logical and rule governed) and to place his research within the context of linguistic study.

From the 9th through the 13th weeks of the course, students examined the evolution of English, its many changes, its extensive borrowings from other languages and dialects, and the many unsuccessful attempts to legislate language use and language change. They read Roger Shuy, William Labov, and Geneva Smitherman; discussed language variation and change; and worked extensively with the concept that "nonstandard dialects of English, like all human languages, are rule-governed; they are not corruptions or inferior versions of Standard English" (Clark, Eschholz, & Rosa, 1998, p. 313). A key reading was an essay entitled "Speech Communities," authored by Roberts (1998), which asserts:

> Now let us pose a delicate question: aren't some of these speech communities better than others? That is, isn't better language heard in some than in others? Well, yes, of course. One speech community is always better than all the rest. This is the group in which one happens to find oneself. . . . As a practical matter, good English is whatever English is spoken by the group in which one moves contentedly and at ease. . . . If you admire the language of other speech communities more than you do your own, the reasonable hypothesis is that you are dissatisfied with the community itself. It is not precisely other speech that attracts you but the people who use this speech. Conversely, if some language strikes you as unpleasant or foolish or rough, it is presumably because the speakers themselves seem so. (p. 274)

At this point in the term, it became evident that students were hearing, but not always believing; Jeremy was not the only one who was not buying the linguistic position on language and dialect. On a quiz given in mid-November, 12 of the 25 students answered the following question incorrectly:

According to the text, what is the most likely explanation for objecting to a dialect?

a. the sounds of the dialect are difficult to comprehend   6
                                                                   (responses)
b. the vocabulary of the dialect is difficult to comprehend   1
c. the syntax or grammar of the dialect is difficult   5
      to comprehend
d. the people who speak the dialect are not viewed favorably   13
      (the correct response, according to the text and class discussions)

(On the final exam for the course, when this question was repeated, only seven students answered this question incorrectly, but this number still represents 25% of those taking the exam, and the concept was one that had been a major theme of the course. On the final, four students chose syntax, two chose sounds, and one chose vocabulary.)

Perhaps the most telling measure of how deeply held were students' beliefs in the myths of language were the responses I received from students' in-class writing, elicited during the 14th week of the 15-week term. Students were given the following prompt: Imagine that you're at a party, and you've met an old friend. You've just confessed that you're taking a linguistics course. Your friend becomes impassioned and begins to lament the horrible changes that have recently occurred in the English language. He/she brings up the California decision to include Ebonics in teacher education, the growing use and acceptance of "substandard" dialects (like Pittsburghese), and the increasing inability of English speakers to correctly use *who* and *whom*. All of these examples are given as evidence of the mess that English has gotten itself into. He or she insists that the only solution is political activism on the part of those, like yourself who know how to fix the language, and adoption of a constitutional Amendment that would make English the official language of America. Reply thoughtfully, citing key concepts that we have studied.

Thirteen of the 25 students who responded to this prompt defended at least one popular language myth—arguing emphatically *against* positions we had read and reviewed in the textbook and in class discussions. In two instances, students actually cited the text as the source of their folk-linguistic beliefs or myths about language.

From a content analysis of students' responses, four prevalent (or highly resistant) myths remained firmly in place as students thought about language. Two myths readily defended by students were the beliefs that there is a single standard variety of English that can be identified and held constant, and that those varieties of English that differ from the standard variety are inferior. Students supporting these myths commented that, "Webster's dictionary set the standard for the English language and I don't think it should be strayed from," "We are losing proper English dialect," or "We have to stick with straight English." Jeremy, the student who was researching the Pittsburgh dialect, elaborated: "Today we have the dialects of the Italian New Yorkers, Pittsburghese, Ebonics, Spanglish, and none of them are clear enough to be considered a 'true language'." Another student developed this idea further, writing: "In my eyes, the English language has been extremely bastardized. When I hear someone say, 'Yo, I'm goin' dan to ma crib wif my homies for a bootie call' or 'I'm gon dantan to warsh my car,' it makes me cringe, especially given my love of the English language."

The third myth that students frequently defended, related to the first two, is that those who do not speak standard English have chosen not to do so, and that choice reveals character flaws in those speakers. In support of this belief, one student wrote, "The English language is a mess because of things like Ebonics and Spanglish and foreigners speaking incorrect English and passing that on to their children." Another student attempted to defend his position on Ebonics in these words: "This [Ebonics] is black English mixed with American English. I believe it is lazy on their part as well as our part for letting these groups of people form these languages." A third student speculated on the reasons behind language choices that he saw as subversive: "Why do they want to teach their children to speak 'garbage' when they can speak a well refined form of the English language? I guess we will never know why some people want the language to regress to a substandard form maybe its incompetence or fear of too much power [sic]." These perceptions of dialect variation were highly consistent with students' views at the start of the course and contrary to the prompt's directions asking students to cite key concepts studied in class. Responses like these reflected no clear application of linguistic knowledge or the scientific study of language. Instead, when asked to imagine themselves in a social situation where language issues were being debated, many students fell back on deeply held language myths.

Many students also argued that dialect and language diversity was a threat to national unity. In support of this position, one student explained:

> These people whom are fluent in two languages are meshing together two very different languages to create this Spanglish. This could cause problems being people pick and take from each language very inconsistently. What one person would say could be the complete opposite of what another would say. . . . The languages need to be standardized creating unity as a country.

Other students responded from a more personal perspective: "While I support immigration, I will say that it is bothersome to have to interact with individuals living in my own country who can't speak English," and "If people want to live in America, then they should be prepared to live and speak the way America does. America shouldn't have to change for them." There were many elaborations on this theme:

> English does need to be made the official language of America . . . by the year 2020 about half of the population will speak some form of Spanish. I feel this is a major problem to the people like you and I [sic]. I don't speak Spanish and I don't want to learn it. We have to look at the rights of the American people, the people who were here first. . . . When my grandparents came over from Serbia, they didn't speak any other language but English. They knew how lucky they were to be in America and they did not take it for granted. Today's immigrants should learn a history lesson.

One student tried to work out a creative solution to the tensions she perceived among languages and dialects, but in the end she found her creativity unequal to the challenge:

> Maybe we can generalize teaching of dialects and Ebonics. We could also limit who gets to teach/learn Ebonics. My suggestion: people from the western side of the US be taught Ebonics. The eastern side of the US can be taught dialects. Of course, people travel, but we know enough to be able to communicate with people with such different speaking abilities. Maybe a Constitutional Amendment is necessary. Just think, if all these new "substandard" dialects come into play, soon there will be too many, and no one will be able to communicate effectively.

Finally, students who defended one of the folk beliefs about language were also likely to argue that the knowledge and use of standard English would ensure economic opportunities and good jobs. They argued that those who do not speak standard English "will be eaten alive by the working world that is intelligent enough to be able to speak to one another using proper English." These students viewed the school system as bearing the ultimate responsibility for teaching standard English: "The school is not doing their job of preparing students for college or a job by teaching them sentences such as 'we be going down to da field.'"

From other data that I gathered from the class, I attempted to explore what might have made these 13 students different from their peers who were more ready to accept linguists' views about language. One key difference between students who continued to believe in popular ideas about language (rather than linguistic ways of thinking about language) is that these students were more likely to report themselves as being familiar with and likely to use the local Pittsburgh dialect. In a survey given to students near the end of the course, two of the survey items asked students to assess how frequently they used features of the

Pittsburgh dialect (the use of *yinz* and the *need* verb construction). Only 2 of the 16 students (12.5%) whose test responses suggested they accepted or understood linguistic views of language variation described themselves as frequent to very frequent users of Pittsburghese. However, of those students who appeared *not* to accept or understand linguistic views about language, 6 of the 13 (46%) described themselves as using features of the Pittsburgh dialect frequently to very frequently. Although the sample size of this research is too small to be able to draw generalizable conclusions, these results suggest that those most likely to hold myths about language may also be those most likely to speak nonstandard varieties of a language.

How then can we understand these students and their persistent beliefs in the powerful, popular myths about language? Lippi-Green's (1997) book, *English With an Accent,* is helpful here. She argues, "To make these two statements: *I acknowledge that my home language is viable and adequate* and *I acknowledge that my home language will never be accepted* is to set up an unresolvable conflict" (p. 186). The conflict must be that much greater when it is placed in the context of a required college course and a degree program, which, for many students, is only being endured so as to get a good job. For many students, the academic position, the linguists' position, is contrary to their lived experience. Their dialect is not accepted. They are mocked, they are corrected, and they read in the local newspapers and magazines that their dialect will mark them for low-status jobs. Nor are negative perceptions about speech varieties limited to Pittsburgh and Pittburghese: A *Business Week* job seeker's tip published in 2000 advised job seekers to "lose the accent," citing research findings that speakers with "identifiable accents, such as a heavy Southern drawl," are more often recommended for lower level jobs compared with those "with a less identifiable accent, such as that found in the Midwest" ("Job Seekers' Tip," 2000, p. 16). The more-or-less-identifiable description is ironic given that the less-identifiable accent *is* able to be identified as midwestern. Perhaps a better indicator of an accent's acceptability is the social class, privilege, and status possessed by those with whom it is identified. Pittsburghese is strongly identified with the working class, particularly those in the steel industry; as such, it is not perceived as a high-status accent. Atkins' (1993) research confirmed that employment recruiters made character determinations based on speech habits, judging candidates with Appalachian and African-American Vernacular English accents to be "unorganized," "lazy," "inferior," and "unprofessional" (as cited in Cargile, 2000, p. 165).

In the local news stories on Pittsburghese, the dialect is most often complemented and affirmed by those who do not use it or who can easily code shift to a more standard variety of English. Actual speakers of Pittsburghese (and other nonstandard dialects) are perhaps, like Jeremy, more familiar with the ridicule and prejudice that accompany the use of terms like *gumband* and *yinz* (the plural form of *you,* the Pittsburgh equivalent of *y'all*). For these students, popular myths of language have a certain utilitarian value. If students can persist in believing in popular myths of language, they can hold onto the powerful hopes that these beliefs promise, hopes of real-life rewards, promises of national unity, order, acceptance, and salaried employment. The popular myths about language have clearer moral values: They label *good* and *bad* languages and *good* and *bad* speakers, and they promise that those who learn to speak standard English will live happily ever after. Linguists' explanations give far less assurance. They do not offer easy answers or comforting sentiments in proclaiming: *Language is good or bad depending on contexts. Things change. Nothing is certain. Social class and prejudice shape perceptions, approval ratings, and rewards more than any inherent characteristics of language.* As long as our culture continues to behave as if folk-linguistic beliefs about language are true (in classrooms, in hiring, and in the media), then one linguistics course attempting to change beliefs in those popular myths may have a limited chance of successfully altering views of language and dialects.

Almost 30 years ago, the CCCC resolution and position statement ("Students' Right," 1974) acknowledged that, "The English profession, then, faces a dilemma: until public attitudes can be changed—and it is worth remembering that the past teaching in English classes has been largely responsible for those attitudes—shall we place emphasis on what the vocal elements of the public thinks it wants or on what the actual available linguistic evidence indicates we should emphasize?" (p. 1). The resolution confidently determined that the English profession would best meet the needs of students, the public, and the future by acting on the available linguistic evidence. Students' right to their own languages was affirmed, as was teachers' responsibility to gain the "experiences and training that will enable them to respect diversity" (p. 1). My own research and experience, however, suggests that teacher knowledge and student exposure to and interaction with linguistic principles may not be enough. We may need to be more intentional in training teachers and introducing linguistic concepts into our classrooms. As Wilson (2001) has noted in a recent *English Journal* article, "It is rare to find a focus on language as a living, breathing, sociocultural phenomenon in secondary classrooms. . . . With little discussion of English beyond the traditional or transformational grammar course, we've been offering up a study of the language too frequently isolated from the individuals who actually use it" (p. 31). Wilson attempts to address this educational lapse and suggests helpful strategies for integrating the sociocultural study of language into the classroom. But perhaps even this focus on language in the secondary classroom comes too late. Students' beliefs and attitudes about language may be shaped much earlier, yet rarely are elementary teachers educated in linguistics and rarely are sociocultural language issues and concepts introduced by elementary teachers to younger students. Although requiring a single course in linguistics of secondary education majors is not enough to overcome all student resistance to folk myths about language, many students do begin to appreciate the complexities of language diversity and language issues. However, at my university, as at many others, elementary education majors are not required to take even a single course in linguistics. Although elementary education majors are frequently required to take courses in reading and language arts methods, without coursework in linguistics, these students often miss the opportunity to develop a more nuanced and informed theory of language. This seems particularly troubling because these are the teachers who are responsible for early literacy teaching and for laying the foundation for students' later attitudes and experiences as they relate to linguistic diversity.

This exploratory research suggests that if we are to continue in attempting to support students' right to their own languages, we must acknowledge that merely teaching and learning about language and linguistic theory are most probably not sufficient for changing language myths and attitudes that are widely supported by socioeconomic pressures. We must acknowledge that mythic beliefs often have strong psychological motivations, and that mythic beliefs about standard English in America may well be intertwined with the larger metanarrative of the American Dream. Further research at all grade levels that investigates what students believe about language, what they learn about language, and what they resist learning about language is needed if we are to realize the goal of ensuring all students' rights to their own language.

REFERENCES

Cargile, A. C. (2000, September). Evaluations of employment suitability: Does accent always matter? *Journal of Employment Counseling, 37,* 165. Retrieved July 22, 2003, from InfoTrac College Edition database.

Clark, V. P., Eschholz, P. A., & Rosa, A. F. (Eds.). (1998). *Language: Readings in language and culture* (6th ed.). New York: St. Martin's.

Daniels, H. (1998). Nine ideas about language. In V. P Clark, P. A. Eschholz, & A. F. Rosa (Eds.), *Language: Readings in language and culture* (6th ed., pp. 43–60). New York: St. Martin's.

Fox, M. (1999, December 12). Good, bad, and ugly are all myths. *New York Times Magazine,* p. 40. Retrieved April 12, 2000, from ProQuest Direct Academic database.

Job Seeker's Tip: Lose the Accent. (2000, September 11). *Business Week,* p. 16. Retrieved July 22, 2003, from InfoTrac College Edition database.

Kloman, H. (1992, February). The truth and consequences of Pittsburghese: How you say downtown can affect your career. *Pittsburgh Magazine,* pp. 40–43.

Lippi-Green, R. (1997). *English with an accent: Language, ideology, and discrimination in the United States.* New York: Routledge.

Niedzielski, N. A., & Preston, D. R., (2000). *Folk linguistics.* New York: Mouton de Gruyter.

Roberts, P. (1998). Speech communities. In V. P. Clark, P. A. Eschholz, & A. F. Rosa (Eds.), *Language: Readings in language and culture* (6th ed., pp. 267–276). New York: St. Martin's.

Students' right to their own language. (1974, Fall). *College Composition and Communication* [Special Issue], 25.

Wilson, M. (2001, March). The changing discourse of language study. *English Journal, 90*(4), 31. Retrieved July 22, 2003, from ProQuest Direct Academic database.

Zallon-Conway, R. (1998, October 12). Words n'at: Our dialect defines us, but is that good or bad? *Beaver Valley Times,* pp. C1, C5.

9

DEVELOPING AN ONLINE WRITING TUTOR

The Interaction of Design Principles and Assessment

John R. Hayes

Diana M. Bajzek

Susan Lawrence

Erwin R. Steinberg

This chapter describes a work in progress—an online basic writing tutor for engineering and science students. At this point, we have created two modules: an Audience Module to teach technically oriented writers better ways of communicating with nontechnical readers, and a Thesis Statement Module to teach the writing of more effective thesis statements. We have assessed and revised both of these modules. Much of this chapter focuses on the way design principles and assessments interact to shape the final product.

Why build an online writing tutor? Several considerations have led us to undertake this project. First, there is a need. The composition instruction that engineering and science students typically receive is often not sufficient to solve their writing problems. In some cases, this may be because students believe that writing courses are not relevant to their professional careers, and, thus, they are not motivated to work hard in college composition courses. In other cases, it may be that the students' writing problems are so serious that one could not expect one or even two college composition courses to solve them. This might be the case, for example, if the student's first language is not English. Whatever the source of the difficulty, our writing tutor is designed to be a resource for engineering and science faculty so that some or all of their students can receive additional writing instruction without cost of time or energy to engineering and science faculty.

Second, we believe that our tutor has some instructional advantages:

1. It can provide immediate feedback, which is often difficult to do in traditional classrooms.
2. It can provide essentially unlimited practice.
3. Because it focuses on writing examples taken from engineering and science, our tutor can make composition seem more relevant to engineering and science students. The tutor can reinforce concepts taught in composition courses by applying them to familiar materials.
4. It can be used at home, in dorm rooms, or in writing centers at times of the student's own choosing.
5. It can be used to address just those problems that individual students or their teachers identify. The student does not have to sign up for a whole semester of instruction to deal with what may be a circumscribed problem.

Finally, we have a scientific agenda. We want to test a pedagogical strategy we call *judgment training* that appears to be well adapted to use with online tutors. We believe that such training may be a useful strategy for teaching writing in many contexts. We hope that by evaluating the judgment training strategy, we can learn something about the process of learning to write.

THE NEED FOR ADDITIONAL BASIC WRITING INSTRUCTION IN SCIENCE AND ENGINEERING STUDENTS

It has long been recognized that engineers and scientists need writing skills on the job (Barrass, 1978; Sageev, 1994; Wunsch, 1982). Indeed, the Accreditation Board for Engineering and Technology (ABET), in its 2001–2002 criteria for accrediting engineering programs, specified that, "Engineering programs must demonstrate that their graduates have an ability to communicate effectively." Many instructors, concurring with ABET, recognize the importance of writing for careers in engineering and science, and are concerned with the quality of their students' writing (Ammer, 1998). The results of a survey of science faculty attitudes about student writing abilities at Carnegie Mellon University led the authors (Young & Gordon, 1995) to draw the following conclusions:

1. Science faculty believe that slightly fewer than a third of all their students graduate with the writing abilities the faculty think are important. Virtually none of the faculty believes this is an acceptable situation.

2. Three of the abilities all faculty think students should acquire at the university level are: (a) write with grammatical correctness, (b) clear and coherent sentences, and (c) organize paragraphs and sections logically. Faculty members feel that the percentage of their students who graduate with these abilities is unacceptably low. Because of the nature of these abilities, we would call the problems students seem to be having "problems of basic intelligibility." The issue, in other words, is not of students not writing eloquently or creatively enough, but one of students simply not writing intelligible prose.

3. Time is a major part of the overall problem. Professors cite a lack of adequate time to integrate writing activities more fully into their courses.

Even if time were available, many engineering and science faculty members would not feel comfortable teaching writing skills. As Pemberton (1995) notes, "successful, publishing academics do not think of themselves as writers, and consequently, doubt their own ability to comment on and respond effectively to student writing" (p. 120). According to Russell (1991), lack of time and lack of inclination to teach writing have hindered the development of writing-across-the-curriculum programs in many colleges.

Many engineering and science students are not acquiring the basic writing skills they will need on the job. Further, engineering and science faculty cannot and should not be expected to provide the needed instruction. The need, then, is to provide an effective but inexpensive method for delivering writing instruction to engineering and science students without requiring engineering and science faculty to teach writing.

WHY AN ONLINE COMPUTER-BASED TUTOR?

The most important reason to consider using a computer-based tutor is cost. Human writing instructors are expensive, and many universities are increasingly reluctant to increase composition staff or fund writing centers. Further, putting the computer-based tutor online provides additional economies because it requires neither class time nor classroom space. It is also convenient for students because they can use it at times and places of their own choosing. Of course, we do not expect a computer-based tutor to provide the sensitive, flexible kind of instruction that a human teacher can provide. However, there are instructional tasks that a computer-based tutor can do very effectively. For example, such tutors can provide immediate feedback, something that a human instructor with 20 or more student papers to grade is hard pressed to do. Further, tutors can provide as much practice as any student may need. When instructional resources are limited, there is no reason that an expensive human instructor should be required to do a repetitive job that can be done more cheaply by a computer.

ARE THERE OTHER ONLINE OR COMPUTER-BASED TUTORS THAT DO THE SAME JOB?

There are three existing tutors that might be compared to the Carnegie Mellon Writing Tutor. First is the Rogue Community College Online Writing Lab (OWL). OWL, available through the Web, provides an impressive body of declarative writing instruction relevant to a wide variety of academic disciplines. It also provides scaffolding in the form of general advice about writing strategies. First-year assessment results for OWL have been very positive. It appears to provide a substantial improvement over prior instructional practice.

The main difference between OWL and the Carnegie Mellon Writing Tutor is that OWL provides feedback through Internet connection between students and human tutors. In contrast, the Carnegie Mellon Writing Tutor provides expert-based feedback without the intervention of a human tutor. The Carnegie Mellon Writing Tutor should provide instruction at substantially lower cost to the institution than OWL or other online writing labs that require the intervention of a human writing instructor.

A second tutor, Calibrated Peer Review (CPR), provides a Web-based resource for facilitating peer review, thus relieving instructors of some of the burden of evaluating papers. One of the central features of CPR is a procedure for qualifying students to evaluate papers. Thus, CPR shares a main goal with our tutor to improve students' ability to evaluate text. In CPR, students are required to evaluate three papers with some level of accuracy before they can qualify as peer reviewers. However, CPR appears to provide reviewers with minimal writing instruction. Reviewers are graded on their answers to questions such as, "Is the essay well organized?" and "Is the text grammatically correct?" Three evaluations of students' responses to such questions do not seem enough to teach students to evaluate organization or grammaticality. Rather it seems likely that CPR works by selecting students to be judges who can already make these judgments, rather than by teaching students to make them. Nonetheless, identifying students who can make accurate comments on papers should be seen as useful. However, as noted earlier, teachers' comments on papers have not proved to be an effective instructional strategy. Calibrated peers' comments may be no more effective. Both CPR and the Carnegie Mellon Writing Tutor are cost-effective. However, we believe that the Carnegie Mellon Writing Tutor provides more thorough and effective writing instruction.

The third tutor is the Cognitive Tutor for Writers (CTW), a computer-based tutor developed by Rowley, Carlson, and Miller (1998). This tutor provides declarative instruction and scaffolding for students, but not feedback. It is intended for use as a supplement to teacher instruction in high school classes. It has been carefully evaluated and appears to provide statistically significant gains in writing performance for inner-city children. However, it is intended as an occasional supplement to classroom instruction. Its designers did not intend it to be used as a stand-alone teaching aid.

At present, it appears that there are no other computer-based writing tutors that will satisfy the same goals as the Carnegie Mellon Writing Tutor, which is to provide low-cost, high- quality writing instruction in a stand-alone tutor.

JUDGMENT TRAINING

Let us now turn to the core instructional concept underlying the tutor: judgment training. By *judgment training*, we mean instruction that is aimed at providing students with skills that allow them to more accurately evaluate the quality of their own texts and those written by others. The familiar procedure in which composition teachers write comments on student's essays may be thought of as an example of judgment training. Presumably, the composition teacher's intention in commenting on text problems, such as lack of organization or wordiness, is to help their students recognize and fix such problems when they encounter them in later texts. The teacher's goal, then, is to provide students with judgmental skills that they will take with them when they write or edit new texts.

This goal is obviously important for writing instruction. Scholars such as Graves (1994) and Tierney et al. (1991) stress the importance of teaching students to evaluate their own writing. If writers fail to perceive problems in their texts, they can not take action to fix them. Hayes, Flower, Schriver, Stratman, and Carey (1987) found that freshman writers often failed to detect problems that were immediately evident to more advanced writers. For example, they observed that some freshman writers failed to find any fault in sentences such as, "Many naive women possess the assumption that it is necessary that they be superlative athletes in order to successfully be a member of a varsity team" and "In sports like fenc-

ing for a long time many of our varsity team members had no previous experience anyway." The problem was not inattentive reading. The freshman might read
these sentences over word by word as many as eight times and still evaluate them
as *good*. Rather, many of the freshmen appeared to be persistently insensitive to the
problems in the text.

Unfortunately, teachers' comments on students' papers do not appear to be
effective. Hillocks (1986), who provides the most complete discussion of these
issues, reviewed four procedures for teaching students to evaluate their own
writing:

- teachers commenting on students' final drafts,
- teachers commenting on students' intermediate drafts,
- students studying models of writing, and
- students being taught sets of evaluative criteria.

Concerning the first two procedures, Hillocks reviewed the available literature
and concluded that, "The available research suggests that teaching by written
comments on compositions is generally ineffective" (p. 167). One can imagine a
number of factors that might make the commenting procedure ineffective. First,
of course, students may fail to read the comments at all, being interested only
in their final grade. Alternatively, if students do read the comments, they may
not understand them. For example, they may not know what aspects of their
writing teachers are referring to when they write *awkward* or *parallelism* in the
margin. Finally, the teacher may have relatively few opportunities to comment
on any particular text problem for each student during the course of a semester.
If a student receives 5 or 10 comments on organization or wordiness over the
course of a semester, that may not be enough to make a difference in the student's writing.

In the procedure in which students study models of writing, students might
be asked to read models of good writing, read and identify features of good (and
sometimes poor) writing, to attempt to imitate examples of good writing, or all
three. Concerning teaching through the imitation of expert models, Hillocks
(1986) reported that the results of studies evaluating this method were mixed,
with some studies showing gains but others not.

The final procedure—teaching students sets of evaluative criteria—differs
from the procedures just described in one critical way. It includes specific tests to
ensure that the students have acquired and can apply the criteria. The first three
procedures attempt to teach students to recognize criteria relevant to writing
quality by exposing the student to teacher comments or written models. Only the
fourth procedure assesses whether the student has attended to the criteria and can
apply them.

Hillocks (1986) reported positive results for this procedure. Summarizing his
review of a number of studies (Benson, 1979; Clifford, 1981; Farrell, 1977; Kemp,

1979; Rosen, 1973; Sager, 1973; Wright, 1975), he says, "As a group, these studies indicate rather clearly that engaging young writers actively in the use of criteria, applied to their own and others' writing, results not only in more effective revisions but in superior first drafts" (p. 160). That students' first drafts improve is important because it suggest that students are applying the criteria to their own text production.

Sager's (1973) study of sixth graders in inner-city schools provides a clear illustration of an effective procedure for teaching quality criteria to students. Students in the experimental group were taught to use scales focusing on four aspects of writing quality: vocabulary, elaboration, organization, and structure. Each scale had four values ranging from 0 (*poorest quality*) to 3 (*best quality*). A high score on vocabulary was given to essays that had a variety of new and interesting words, rather than just common overworked ones. A high score on elaboration was given to essays that had an abundance of related ideas that flowed smoothly from one idea to the next. A high score on organization was given if ideas were arranged in a way that was interesting and easy to follow and a high score on structure if the story could be read aloud with ease. Students, working on one scale at a time, learn on one day what features earned a 0 and on other days what features earned 1, 2, or 3.

In introducing each scale, the teacher led a discussion of the features that a specific composition did or did not have. Students then received extensive practice in rating compositions both by themselves and in small groups. Differences of opinions about ratings were discussed, and an attempt was made to achieve consensus in the class. If the compositions did not receive a 3, the students suggested improvements and made revisions. At first the students rated one component at a time, then two components, and finally all four. Toward the end of practice, students rated compositions individually to assess agreement without discussion. The estimated reliability of the scale when used by the children was .99, with component reliabilities ranging from .96 to .98. Students in the control group studied the same four components of composition, but followed the standard school curriculum. Both groups studied 45 minutes a day for 5 days a week for 8 weeks.

By comparing pre- and posttest essays, Sager (1973) found that the experimental group made significantly greater gains than the control group on all four aspects of writing quality—that is, vocabulary, elaboration, organization, and structure. Hillocks (1986) calculated that the experimental/control effect size was .93 and the pre/post effect size for the experimental group was .82.

Many of the studies reviewed by Hillocks that explored the teaching of criteria were flawed in one way or another. In several of them, the effect of teaching criteria for quality was confounded with one or more other variables (Benson, 1979; Clifford, 1981; Farrell, 1977; Wright, 1975). Clifford, for example, listed 10 variables other than training on criteria for quality that differentiated his experimental and control groups. In an apparently unconfounded study, Rosen (1973), teaching students organizational skills, found significantly greater gains in the treatment group than in the control group. However, her results raise some questions because the experimental group also showed greater gains than the control group on most of the variables measured including punctuation, mechanics, and spelling—aspects of writing that she did not teach. In one of the studies, Kemp (1979) appears to have been focused on teaching stages of the writing process, rather than criteria of writing quality. In the Sager study, the results may be questioned because the researcher taught all of the experimental students, but others taught the control students. Despite the presence of problems, however, the studies as a group do suggest strongly that teaching criteria for quality can improve students' writing.

Two additional studies lend support to this conclusion. In a study by Rosow (1996), second graders were taught to use scales focusing on three aspects of writing quality: focus, detail, and organization. Each scale had four values ranging from 0 (*poorest quality*) to 3 (*best quality*). Rosow's instructional procedure was quite similar to that used by Sager. The objective of the research was to determine whether the students could learn to rate their own compositions on focus, detail, and organization as adults would rate them. Although there are some weaknesses in the author's data analysis, the results do suggest that the students were able to evaluate at least the organization of their compositions as adults did.

A study by Schriver (1992) used a different method to teach college students to judge the quality of texts. Schriver constructed a sequence of 10 lessons on writing clarity. Each lesson was constructed as follows. First, participants read an unclear text and underlined those aspects of the text that they thought the intended readers of the text would find unclear. Second, the participants read a think-aloud protocol of an intended reader attempting to understand that text. Third, the participants were asked to revise their initial judgments of clarity on the basis of the protocol.

The experimental group, consisting of five classes, studied the 10 lessons as part of a writing curriculum. The control group consisted of five classes that used the standard writing curriculum that included peer critiquing, role playing, and so on.

Participants were pre- and posttested by asking them to identify features in two popular science texts that students would find unclear. Schriver (1992) identified the text features that readers actually found unclear by collecting think-aloud protocols from 20 readers. Thus, she could determine whether the participants' predictions were accurate. The experimental group showed significant gains in predicting what readers would find unclear. The control group showed no change.

The subject populations in the studies reviewed here range from second grade to college. This range suggests that the benefits of teaching students to recognize and apply criteria of text quality may apply to a broad range of writers. Further, at least some of the studies indicate that the benefits transfer to the students' own writing.

PEDAGOGICAL PRINCIPLES USED IN THE DESIGN OF THE TUTOR

In addition to implementing the judgment training strategy in designing the tutor, we have also relied on the following six pedagogical principles.

1. Provide the student with clearly defined goals and motives
   Many science and engineering students will not take a lesson on writing seriously if they are not convinced of its relevance to themselves. Pilot testing of an earlier version of the tutor indicated that motivation was an important condition for learning. Therefore, the introduction to each module explains why the topic of that module is important for engineering and science professionals. It also clearly explains what skills the student can expect to acquire as a result of studying the module and how much time it will take them to complete the module.

2. Integrate instruction with practice
   Each module consists of two parts, an instructional section and a practice section. The instructional section introduces the text feature to be studied, presents a sequence of texts in which the text feature varies widely, and discusses the basic principles and strategies for evaluating the quality of the text feature.

   In the practice section, the student is presented with a sequence of exercises and asked to evaluate each of them by applying the rules and principles presented in the instructional section. Schneider (1985) recommends that many practice trials be provided in skill training. The number of available exercises must be large enough so that most students can make judgments accurately by the time they finish the practice section. How many exercises are required must be determined empirically and will probably differ from module to module. We assume that most students will not need to work through all of the exercises before they learn the skill.

3. Decompose complex skills
   Some writing skills, such as identifying whether a text is appropriate for a general audience, are quite complex. For example, a text may be inappropriate for a general audience because some critical terms are undefined. It may also be inappropriate because, although it has no undefined terms, it is written at such a high level of abstraction that the general reader can not grasp its meaning. It

may be inappropriate, even if it is written clearly, because it fails to provide the reader with a reason to be interested in the topic.

There is a controversy in the instructional literature about whether practicing the parts of a skill is an effective way to teach a complex skill. Gagne and Briggs (1974) emphasize its value, but Brown, Collins, and Duguid (1989) emphasize its failures. Schneider (1985) cites data indicating that teaching part skills can, in fact, promote the acquisition of a complex skill. We believe, for example, that judging whether a text is appropriate for a general audience is one of those complex skills that can benefit by practicing part skills. In particular, we believe that it consists of part skills such as identifying undefined terms, identifying abstract language, and identifying useful examples, each of which can be practiced separately.

In teaching complex skills, the tutor teaches each of the component skills, but also teaches the student to combine their evaluations of the separate components into an overall judgment of the text. Thus, the tutor provides both part- and whole-skill training.

4. Promote active participation

Schneider (1985) emphasizes the importance of learners' active participation in the instructional process. He says, "Active participation is enhanced if subjects need to respond every few seconds . . . Without these [responses] subjects' observation becomes passive and there is little improvement with practice" (pp. 297-298). Constructivist learning theorists strongly agree that students' active participation in learning is a critical factor determining the effectiveness of instruction. If students are not required to respond to the instructional materials, they may not give full attention to the learning task. The proposed tutor is designed, therefore, to promote students' active participation in learning by requiring them to make frequent evaluative judgments of texts in both the instructional and practice sections of each module.

5. Provide students with scaffolding

Scaffolding—the process of providing support to students as they are acquiring a skill—is also widely recognized as an important aid to instruction (Collins, Brown, & Newman, 1989; Farnham-Diggory, 1992). The Carnegie Mellon Writing Tutor provides scaffolding in two forms: (a). Students will have ready access to summaries of the rules and principles presented in the instructional section, and (b) when students make judgments of a text, they will be provided information helping them to evaluate their answers.

6. Provide immediate feedback

One of the most reliable results in the literature on learning is that quick feedback promotes learning. As their third principle in the design of computer-based tutors, Anderson, Boyle, Farrell, and Reiser (1984) recommend that immediate feedback be provided for errors. The tutor provides students with timely feedback on all of their responses.

THE TUTOR

In its final form, the tutor consists of independent instructional modules, accessible in any order, each focused on specific writing topics that have been identified by engineering and science faculty members as important for their students or by writing centers as common student writing problems. At present, we anticipate that the tutor will include modules on the following topics:

Addressing a general audience
Providing adequate thesis statements
Writing clearly
Providing logical organization
Using articles appropriately
Revising
Citing sources and avoiding plagiarism
Punctuating accurately
Avoiding wordiness
Improving graphics

Each tutor module consists of two parts: an instructional section and a practice section. The instructional section introduces the writing topic and presents the basic principles and strategies for carrying out the module's writing tasks. The choice of principles and strategies is based on available research. For example, the revision module makes use of strategies shown by Wallace and Hayes (1991) and Wallace, Hayes, Hatch, Miller, Moser, and Silk (1996) to produce improved revision. The clarity module uses strategies that Schriver (1992) developed and tested—strategies that significantly improve writers' abilities to identify text that will confuse readers. The modules on organization, thesis statements, and addressing a general audience make use of strategies evaluated for effectiveness by Felker, Pickering, Charrow, Holland, and Redish (1981) and Hillocks (1986).

In the practice section, the student is asked to apply the rules and principles presented in the instructional section to a sequence of exercises. In these exercises, they read a text and evaluate it for its adherence to the principles outlined in the instructional section. Then, as feedback, they are shown how an expert writer responded to the same exercise

ADDRESSING A GENERAL AUDIENCE: AN ILLUSTRATION OF HOW THE PEDAGOGICAL PRINCIPLES ARE APPLIED IN THE MODULES

The Audience Module is designed to address a common writing problem that occurs when technically sophisticated writers attempt to address general or non-technical audiences. The problem is that technically sophisticated writers often overestimate what general audiences know. The result is that the audience may be confused by unfamiliar terms and concepts and may have no idea why the topic is important.

The module starts by discussing the professional importance of addressing a general audience. It points out that, on the job, a scientist or engineer typically has to communicate with many people who are not specialists in their field: bosses, clients, and possibly coworkers on multidisciplinary teams. This is an application of Principle 1: Provide clearly defined goals. Then the module introduces five principles for writing clearly to general audiences:

1. Define unfamiliar terms
2. Clarify abstract language
3. Use concrete examples and commonsense analogies
4. Catch the reader's interest early
5. Explain why the topic is important

This is an application of Principle 3: Decompose complex skills.

Each principle is explained and illustrated. Figure 9.1 shows some of the material explaining and illustrating the principle, "Use concrete examples." After each principle is illustrated, the student is asked to answer a few questions relevant to the principle. For example, after students read the material in Fig. 9.1, they are asked to decide whether several sample sentences would profit from concrete examples (See Fig. 9.2). This exercise is an application of Principle 2: Integrate instruction with practice; and Principle 4: Promote active participation.

After each decision, the student receives immediate feedback in the form shown in Fig. 9.2. This is an application of Principle 6: Provide immediate feedback

FIGURE 9.1. A screen that illustrates the principle, "Provide concrete examples."

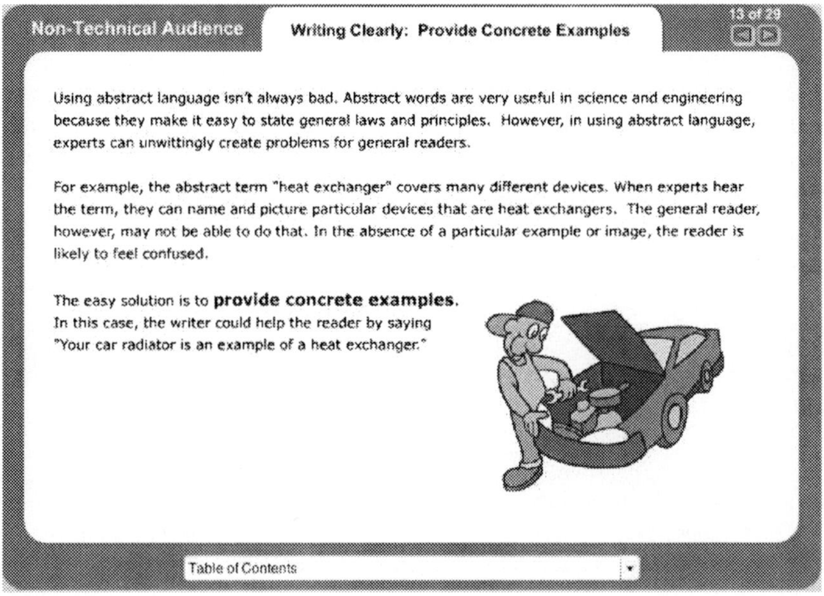
Non-Technical Audience
Writing Clearly: Provide Concrete Examples
13 of 29
Using abstract language isn't always bad. Abstract words are very useful in science and engineering because they make it easy to state general laws and principles. However, in using abstract language, experts can unwittingly create problems for general readers.
For example, the abstract term "heat exchanger" covers many different devices. When experts hear the term, they can name and picture particular devices that are heat exchangers. The general reader, however, may not be able to do that. In the absence of a particular example or image, the reader is likely to feel confused.
The easy solution is to **provide concrete examples.**
In this case, the writer could help the reader by saying "Your car radiator is an example of a heat exchanger."
Table of Contents

FIGURE 9.2. An exercise designed to promote the student's active participation in learning the principle, "Use concrete examples."

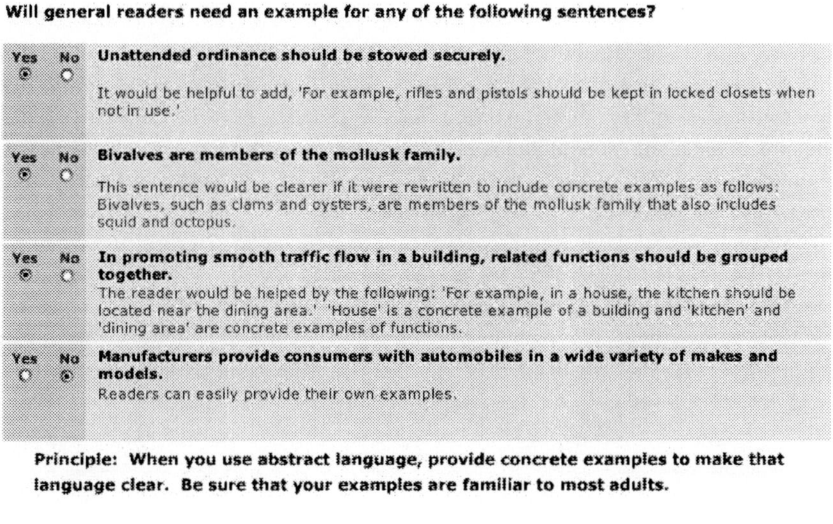
Will general readers need an example for any of the following sentences?
Yes No
Unattended ordinance should be stowed securely.
It would be helpful to add, 'For example, rifles and pistols should be kept in locked closets when not in use.'
Yes No
Bivalves are members of the mollusk family.
This sentence would be clearer if it were rewritten to include concrete examples as follows: Bivalves, such as clams and oysters, are members of the mollusk family that also includes squid and octopus.
Yes No
In promoting smooth traffic flow in a building, related functions should be grouped together.
The reader would be helped by the following: 'For example, in a house, the kitchen should be located near the dining area.' 'House' is a concrete example of a building and 'kitchen' and 'dining area' are concrete examples of functions.
Yes No
Manufacturers provide consumers with automobiles in a wide variety of makes and models.
Readers can easily provide their own examples.
Principle: When you use abstract language, provide concrete examples to make that language clear. Be sure that your examples are familiar to most adults.

HOW FORMATIVE ASSESSMENT MADE US RETHINK
THE DESIGN OF THE AUDIENCE MODULE

When we had our first working version of the Audience Module running, we recruited 10 students to try it out. Their task was to work through the module and comment, as they worked, on anything they liked, anything they disliked, and anything that confused them.

Results for the Instructional Section

In general, the participants responded positively to the instructional section of the module. The formative evaluation revealed a variety of minor problems. These included:

- a number of typos, .
- an example that did not work, and
- the onscreen robot that was intended to make the interface seem user-friendly, but actually annoyed a number of the participants.

These problems were easily fixed.

However, formative assessment also revealed a major problem. In the discussion on defining terms, the module suggests that words such as *torque, enzyme, maser, titration,* and *entropy* may require definition when included in texts for a general audience. Some of our participants said that we were being too hard on the audience, and that most would know those words. Clearly the module was not being persuasive about one of the central principles that the module addresses— namely, that general audiences may not know some terms that are quite familiar to those with technical educations.

To deal with this problem, we did two things. First, we conducted a study, to be published elsewhere, demonstrating that the greater a person's familiarity with a technical term, the more he or she overestimates the percentage of people in the population who also understand that term (see Table 9.1). Both statistically and practically, the difference is highly significant.

Second, we added the exercise shown in Figure 9.3 to the module. In this exercise, the student is asked to estimate the percentage of college graduates who know each of the words on the left. When the student makes a choice, the correct answer is shown on the right. (The answers are derived from Dale & O'Rourke, 1981.) We are now assessing the effectiveness of this kind of exercise to improve the accuracy of students' estimates of other people's knowledge of technical terms.

TABLE 9.1. The Greater a Person's Familiarity With a Term, the More They Overestimate the Percentage of People Who Also Understand the Term.

	Rater's familiarity with the term			
	Not at all	I've heard it	I think I know it	I'm sure I know it
Percent Overestimation	-1.02	8.82	13.4	28.10

FIGURE 9.3. Exercise Designed to Improve Students Estimate of Other People's Knowledge of Technical Terms.

Try to guess what portion of College graduates know the meanings of the following terms: (The answers the tutor provides are based on surveys of US college graduates.)

quadratic	○ 19%	○ 41.5%	○ 57%	● 86%	○ 99%	41.5%
Arrhythmia	○ 19%	○ 44%	● 58%	○ 78%	○ 96%	19%
dicotyledon	○ 21%	○ 38%	○ 52%	● 73%	○ 99%	52%
electrolyte	○ 17%	○ 36%	○ 59.5%	○ 82%	● 95%	59.5%
anion	○ 17.5%	○ 33%	● 51%	○ 76%	○ 95%	17.5%
scintillate	○ 19%	○ 31%	○ 55%	○ 73%	● 92%	19%
syndrome	○ 31%	○ 42%	○ 58%	● 82%	○ 98%	58%
quadrant	○ 22%	○ 34%	○ 63%	○ 82%	● 98%	34%
viscous	○ 17%	○ 35.5%	○ 55%	○ 74%	○ 100%	

Results for the Practice Section

Although participants were fairly positive in evaluating the instructional section of the Audience Module, the same was not true of the practice section.

In our first version of the module, patterned on some of the studies described earlier, the practice section involved a sequence of texts and a set of six questions about each text. Five of the questions concerned the principles listed previously, and a final question asked the student to provide a holistic evaluation of the text's quality on a 4-point scale. For example, participants might be asked to specify which in a list of terms from the text should be better defined for a general audience or whether particular passages were too abstract for the audience. Participants were given feedback immediately after completing each question— both visually, by marking answers right and wrong on screen, and auditorily, by an onscreen robot that provided auditory instructions and feedback.

Generally, participants found the exercises dull and repetitious. The reason, we believe, is that they were asked to answer six similar questions about each text. Further, many found the prescriptive feedback annoying and overly precise. For example, they might ask, "Why was a quality rating of 2 definitely wrong and a quality rating of 3 definitely correct?" Certainly a valid complaint.

In response to the participants' critiques, we completely reorganized the practice section. We abandoned the strategy of asking students to answer a fixed set of questions about each text. Instead, we adopted a three-step pattern for each exercise.

- The first step (see Fig. 9.4) was to present a text on the left and to ask the student to check off the major problems with the text on the right. Most texts had one or two major problems.
- The second step was to show another two-page spread (see Fig. 9.5). The left-hand page presented the original text with annota-

FIGURE 9.4. The student is shown a student-written text and asked to evaluate the text's problems.

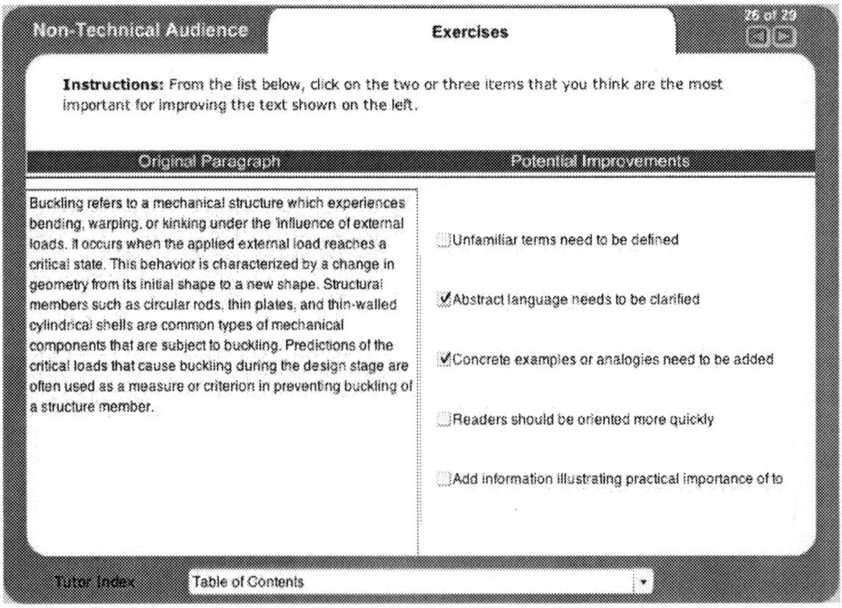

FIGURE 9.5. On the left, students are shown an annotated version of the original text. The numbered comments are color coded to indicate which parts of the text they refer to. On the right, students are shown a revised version of the text. Comments explaining why changes were made in color-coded sections of the text may be viewed by scrolling the text.

Non-Technical Audience	Exercises	27 of 29

Instructions: The expert's reasons for marking and changing the text are shown in numbered comments under the text. The comment refers to the parts of the text that matches it in color.

Experts Comments on Original Paragraph	Experts Version of Paragraph
Buckling refers to a mechanical structure which experiences bending, warping, or kinking under the influence of external loads. It occurs when the applied external load reaches a critical state. This behavior is characterized by a change in geometry from its initial shape to a new shape. Structural members such as circular rods, thin plates, and thin-walled cylindrical shells are common types of mechanical components that are subject to buckling. Predictions of the critical loads that cause buckling during the design stage are often used as a measure or criterion in preventing buckling of a structure member. 1. This sentence is very abstract. Abstract terms such as "mechanical structure" and "external loads" need examples. 2. The term "critical state" should be better explained. 3. This sentence is ambiguous. Is it buckling that occurs	Buckling is the bending, warping, or kinking that happens to mechanical structures such as a beam or car frame when they are subjected to strong loads or forces such as occur in collisions or when the structures are loaded heavy weights. More specifically, buckling occurs when such a load causes the structure to reach a "critical state," the point at which the structure cannot return to its original geometry from the structure's initial shape to a new shape: under enough weight, for example, the straight line of a board may change to a curve. Structural members such as circular rods, thin plates, and thin-walled cylindrical shells are common types of mechanical components that are subject to buckling. In order to build structures that resist buckling, engineers make calculations that predict critical loads, and design their structures accordingly.

Tutor Index	Table of Contents

tions by an expert writer listing major problems with the text. The right-hand page presented the expert's revision of the original text with annotations by the expert explaining why the changes were made.

- In the third step (see Fig. 9.6), students were shown the judgments they had made about the text in Step 1 and asked to judge how well their judgments matched those of the expert.

A second round of formative assessment with 10 new students indicated that, in the new version of the module, students continued to have a positive view of the instructional section, but, most important, they now also had a positive view of the practice section.

Because the results of the formative assessment led us to make extensive revisions, we have not had time to carry out a summative assessment of the Audience Module. We hope this assessment can be carried out in the fall of 2006.

FIGURE 9.6. On the left, students are shown the diagnosis of the text problems they made before seeing the expert's revision. On the right, they are asked to judge how well their judgments match those of the expert.

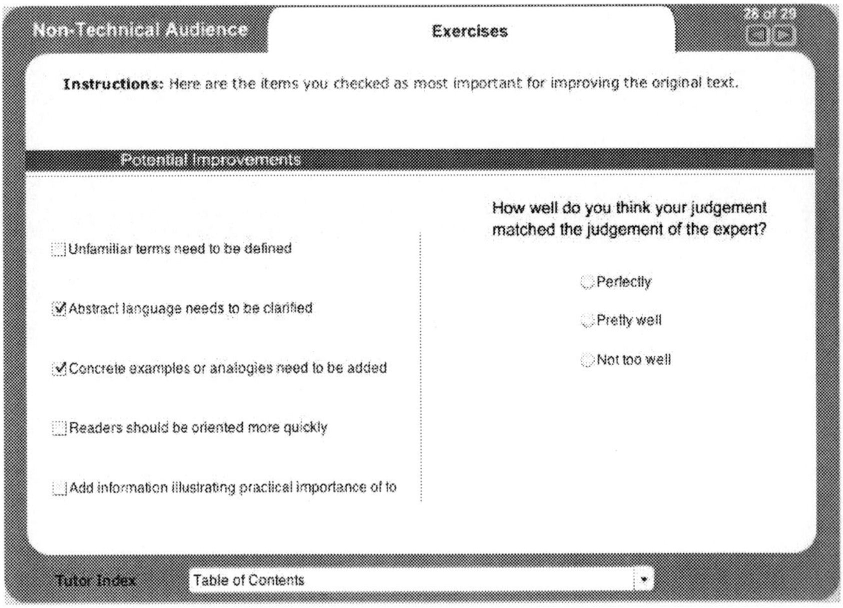

ASSESSMENT OF THE THESIS STATEMENT MODULE

The Thesis Statement Module

The objectives of the Thesis Statement Module are to: (a) help students recognize that thesis statements provide a useful tool for making texts easy to understand, (b) help students write more effective thesis statements, and (c) encourage students to use thesis statements in their own texts. The Thesis Statement Module, like the Audience Module, consists of an instructional section and a practice section.

Instructional Section. The instructional section presents these principles:

1. Thesis statements are statements that tell the reader what the text will be about.

2. They help readers to decide whether they want to read the text; if they decide to read, they help the reader understand the text.
3. They should be placed early in the text.
4. Pointers i.e., explicit statements such as "I intend to show . . ." and "The purpose of this memo is . . .") enhance the effectiveness of thesis statements.

Practice Section. The script for the Thesis Statement Module was written after we assessed the Audience Module. Therefore, we were able to use the revised design of the Audience Module practice section as a template for the practice section of the Framing Statement Module.

Formative Assessment

Procedure. Ten students, recruited through the Psychology Department experiment pool, were asked to work though the Thesis Statement Module and comment on anything that occurred to them such as things they liked, things they did not like, and things that confused them. They were also asked for summary comments after they completed the module.

Results. Generally, the formative assessment indicated that the students liked both the text and format of the module. Specifically, students commented positively on the clarity of the text and identified specific sections (e.g., the section on pointers), as particularly helpful. Some said they liked "the flow" of the material. The practice section of the Thesis Statement Module did not receive the negative feedback that we had received in response to the first version of practice section of the Audience Module. We believe this is because the practice section of the Thesis Statement Module was modeled on the revised and improved version of the practice section of the Audience Module.

In addition, the results of the formative assessment provided valuable information concerning a number of low-level problems with the tutor text and interface. These included: (a) the identification of a number of typos, (b) the recognition that the scroll bar used in the examples in the practice section needs to be made more visually evident (several students failed to notice that the example texts could be scrolled), and (c) a suggestion for a change in the options available for answering questions.

The formative assessment also revealed a problem that is important for the writing tutor as a whole. Some students reported that their high school teachers had taught them to avoid first person and to use passive voice when writing about scientific or technical topics. Although some journals forbid the use of first person and discourage active voice, this practice is changing, especially concerning the use of active voice. Further, there are many kinds of writing that scientists and engineers may engage in where first person and active voice are quite appropriate.

It seems probable that the tutor needs a module that specifically discusses the use of active and passive voice and of first and third person in scientific writing.

Summative Assessment

One aspect of the tutor that might be considered problematic is that it requires students to evaluate texts they did not write, and it does not require students to produce and evaluate their own texts. The question is, "Will the evaluative skills that students acquire by practicing with texts they did not write transfer to their own texts?" Research summarized by Hillocks (1986) and Hayes (2004) indicates that such transfer can be achieved. This transfer question is addressed here.

To assess the effectiveness of the module in a real classroom setting, we compared students' use of thesis statements in two presentations of the same class. In one presentation, fall 2004, the tutor was available to students; in the other, fall 2002, it was not. The course, "Introduction to Intelligence in Animals and Machines," is a large introductory course that draws students from all of the colleges on campus. In this course, students are required to write a five-page research paper on any 1 of roughly 30 topics in psychology. The instructions for writing the paper were identical in 2002 and 2004 and indicated that 5% of the grade would depend on providing a clear thesis statement. In 2004, the instructor announced that the Thesis Statement Module was available on the course Web site, but that its use was not required. In addition, in section meetings, the teaching assistants encouraged students to use the module when writing their papers. At the beginning of the Fall 2002 and Fall 2004 semesters, we asked students for permission to copy the first page of their essays for research purposes. We then copied the first pages of the essays and removed any marks identifying the student and the semester. The first pages were then randomly intermixed and blind-graded for the presence or absence of a thesis statement and the presence or absence of a pointer. Table 9.2 shows the percentage of thesis statements and the percentage of pointers in 2002 when the module was not available and in 2004 when it was available. The difference in the percentage of thesis statements was significant ($X^2 = 16.153$, $df = 1$. $p < .001$), as was the percentage of pointers ($X^2 = 4.807$, $df=1$, $p < .05$).

TABLE 9.2. Percentages of Thesis Statements and Pointers Employed by Students Who Did and Did Not Have the Tutor Available.

	% Thesis Statements	% Pointers
2002 Tutor not available	39.5	19.4
2004 Tutor available	61.9	30.2

The improvements both in the use of thesis statements and of pointers are substantial from an instructional perspective. We feel that these gains would be even larger if students had been required to use the tutor, rather than simply having it available.

The assessments procedures that we have described can answer this question; "Will the tutor be effective when it is used?" However, they will not answer this question; "Will instructors and students actually make use of the tutor?" To answer this question, we plan to collect data on the frequency with which the tutor is used once it is deployed at Carnegie Mellon and on the other campuses. Because access to the tutor will be through a Carnegie Mellon server, it will be easy to collect such data both locally and at the distant campuses.

In addition to collecting frequency-of-use data, we will conduct surveys of faculty and students using the tutor to determine the degree of faculty and student satisfaction with the tutor and to obtain suggestions for its improvement.

VARIOUS WAYS IN WHICH THE TUTOR MAY BE USED

We anticipate that the tutor may be used in a variety of ways. One possibility is that individual students, concerned with their writing skills, may choose to use the tutor on their own. Another possibility is that instructors may require their classes to use the tutor before a writing assignment. A third possibility is that an instructor may require students who have specific weaknesses in writing to use particular tutor modules (e.g., the module on organization). A fourth possibility is that the tutor may be used as supplementary instruction in writing centers.

To help instructors keep track of students' tutor use, the tutor can print out a certificate indicating the student's level of performance on each module. If they wish, instructors can require that students turn in the certificates so they can check on students' tutor use.

WHO CAN BENEFIT?

Potentially, the tutor can help many students who are now not receiving adequate instruction. Because the tutor will be readily accessible through the Web, it can be useful for all 2- and 4-year colleges in English-speaking countries. We believe that most engineering and science students can improve their communication skills by using the tutor. However, those who are likely to receive the greatest benefits are underprepared students and students for whom English is not their first language. Educational institutions will also benefit because the tutor is a cost-effective way to deliver writing instruction to science and engineering students.

SUMMARY

We have argued that engineering and science students are not acquiring the basic writing skills in college that they will need in their professional careers. To help solve this problem, we are developing an online basic writing tutor that presents writing principles, allows students to practice the application of those principles, and provides them with immediate feedback. The primary instructional strategy underlying the tutor is judgment training—that is, teaching students to evaluate texts.

So far two modules have been completed. The Thesis Statement Module has been assessed and shown to increase students' use of thesis statements in papers they wrote for a psychology course. Formative assessment of the Audience Module has led to extensive revision and reorganization. The moral we take from this experience is that even if you use good design principles and make use of the literature, you can still create a tutor that does not work. Assessment is an essential step in tutor design!

POSTSCRIPT

Dick Hayes

I got to know Bill Smith in the early 1980s when he was at Pitt and I was across the street at CMU. It was an exciting time. The promise (or threat) of empirical research in writing was causing enthusiasm in some and fear and loathing in others. Bill and I were natural allies because, as empirically oriented souls, we were on the same side of this deep cultural divide. It is nice to have an ally who is friendly, funny, and very smart.

Bill is a brilliant experimenter. I was blown away when I read his article with Warren Combs on covert cuing in sentence combining (Smith & Combs, 1980). The central insight in the article was that an educational procedure, such as instruction in sentence combining, might have its effect either by increasing skills or conveying a covert message. As the authors put it, "Thus, students may not be learning *how* to construct longer, more complex sentence from SC practice, but rather that they *should* do so" (p. 19; italics original). In fact, the authors found that simply telling students that their audience consisted of highly intelligent people who were influenced by long, complex sentences changed the students' writing in much the same way as 2 hours of instruction in sentence combining. The point was not to disparage sentence combining, which they were careful not to do, but rather to point out a general problem in understanding the efficacy of educational procedures. Are students being taught new skills or are they being cued to apply

skills they already have? The question is relevant to lots of educational procedures. Indeed, it is relevant to the tutor described in this chapter. Did the Thesis
Statement Module teach students how to write thesis statements or did it just
remind them that they should write one? We do not know the answer yet, but it is
important for us to find out because it will help us understand how the tutor is
working.

Bill once said to me that if a student has written one good paper, then he or
she can write. This struck me as a neat insight. I realize now that it was of a piece
with the sentence-combining study and indeed may be a Bill Smith theme. Bill is
acutely aware that students may not reveal their skills unless they have a good reason to do so. One of the teacher's difficult tasks is to figure out how to get students
to exercise the skills they already have.

I end with a story that may not be widely known. I believe it is a true story
because Bill told it to me and because it fits with his skeptical turn of mind. My
memory of the details, however, may have gotten a little ragged with time.

Bill's colleagues, like most writing instructors, believed that they should grade
students' essays on the quality of the writing and definitely not on whether they
agree with the students' politics or point of view. This is certainly an admirable
aspiration, but Bill wondered if real, human instructors actually grade that way. So
he crafted an essay arguing that, all things considered, Hitler really was not such a
bad guy. He made sure that the punctuation was perfect, the style impeccable, and
the organization rigorously logical. Then he inserted the essay surreptitiously into
the placement essay grading process, where it was graded by a number of writing
instructors. Lamentably, no one gave this very well-written essay an A.

The field of composition needs (but does not necessarily deserve) more people like Bill Smith.

REFERENCES

Ammer, J. J. (1998). Peer evaluation model for enhancing writing performance of students
with learning disabilities. *Reading and Writing Quarterly: Overcoming Learning Difficulties,*
14, 263-282.

Anderson, J. R., Boyle, C. F., Farrell, R., & Reiser, B. (1984, June). Cognitive principles in the
design of computer tutors. *Proceedings of the sixth annual conference of the Cognitive
Science Society,* Boulder, CO: Institute of Cognitive Science, University of Colorado.

Barrass, R. (1978). *Scientists must write.* London: Chapman Hall.

Bartlett, E. J. (1981). *Learning to write: Some cognitive and linguistic components.* Washington, DC:
Center for Applied Linguistics.

Benson, N. L. (1979). *The effect of peer feedback during the writing process on writing performance,
revision behavior, and attitude toward writing.* Unpublished doctoral dissertation,
University of Colorado at Boulder.

Brown, J. S., Collins, A., & Duguid, P. (1989). Situated cognition and the culture of learning. *Educational Researcher, 33,* 32-42.

Clifford, J. (1981). Composing in stages: The effects of a collaborative pedagogy. *Research in the Teaching of English, 15*(1), 37–58.

Collins, A., Brown, J. S., & Newman, S. E. (1989). Cognitive apprenticeship: Teaching the craft of reading, writing, and mathematics. In L. B. Resnick (Ed.), *Knowing, learning, and instruction: Essays in honor of Robert Glaser* (pp. 453-494). Hillsdale, NJ: Lawrence Erlbaum Associates.

Dale, E., & O'Rourke, J. (1981). *The living word vocabulary: A national vocabulary inventory.* Chicago: World Book-Childcraft International.

Farnham-Diggory, S. (1992). *Cognitive processes in education.* New York: Harper & Row.

Farrell, K. J. (1977). *A comparison of three instructional approaches for teaching written composition to high school juniors: Teacher lecture, peer evaluation, and group tutoring.* Unpublished doctoral dissertation, Boston University School of Education.

Felker, D., Pickering, C. V., Holland, M., & Redish, J. C. (1981). *Guidelines for document designers.* Washington, DC: American Institutes for Research.

Gagne, R., & Briggs, L. J. (1974). *Principles of instructional design.* New York: Holt, Rinehart & Winston.

Graves, D. H. (1994). *A fresh look at writing.* Portsmouth, NH: Heinemann.

Hayes, J. R. (2004). What triggers revision? In L. Allal, L. Chanquoy, P. Largy, & Y. Rouiller (Eds.), *Revision of written language: Cognitive and instructional processes* (pp. 9-20). Dordrecht, The Netherlands: Kluwer.

Hayes, J. R., Flower, L., Schriver, K. A., Stratman, J. F., & Carey, L. (1987). Cognitive processes in revision. In S. Rosenberg (Ed.), *Advances in applied psycholinguistics: Vol. 2 Reading, writing, and language learning.* Cambridge, England: Cambridge University Press.

Hillocks, G. (1986). *Research in written composition: New directions for teaching.* Urbana, IL: ERIC Clearinghouse on Reading and Communication Skills and National Conference on Research in English.

Kemp, J. H. (1979). *A comparison of two procedures for improving the writing of developmental writers.* Unpublished doctoral dissertation, University of Georgia.

Pemberton, M. (1995). Rethinking the WAC/Writing Center connection. *The Writing Center Journal, 15*(2), 116–133.

Rosen, M. (1973). *A structured classroom writing method: An experiment in teaching rhetoric to remedial college English students.* Unpublished doctoral dissertation, New York University.

Rosow, E. G. (1996). *The effects of analytic assessment strategies on second graders' ability to identify revision needs in their writing.* Unpublished doctoral dissertation, University of Connecticut.

Rowley, K., Carlson, P., & Miller, T. (1998). A cognitive technology to teach composition skills: Four studies with the RWISE writing tutor. *Journal of Educational Computing Research, 18*(3), 259–296.

Russell, D. R. (1991). *Writing in the academic disciplines, 1870–1990.* Carbondale: Southern Illinois University Press.

Sageev, P. (1994). *Helping researchers write... so managers can understand.* Columbus, OH: Battelle.

Sager, C. (1973). *Improving the quality of written composition through pupil use of rating scale.* Unpublished doctoral dissertation, Boston University School of Education.

Schneider, W. (1985). Training high-performance skills: Fallacies and guidelines. *Human Factors, 27*(3), 28–30.

Schriver, K. A. (1992). Teaching writers to anticipate readers' needs: A classroom-evaluated pedagogy. *Written Communication, 9*(2), 179–208.

Smith, W. L., & Combs, W. (1980). The effects of covert and overt cues on written syntax. *Research in the Teaching of English, 14*, 19–38.

Tierney, R. J., Carter, M. A., & Desai, L. E. (1991). *Portfolio assessment in the reading-writing classroom.* Norwood MA: Christopher-Gordon

Wallace, D., & Hayes, J. R. (1991). Redefining revision for freshmen. *Research in the Teaching of English, 25*, 54–66.

Wallace, D., Hayes, J. R., Hatch, J. A., Miller, W., Moser, G., & Silk, C. M. (1996). Better revision in eight minutes? *Journal of Educational Psychology, 88*, 682–688.

Wright, N. J. (1975). *The effect of role playing on the improvement of freshman composition.* Unpublished doctoral dissertation, Texas A&M University.

Wunsch, D. R. (1982). The effects of written feedback, rewriting and oral group feedback on business letter writing ability. *The Delta Pi Epsilon Journal, 24*, 29–38.

Young, R. E., & Gordon, J. (1995, March 10). *Mellon College of Science Faculty Survey of Student Writing Abilities.* Unpublished manuscript.

IO

PEDAGOGICAL TRANSFORMATIONS IN A MYTHIC AGE

Joan Latchaw

UTOPIA REVISITED

Technological progress and sophistication are the crowning glory of American society, shaping our national consciousness, discourse, and economy. The myth of *technology as progress*, what Michel Foucault might call a statement, underlies and provides a context for discourse in particular fields and disciplines. Always existing in a network, statements play an integral role in defining a discipline. In education, technology as progress comes to mean "technological literacy is necessary for success." Statements determine what topics and issues are acceptable, what constitutes the truth, and who is allowed to speak. Statements about technology regulate the prevailing rhetorical discourse that emerges in newspapers, TV magazines, and travel brochures: Powerful metaphorical phrases, such as the "global village," "technology as the new frontier," and "America as the land of opportunity," serve as "*totalitarian theories.*"[1] They shape the way we think, act, and make decisions.

The technology myth gets played out in national educational policies like Bill Clinton's Technology Literacy Challenge goals, which received broad recognition and support despite the failure to affect social and curricular reform. Other initiatives include wholesale adoption of course software packages, such as Blackboard and WebCt, laptop computers for every child, creation of computer labs, and computer-based reading programs. These kinds of actions, what Foucault (1988) calls *tiny, local events* produce truth claims, articulations of right thinking and action.[2] Truth, according to Foucault, marks differences between what we say. I argue that a certain set of truth claims about education (what people say) determine educational policies, practices, and perspectives. These truth claims shape right thinking and action—not in an absolute sense, but what people and institutions perceive and articulate as proper and virtuous. Such claims lead to hardware and software development, which people *believe* enhances critical thinking and literacy skills.[3] These beliefs have not been substantiated by research (Mergendollar, 1996; Segal, 1996; Selfe, 1999a, 1999b). However, truth claims, by definition, need no proof; rather, truth is generated and sustained by discourse.

This deep faith in the power of technology contributes to a *utopian patina* (Rouzie, 2001), which masks the complexity of social dynamics in online environments, the negative effects on individual students, the pressure of institutional initiatives, and the power hierarchies always present between teachers and students.

---

[1]Foucault (1980) particularly faults psychoanalysis and Marxism for producing a "halo of theory that would unite" fragmentary knowledges, arguments, and discourses into a false "solid and homogeneous theoretical terrain" (p. 87). Foucault's project is to expose disciplinary regulation and create challenges "against the institutions and against effects of the knowledge and power that invests scientific [and other disciplinary] discourse" (p. 87). Foucault calls for a genealogy of knowledge, which would break the silence imposed by theory and lead to strategic action. He provides a mechanism for movement based on the belief that culture is "constituted first and foremost as an open, altogether undecided game with changeable, reversible rules and interactions and 'in such a way that none of these interactions appear to be of priority or absolutely totalizing. Any of them can enter a game which goes beyond them; and conversely, any of them can have an effect, however locally limited it may be, on another to which it belongs and by which it is surrounded'" (Nilson, 1998, p. 66). Foucault's insistence that all people can enter a game and exercise power in locally situated situations is fundamental to my argument about and analysis of teaching with technology.

[2]Foucault does not use truth in an ontological or epistemological sense. Rather Foucault follows Nietzsche, who embarked on a process of truth-telling (see Nilson, 1998, chap. 6). For Foucault, this process includes "care of the self" (a critical elaboration, modification, and transformation of the self) and intellectual engagement with society in order to "oppose the conservative power which prescribed truth as creed and certainty" (Nilson, 1998, p. 90). Truth, therefore, is relative, historical, unstable, conventional, disciplinary, and linguistic.

[3]In the early 1990s, I witnessed the demonstration of an IBM-produced software package for beginning readers. Its interface and graphics were visually stimulating, with various colored syllables falling from the top of the screen. Young readers were asked to quickly combine the

Consequently, many teachers adopt computer-mediated communication (CMC) technology under pressure; face tensions and conflicts, sometimes requiring immediate attention; and confront disgruntled students, who find little value in these novel practices. For example, teachers are not always aware of disputes, which develop outside their field of vision. Even when conflicts arise under the teacher's watchful eye, the speed of dialogue (often unconstrained in digital environments) can create a momentum, which sweeps the emotions and silences the intellect. Analysis, discussion, negotiation, and resolution are extremely difficult to accomplish under such strained circumstances.

At a more insidious level, teachers and administrators mistakenly come to believe that technology *is* pedagogy. That is, the marketing of the courseware to administrators, school systems, and faculty suggests an inherent and coherent pedagogical design—driven more by technological expertise and capability than educational theory.

Demythologizing progress requires constant attention to critical inquiry—for teachers, scholars, administrators, and government officials. Through Foucault (1980), who was deeply committed to making people less vulnerable to criticism of "institutions, practices, discourses" (p. 80), I probe society's belief in technological progress from an educational perspective, trace a brief history of composition's developing truth claims, challenge some disciplinary assumptions and practices based on the truth claims, and propose guidelines and directions that might serve as an alternative set of truth claims.

MYTHIC ENCULTURATIONS

Because we are bombarded with claims about technology-rich education from the media, school boards, and software developers, we are enculturated through discourse to accept certain educational policies or precepts as an ultimate unquestioned good.[4] For instance, rhetorical phrases such as "Clinton's Technology

---

syllables to form words. When asked about the theory underlying the reading program, the facilitator of the session said the program was based on phonics. When asked how children would then learn to combine words that were not phonetically intuitive, she answered, "They just do," and had no research to substantiate that claim. (It appeared that neither the developers nor the presenter had a clear theoretical or pedagogical understanding of the application.) This answer is disturbing, particularly when the "consumers" of such software, such as administrators and elementary education teachers, have little or limited knowledge of linguistic, reading, or educational developmental theories. It was equally disturbing that the application was so visually rich that thinking "through to theory" was a challenge, even if viewers did have such knowledge.

[4]I am not discounting the value of public policy goals in providing universal access to children and families: for Internet communication, knowledge gathering (i.e., medical conditions, housing opportunities), research, word processing, business applications. Rather, I lament lost opportunities for learning, which would result from computer applications informed by greater critical and pedagogical expertise and experience.

Initiative" and Bush's "No Child Left Behind," along with other discursive elements, like slogans, proverbs, maxims, or symbols, become cultural artifacts, which
ultimately serve as "object[s] of interpretation" (Prado, 1995, p. 132). Educators
interpret the presidential slogans to mean that children with computers learn
more efficiently and effectively, that children who acquire digital literacy early are
more likely to succeed professionally, and that technologically savvy citizens will
eliminate social problems. Slogans like "No Child [will be] Left Behind" also have
a powerful affective quality, appealing to pathos. The phrase has a strong rhetorical appeal, in its grammatical construction, as an appeal and a promise. Someone
(unnamed and yet to be determined) will not allow children to be neglected.
"They" or some imagined institution or force will take action to avoid such neg-
lect, easily associated with physical or emotional abandonment. The implied
imperative spreads the responsibility to everyone: parents, institutions, and concerned citizens. It subtly implies guilt for those more culturally advantaged. The
goals and expectations embedded in such slogans circulate as truth claims, which
become normal and desirable.

Influenced by the Clinton and Bush slogans, school administrators begin to
take some of these truth claims as personal beliefs, espousing them to other
administrators, faculty, and businesses. Not uncommonly, administrators make
deals with corporations, such as IBM and Apple, which sometimes subsidize computer acquisitions and software for entire school districts. Such activities at the
local level, in turn, determine the control and shape of discourse. For instance,
teachers committed to the truth claim that schools should train students in digital
literacies talk to other teachers, parents, and students about incorporating Power
Point presentations, online discussions, and peer response applications into their
courses, using multimedia in lectures, and collaborating with technology support
staff. In turn, many high school students, assigned Power Point presentations or
Web pages as part of coursework, come to expect even more sophisticated technologies at the college level. These expectations, now considered normal, get
expressed to college administrators and teachers who respond accordingly
through administrative decisions.[5]

Such chaining of events through discourse is an example of what Foucault
calls *normalization*, a regulative and corrective mechanism, which operates through
enculturation. (Foucault is primarily concerned about normalization in science,
government, psychiatry, and law.) The social body within a particular discipline
imposes "disciplinary coercions whose purpose is in fact to assure the cohesion of"

---

[5]The decision to adopt Blackboard at my university was based primarily on student needs and
expectations, a surprising discovery given my skeptical attitude about unilateral administrative
decisions about technology; these attitudes were not unfounded given prior directives about distance education and the adoption of Lotus Notes. However, I began to question my own truth
claims about external and hierarchical forces of power concerning imposed technologies in
higher education.

the social body through natural rules or codes, that is norms (Foucault, 1980, p. 106). Because they are naturalized, norms are generally not articulated. In this country, people submit themselves unknowingly to ideas about technology, education, and governance, which get reified through discourse. Normalization is powerful because it is invisible and occurs through common networks of relations—from personal conversations to disciplinary decision-making bodies to documents, such as mission and policy statements. Critical reflection becomes difficult and exceptional when ideas, beliefs, and/or actions *seem* internally motivated, informally expressed, and smoothly executed.

Normalization is powerful in producing conformity, especially when neither the pressures nor the consequences of noncompliance are recognized. At my university, Information Technology Services (ITS) offers the faculty monthly workshops on various functions and features of the Blackboard system, technology roundtable discussions, and presentations by faculty who have integrated the software into their courses. The courseware provides a repository for course materials; incorporates easy communication features such as e-mail, discussion boards, and archives; and includes administrative functions such as grading sheets. The computer support staff reports that students are learning in new and exciting ways and point to nationally recognized programs like the online aviation curriculum. They also report that the number of Blackboard courses has grown in the last year from 450 to 1100, over a 100% increase. The Blackboard ITS services are represented as strictly voluntary, and, on a literal level, they are.

However, if the Blackboard faculty continues to grow exponentially, the number of nonusers will eventually become abnormal, in the Foucauldian sense. The pressure to conform is an example of Foucault's (1978) notion of biopower, the creation of self-regulatory docile bodies who, having been enculturated, take it upon themselves to remain "good, healthy subjects" (pp. 143–144). Resisting bodies, failing to incorporate technology into courses, may eventually be considered pedagogical derelicts or reactionaries. Even nonresistors, innocent of technology's influence, may be adversely affected. At my institution, current attitudes about technology are subtly influencing tenure and promotion decisions, unknowingly to the applicants. During a recent college-wide promotion and tenure committee meeting, I noted that group members always mentioned implementation of Blackboard and other technologies as an automatic good. Recognized as innovators, these faculty members are rewarded with enhanced reputations, status, and economic conditions. The implication that technology is pedagogy profoundly affects public school systems, universities, individual scholars, and particular disciplines.

It would be far more productive to imagine technology as "a stalking horse for profound pedagogical change" (Mergendollar, 1996, p. 44). The Accelerated Reader program, widely adopted in elementary and middle-school systems, is lauded for motivating students to read more and for simplifying the teacher's work. Each child reads a book of her choice, based on a pretest, and then takes a multiple-choice quiz on the computer. The student's progress is tracked on a point system, which the teacher uses to calculate a reading grade. Although the advantages cannot be denied, they eclipse ideologies, policies, and pedagogies driving educational systems.

Some sequential stalking can expose ideologies and assumptions, which need reexamination. First, as my colleague Carol Lloyd noted, the pretest reflects hierarchical structures. Schools track students, sorting them into perceived abilities, a highly controversial practice, which establishes power differentials and sets the mark for achievement.[6] Second, the technological innovation signals a backward pedagogical shift, from classroom discussion—ideally a forum for exchanging ideas and thinking analytically—to knowledge telling and information gathering. Third, students are more likely to be motivated by grades than interest or joy in reading. For Lloyd, the technology triggered a series of ideological questions: What *is* reading? Why do we read? Why do we teach children to read? What does it mean to be innovative?

COMPOSITION'S CIRCULATION OF TECHNOLOGICAL TRUTHS

By adopting innovative courseware hastily, mandating computerized writing classrooms, and overvaluing peer critique, Composition Studies pictures itself as a technologically and pedagogically progressive discipline. This vision has created a whole new layer of issues and problems. In CMC interactions, lines of power and authority between teachers and students (and among teachers collaborating in online environments) sometime become confused, obscured, and unclear; crisis management impedes course goals; community expectations and conventions subsume rights and concerns of individual students and teachers; and identity issues often disrupt the learning environment.

From my own experience as a teacher using CMC and from an emerging body of research, I am convinced that utopian visions of technology have *not* been realized and will not be as long as a number of truth claims about pedagogy remain unaccounted for in the clamor to build "smart classrooms" and construct ever more lucrative distance learning programs. Teacher/scholars expressing ideas about the power of technology are thought to be speaking the truth, which means "making the right moves in a discourse, where 'right' is that dictated or tolerated by a truth-regime's criteria for what is acceptable, that sanctioned or excluded by its mechanisms for distinguishing truth and falsity, and that which is

---

[6]Mike Rose (1989) tells a poignant story in *Lives on the Boundary* about two accidentally "switched students" who were placed in the wrong track in elementary school. The remedial label and corresponding curricula adversely affected one of the students for many years.

in accordance with its belief-determining expert judgments" (Prado, 1995, p. 124). The following set of statements functions as truth claims, defining and giving the illusion of unity to the field of composition:

- Computer technology cultivates critical thinking,
- Educators should teach computer literacy,
- Computer technology creates a community of learners,
- Computer technology encourages egalitarianism,
- Computers promote student-centered learning, the optimal academic environment, and
- Computer technology improves writing.

My discussion tracing the development of these claims, review of research, and analysis of listserv dialogues reveal that terms like *egalitarianism* and *community* mask disparities and disciplinary disputes. We need to test these truth claims because they drive research projects and classroom practice and distort the discipline's view of itself.

Clearly truth claims are sanctioned by those in positions of power because computer labs and personnel continue to be funded even in times of financial crisis, because many English Departments are teaching first-year composition in computer labs despite inconclusive evidence that using computers improves writing, and because many teachers rely heavily on peer editing workshops and online discussions despite little evidence of their effectiveness.

These practices and initiatives will go unquestioned unless we examine how truth is "produced and transmitted" under the control of "political and economic apparatuses," such as the university, writing, and media (Foucault, 1980, pp. 131–132). Foucault explains that truth is produced by "multiple forms of constraint" and induces "regular effects of power" (p. 131). Although power might suggest domination through hierarchical structures, Foucault means regular in the sense of normalization. Truth is constrained at many levels: by administrations, individual scholars, and mass media. Universities constrain truth by circulating mission statements and directives, which then induce effects of power, such as offering (or withholding) particular technology resources and services. Scholars (Foucault's specific intellectuals) constrain truth by propagating certain ideologies and discourses about technology, which affect the masses and, in that way, exert local forms of power. For example, an interrelated network of administrators, scholars, and university structures argue compellingly and produce funds for technological innovations, which in turn creates pedagogical discourse sanctioning the actions. Current pedagogical conversations not only reflect local situations and interests, but embody a decades-old history of educational reform.

Two important developments—the critical thinking movement and what composition theorists call the process movement—have drastically changed ideas about the nature of learning. The phrase *active learning* is generally interpreted to mean peer response, team projects, e-mail collaborations, and student-driven discussion. In some cases, students help construct course materials and decide curricula. From the shift in classroom practices (i.e., lecture to discussion) and curriculum development, discourse about student empowerment evolved. Teachers have turned notions of student empowerment to pedagogical advantage; student-centered learning has become nearly sacrosanct in English departments. Educators, particularly composition teachers and scholars, believe that if teachers resist leading students toward predetermined positions and if they restrain their own voices, then students will think more independently. CMC discourse asserts that when teachers "get out of the way," students will be freer to converse and think critically. Student-centered discourse circulates the notion that teachers create hierarchies and power imbalances, and if they remove themselves those imbalances will disappear. With discussion replacing lecture, student presentations and projects superceding exams, and student-driven listservs and newsgroups, these assumptions are somewhat merited. But they do not reflect the reality of most college classrooms and the student–teacher dynamic in general.

For the most part, the humanities and social sciences are adopting student-centered pedagogies reinforced by discourse about network theory. Over the last 15 years, teacher/researchers in computers and writing have developed and disseminated the idea that networked classrooms help create a community of learners, which empower students and reduce the teacher's authority. A whole cluster of truth claims traversing social, political, and cultural territory emerged, as represented by the following statement: "Networking's main advantage is the egalitarian quality of the participants' discourse, the dissolving of certain inequities—produced by gender, class, ethnicity, and personality differences—that exist in normal classroom discussions" (Eldred, 1989, p. 53). The egalitarian theory holds sway because liberationist theories inform it: social construction of knowledge, feminism, postmodernism, postcolonialism, communitarianism, and cultural studies. These theories have hegemonic sway in universities to the extent that they ironically function as totalitarian theories. Selfe (1990), an intellectual giant in computers and composition, reinforced the importance of theory, when she said that grounding perceptions of the changes that occur in networked classrooms within a theoretical framework assures the validity of our practice. In many respects, she is right because practice alone relies too heavily on anecdotal "evidence."[7]

---

[7]Selfe and Selfe's (1994) "The Politics of the Interface" is a good example of theorizing the technology. Although much has been written about hypertext, including some disadvantages, the perceived advantages far outweigh the risks. Selfe (1999b), in *Technology and Literacy in the Twenty-First Century*, has opened spaces for scholarship on access. In "Lest We Think the Revolution is a Revolution" (Selfe, 1999a), she analyzes advertisements for computer technology through a Cultural Studies lens, drawing some surprising conclusions about America's dominance in world markets and worldview.

However, theory alone makes invisible the tiny local events that might challenge it and maintains the illusion of disciplinary integrity. In the following case study, egalitarian theory would claim empowerment for women, but experience, analysis, and a small body of research suggest a more complicated reading. By performing close readings of tiny local events on listservs and other digital communications, we can, as Foucault asserts, "fracture the smooth totality of [the] disciplinary tradition's picture of itself or . . . its constitutive elements" (Prado, 1995, p. 25).

DISCIPLINARY DISRUPTIONS

It is important to isolate significant moments in specific situations that test ideas, truth claims, and knowledge particularly because conflicts and problems arising from CMC interactions are not always analogous or similar to those surfacing in traditional classrooms and models, and because universal principles of ethics obscure the *particular* circumstances, which provide the key to ethical situations. A number of important scholarly voices have begun examining perils and risks of teaching with technology in the classroom, "to unearth factors or events . . . anomalies and suppressed items, which yield a new picture of whatever has previously gone unquestioned . . ." (Prado, 1995, p. 25).

Some scholars have begun this process by reminding us what research has and has not accomplished. In a 2001 *College Composition and Communication* article, Rouzie found little consensus about the benefits versus risks associated with online class discussions. Although he reported greater challenges to CMC's utopian patina, much of the scholarship paints synchronous discourse as egalitarian and dialogic.

Other scholars challenge the utopian patina by shifting the focus away from established truth claims. Cynthia Selfe has recently shifted our gaze from pedagogical to socioeconomic/political issues. In *Technology and Literacy in the Twenty-First Century*, Selfe (1999b) made problems of technological access visible by exposing how the Clinton plan ignored inequities across school districts and socioeconomic groups. Minorities do not have the same kind of access to computer technology as White, middle-class families. These realities have been suppressed due to utopian visions of technology. Selfe's newly constructed metaphors, calling for *technological literacy* and *the importance of paying attention*, have opened spaces for new directions in scholarship.[8]

---

[8]Selfe (1999b) defines *technological literacy* as a "complex set of socially and culturally situated values, practices, and skills involved in operating linguistically in electronic environments, including reading, writing, and communicating" (p. 148). It demands a reflective awareness on the part of scholars and teachers. Selfe urges educators to "pay attention" to the technology-literacy link, which she relates to issues of access.

Feminist scholars are yielding a new picture of gender communications by unmasking essentializing tendencies of scholars and teachers. Takayoshi's (2000) important feminist study, "Complicated Women: Examining Methodologies for Understanding the Uses of Technology," disrupts the essentialized gendered constructions apparent in the current research on gender and technology.[9] Takayoshi problematizes the narratives of empowerment and oppression by analyzing one female student's experience of and discourse about communicating in an online environment. The resulting analysis demonstrates a more complex understanding of how women negotiate virtual communications than the utopian narratives suggest. In adopting a skeptical stance of her own assumptions and research methods, Takayoshi warns against polarized thinking, which groups people into technophiles or technophobes, oppressors or victims.

Likewise, Romano's (1993) study, "The Egalitarianism Narrative: Whose Story? Which Yardstick?", unearths important insights about research methods, privileged discourse, and events that test theory. Truth claims about community and student-centered learning rely on a discourse heavily invested with the terms *marginalization* and *egalitarianism*. Romano rightly reveals that these highly politicized, theoretically weighty, uncontested words signal teachers' and researchers' own politics and interests, not generally privileging a politics and articulation of difference and liberation.

Interestingly, half the class (Mexican Americans) participating in a Daedalus Interchange discussion about Luis Valdez' *Los Vendidos*,[10] refused the ethnic label and subject position that Romano offered. In fact, one student, during a discussion about Mexicans, identified herself as an American citizen, highly offended by French and German people she met in Massachusetts, who expressed dislike for Americans. Romano's students, like Takayoshi's, were a much more diverse, heterogeneous group than one might expect. Throughout one Interchange session, individual students revealed different aspects of the self depending on changing context, rhetorical situation, and personal interests. Because the construction of the self is unstable and unpredictable, according to Romano, then so are our claims about technology and composition and sociocultural identities. Romano reminds us that compositionists must move between theory and practice, "not allowing the anecdote to undermine the importance of theorizing the discipline, yet preventing that theory from lulling its believers to rest easy in their doctrine." Romano warns against egalitarianism as a grand narrative and uses tiny local events, like the Daedalus exchange, to test theory, searching out incompatibilities

---

[9]This body of research, alluded to by Rouzie (2001), supports the contention that women in digital environments feel more empowered: to speak without fear, to switch genders, to feel less encumbered by bodily image, and to challenge and try out new ideas.
[10]The play, written in the late 1960s, focuses on Mexican American farm workers in California during the grape strikes. Romano chose the play, which caricatures a number of Mexican American stereotypes (farm worker, revolutionary, entrepreneur, educated middle class), to inspire discussion among students who would, she assumed, relate to the events and portrayals.

that will positively alter what Foucault calls "regimes of truth": in this case, the discipline of composition.

Hawisher and Sullivan (1998), in revisiting the egalitarian narrative, refused to characterize digital communications as either utopias or dystopias. Rather, they designed a study to determine the complex negotiations women must undergo to establish online presence. They tested whether the e-spaces women occupied could be considered heterotopias: According to Foucault, "countersites where culture is represented, contested, and inverted" (cited in Hawisher & Sullivan, 1998, p. 173).

The purpose of the list, woman@waytoofast, was to provide "an occasion for . . . women in composition studies to discuss how they would like an e-space constructed and to model the kinds of values and actions they might expect of e-space participants" (Hawisher & Sullivan, 1998, p. 181).[11] The women expressed genuine concern for each other, although some women, surprisingly, lost interest in issues of violence and harassment, and a few others felt disaffected (misunderstood). Hawisher and Sullivan noted a fusion of public and private space, which was satisfying for some but burdensome and anxiety producing for others (due to time commitments). However, the women created alternative plans of action for combating attacks against women online. The researchers concluded that e-spaces are not yet heterotopias, but that women must continue to harness these spaces "as sites for feminist power . . . rethinking . . . public and private space . . . through mediation, persuasion, and acts of kindness" (p. 195).

Takayoshi, Romano, and Hawisher and Sullivan, in challenging notions of egalitarianism, suggest that researchers interrogate what counts as equality and right action in digital environments. Porter (1998), in *Rhetorical Ethics and Internetworked Writing*, demonstrates that localized environments represent communities, which are by nature both rhetorical and ethical. Porter's contributions are significant in indirectly exposing the flaws in the truth claims I identified, advocating a situated ethics, and providing questions and guidelines for negotiating in CMC environments.

As I previously discussed, truth claims about education and technology make invisible a whole set of mechanisms and issues that crucially affect learning environments. Porter reveals these complexities by showing, through a detailed tracing of rhetorical and ethical theory, that teaching computer literacy or integrating computer technology into courses requires knowledge about the dynamics of social interaction, community formation, rhetoric, and identity politics. That is, computer literacy is not just a set of skills, but a way of thinking critically about technology. If this is true, then computers do not have the kind of agency implied in the truth claims.

---

[11]Hawisher and Sullivan studied 30 women in composition studies. An online discussion of 27 women ensued after each was interviewed twice. The entire study, including interviews, was conducted online.

The particular circumstances of digital environments reveal "writing as social action with legal and ethical implications" and writing as a process constituting acts of power within an already dynamic set of power relations; it raises . . . political and ethical questions: To whose benefit am I working/writing? To whose advantage/disadvantage?" (Porter, 1998, p. 145). These questions seems best answered by analyzing how power relations shift through a netlike organization, "how individuals are always in the position of simultaneously undergoing and exercising this power" (Foucault, 1980, p. 98). Such shifting dynamics are dramatic and rapid in online or hybrid classrooms, where flaming, dissent, mutiny, subjugation, and negotiation are made visible in processes of knowledge construction and identity politics. I am convinced, from my experience with listserv dynamics, that power is unstable, reversible, and negotiable, as Foucault insists. When students took control or when I felt powerless or subjugated, it felt as if power were a commodity, an unstoppable force. In some cases I took immediate action to reverse such situations, whereas in others I did not. On reflection, it is clear that individual teachers and students sometimes feel dominated and helpless. Such reactions prevent productive discourse and action. I examine such moments in the analysis section, a prelude to creating a list of guidelines for building community rhetorically and ethically.

A BALANCE OF NEEDS:
CARE OF THE SELF AND THE COMMUNITY

Foucault's *technologies of the self* can guide educators in caring for both students' and teachers' personal and professional identities, interests, and knowledge, and the ethos of the classroom community. Foucault (1988) urges that individuals be permitted to "effect by their own means or with the help of others a certain number of operations on their own bodies and souls, thoughts, conduct, and way of being, so as to transform themselves in order to attain a certain state of happiness, purity, wisdom, perfection or immortality" (p. 18). *To be permitted* suggests that the community allow, if not invite, members to strive for transformation. In classrooms, this means teachers creating a safe environment for and encouraging individually motivated exploration (asserting views, testing new ideas and identities) and change. Some students are easily disposed to asserting their views, testing new ideas, and exploring their identities—depending on the situation or task. Students sometimes need more help of others to challenge or prod them toward deeper intellectual engagement. For reasons of motivation, discouragement, or encouragement, students may need help in the form of praise, guidance, or gentle reminders about potentially transforming their minds, material/physical conditions, or behavior. Other students may be unprepared, resistant, or uninterested in the deep, critical, verbalized self-reflection that Foucault favors. Yet others may be performing operations on their "souls, thoughts, and conduct" unbeknownst to members of the community.[12] Bias toward outward expression of professional and personal growth may be unfair to those who profess silent participation.

The teacher can play an important administrative role in helping others by negotiating appropriate rules and behavior patterns, sensitively considering students' various needs and capabilities, and developing a pedagogy that supports academic and personal transformation; that is, exploiting the concept of student-centered classrooms in ways that strengthen an *ethic of caring*. Porter relates a feminist *ethic of caring* to Foucault's concept of relying on the help of others, drawing on the work of Nel Noddings. Noddings, who calls for an active engagement in the welfare of others, offers a model of caring that is personal, situation-specific, and dialogic, pairing "the 'cared-for' and the 'one-caring' in a mutually supportive relationship" (Porter, 1998, p. 93).[13] Such an approach challenges the notion that teachers should strive for objectivity and neutrality, attributes that many wrongly equate with justice and fairness.

Building and maintaining community through an ethic of caring requires personal engagement, particularly in contentious situations. In fact, disagreement, discord, and temporary havoc are endemic to the process and sometimes necessary for change. Such situations occur, according to Foucault (1980), because people are constantly entangled in a network of power relations, sometimes exercising power, sometimes being constituted by or undergoing it. The following analysis of a graduate composition theory course explores both teachers' and students' responsibilities in creating a space for negotiating knowledge, power, ethics, behavior, and personal growth.

Individuals need space for negotiation to ascertain and carry out the types and numbers of operations needed for transformation. The face-to-face graduate class limited the number of operations in terms of engaging *the body* as a gender experiment in identity. The concept of *the body* becomes complicated in hybrid classes (both digital and face-to-face interaction). Residing in a dual world, the body becomes a curious construct, interacting with real people, codes and signals representing real people, and an imagined version of individuals and/or groups. The class, becoming trapped in a melee about reality, truth, and identity, failed to imagine individuals reconceiving their identities: by layering new qualities onto their virtual personas, which might become integrated into their personalities, by

---

[12]I do not mean to suggest that individuals are necessarily disposed to particular behavior patterns or possess character traits, which determine classroom interaction, styles of learning, or intellectual growth. Students may, in fact, exhibit periods of expressiveness, resistance, disinterest, or openness depending on classroom conditions, tasks, and life situations.

[13]Porter (1998) distinguishes feminist ethics of caring from deontological and utilitarian systems, which are based on universal and abstract principles. Noddings takes issue with generalized ethics because they are impractical and impersonal and claims that an ethics of caring represents the highest form of ethical reasoning.

changing attitudes, subtracting faults, and so on. Changing perceptions about the self can markedly alter ways of thinking, self-esteem, and behavior patterns if they are encouraged (Burns, 1980; Maturana & Varela, 1987).

CYBERSEMINAR CONUNDRUMS

Monica and Kelli were graduate students in "Cyberseminar for Composition Theory," a collaboratively conceived joint project among three universities: NDSU, IUPUI, and Cal State San Bernardino. The three teachers (Joan, Jeff, and SusanMarie), long-time friends and colleagues, wanted to help our master's-level students, not generally bound for PhD programs, see theory as integral to their classroom practice and future professional lives. The decision to collaborate was based on a review of research, similar student populations, and common institutional departmental and course goals. Kayany and Rowley's (1994) analysis of professional discourse in "Forums in Cyberspace for Theoretical Debate" provided the rationale for using CMC. The researchers concluded that asynchronous forums support the dialectic learning process conducive to academic debate, which is highly dependent on theory. Theory, we believed, enriches practice, consciously or not, because it informs pedagogy and politics of the classroom.

The classes convened on the separate campuses at roughly the same time on Thursday evenings, and they shared a common reading list, major assignments, listserv discussions, and electronic debate. The course focused on controversies in composition. My analysis of the classroom and listserv was based on classroom observation, listserv discussions, student conferences, and private conversations. In the interaction between the students' real and virtual classroom engagements, conflicts developed that challenged any simplistic or romantic notions of technology as a neutral or benign tool, easily portable into traditional pedagogy.

Monica, a woman in the NDSU class, was an intelligent, shy, eager, but easily intimidated student. In class discussions, Monica confessed her reluctance to participate in listserv discussions. Aside from Monica's personal lack of self-confidence, the NDSU group felt that the Cal State students were more theoretically savvy, knowledgeable, and sophisticated. Less than 1 month into the course, Monica asked for the help of others on the listserv in clarifying a difficult passage by Jonathan Culler. John, one of the Cal State students, glossed the passage, helping Monica put theory into practice, exactly the kind of move we hoped students would make. Subsequently, Monica asked her electronic colleagues how a deconstructionist would approach "Chief Red Jacket and the Missionary." A number of theoretical missteps caused Monica considerable anxiety: "Trying to comprehend this material reminds me of a Far Side cartoon I saw once: a young man in a classroom raised his hand and asked to be excused because his brain was full. That's how I'm feeling this week." This self-parodic anecdote not only reveals Monica's humility, but her dogged persistence and willingness to engage in hard, intellectual work. Monica was unaware that her informal style, intellectual reticence, humor, and request for knowledge and creativity created a comfortable space for theoretical engagement.[14]

Monica expressed her feelings of intellectual inferiority to me privately and, on occasion, to the NDSU class. During a face-to-face discussion in class about online identity, Monica contemplated adopting a male pseudonym. At this point in the term, she had courageously tested new ideas in a public forum and exposed her fears and perceived shortcomings. A male name, she reasoned, would signify a new persona, a linguistic vehicle for masculine qualities Monica associated with confidence, assertiveness, and self-esteem. The name change, effecting a shift in Monica's conduct and way of being, might be the first operation in her process of transformation. Monica needed the sanction of her closely knit classroom community to embark on this experiment, which she implied could bring her greater happiness, comfort, and wisdom. In caring for herself, Monica was actively engaging in "taking pains with [herself]."[15] Writing herself, through a new signifier, held the promise of Monica discovering and developing an alternative "real life" persona: a transference of new conduct and behaviors from the virtual world to the real world.

The experiment shattered in a battle of wills between Monica and another female student, Kelli, who insisted, in class discussion, that pseudonymous discourse was dishonest.[16] Kelli, unlike Monica, has a robust self-esteem, is assertive in her opinions, and is intellectually confident. She argued that masking identity is morally and ethically corrupt, and that listserv members had the right to know "who each other is," implying that the good of the larger community (joint listserv) would be compromised. (Exactly how Monica's "deception" would impair the communal integrity of the listserv was never entirely clear.) For Kelli and some other class members, honesty became a moral imperative, a universal, rigid principle. The opposing faction was willing to grant "ethical authority to local practice and the conventions of [a] particular communit[y]" (Porter, 1998, p. 19).

---

[14]A student in the Cal State class "lectured" to the listserv on a theory, which he incorrectly glossed some time after correctly explaining Culler's passage. His error led to a series of events that eventually changed the dynamics of the listserv in positive ways: by leveling the playing field. However, it caused the student considerable angst and a reconsideration of his position in the class and his future career goals.

[15]Through linguistic analysis, Foucault (1988) conjoins the notion of self, as a reflexive pronoun, to identity. In analyzing Alcibiades' concept "taking pains with oneself," Foucault interrogates the meaning of self: "*auto* means the same, but it also conveys the notion of identity. The latter meaning shifts the question from 'What is this self?' to 'What is the plateau on which I shall find my identity?'" (p. 25).

[16]I learned a lesson in essentialism. Expecting the women to operate out of an ethic of caring, I was surprised that the conflict arose particularly because Monica was the older of the two. Clearly not all women are feminists or feminists in the same way.

This latter group was likely familiar with conventions of electronic discourse, particularly pseudonymous communication, a commonly accepted practice in electronic forums, such as chatrooms and discussion boards. The philosophical debate eclipsed technological and psychological issues, crucial to negotiating identity *in this situation*. Had we discussed the matter through the rhetorical lens of Chaim Perelman or Stephen Toulmin, students would have understood that honesty is not always the best policy, particularly in ambiguous political situations.

Because of my own penchant for philosophical meandering, I missed the opportunity to help both Monica and Kelli see that "we should give ourselves [as individuals] more care than anything in the world" (Foucault, 1988, p. 22). Had I been more aware of Foucault's and Noddings' theories about individuals' psychological and spiritual transformation, I would have asked Monica why a masculine persona conferred a better self-esteem. Would it give her more rhetorical confidence in raising issues and challenging opinions on the listserv? Would the identification with masculine qualities of assertiveness change her self-image as a shy, reticent, inadequate person? Would she use another identity to obscure a part of herself or to be more honest about herself?

These questions might have generated a dialogue, potentially effecting the good of individuals and the good of the community in profound ways. Kelli could have gained the help of others to see Monica's position and, in turn, investigate her own motivation for so strongly adhering to an abstract principle. Instead, Kelli's resolute stance only served to emphasize and reinforce Monica's insecurities. Ultimately, Monica gave up, submitting to domination and objectification, which Foucault calls "technologies of power," commonly in dialectic with "technologies of the self." Monica was governed, finally, by Kelli and her supporters in the debate, and lost the opportunity for reaching a new "plateau of identity."

Reflecting back on this incident through a Foucauldian (1988) lens, I see the "relation between taking care of the self and defective education" (p. 30). I am wondering why I did not come to Monica's defense, why I did not foreground the classroom dynamic, identifying which students were exercising power and which were subjected by it. Exploring power relations might have generated knowledge about psychological, philosophical, and educational factors affecting digital communication *and* created a greater awareness of personal transformation.

As I write this analysis, I remember a distant pedagogical moment: a neophyte TA being observed as a composition instructor. The class, in discussing a reading that students would incorporate into a writing assignment, took a lengthy sidetrack into philosophical debate. The evaluator commented that I wasted precious class time on a tangential point. I realize, at this writing, my pedagogical weakness in being magnetized to all things philosophical. Although the debate about honesty and naming was interesting, it obliterated Monica's purpose, making it impossible (given who she was) to continue acting out of care of the self.

Another defect was in sanctifying student-centered discourse, whereby, in theory, students mediate, negotiate, and come to consensus. The classroom dynamic offered no room for compromise. If I could rewrite the scenario, I would theorize the conflict, asking students to read excerpts on communitarian theory and care of the self. In preparation for further debate, students could speculate on the value of caring for oneself in general and in particular (for themselves and Monica). We could then weigh individual rights and concerns against the common social good. Consensus or not, I would insist that Monica's decision is finally her own, and that the class should allow her courageous search for identity.

OPENING TO TRANSFORMATIVE VISIONS

Teachers of the cyberseminar confronted equally compelling dilemmas around relations of power and knowledge manifested on the listserv and reverberating in the respective classrooms. Control of discourse (through length of posts, style and tone, modes of address, knowledge sharing) shaped teachers' and students' perceptions of others' intelligence, personalities, and self-image. These listserv conundrums are beyond the scope of this chapter, but they, along with the Monica/Kelli analysis, reminded me that theory induces both blindness and insight.[17]

Any theoretical lens necessarily narrows one's perspective by blocking out truths invisible to the eye or mind. Foucault and Porter illuminate truths about relations of power and knowledge for individuals and communities. A feminist ethic of caring provides a psychological lens, an opening into particular individuals' personalities, principles, and needs. However, none of these theories addresses a consideration of values that explores the "existential nature of the individual, . . . the social formation of values," and the distinction between the two. "It may be easier to determine what people value, but what is often most crucial is why they do so" (Begley, 2000, pp. 236–237). The hypothetical questions I posed to Monica and Kelli would ideally root out motivations for developing and maintaining particular values. Such knowledge would likely create greater understanding among members of the community, thus greater opportunity for individual transformation and social change. In other situations, where consensus and negotiation are not possible, alternative models should be imagined.[18] Shifting visions becomes difficult when truth claims about problem solving and resolution get reified through discourse. All teachers, but especially those who collaborate and negoti-

---

[17]"Monica" has read this analysis and, according to her recollection of events and personal responses, corroborates the accuracy of this narrative.

[18]Begley (2000) sites the dilemma school organizations encounter in Canada, where administrations apply social pressure on educational stakeholders to become involved in decision-making processes. Consensus often cannot be reached because of conflict of values, which renders obsolete "the traditional rational notions of problem-solving" (p. 239). Administrators must settle for responding to situations, rather than resolving them for all parties.

ate among various communities electronically, should consider "how the personal values of the individual might conflict with those of the community" (Begley, 2000, p. 238). Values research provides another layer of complexity in examining online communities, when it considers individual and organizational motivations, attitudes, goals, and expectations.

After taking these various theoretical perspectives into consideration and testing them against the practice of everyday life in the classroom, I developed a set of guiding observations to attempt educational reform in the digital age:

- *Students' and teachers' online personas can create a hierarchy or shift in power relations that may or may not promote a constructive learning environment.* Adopting a new persona might involve complex negotiations, which may or may not satisfy the community. The good of the individual must be balanced against the good of the community. More attention should be given to the care of the teacher, who, in the drive for student empowerment, sometimes suffers the slings and arrows of student rage, disrespect (particularly online), and outright revolution. In online collaborations with other classes, one teacher can feel intimidated by another's knowledge or discursive ease.

- *Power relations, consciously experienced or not, exert strong control among teachers and students.* The control may be externally or internally perceived and determined or motivated by individual goals, expectations, values, and personalities. Foucault's distinction between states of domination and relationships of power is helpful in revealing the degree to which relations of power are fixed or flexible. Research in educational and developmental psychology might add another layer of meaning to power relations that critical theorists view as primarily social, cultural, and political processes.

- *Various voices and ideas must be tested, checked, and challenged, as well as nurtured and encouraged, to create a productive learning environment.* When encouraging personal transformations through education, an uneasy tension can develop between the cognitive and affective. For instance, challenging students to push their ideas beyond expected boundaries sometimes causes crises of identity and self-esteem or, in some cases, retribution against the teacher. Furthermore, it is sometimes beyond the teacher's knowledge to determine students' psychological dispositions, habits of mind, or background knowledge in 10 or 15 weeks. When such difficulties arise, I believe it is most productive to make the problem visible, thus open for critical examination.

- *Instructors can teach ethics as the need arises.* Schooling students in proper Netiquette can help create respectful, comfortable educational settings. But good manners do not always translate into ethical behavior and are sometimes ignored in digital environments. Porter (1998) developed the concept of rhetorical ethics particularly aimed for internetworked writing situations (see Porter, 1998, pp. 68–69, for a set of heuristics to determine how the writer identifies "what is good and desirable" for a given situation). When the need arises, ethics cases from research, teacher experience, or fictional constructions can be tested against current conflicts or problems.

- *Teachers can make significant contributions to scholarship on the rhetoric of digital environments.* Some participants perceive digital communications as speech acts, some as written text, some as a hybrid form. A Derridean exploration of speech and writing could be a productive direction for further research. The form of discourse can shape the learning environment in significant ways. I suspect that students become normalized to particular discursive patterns, unarticulated rules and codes, styles of expression, and so on. A greater understanding of digital interactions could make online communities more effective for students' intellectual and personal growth.

PEDAGOGY REVISITED

As eager young teachers, graduate school buddies commonly haunt each other's classrooms, exchange stories, and share assignments. As one of a triumvirate, I would spend long hours convincing the other two about an approach, a technique, or a favorite essay. I became crestfallen when my suggestions bombed. After teaching for 20 years, I occasionally try on another teacher's pedagogy. More often than not it fails, sometimes miserably. I continually ponder, "Why isn't pedagogy more transferable?" Recalling past experience, I suspect passion for a particular work, excitement over a newly conceived activity, or curiosity about a fresh theoretical approach would reflect an individual teacher's intellectual development, creativity, or deepest values. As Begley has convincingly argued, values and motivations are personal; it stands to reason then that values, which necessarily underlie pedagogies, are not easily transferable.

What is utopia for one course, teacher, or group of students may prove a dystopia for others. This problem is complicated by the use of computer technologies, which are neither value free nor theoretically neutral. In fact, particular pedagogies are imported along with computer applications, as my example about reading programs demonstrates. I am not arguing against integrating computer technology in educational courses and curricula. Rather I am arguing for teachers to consider a triangulation of values: pedagogy, research, and technology.

Computer technology might reveal deep pedagogical fissures in an educational curriculum; innovative teaching techniques in traditional classrooms might lead to new developments in hardware or software; successful computer programs might lead researchers to new scientific knowledge. Implicit in the triangulation metaphor is the notion of necessary collaboration: via face-to-face, virtual, or textual interaction. I have lived this lesson primarily because Bill Smith taught me that synthesis and collaboration are more interesting than isolation and difference, and because of his unrelenting belief in people, their good intentions, and inquisitive spirits. These values are more likely to direct us toward our pedagogical dreams than abstract or universal principles.

ACKNOWLEDGEMENTS

My sincere gratitude to Tracy Bridgeford and Elizabeth Drescher, friends, and colleagues, who read many drafts tirelessly and cheerfully—at various levels of development. Their guidance and friendship reinforce my belief that composing is, for many scholars, a necessarily collaborative effort, and that intellectual endeavors and affective factors are essentially interwoven.

REFERENCES

Begley, P. (2000). Values and leadership: Theory development, new research, and an agenda for the future. *The Alberta Journal of Educational Research, 46,* 233–249.

Burns, D. D. (1980). *Feeling good: The new mood therapy.* New York: Signet-Penguin.

Eldred, J. C. (1989). Computers, composition pedagogy, and the social view. In G. E. Hawisher & C. L. Selfe (Eds.), *Critical perspectives on computers and composition instruction* (pp. 201–218). New York: Teachers College Press.

Foucault, M. (1972). *The archeology of knowledge & the discourse on language* (A. M. S. Smith, Trans.). New York: Pantheon.

Foucault, M. (1978). *The history of sexuality* (Vol. 1: R. Hurley, Trans.). New York: Pantheon.

Foucault, M. (1980). *Power/knowledge: Selected interviews & other writings* (C. Gordon, Ed.). New York: Pantheon.

Foucault, M. (1988). Technologies of the self. In L. H. Martin, H. Gutman, & P. H. Hutton (Eds.), *Technologies of the self: A seminar with Michel Foucault* (pp. 16–49). Amherst: University of Massachusetts Press.

Hawisher, G. E., & Sullivan, P. (1998). Women on the networks: Searching for e-spaces of their own. In S. C. Jarratt & L. Worsham (Eds.), *Feminism and composition studies: In other words* (pp. 172–197). New York: Modern Language Association.

Kayany, J. M., & Rowley, M. W. (1994). *Synchronous and asynchronous forums in cyberspace for theoretical dialectic.* Paper presented at the AEJMC Convention, Communication Theory and Methodology Division, Atlanta.

Maturana, H. R., & Varela, F. J. (1987). *The tree of knowledge: The biological roots of human understanding.* Boston: New Science Library.

Mergendollar, J. R. (1996). Moving from technological possibility to richer student learning: Revitalized infrastructure and reconstructed pedagogy. *Educational Researcher, 25*(8), 43–46.

Nilson, H. (1998). *Michel Foucault and the games of truth* (R. Clark, Trans.). New York: St. Martin's Press.

Porter, J. (1998). *Rhetorical ethics and internetworked writing.* Greenwich, CT: Ablex.

Prado, C. G. (1995). *Starting with Foucault: An introduction to genealogy.* Boulder, CO: Westview.

Romano, S. (1993). The egalitarianism narrative: Whose story, which yardstick? *Computers and Composition, 10*(3), 5–28. Retrieved July 2003 from, http://corax.cwrl.utexas.edu/cac/a...s/v/10/10_3_html/10_3_1_Romano.html

Rose, M. (1989). *Lives on the boundary: The struggles and achievements of America's underprepared.* New York: The Free Press.

Rouzie, A. (2001). Conversation and carrying-on: Play, conflict, and serio-ludic discourse in synchronous computer conferencing. *College Composition and Communication, 53*(2), 251–299.

Segal, H. P. (1996). The American ideology of technological progress: Historical perspectives. In S. T. Kerr (Ed.), *Technology and the future of schooling: Ninety-fifth yearbook of the National Society for the Study of Education* (pp. 28–48). Chicago: University of Chicago Press.

Selfe, C. L. (1990). Technology in the English classroom: Computers through the lens of feminist theory. In C. Handa (Ed.), *Computers and community: Teaching composition in the twenty-first century* (pp. 118–139). Portsmouth, NH: Boynton/Cook.

Selfe, C. L. (1999a). Lest we think the revolution is a revolution: Images of technology and the nature of change. In G. E. Hawisher & C. L. Selfe (Eds.), *Passions and pedagogies and 21st century technologies* (pp. 292–322). Logan: Utah State University Press.

Selfe, C. L. (1999b). *Technology and literacy in the twenty-first century: The importance of paying attention.* Carbondale: Southern Illinois University Press.

Selfe, C. L., & Selfe, R. J. (1994). Politics of the interface: Power and its exercise in electronic contact zones. *College Composition and Communication, 45*(4), 480–504.

Takayoshi, P. (2000). Complicated women: Examining methodologies for understanding the uses of technology. *Computers and Composition, 17*, 123–138.

11

INSISTENT/RESISTANT

Re/visiting the I/Search

J. Bradley Minnick

Julie Aungst

> Accordingly, Perkins (1986) argues that we should recast learning as a process of design. Through the design process, students experience knowledge as a human creation that is a response to human needs and problems. This knowledge will necessarily have a situation-specific function and structure and will be revised as new problems, situations, information, and viewpoints arise.
> (Wilhelm & Edmiston 1998, p. 91)

WORSE FOR THE WEAR

Consider Mary, an intern teacher enrolled in a fifth-year Masters in the Art of Teaching (MAT) program at a prominent eastern university. This graduate program enables interns to teach for 25 to 30 hours per week on-site in an English classroom (6–12) and as an apprentice to a cooperating teacher for an entire school year while completing university course work in the evenings. University course work includes: the Teaching of Literature, the Teaching of Grammar and Usage, and the Teaching of Writing. Mary has interviewed and accepted internship work in a sixth-grade classroom at the university's laboratory school.

At the beginning of the year, Mary's cooperating teacher hangs a chart in the room depicting the cartoon cat Garfield whose furry index finger stoically points to the phases of the writing process: prewriting, writing, revision, and editing. Mary, like many of her sixth-grade students, has the chart memorized. Unfortunately, after a few weeks, Garfield's once-grinning face seems to look worse for the wear.

In English classrooms across the country, the process approach to writing is seemingly everywhere. This proliferation of the writing process has come a long way the 1960s, when D. Gordon Rohman (1964; Rohman & Wiecke, 1965) introduced the notion of a composing process and offered a theoretical framework for describing it. Rohman's process included "Prewriting, Writing, and Rewriting," focusing on a student's attention on the time prior to completion of the first draft, which had been neglected by previous modes of instruction.

In the early 1970s, Emig (1971) took a more sophisticated view of the composing process, recognizing that it was recursive and that overlap could occur among Rohman's three stages. Emig's work subsequently stimulated both researcher's and practitioner's attention toward a process approach to writing. Our intern Mary's mentor teacher embraces Emig's approach and assigns her a unit on research writing, engaging her in the process of helping students to compose I-Search papers. Like many novice teachers, Mary embarks on a journey—a journey complete with wrong turns and misjudgment—a journey that will take her through her own I-Search on her quest to find good pedagogical practices necessary to teach her sixth-grade students effective research writing.

THE I-SEARCH

The I-Search paper, designed by writing specialist Macrorie (1988), suggests that students who are learning to write research should engage in the process of research question design and data gathering as authentic researchers would—that is, they should work through the process of writing by designing solid research questions on a topic about which they want to learn. Then, with help from the teacher, the student determines possible ways to answer the questions posed, which may include anthropological data-gathering techniques such as observing people or cultures; close reading by analyzing a variety of texts; and, journalistic endeavors such as interviewing subjects who are knowledgeable and able to talk in meaningful ways about the student-selected research topic. After initially developing a question, considering how to answer the question, and compiling data, the student is then to write about his or her findings using the first-person perspective—chronicling the experience without hiding the subjectivity and viewpoint inherent in the writing of it.

Students use the I-Search format, then, to engage in the process of research and what research is good for: searching for and developing embryonic forms of ethnography, conducting traditional book scholarship, attempting to understand the phenomenological, exploring oral histories, and engaging in action-based research, thus providing possibilities for cross-curricular work. Possible topics and questions developed by students are as various as the research methods used to conduct the I-Search. One effective prewriting method is keeping a journal.

THE JOURNAL

As part of her course work at the university, Mary has read Peter Elbow (1973, 1986) and embraced the notion of asking her students to free write, especially in journals that she responds to positively and promptly. She has utilized Gabrielle Rico's (1983) clustering techniques in order to enable her sixth graders to gener-ate ideas for their journals. She has incorporated 20-minute mini-lessons when teaching her students valuable revision and editing skills, and, as Nancie Atwell (1987) suggests, Mary has asked her students to keep a record of her mini-lessons in their journals. She too keeps a journal of her internship experiences.

Mary has engaged in 10-minute writing conferences with her students and has shown them how to conference with each other in more or less meaningful ways as Donald Murray (1968) recommends, writing down the results of the con-ferences in her teacher journal. In addition, Mary's writing classroom is orderly and organized in a way that would make Lucy Calkins (1991) proud. She has set up clusters of desks that she calls learning centers. Here, students write poems and stories in response to a variety of stimuli, including everyday items, pictures, and background music. Her students organize their writing and put it in writing portfolios. These portfolios are alphabetized by student name and neatly stacked in crates located in the rear of the classroom; she and her students assess papers using holistic grading and writing rubrics they develop, collaboratively designing them based on criteria they collectively put forth.

And, it all seems to be working.

Mary's students, for instance, seem able to write presentable papers; they are often able to solve writing problems on their own and are self-directed when achieving their writing goals. They are so self-directed, in fact, that they often resent any overt teacher direction.

Bottom line: Her students are resistant in good ways.

Now, however, it is time for her students to flex their writing muscles and engage in the process of writing research papers. This, of course, presents a dif-ferent set of problems for her and her students—particularly those students who would rather spend their time writing self-directed poetry and stories. Because many of her students are used to self-directed writing and self-generated topics, they are, at first, both resistant and resentful of the I-Search assignment, or any assignment for that matter, and its methodology. School-based assignments just do not figure into the "authentic" writing that they have been doing or told they would be able to do, nor do teacher-based assignments seem much fun. In fact, at first, the I-Search seems a lot like the traditional research paper dusted off and renamed.

How, then, can Mary help her students move beyond self-directed narratives and enter into the academic discourse necessary to write the I-Search paper?

What follows is Mary's I-Search journal. In it she searches for a way to help her students who are having problems in writing their own I-Search papers. Mary describes her frustration in her initial I-Search writing conferences with one of her students, Evan.

Evan is as resistant as Mary is insistent.

Mary writes:

> Evan is having a difficult time understanding the weaknesses inherent in his I-Search paper. Evan is a very grade conscious, meticulous student and often writes what he expects to be teacher-pleasing, flowery prose. Evan is doing his mini-I-Search paper on classical music. We are just in the first week and he is already complaining that his partner has been of no help, that he has had to do most of the work himself.
>
> As we talked about his initial draft, I note that he uses a number of musical terms, but doesn't define any of them. From our talk, I am not sure that he knows the meanings of at least some of the terms. As delicately as possible, I try to explain to Evan that he needs to define the terms that he uses in his paper.
>
> But, Evan is insistent and resistant. He insists that he knows what the words mean, and that he can't define them exactly in the paper because it will ruin the "artistic gains" he is trying to make. He is proud of his first draft and he resists any comments that will force him to change it.
>
> I can be insistent, too. I try to convince Evan that from a reader's perspective the meanings of the words are not clear. When I continue to emphasize that, from a reader's perspective, the meanings of the words are not clear, I can see him getting more and more upset. So we insist and resist each other. I become more frustrated. Evan becomes upset. We never reach an understanding, debating this issue until the end of the period. With nothing resolved, Evan leaves the class close to tears.

RESEARCH WRITING AS DESIGN

Writing teachers often attempt to move beyond personal writing or toward what Bruner (1985) calls a paradigmatic approach to writing, without much success. Mary is experiencing this challenge. According to Bruner, two distinct forms of writing exist: narrative and paradigmatic. Narrative emphasizes personal narratives or turning the stuff of life into narrative events, evincing through writing, it is hoped, coming to a personal understanding of self and self in relation to other. Paradigmatic writing, in contrast, traditionally involves school-based essay writing and argumentative writing necessary for producing a text-based literary critique. According to Bruner, the narrative and paradigmatic each has its own discourse rules, format, and style.

Educator John Mayher (1987), in contrast to Bruner, does not see the clear distinction Bruner does between narrative and paradigmatic writing. In Mayher's view, there is a blurring between the narrative and paradigmatic. Mayher suggests that the process of composing an essay is essentially the process of composing the story of something in a form that appears paradigmatic yet enables students to move toward inquiry-oriented critical encounters with their own and others' texts. It is this blurring of the lines between narrative and essay combined with learning as design that holds tremendous promise for a teacher of writing. That is— students need to find a narrative link between story and essay.

How, then, does a teacher of writing help students find this narrative link?

Certainly there is the process of writing; that process involves the development of self-selected topics, drafting, redrafting, and revision similar to the traditional writing process. However, in helping students move from story to research to research essay, teachers may consider revisiting Macrorie's I-Search process combined with learning as design elements, providing engagement for students who are beginning research writing.

Lehrer (1991, 1993) describes a complex process of design in which

> students must integrate and orchestrate a whole complex of skills as they go through a recursive process of asking questions, decomposing problems, collaborating to manage the design project, finding information, developing information (e.g., through interviews, surveys, drama), selecting and analyzing information, organizing information, representing information, evaluating the design through feedback, revising, and presenting the product. (For a fuller discussion and examples of the design process and illustrations of its use with hypermedia, see Wilhelm, 1995; Wilhelm & Friedemann, 1998.) (Wilhelm & Edmiston, 1998, p. 93)

Wilhelm and Edmiston's work is clearly designed with process drama in mind— that is, it is intended to engage teachers and students with writing by using improvisational dramatic structures, reflective reading, writing, simulations, and critical inquiry tasks as tools for learning. Research as design attempts to have students use writing for what it is good for—the expression of ideas and concepts. "In design, students are encouraged to create various representations of a single idea. ...Janvier (1987) has found that multiple and linked representations of ideas provide the cornerstone of true understanding, because students will then see how ideas are situated and what kinds of work those ideas can do" (Wilhelm & Edmiston, 1998, p. 92). It is in this vein, as design, that Mary resisted, re/visited, and re/searched Ken Macrorie's conceptualization of the I-Search paper in terms of her own work with her middle-school students. The I-Search, then, is an essential narrative link allowing metacognitive exploration without the forced objectivity all students fear when searching for the words to present suitable research. Mary's I-Search journal will assist her in helping her students complete their first research paper; she also believes it will assist her in understanding and helping them with the writing problems they discuss with her during writing conferences.

MARY'S "MY QUESTIONS"

Teachers should write along with their students. It is, of course, the same with the I-Search. Through Mary's words that follow, we see that she has embarked on her own I-Search writing journey. She has posed a problem (the case of the resistant Evan), suggested parameters for research (learning more about the design of the I-Search paper), and considered how she might solve the problem she has posed (Flower, 1981).

Mary writes:

> I actually stumbled upon the I-Search by accident. What I mean is that I was told to teach the project—I did not choose to teach it. My mentor teacher uses the project every year with his middle school students. This year, it became my responsibility.
>
> When he told me that he wanted me to teach the paper, I knew nothing about the I-Search process. I had read some of Ken Macrorie for my Teaching Writing course and knew of the idea behind the I-Search, but I knew absolutely nothing about how it would materialize in an actual classroom setting. I was nervous, overwhelmed, and I felt as if I was in way over my head.

Mary recognizes that she can be resistant in her own writing and teaching, too. Novice teachers are more apt to attempt new and difficult teaching tasks when their possibilities of failure are reduced and a safe space for failure is established. This safe space for failure is also essential when students embark on new and potentially threatening writing tasks. Like the resistant Evan, Mary is, at first, nervous and overwhelmed with the prospect of this I-Search task.

In addition, unlike Atwell's (1987) conception of self-selected research, Mary is, as is often the case in the real world of student teaching, unable to select her own methodological approach. Instead, she has been assigned a writing task by her cooperating teacher—that of helping students through the I-Search paper process. This is also a potential source for frustration and resistance.

Mary writes about this frustration in the journal entry that follows:

> I made a lot of mistakes along the way. The first one set the project back an entire week. In an attempt to acclimate the sixth graders to the I-Search process, I had planned on leading them through a "mini-I-Search" in which they would use their classmates as their sources.
>
> As I had envisioned it, the students would first identify an area of expertise or interest. Then the students would choose partners based on which student's area of expertise they found most interesting. (Evan's chosen partner, for example, had identified classical music.) Finally, the students would pose a question about their partner's area of expertise, interview their partner, and then write about what they had learned in their interview.

Mary uses her journal here to describe her initial attempt to have students perform the prewriting task of engaging in the mini-I-Search. She hopes this role playing of interviewers and interviewees will engage students in the I-Search process and allow for much needed I-Search interview practice. However, things do not go as planned.

Mary writes:

> When we actually began the mini I-Search, it turned out that none of the students seemed to know enough about their "area of expertise" to feel comfortable being interviewed by their partner. For many, the resulting first drafts lacked just about everything—substance, interest, and energy. Then, there were a few like Evan who essentially wrote a draft of a paper that would look and sound like what they expected a teacher to be looking for and ignored their interviews. What a disaster!

In her initial expectation failure of her mini-I-search, Mary may have done best to heed Moffett's (1994) student-centered advice concerning the process of rippling. According to Moffett, rippling is "an informal, continuous tutorial of some knowledge or skill that everybody is at once receiving from the more experienced and transmitting in turn to the less experienced" (p. 168). When students are essentially at the same level of experience, little rippling can take place. "Mixing ages and mixing levels of experience within the same age is what sets ripples going if participants are free to choose what they do and to interact while carrying out what they choose" (Moffett, 1994, p. 169).

In Mary's mini-I-Search design, which began in an ambitious direction, the students are not experienced enough with working through the I-Search process to even attempt a mini-version of it, let alone to participate in mock interviews.

Mary writes:

> I finally decided to ditch the idea because the students were becoming more confused about research writing than they were learning, and the "mini-I-Search" was not providing an adequate introduction to the actual I-Search paper. So, at the end of the week, I put on the brakes. I needed a different approach to get the project started again.

Mary quickly realizes that her students have been asked to embark on this mini-I-Search task prematurely. They have not gathered the appropriate data to begin writing, let alone talk about their work at a metacognitive level. Mary, then, must back up to build up (Tharp & Gallimore, 1988, p. 245). That is—Mary must back-up from her initial design for helping students with their I-Search papers, which was off the mark, and build a more carefully constructed scaffold as a supportive structure for them. Mary begins to explore the techniques of scaffolding.

Wood, Bruner, and Ross (1976) describe scaffolding as a metaphorical structure, much like a painter's scaffold, that is built by the teacher and used to assist students in their learning. Scaffolding learning has been called a variety of names, including *assisted learning* and *cognitive apprenticeship*. According to Wood, Bruner, and Ross (1976), scaffolding is "a process that enables a child or novice to solve a problem, carry out a task, or achieve a goal that would be beyond his [or her] assisted efforts" (cited in Graves & Graves, 1994, p. 10).

To explain how scaffolding works in teaching a child a new skill, Graves and Graves (1994) use the example of a parent teaching a young child to ride a bicycle with the assistance of training wheels:

> Training wheels are supportive; they enable a novice bicycle rider to do something he or she might not otherwise be able to do—ride a two wheeler. Equally important, training wheels are temporary, and they can be gradually raised so that the budding bicycle rider increasingly assumes the task of riding the two wheeler with less and less support from the scaffold. (p. 10)

According to Anderson (1989), a scaffold, then, "is a temporary and adjustable structure that allows accomplishment of a task that would be impossible without a scaffold's support" (cited in Graves & Graves, 1994, p. 10).

According to Graves and Graves, closely aligned with scaffolding is what Russian psychologist Vygotsky (1978) called the zone of proximal development. Vygotsky explained that, "at any particular point in time, children have a circumscribed zone of development, a range within which they learn. At one end of this range are learning tasks that they can complete independently; at the other end are learning tasks which they cannot complete even with assistance. In between these two extremes is the zone most productive for learning, the range of tasks at which children can achieve if they are assisted by some more knowledgeable or more competent other" (Graves & Graves, 1994, p. 11).

Both the concepts of scaffolding and zone of proximal development provide the foundation for Mary to make decisions about the selection and arrangement of instructional strategies and activities to support her students. (Note: It is the teacher developing the shape of the scaffold based on the students' needs that allows for teacher–student problem solving.) However, it is clear that Mary still needs to understand her own role in implementing those strategies and activities. According to Graves and Graves (1994), "When tasks are difficult or students are learning to do something they have not done before, it is appropriate for teachers to do much of the work—to heavily scaffold students' efforts. With easier tasks or when students are working on tasks with which they have had some experience, it is appropriate for teachers to reduce the amount of assistance they offer—to gradually dismantle the scaffolds they use to assist students" (p. 11).

Part of Mary's task in rethinking her I-Search instruction is to decide what kind of assisted learning experiences will likely be most useful as a scaffold to enable her students to understand and complete their I-Search projects. A second part of Mary's task is to make informed decisions about her students' zones of proximal development relative to their I-Search projects and then to select and adapt particular activities and lessons that best fit her students' actual learning zones. A third part of Mary's task is to consider how to gradually release responsibility so that students can begin to do the work themselves with little teacher assistance. The "gradual release of responsibility" provides a productive heuristic for making decisions about adjusting the amount of teacher assistance being provided.

Pearson and Gallagher (1983) explain "that effective instruction often follows a progression in which students gradually assume increased responsibility for their learning" (cited in Graves & Graves, 1994, p. 11). As described by Graves and Graves (1994), the gradual release of responsibility model allows for a "temporal sequence in which students gradually progress from situations in which the teacher takes the majority of the responsibility for their successfully completing a reading task to situations in which students assume increasing responsibility . . . and finally to situations in which students take total or nearly total responsibility for completing tasks" (p. 11).

Mary finally decides that a brainstorming session on topics of special interest and questions about those topics will give her insight into her students' special interests and their abilities to pose questions as well as enable her to scaffold by modeling question-posing at different levels of complexity for students who need assistance. Moreover, her students have brainstormed before and have both enjoyed it and participated actively.

In her journal, Mary writes about the second time through the I-Search process with students. (Note how Mary begins to consider what kinds of prewriting activities she might use to help her understand something about her students' areas of interest.)

Mary writes:

The second time through the I-Search, I was much more explicit with regard to the requirements of the project. I re-began the unit by having the class brainstorm possible topics for exploration: What is the one question to which you genuinely know the answer?

Although the class was only required to brainstorm twenty questions, most of the students reached the one hundred level. Some of the questions were nonresearchable (such as why are girls so weird?) and others were more focused (such as what is AIDS?).

As a class, we discussed various factors that contribute to designing a researchable question. (Does this question have an answer? Would this questioning lead to sources—both primary and secondary?)

After the discussion and whole-class practice with some of their own questions, the students worked on their own and in small groups through a process of elimination to narrow their focus to one possible question to research. This question became their "search question" and would serve as their guide throughout the rest of the unit.

In this instance, after Mary finishes having students brainstorm possible I-Search questions, she provides her students with a set of questions or shaping directions that might act as scaffolds to guide them in creating and organizing their I-Search papers. Basically, Mary and the class consider the kinds of questions necessary to produce good research, and Mary provides guidelines as supporting mechanisms for her students.

She continues to develop "during writing" activities for students. For example, in the journal entry that follows, Mary describes how she asks students to work through the phases of the process with her step-by-step, clearly moving them to develop clearly articulated research questions as the basis for beginning their I-Search papers.

Once their search questions were selected, I asked the students to draft the first section of the I-Search paper: My Questions. In this section, I asked the students to state clearly what their search question was, to explain why they were interested in their topic, and to identify what they knew about the topic before they began researching.

Writing this section provided a nice lead into the project because, without being consciously aware, the students were beginning to select possible areas for library research and organizational structures for the later sections of the paper.

Mary scaffolds students by asking them to develop their own "My Questions" section, in which they are to design a research question, describe why the topic is important to them, and what they know about the topic before they begin. The design of a relevant research question is imperative for any research, but in this case, Mary also guides students by asking them to pay attention to the reasons they selected their research question and to take note of their prior knowledge. Mary's own search into her own pedagogy begins to make a difference in the classroom. She realizes that only after this support has been established are her students ready to go to the library. Answering these questions acts as an instructional support for the students and for Mary, who, upon reading about the reasons they are interested in the research and their background knowledge, may better go about assisting them.

Mary writes:

> Once all of the "My Questions" drafts were completed, I took the students to the library. Fortunately, I had the help of the school librarian, who assisted the students who needed it with the necessary skills to begin to use the library. Between the two of us, my cooperating teacher, and my university supervisor, my students were able to get the help they needed to locate materials. They then spent three weeks in class reading their sources, taking notes, and preparing for and conducting their interviews. Everyone worked at his or her own pace, but deadlines were posted on the wall calendar to keep the class on track.

Further, as her students write their notes and prepare for their interviews, Mary also has the students work on the section of the I-Search paper that documents their research procedures. Again, Mary decides to take an active role in scaffolding her students' learning by providing them with a set of questions that they can ask themselves to help them decide what is important information to include and what is not as important.

MARY'S "MY SEARCH PROCESS"

Mary discusses how she moves her students through the second section of the I-Search process by providing students with specific guidelines and then gradually releasing responsibility.

Mary writes:

> During these three weeks, the second section of the I-Search paper, "My Search Process," was assigned. In this section, the students were asked to document steps in their research process. Some questions they were invited to explore were: How did you locate your sources? What sources did you start with? How did these sources lead to other sources? What are some major breakthroughs/problems in your research? How did your search question change? Generally the students did a thorough job with this section because they wrote it as if they were telling a story—a form of writing with which

these students were very familiar. Some students needed to be pushed to elaborate more, but elaboration was always encouraged as if it meant adding more detail to the story.

In that writing tasks are usually of different levels of difficulty for different students, Mary's "search task" takes on a number of complications for her students. Mary next writes in her journal about how she requires students to "talk about" their work and asks students to create a "visual map" that will allow them to "diagram their question." This visual representation is yet another form of guided instruction providing her writers a way to read and revisit the world of their I-Search processes.

> When the majority of the class was ready, I instructed them to write the "What I Have Learned" section. This section required the students to talk about three or four major answers to their search question. Most of the students had never written a research paper before; therefore, I decided to use a visual map that my cooperating teacher had given me to help the students organize their information. The map showed students how to diagram their question, provide possible answers to that question, and provide supporting details for each answer. The maps were difficult for the students because they were unfamiliar with the format, but they seemed to organize all of their information. The real problem came when the student submitted their written drafts of the section. Regardless of how the students structured their information on the visual map, when they wrote their papers, their facts were scattered and disjointed.
>
> In many cases, the information written in the draft had little to do with the students' search questions. I realized again that I had overestimated what my students knew about and could do in organizing all of the information they had gathered in their research into the form of the I-Search paper.
>
> Once again, I put on the brakes, backed myself up. I tried to address the problem by showing the class how to write an outline, and required each student to write an outline for their paper. I wanted the students to try writing the next draft of their papers from their outlines. The drafts were a little better this time, but still not what I hoped they would be. The students' problems seemed to be much more individualized.
>
> One student didn't answer her search question, another needed to make transitions between ideas, and still another had disjointed information. There seemed to be so many problems—more than I had anticipated—I had no idea how I was going to address them all in one classroom and still stick to the deadlines I had created for the project.

To address the disorganization of her students, Mary moves too quickly from the visualization to the writing stage. She again backs up and takes the more formal approach of asking students to prepare outlines. This is, admittedly, a stab in the dark and harkens back to the ways we were taught to write a traditional research paper; Mary is at a loss; asking students to outline is her attempt to help them become better organized.

Mary has made another mistake. Students write drafts from their outlines, but they are "not what" Mary hopes they will be. Mary realizes that it is important for her to understand what each student perceives as the problems in his or her draft so she can adjust her response and advice reasonably to address students' needs. Rather than provide her students with a general list of scaffolding questions that each should answer, Mary decides to have her students write down questions they have in the margins of their own papers and at the end write down questions the reader (peer or teacher) is to consider concerning the draft.

MARY'S "WHAT I HAVE LEARNED" SECTION

At this stage, Mary feels it is important for her students to learn to ask their own questions about what they perceive to be the problems in the I-Search papers they have written. She also hopes that their questions will give her more insight into what her students are learning and cues as to where she should focus her attention in the individual writing conferences. In her journal, she describes how she asks her own questions in the conferences that she conducts with students.

Mary writes:

> I scheduled individual conferences with each of my students. I allotted five to eight minutes per conference, and required that each student bring to the conference at least one question that he or she had concerning the I-Search draft or process. While I was conferencing with students, the rest of the class was involved in peer-conferencing, revising drafts, or working on their final copies.
>
> One of my students, Carrie, was having a hard time organizing the information in her paper on anorexia. In her paper, she changed topics often and didn't categorize similar information together. She came to the conference wanting to know how she could fit all of her factual information together in the same paper. Specifically, her "during writing" questions were: In what order should I talk about my information, and how should I organize it?
>
> I noticed that her paper focused on the causes, effects, and symptoms of anorexia, so I asked her to skim through her paper and make note of all the times she wrote about those three areas. Once she was done, I asked her if she felt these areas followed any specific order in the stages of anorexia. She felt that first an anorectic would show symptoms, then they would discover the causes of the disease and the effects that followed. I then asked her why she didn't write about all of the symptoms first, the causes second, and then the effects last? She looked at me for a second and then she broke out into a smile, "I don't know, but that's a really good idea!" Carrie's "during writing" confer-

ence ended quickly then and her problems with organization—at least with this paper—were solved.

Ellen's search question was as follows: What are the effects of cigarette smoke on the people who smoke and the people and animals around them? The question was long, awkward, and slightly confusing, particularly because Ellen used the term *second-hand smoke* throughout her paper to refer to the smoke exhaled by the smoker. I had commented on her draft that her question needed to be revised, but I didn't know how to go about getting her to revise it so that she used the term *second-hand smoke*. When she came to the conference, the first question she asked me was: What should I do with this search question? I approached the question by explaining that because she used the term *second-hand smoke* in her paper, she should include the term in her search question. I then asked her to revise the question using the word. She sat at the table staring at her paper and then said, "I don't know what I could do." I tried to push [her] further to revise the question, but I was not very successful. She seemed unwilling to put any more effort into revising the question. If I had this conference to do over again I think I would have had her work on her question at her seat and then [I would have] checked on her later to monitor her progress.

By looking closely at the questions that students ask during the writing conference, Mary enhances her understanding of her students. Then, by suggesting strategies for individual students with respect to their particular needs, Mary is able to help provide appropriate scaffolds (although as in Ellen's case not always successfully) for her individual students as they try to work to solve problems in their writing. Mary finds that the best way to help students during writing conferences with them is by asking them to pose their own questions instead of her posing questions for them.

Mary writes:

> Overall, the conferences were a success, both for my students and for myself. My students found the answers that they were looking for, and I learned how to encourage my students to solve their own [writing] problems.
>
> Having students pose their own questions about writing allowed me to start at the level my students were on and to work up from there. Time was not wasted teaching transitions to a student who did not need that lesson. By allowing the students to pose their own questions, my teaching could be individualized to meet the needs of each child.

WHAT WE HAVE LEARNED

Mary's My Search, in the end, provides a conflict between teacher-directed and constructivist ways of conceptualizing writing instruction, especially during writing conferences. Her own I-Search question might be revised from: How, then, can I help my students to move beyond their narratives and enter into the academic discourse of the research paper? to How can I mediate between a teacher-centered and a student-centered approach when asking students to write research?

In the book *Strategic Reading*, Wilhelm, Baker, and Dube (1997) describe how in traditional reading classrooms (and writing classrooms) teachers spend most of their time assigning and evaluating. They assign writing topics, students write for them, and they evaluate student writing, tossing in some peer-editing for good measure. This assign-and-evaluate approach is echoed by other researchers (Durkin, 1979; Hillocks, 1986; Nystrand et al., 1997; Tharp & Gallimore, 1988).

In considering the teaching process in context with the process of teaching reading (and teaching writing), Wilhelm, Baker, and Dube suggest (1997) that: " . . . the Vygotskian-inspired, sociocultural-based, learning-centered model . . . was so radically different from the two most dominant models of teaching and learning (teacher-centered and student-centered) that most people had never considered it" (p. 26).

For Mary, teaching the I-Search paper is not an either/or proposition. On one side in the teacher-centered class, the teacher pontificates and provides what she considers to be essential information on how to do the I-Search, and it is the students' responsibility to take in the information, use it, and transmit something back. On the other side in a student-centered classroom, "proponents of this view often cite constructivist notions by arguing that learning is in the province of learners, who must necessarily construct their own understandings. Knowledge is acquired by learners in the process of their self-initiated inquires and personal investigations" (Wilkins, Baker, & Dube, 1997, p. 27). In this view, students work through the process on their own and in groups, discovering for themselves what writing is good for.

Wilhelm, Baker, and Dube (1997) suggest that neither model best serves students. Instead, they suggest a model that is "two sided and required mutual effort and responsibility on the part of learners and teachers . . ." (p. 26). In this model, teachers and students work together in collaboration with the teacher to provide the appropriate guidance based on the needs of learners.

Helping novice teachers learn about and use a repertoire of instructional strategies, techniques, activities, and approaches is a primary goal of many preservice teacher education programs. Expanding on that repertoire is also a major feature of postcertification workshops and in-service programs for experienced teachers. Knowing about important and useful instructional techniques for developing children's literacy is essential for every English Language Arts teacher; however, this is just a beginning. The successful teacher knows how to implement strategies and techniques in service of content and with respect to theory. Scaffolding, zone of proximal development, and gradual release of responsibility have long been recognized as powerful theories in understanding the implementation of effective instruction. In this case, they serve as mediated tools to enable Mary to help students to eventually pose questions that enable them to write their own I-Searches. The employment of strategies and techniques, then, without theoretical ways of thinking and knowing about the teaching of writing is vapid pedagogy. Without concentration on key questions that we pose to guide us, we quickly see, as students, that we have little to contribute in terms of making meaning through writing as a self-reflective, self-creating, self-searching process. Without something concrete to work with, every teacher knows that all of the strategies in the world will not do students much good.

Mary uses a range of strategies and activities (e.g., brainstorming, guiding questions, outlining, organizational prompts, and conferencing) to assist her students through the I-Search research process. She moves from generating her own questions to recognizing the importance of student-generated questions first to help her target students' zones of proximal development relative to the I-Search task and then to assess their knowledge of their topics. Through student-generated questions developed for the teacher–writer conferences, she gives her students increasing personal responsibility for their own learning. In doing so, she monitors and adjusts the amounts and kinds of responses she provides individual students.

Mary writes:

> The final product of the I-Search was a success. I noticed a substantial improvement in the growth of the sixth graders as writers, and I attribute this directly to their question-posing. When I do teach the I-Search again next year, I will definitely start with students posing questions.

Mary's own search has led to the successful pedagogical style informed by the writing needs of her sixth-grade students. Although it was not an easy journey, searching for the proper pedagogy seldom is. However, her own narrative research, her I-Search teaching journal, has provided her, and us, with examples of insistence and resistance, revisiting and revising, and a necessary narrative design link for reflective examination.

REFERENCES

Anderson, L. M. (1989). Classroom instruction. In M. C. Reynolds (Ed.), *Knowledge bases for the beginning teacher* (pp. 101–111). Oxford, England: Pergamon.

Atwell, N. (1987). *In the middle: Writing, reading, and learning with adolescents*. Portsmouth, NH: Heinemann.

Bruner, J. (1985). *Actual minds possible worlds*. Cambridge, Ma: Harvard University Press.

Calkins, L., with Harwayne, S. (1991). *Living between the lines*. Portsmouth, NH: Heinemann.

Durkin, D. (1979). What classroom observations reveal about reading comprehension instruction. *Reading and Research Quarterly, 14*(4), 481–533.

Elbow, P. (1973). *Writing without teachers*. New York: Oxford University Press.

Elbow, P. (1986). *Writing with power: Techniques for mastering the writing process.* New York: Oxford University Press.

Emig, J. (1971). *The composing process of twelfth graders* (NCTE Research Report No. 13). Urbana, IL: NCTE.

Flower, L. (1981). *Problem-solving strategies for writing.* New York: Harcourt Brace Jovanovich.

Graves, M. F., & Graves, B. (1994, Fall). Scaffolding children's learning. *Missouri Reader.*

Hillocks, G. (1986). The writer's knowledge: Theory, research and implications for practice. In D. Bartholomae and A. Petrosky (Eds.), *The teaching of writing: 85th Yearbook of the National Society for the Study of Education* (pp. 71-94). Chicago: University of Chicago Press.

Janvier, C. (1987). Representation and understanding: The notion of function as an example. In C. Janvier (Ed.), *Problems of representation in the teaching and learning of mathematics* (pp. 67-81). Hillsdale, NJ: Lawrence Erlbaum Associates.

Lehrer, R. (1991, April). *Knowledge design in history.* Paper presented at the annual meeting of American Educational Research Association, Chicago, IL.

Lehrer, R. (1993). Authors of knowledge: Patterns of hypermedia design. In S. Lajoie & S. Derry (Eds.), *Computers as cognitive tools* (pp. 197–227). Hillsdale, NJ: Lawrence Erlbaum Associates.

Macrorie, K. (1988). *The I-Search paper.* Porthsmouth, NH: Heinemann.

Mayher, J. S. (1990) *Uncommon sense theoretical practice in language education.* Portsmouth, NH: Bonyton/Cook Heinemann.

Moffett, J. (1994). *The universal schoolhouse spiritual awakening through education.* San Francisco: Jossey-Bass.

Murray, D. (1968) *A writer teaches writing: A practical method of teaching composition.* Boston: Houghton-Mifflin.

Nystrand, M., with Gamoran, A., Kachur, R., & Prendergast, C. (1997) *Opening dialogue: Understanding the dynamics of language and learning in the English classroom.* New York: Teachers College Press.

Pearson, P. E., & Gallagher, M.C. (1983). The instruction of reading comprehension. *Contemporary Educational Psychology, 8,* 317-344.

Perkins, D. N. (1986). *Knowledge as design.* Hillsdale, NJ: Lawrence Erlbaum Associates.

Rico, G. L. (1983) *Writing the natural way: Using right brain techniques to release your expressive powers.* Los Angeles: J. P. Tarcher.

Rohman, D. G. (1965, May) Prewriting: The stage of discovery in the writing process. *College Composition and Communication.*

Rohman, D. G., & Wiecke, A.O. (1964). *Pre-writing* (USOE Cooperative Research Project No. 2174). *The construction and application of models for concept formation in writing.* East Lansing, Michigan State University.

Tharp, R. G., & Gallimore, R. (1988). *Rousing minds to life.* Cambridge, England: Cambridge University Press.

Vygotsky, L. S. (1978). *Mind in society.* Cambridge, MA: Harvard University Press.

Wilhelm, J. (1995). Creating the missing link: Teaching with hypermedia. *English Journal, 82,* 34–40.

Wilhelm, J., Baker, T. N., & Dube, J. (1997) *Strategic reading: guiding students to lifelong literacy.* Portsmouth, NH: Heinemann.

Wilhelm, J., & Edmiston, B. (1998). *Imagining to learn inquiry, ethics, and integration through drama.* Portsmouth, NH: Heinemann.

Wilhelm, J., & Friedemann, P. (1998). Drama and doing the right thing. *Journal of Research in Rural Education, 13*, 1–11.

Wood, D. J., Bruner, J. S., & Ross, G. (1976). The role of tutoring in problem solving. *Journal of Child Psychology and Psychiatry, 17*(2), 89–100.

12

HALLMARKS
OF TEACHER PREPARATION

The Field Center

Dawn Latta Kirby

Dan Kirby

In the early 1970s the Department of Language Education at the University of Georgia (UGA) located in Athens, Georgia—approximately 60 miles north of Atlanta—was under pressure to convert its teacher education program to a competency-based teacher education licensure program. If the subtlety of that change escapes you, remember the 1970s. Teachers were once again the reason that SAT score were falling and Johnny could not read. As the perennial scapegoat for teacher's failures, schools of education were under pressure to fix the problem. Without going into tortuous detail here, critics of education—people who need no credentials to speak their minds—suggested that teacher education programs were to blame for the miserable performance of school children because those programs had low standards and turned out teachers who had little expertise. Into this blame game came a group of behaviorist political opportunists who suggested that the way to correct the problem of low standards for teacher education graduates was to create a series of assessments that could verify that potential educators had specific competencies and were prepared to succeed at raising scores and fixing whatever was wrong with America. What escaped these critics were the problems of low pay for teachers, few incentives for excellence, and the American ideal that all children, however poorly they were prepared to learn, should be held to the same standards as those children who enjoyed substantial economic advantage.

Education aficionados who can recollect the days of the Competency-Based Education (CBE) fervor might also remember that the central tenet of that kind of program was for teacher education students to demonstrate in clinical settings their ability to perform successfully a rather ominous list of teacher tasks and behaviors. CBE as it was originally conceived placed an enormous burden on clinical teachers not only to observe their student teachers extensively, but also to make sophisticated judgments as to the quality of student teacher performances. CBE further held the false assumption that all of the performances and decisions that teachers must make in any given day could be quantified and arrayed on a simple checklist. Therefore, programs nationwide developed long, elaborate checklists of skills upon which student teachers were to demonstrate competencies and with which clinical teachers were to observe and check off such performances as satisfactory. The notion that the subtle elements of successful teaching can be captured in a behaviorist checklist belies the fact that great teachers orchestrate a remarkable range of values, beliefs, decisions, and strategies so that their successful performance creates a whole far more significant than the sum of the parts.

Faculty in the Department of Language Education, most of whom were quite skeptical about the atomistic principles of CBE, undertook to design and implement an intensive on-site teacher preparation program for prospective secondary English teachers, a program that would involve university professors and classroom teachers in an innovative partnership. This program became know as the Advanced Professional Education Sequence (APES). Central to the success of this new program was the development of laboratory school sites at which students, professors, and teachers would work together for professional teacher education. These laboratory school sites became known as Field Centers, where 6 to 12 interns might be placed and mentored. In this program, student teachers, who became known as teacher candidates (TCs), in secondary English worked under the supervision of two high school teachers and one college supervisor. TCs daily taught four high school classes, had one planning hour to meet and plan as necessary with their supervising teachers and/or with the college supervisor, and had one planning hour to plan instruction, grade papers, and otherwise prepare to teach. TCs attended faculty meetings and parent conferences, and kept the regular hours of the teachers in the schools where they were placed. College supervisors were an on-site presence in the school at least 3 days per week, observing the TCs as they taught, conferring with the supervising teachers, and lending their content and curricular expertise to the faculty members of the school. Because each TC worked with two supervising teachers, 12 to 24 of the school's faculty were involved in supervising TCs along with the one college supervisor.

COSTS OF THE FIELD CENTER APPROACH

This program was cost- and labor-intensive because the work in the field center counted for the entirety of the quarter's teaching load for the college supervisor. The high schools that participated in the program were located in the greater Atlanta, Georgia, and Athens, Georgia, areas, meaning that the college supervisors often had to drive long distances (60 or more miles one way) three or more times each week to work in the field centers. Therefore, the university reimbursed college faculty for mileage expenses while having to employ additional faculty to cover the on-campus courses not being taught by the full-time college faculty during the quarter that they worked within the field center. Yet the program excelled in producing TCs who had a clear picture of the reality of teaching, its daily demands, and the most effective strategies to deal with students, parents, and the larger community of the school.

BENEFITS OF THE FIELD CENTER APPROACH

The effects of the field center experience for all of its constituents were significant. First, the community, students in the high schools, on-site teachers, and parents all received the heightened educational experience brought about by working directly with college faculty who were well versed in best practice pedagogy and in the most effective means for bringing theory to bear on instruction. College faculty members, in turn, were enriched by direct contact with high school students and by the shared colleagueship with on-site teachers, so that the instructional practices of both faculties improved.

Second, the benefits for the TCs—all of whom were teachers in training, often hoping to be employed in the communities where they student taught— were enormous. Teachers and their TCs had common planning times so they could share lesson plans, talk about issues as they arose, and discuss materials. Trouble-shooting was immediate; if the TC's lesson of the previous day went poorly, the next day's planning period could be used to address those concerns and plan more effectively for the next teaching encounter. Because TCs worked with two supervising teachers on-site and one college supervisor, they received intensive professional modeling and support. They also were able to observe at least two different teaching, classroom management, and grading styles. Because the college supervisor was in the field center site 3 or more days per week, TCs received close supervision and information about teaching from both the college and high school faculty members' perspectives. Finally, TCs learned quickly the demands of a teacher's real day—the hours, energy demands, and various skills that must routinely be part of each professional day in the high school—so that the TCs were less overwhelmed and more realistic about the expectations that would be placed on them, especially during that first critical year of teaching.

TCs also participated in a seminar held one afternoon each week after school hours in order to discuss problems in planning, instructional delivery, management, school climate, or other issues that had arisen during the week. The college supervisor who conducted the seminar for his TCs also could encourage TCs to make comparisons across school and grade settings, among teaching and management styles, and about the administrative climate within each school. Seminars further continued to offer TCs information about teaching that they could walk right into their classrooms the next day and implement. Therefore, TCs were reminded of what they had learned in their preceding college classes and of ways to continue applying that classroom learning to their on-site teaching situations.

Third, for the university, the advantage of this program was more than mere public relations, although that certainly was one key asset of the program. It was tuition-based so students registered and paid for both student teaching and the seminar. Supervising teachers on-site were paid a small stipend for their work with student teachers, but the main benefit for everyone—university, high school, TCs, community, high school students, cooperating teachers, and supervising teachers—was the increased pool of skilled, well-prepared teachers within the educational system and the reputation that the university incurred as being a quality site for teacher preparation. Therefore, graduates from the UGA teacher preparation program were quickly hired, their former undergraduate students and the cooperating teachers who had participated in or heard of the field centers often enrolled at the university for graduate work, and schools became eager to become field center sites to reap the full range of benefits from those professional associations.

FROM WITHIN THE FIELD CENTER: STORIES OF BILL SMITH

Bill Smith played several significant roles in both the design and implementation of the APES at the University of Georgia. First, because he is a good thinker and planner, Bill was instrumental in the initial design of the new program. Hatched on chart paper at retreat sites in the north Georgia mountains, the program was at first little more than the hallucination of a remarkable group of faculty in Language Education. At Bill's insistence, faculty decided to dream *a perfect program* without worrying about whether it was really practical at an implementation level. The program would be delivered at school sites, and university professors would live at those sites for extended periods of time. Clinical teachers would be partners in methods seminars that would be co-taught at the site. High-quality scholarly research would be conducted at the sites, with findings shared with faculty and the community. Graduate students would also be mentored at those sites, serving as field center colleagues with university faculty. Through all of this planning and the subsequent struggles to bring it to implementation, Bill Smith was both a thoughtful critic and an enthusiastic cheerleader.

Once several field centers were operational, Bill insisted that he wanted to direct a field center. The Language Education faculty kidded him, suggesting that he did not really know much about schools or teacher education. "You're a linguist," we scoffed. "You wouldn't last a week in the real world of the public schools. Besides, you're an idealist, and you'll make teachers mad." Dan was a colleague of Bill Smith, and they both managed field center sites in the greater Atlanta area. Bill was a natural in a field center setting. Although he was probably more at home in a doctoral seminar, pursuing esoteric linguistics questions with hungry doctoral students, Bill insisted on being included among those who lived a portion of their professional lives each year in the high schools of suburban Atlanta. Because Bill did not have any recent public school teaching experience, he was free to size up any instructional or political issue with the eye of a researcher. If a school practice seemed inappropriate or wrong-headed to him, Bill was quick to engage both TCs and teaching professionals in a spirited discussion about why circumstances had to be that way. Bill's irreverence for mindless school practice and his willingness to engage in heated discussions without rancor made him a favorite among all who participated in his field center. During those years in the field center, Bill was able to observe and critique teaching acts in their purest form without muddying his analysis of those acts with the compromised view of the educational insider.

Dawn was a TC in an urban high school in Atlanta that was the site of Bill's inaugural field center during the spring of 1974. Dan and Bill often invited their two groups of TCs, as well as students in other junior- and senior-level English education courses, to meet with them for informal gatherings in order to discuss professional issues and develop a spirit of community among the students within the teacher preparation program. Dan and Bill therefore developed curriculum and instructional methods together, and Dawn experienced the program first-hand with Bill as her college supervisor.

Bill was a knowledgeable, devoted, if mischievous college supervisor. On one particular occasion, Dawn became frustrated with the grading practices of one of her high school cooperating teachers who wanted her to count off points in students' compositions for each mistake and surface error that the students made. Dawn preferred to concentrate on the quality of the writing, with the result that the cooperating teacher thought that Dawn's grades on the high school students' papers were inflated. When Dawn went to Bill with the controversy, he immediately whipped out a pen and a tablet of paper and explained the solution of the split grade to Dawn: The top grade would be awarded for content, and the bottom grade would represent correctness within the paper. This concept was new to Dawn in 1974 and satisfied both the cooperating teacher and Dawn. Further, it showed Bill's ability to think of solutions that implemented current best practice and theory and that maintained a professional stance for everyone involved in the discussion.

On another occasion, one of Dawn's cooperating teachers told Dawn that she was displaying too much high energy in the classroom; the cooperating teacher was concerned that Dawn would not be able to maintain that level of energy throughout a career of teaching, so the veteran teacher wanted Dawn to prove that she could be an effective teacher even if teaching in a more subdued manner. Bill conveyed this message to Dawn, indicating that he, too, wondered if Dawn could accomplish this task. The next day, Dawn went into the class and taught while utilizing a lower energy level. Dawn sat down while teaching, did not crack any jokes, lectured the whole period, made students raise their hands to speak, and otherwise moderated her teaching style. Both Bill and the cooperating teacher were pleased that the lesson was nonetheless effective while being less demanding on Dawn's personal energy. Now, when Dawn is feeling less energetic or even a bit under the weather, she knows that she can still be an effective teacher; and perhaps it is this ability to moderate energy on some days that has helped Dawn to remain happily in teaching even now without experiencing significant burnout. But to this day, Dawn will maintain that high energy is one of the hallmarks of most of her teaching days.

The mischievous side of Bill also surfaced during Dawn's student teaching experience in the field center that Bill supervised. Bill admonished Dawn and the other two TCs under his supervision not to gather in the teacher's lounge and engage in unprofessional talk about students, parents, the school, or our lives. We TCs nodded our understanding and minded our professional Ps and Qs in the teacher's lounge while in the company of other teachers in the school. When we three TCs were alone in the teacher's lounge, however, we rather ignored Bill's admonitions and discussed whatever topics we had on our minds—which might include our recent dates or opinions of various students or teachers. One Monday, we TCs noticed some books out of place on the book shelves in the teacher's lounge, but we didn't think much about it, and we proceeded to discuss our weekend activities with each other. When the bell rang, we filed out to teach our classes. However, at the weekly seminar, Bill displayed an uncanny knowledge of our most recent weekend activities. We were stunned. When he saw the puzzled looks on our faces, he reminded us that the teacher's lounge was a professional setting and that we all wanted to present ourselves in the best light while in the school in order to receive good recommendations and become gainfully employed. Then he brought a small cassette recorder from his briefcase, hit the "play" button, and watched us TCs as we heard ourselves on the tape, gabbing about our weekends. The point was well made. Talk from that time on remained strictly professional while we were in the teacher's lounge.

Bill was also known for his subtle baiting of students who sat in TCs' classes at the high school. One of Bill's favorite tricks was to seat himself in a student desk near the rear of a classroom among the 10th graders who hid out back there. As the TC ventured deep into a lecture on a scene in *Hamlet* or tried to explain the subjunctive, Bill quietly encouraged students around him to raise their hands and ask the TC difficult questions. "What exactly was Hamlet's relationship with his mother?" or "Isn't the use of the subjunctive anachronistic?" or "Why should we use the subjunctive when no one on TV or in the papers uses it?" Bill loved to see whether the TCs could deal with spontaneous questions and how well they handled surprises in the classroom.

In his role as instructional coach, Bill was an avid note taker in the TCs' classes, usually scripting the entire lesson. When he sat down with a student teacher after observing a lesson, he had detailed observation notes and posed challenging questions to the TC. "Why did you ignore that kid in the third row?" or "How else might you have responded to the student who didn't see why she had to know the subjunctive?" or "What's your plan for energizing that group of learners tomorrow when you're back in that class?" If a TC denied a particular bad behavior, Bill would reread his transcript to the TC, saying, "Maybe I got this wrong, but what I heard you say was. . . ." TCs soon learned to confess failings quickly and honestly, knowing that Bill would offer caring, professional advice and continue to make us think by posing the types of higher level questions that only researchers seem able to compose.

In all encounters with TCs, Bill remained strictly professional. He held enormously high standards, but he was always friendly, caring, and an intelligent mentor. TCs were encouraged to conduct their own mini-inquiry or mini-research studies during their teaching. Bill helped his TCs to identify an issue or a concern in their teaching that they wanted to improve, and then to construct possible solutions and options. TCs asked questions such as, "What if I taught this material this way?" or "What if this activity came first during my lesson?" or "What if I used these materials instead of those older ones?", and then noticed the results of their new actions. Often the results improved their teaching, their students' learning, and their abilities to think and act like the professionals they wanted to become. Bill was an ideal model of reflecting, applying knowledge, and monitoring results to improve pedagogy.

On one memorable evening, Bill and his wife Sue invited Bill's three TCs to their home for dinner. We TCs arrived, naively expecting a rather stuffy evening. What we got was just the opposite. Bill and Sue were interesting conversationalists, caring hosts, and fabulous cooks. They treated the assembled TCs as their professional equals while still sharing insights about careers and professional choices with the TCs. We TCs were offered fine wine—not the usual college fare—and it was on this occasion that Dawn first sipped the Napoleon brandy that Bill always has on hand at home. This night is a hallmark in Dawn's professional life because it taught her that teachers can be caring, humane, and very real with their students in appropriate ways while still maintaining the attitude of the professional guide and mentor. It is a lesson that Dawn has tried to carry into her interactions with her adult students.

The most important lessons from within the field center are those of professionalism and mentoring. The caring attitudes and professional demeanors that both Dan and Bill managed to convey to all of their students have become note-worthy in all of their students' careers. Bill and Dan were the mentors for their students that their former TCs are still trying to emulate 30 or more years later.

LONG-TERM EFFECTS

The long-term effects of the field center and of the experience with Bill are twofold. Professionally, Dan and Dawn continue to believe that immersion is the best approach to teacher preparation when it is supported by mentoring, nurturing, and critical professional conversations about the contemporary issues of teaching. Dan and Dawn have implemented versions of the field center approach in subsequent work in teacher education for the last 30 or more years, although they both remain heartily skeptical about the CBE tenets that caused its origin.

Personally, Bill remains a friend and colleague across time and space—a gift.

III

BEYOND THE CLASSROOM

13

MENTORING RESEARCHERS

A Tribute to Bill Smith

Suzanne Miller
with Stuart Greene
Dawn Latta
Nancy Mellin McCracken
Michael Moore
Marie Nelson
Connie Ruzich
Nancy Sommers
David Wallace

In the acknowledgment section of my dissertation, written at 3 a.m. on the day I HAD to submit the final version to the University of Pittsburgh, I got the part about Bill Smith just right. It reads, "To Bill Smith who exemplifies and lives the proper spirit of inquiry." If I had had more time, more energy left, I would have explained what I meant. Now, finally, I have the opportunity to elaborate on that dedication. On the occasion of this book to honor Bill's accomplishments and contributions to the profession, we must not forget his role as a mentor to doctoral students. In the past 15 years, it has become clear to me that we can learn a lot from Bill's approach. He profoundly influenced me and, it turns out, many other students to whom I have recently talked. In fact, I believe that what he did stands as an exemplar for that difficult and largely untaught role—of mentor to new researchers.

In speaking to others mentored by Bill Smith, I have been amazed at the clarity of the memories and the lasting gratitude people feel. Bill gave us the gift of time, clearing his schedule for a few hours—2 or 3—on the same afternoon when we ran into a brick wall and needed to talk. He would listen carefully and ask questions to follow the line of our thinking. Perhaps that was the most powerful of his ways—never to take us off the line of our thinking to impose his, but always providing the space for our verbal processing, with his questioning to help us elaborate, sort things out, and consider prospects. He was a consummate collaborator, never afraid of unformed notions or, even, half-baked ideas. Those leaps provoked opportunities to think further together. But he was practical, too. The first time I stayed after class to ask about a research question I was considering for a project, Bill said, "Great question, but it will require a lifetime of research." Then he helped me focus in on a one-semester do-able piece.

In his role as mentor, Bill was not really playing a role at all: He was a passionate researcher intrigued by problems of interpretation, by the possibilities to be considered, by the research questions we had raised. "Huh!" he'd say, "I never thought of it that way." Or, "that's an *interesting* question." Perhaps *that* was the most important—he always took us seriously as thinkers and as researchers, often before we could do that for ourselves.

Bill would tell stories about the life of inquiring into educational questions in ways that conjured it as a genuine option. For those of us coming out of years of public school teaching or master's programs, it was like postcards from another country. From Bill's stories of groups of friends consulting on research at conferences when English education was young, that new kind of life seemed possible for us, too. He always said that nobody, as a child, when asked what they want to be when they grow up, says "an educational researcher." So true. But he helped us envision this odd profession as a real and nourishing one that was within our grasp.

Bill's love was experimental research. But more than almost anyone else I have ever known, he was open to research methods that were not his own. Unlike some from that paradigm (e.g., see Miller, Wilson, & Moore, 1998), he was open to all kinds of methods that got at the research question. He admired the depth of understanding available from qualitative research, and worried, for example, if the quantitative coding scheme I used to describe discussion in my dissertation study might close down other interpretations, might be too narrow a lens. His opening up to multiplicity was at the center of his reflection, his passion, and his engagement in the research life.

In what follows, these and other points are elaborated with stories from the experiences of researchers who were mentored by Bill Smith or observed his mentoring up close.

GENEROSITY

Connie Ruzich, now at Robert Morris University, sees Bill's mentoring as a disposition, as she wrote this memory:

> Bill Smith is one of the most unstintingly generous people I have ever known. Although intensely private, he shares his time and energy and intellect with remarkable openness. My "Bill Smith" story occurred after I left the University of Pittsburgh. As a doctoral student at the University of Pennsylvania, I was in the midst of writing my dissertation, when my dissertation director suddenly left the university. Another Penn professor agreed to accept the titular responsibility of directing my dissertation if my second reader would agree to bear the brunt of the workload. That second reader was Bill Smith. Without compensation, without receiving credit, and without complaint, Bill spent hours reading chapters and suggesting additional lines of inquiry for a student who was no longer at his institution.
>
> Out of his own pocket, Bill picked up all the costs of this support, including the round-trip plane fare to Philadelphia so that he could appear at my defense. After the defense, I attempted to pay Bill's airfare, to offer some small measure of thanks. He refused all payment except one. I can clearly remembering Bill's instructions: "You can only repay me in one way: do the same for other students who you will have the opportunity to help in the future." Long before Hollywood made the film *Pay It Forward*, Bill Smith taught me one of the most memorable lessons of my educational career. Bill reminds us to put aside pointless academic struggles over intellectual property rights and to join with others in the true enterprise of education: learning from one another in ways that can better ourselves and our worlds.

Bill Smith's intellectual generosity was legendary, recurring in many stories of his mentoring. Dawn Latta Kirby, now at Kennesaw State, writes elsewhere in this volume about Bill Smith as mentor to preservice teachers. Here she recalls for us his generous willingness to assist young researchers in research design:

> Even after I had graduated from UGA, Bill and I stayed in touch. After several years, as I went to work on designing my dissertation study on written fluency among high school students, Bill and I met casually at an NCTE conference. Don't remember which one. Anyhow, before I knew it, Bill had agreed to meet me in the hotel lobby after dinner, and we sat there until 3 a.m. charting a design for my dissertation research. I didn't use all of what we had charted, but the idea that he would sit there for 5+ hours, listening to and helping me is amazing to me even to this day. But that's Bill—unstinting in his love of research, his ability to grasp and then convey to others elegant research designs, and his willingness to help novice researchers.

Many of us who have known Bill over the past few decades recalled his love of "charting" research, generating designs to help novice researchers think through possible methods.

RESPECT AND CARING

There was a serious stance Bill had toward doctoral students that many remembered fondly. Nancy Sommers, now at Harvard University, remembers that, "I *loved* going into Bill's office with my questions. He took these questions and me very seriously, probably more seriously than I took myself. His confidence in me made everything possible. I will always be grateful."

This esteem for doctoral students and the possibilities for their intellectual lives was a strong theme in the stories of Bill's students. Joan Latchaw, University of Nebraska (Omaha), has fond memories of Bill as a respectful, caring friend:

> Bill treated students as colleagues, as professionals with good intentions, with motivation, with respect, even when undeserved. For instance, he trusted that projects would come to completion, that ideas would turn into action. He had good contacts for my dissertation, which heavily relied on theories of critical thinking. He was an excellent resource because he talked to the Carnegie Mellon scholars. They were invaluable contacts.
>
> Bill is very disciplined, so we were a good fit. The following has never left me: When I started working on the dissertation he said I must work all the time, taking breaks only to eat and go to the bathroom. Believe it or not, that's pretty much what I did. I had two teenage kids and was divorced, but worked all day every day, became a hermit, took "breaks" to apply for jobs and got the dissertation done in 9 months.
>
> Among Bill's most wonderful qualities was his personality. Bill treated students like friends, at least it seemed to me. I recall a surprise birthday party for him when I lived there and so many students attended and did songs and skits. I always felt at ease in talking about my work, asking for advice. I felt like he cared about me.

The notion of caring has become a central educational foundation (Noddings, 1986), but Bill's inclination to mentor doctoral students with care and respect predated these theories. Creating a feeling of ease in conversations—equalizing power—was Bill's way.

TIME, SPACE, ATTENTION

Stuart Greene, now at the University of Notre Dame, remembers Bill as a mentor who always found the time and place for inquiring with students:

Bill was always willing to give up his time to talk about my research. In fact, I recall that after one particularly stressful time, we spent hours in the library going over a draft of three chapters of my dissertation—line by line. He was never contentious but always questioning, probing, genuinely curious about puzzling issues for which there were no answers. But the time that stands out for me is when he got a suite at a conference for himself and about six graduate students. We practiced our papers in front of each other and tightened our arguments in what was really a four-day seminar. It was quite extraordinary to think of how much time Bill was willing to spend with each of us. Of course, he was in his element—always the teacher, prodding, challenging, asking the tough "so what" question.

Pursuing the tough questions in any forum with students who needed the practice, that was Bill's gift—the time and attention of a critical friend.

SUSTAINING RESEARCHERS
AND COLLABORATION

Nancy Mellin McCracken, from Kent State University, captures Bill Smith's inventive ways of mentoring researchers in her story, which she calls "Peanuts and Marginalia":

I knew Bill Smith when I was at Pitt working on a Post Doc in English Ed. I had just finished my dissertation on teachers' response to students' writing. He read every word and offered wonderful questions and connections. His door was always open and he kept a huge jar of peanuts in their shells for visitors to crack open and eat during our conversations. I got to sit in on his team research group meetings where everyone learned not just how to do research, but how to do it as a research team. And the projects weren't unconnected dummy runs (as Britton used to call writing exercises): Everyone in the group was working toward a common research question. The conversation was energetic, honest, critical, and always with a sense of genuine mutual respect and an underlying spirit of play. Each of us was always clearly more important than any of the small or large research process engaging us at the moment. I've tried to carry that spirit into my research courses in the almost 20 years since then.

One more little telling bit of Bill Smith practice that I've adopted: He freely loaned his books to his grad students and encouraged them to write in the margins. Over the years classics became a palimpsest of readers' responses—scribbled comments and questions in the margins, answered and re-answered at the bottom of pages and all around the text. Reading a book from Smith's shelves was the unique experience of engaging in an asynchronous written conversation with years of doc students and the author. (You should see my copies of Moffett's *Teaching the Universe of Discourse!* I'm on my 4th or 5th copy of Rosenblatt's *Reader, Text, Poem.*) Those books so thoroughly marked up are a symbol for me of what Bill's mentorship was like.

He gave his undivided attention and his razor sharp mind to whatever intellectual question you brought, and he sent you away feeling stronger and ready to go another few rounds. He fed you peanuts in the shell and his marked-up books on composition research. You had to work a little at both, but what sustenance!

The ongoing dialogue with a history sustained many a student in the spirit of play that energized.

CONVERSATIONS FROM AFAR

Many professionals during the past few decades who were not mentored by Bill Smith remembered him fondly as a colleague. Marie Nelson, from National Louis University in Tampa, recalls how her path had crossed with Bill's over many years:

Bill wasn't a mentor of mine in graduate school, mostly because he arrived at the University of Georgia as I was preparing to leave the doctoral program in Language Ed because I couldn't find a (quantitative) dissertation topic that didn't feel like it would waste a year of my time. The year was 1970. Viet Nam was raging. The civil rights movement was in full swing. Ever the activist, I had more important work to do.

By the time I returned to Georgia, in 1978, Bill Smith was at Pitt so I saw him only at conferences. What I remember, however, was not any help he gave to me, but his patient suggestions to students who brought their research for feedback to CEE's L. Ramon Veal Seminar on Research in Language—most of them from institutions that did not offer the solid support I received at UGA.

While it was the emergent designs of grounded theory that attracted me back to graduate school, I was influenced by the creative quantitative approaches to solving research questions that Bill Smith took in his own work—like the study of student revising, in which he had students use invisible ink to tease out the extent to which rereading affected the revising they did. I was also inspired by Bill's flexibility as a thinker. I knew from knowing him at Georgia his first year out of FSU that Bill's dissertation study had been on sentence combining, and that he'd found teaching it made a significant difference in the length and complexity of the sentences students wrote. So I was surprised to learn all those years later (and once again struck by his knack for design) that Bill had published an article in print suggesting just the opposite. Since students will try to give teachers whatever they think teachers want, he reasoned, teaching sentence combining might be largely superfluous, and in fact, he got similar results by giving a writing prompt which simply requested they write longer, more complex sentences.

From the ingenuity of Bill's quantitative designs I learned how to work backward from my own qualitative designs to devise ingenious ways to tease out what I wanted to know. It was this aspect of Bill's intelligence that has most affected my work and the way I work with my own students.

With flexibility, creativity, and ingenuity, Bill influenced Marie and other scholars even from afar.

THE GOLD STANDARD OF COLLEGIALITY

Bill's mentoring can be seen as a sincere form of excellent collegiality. Michael Moore, Professor at Georgia Southern University, remembers Bill as a remarkable mentor—and much more:

I first met Bill Smith when he spoke in one of my doctoral classes as Pitt. Right away his enthusiasm was contagious, and he invited everyone in the class to work with him if we so desired. Bill was the first and only professor I knew to make such an offer. I went to see him sometime afterward and joined his research team. I then took his composition seminar and learned for the first time what a real "seminar" was like. It was then I decided that I wanted to ask Bill to direct my dissertation. There were some politics to work out (Bill was technically in the English Department and I was in Instructional Studies). I approached Bill and asked him if he would chair my dissertation committee. He had one condition. I had to work with him on his projects first. This meant that I would have to delay my dissertation for at least a year. What a great decision on my part.

I worked with Bill on a number of projects, two of which were highly memorable. The first involved our research group that met on Fridays and conducted studies in composition research. We also served each other as informal dissertation and MA advisors. My dissertation fell under regular scrutiny from this group. In fact, when I eventually prepared for my defense, this group conducted a mock defense that was by far the most grueling two hours I have ever spent. My actual defense was such a breeze that I felt guilty.

The other memory was working with Bill on "D" Point Theory. I won't go into the intricacies of "D" Point Theory except to say that it was Bill's way of learning how I think and his way of teaching me how to think. We spent hours and hours working out this theory, eating peanuts, and filling reams of graph paper. We still discuss this theory, replacing the graph paper with napkins from various bars. "D" Point Theory now explains much of the known universe. It has become its own matrix. I have kept every note I've ever taken.

Others have spoken about Bill's gift of time. I don't know where he found it in such quantities. A dissertation meeting with Bill often started late in the afternoon and went until late at night. Bill is the gold standard I follow or attempt to follow on every committee that I am a member. I try to read student work as carefully as Bill did, but I doubt that I do. I would never consider a new research project without subjecting it to Bill's litmus test. Every time this has happened I have come away wondering how I missed so much. No one does it all better.

SMITH SYNDROME

According to David Wallace, the result of Bill's mentoring is "Smith Syndrome," a malady that has infected many of Bill's students. Symptoms include an enthusiastic addiction to empirical research in all its complexities. Eventually sufferers are passing this affliction on to their own students as they listen to them, making them believe that they too are smart enough to sort out the problems of research. Wallace explains his own experience this way:

> The funny thing about Smith Syndrome is that it starts with euphoria about—
> —of all things— research. I noticed my first symptoms on a sunny spring day
> as I walked up a little hill on Forbes Avenue near the University of Pittsburgh.
> I'd just spent an hour in Bill's Cathedral of Learning office, and I was heading back to my little cubbyhole office at Carnegie Mellon, smiling at a sheet
> of paper that Bill and I had just spent the last hour filling with grand plans for
> my dissertations—boxes and lines, hastily scrawled research questions, and
> sample regression equations. After an hour with Bill, the simple research plan
> I'd worked out with Linda Flower and Dick Hayes had mushroomed, sprouting new dependent measures and growing stratified random samples.
> Somewhere deep inside me, I knew this meant a heck of a lot more work, yet
> I was smiling.
>
> At first, I thought the virus that infected me that afternoon must have been
> lurking somewhere in that funny office of Bill's with its slanted ceilings and
> nooks stuffed with book shelves and boxes of data. Months later—far too late
> to save myself—I realized that Bill himself was the carrier, that it was his
> excitement to better understand that had floated across the table and hooked
> me. And it was his certainty that I could do this, that I was smart enough to
> figure out this complicated stuff, that sealed my fate.
>
> I see now that despite my initial infection, I could have escaped the clutches of this malady on my second visit to Bill's office but I hesitated, wondering what was going on in Bill's mind as he leaned back in his chair, stroking
> his chin. And then he got me. "I think what **we** need to do . . . ." **We?** It passed
> by me almost without notice at the time: He wasn't saying "what you need to
> do it"; no, it was we. Suddenly I had a partner, and together we would find
> answers to these problems that had stymied me alone.
>
> I failed to appreciate the subtly of Smith Syndrome at that point. I didn't
> realize that in a physical sense **we** existed only in Bill's office. It was my proj-

ect, my dissertation, so it would be me who got up at the crack of dawn and fought my way through Pittsburgh's surprisingly congested traffic to get to the second research site **we'd** added so that we could compare students from different educational backgrounds. And it was **me** who would spend dozens of hours interviewing the students about their papers so that **we** could compare the student's perceptions of how well they'd fulfilled their intentions with rater's impressions. Yet, somehow I was still happy because I wasn't alone: We needed to better understand.

This thing, in fact, was infecting dozens of graduate students. At Bill's 50th birthday party, I stood solemn before a group of thirty or more of Bill's students who had moments before been happily eating and drinking. I apologized for bringing a moment of seriousness to general levity and explained that I'd been designated to bring them important news about a malady to which they had all been exposed, that the Centers for Disease Control had just identified "Smith Syndrome" and isolated its epicenter as Room 526, Cathedral of Learning, University of Pittsburgh. They laughed—laughed until they cried.

LEAGUES OF CRITICAL FRIENDS

Those of us mentored by Bill Smith remember well this man with an infectious disposition toward inquiry and an intellectual generosity. In his mentoring, Bill provided support for real research apprenticeships, created social networks of fellow researchers, made himself available for any felt reason ("There is no such thing as a dumb question," I hear him saying). He seemed to understand the somewhat predictable cycle of novice researchers sliding from excitement and anticipation to fear and doubt as things inevitably went awry. He anticipated that life would intervene, that energy and nerve might fail—and kept at hand the means of reflection and rejuvenation. Peanuts for some, books and stories for others, and dialogue for all. He fortified us (infected us?) with the attitude that research is important, that becoming a researcher is worth everything we give. More than providing individual attention, guidance, encouragement, and support, Bill nurtured relationships.

Bill's example makes clear the idea that relationships are at the center of successful mentoring. It is not so much what one does as a mentor/teacher, as "what one's actions actually meant to specific others in a specific situation" (Sidorkin, 2002, p. 198).

For many of us, Bill's actions meant the bridge to our future, the just-in-time sustenance that kept us going. Relationship by relationship, he developed a valuing of questioning, wondering, time to figure things out together. In his example and sometimes explicitly, he asked professors-in-preparation to pass it on to future students. In a few decades, Bill Smith's students have scattered throughout the country. As some of us speak together here, it seems clear that he did more than get us through doctoral programs. Bill Smith reenvisioned the process of mentoring researchers by creating a culture of collegiality. We all give him heartfelt thanks for that.

REFERENCES

Miller, S. M., Nelson, M., & Moore, M. (1998, Fall). Caught in the paradigm gap: Qualitative researchers' lived experience and the politics of epistemology. *American Educational Research Journal, 35*(3), 1–36.

Noddings, N. (1986). *Caring: A feminine approach to ethics and moral education.* Berkeley: University of California Press.

Sidorkin, A. M. (2002). *Learning relations: Impure education, deschooled schools, & dialogue with evil.* New York: Peter Lang.

14

GEOGRAPHIES OF HOPE

A Study of Urban Landscapes, Digital Media, and Children's Representations of Place

Glynda A. Hull

Michael Angelo James

Traveling from the University of California, Berkeley, to the adjacent community of West Oakland, one cannot help but observe a changing landscape—from leafy green to grey concrete, from relative affluence to an urban poverty that is stark. Several years ago, we founded a community technology center in the heart of this urban neighborhood that is just a local bus ride from the university campus, yet light years distant in terms of its residents' educational and economic prospects and social futures. Our university–community partnership called Digital Underground Storytelling for Youth (DUSTY)[1] brings University of California undergraduate and graduate students together with youth from the West Oakland community. There they work, play, and create using digital multi-

[1]We gratefully acknowledge the support of the following funders: the U.S. Department of Education's Community Technology Centers program; the University of California's UCLinks Program; the Community Technology Foundation of California; the City of Oakland's Fund for Children and Youth; and the Robert F. Bowne Foundation. We appreciate as well the support of our university and community partners: the Graduate School of Education, University of California, Berkeley; the Prescott-Joseph Center for Community Enhancement; Allen Temple Baptist Church; Cole Middle School; and the Castlemont Community of Small Schools. We

modal, multimedia literacies to cross geographic, racial, cultural, socioeconomic, and semiotic divides. In this chapter, we reflect on our work from the vantage point of 5 years of collaboration to develop and sustain DUSTY, make it responsive to community partners and participants, document its activities, and assess its role. In particular, taking inspiration from recent scholarship in the field of cultural geography (e.g., Harvey, 2000; Mitchell, 2002; Soja, 1996), we attempt here to think spatially as well as historically and socially about West Oakland as an urban neighborhood, and about the role that a community/university collaborative like DUSTY can play in reconstituting images of place and self. We begin by describing the policy and academic backdrops for DUSTY.

PERSPECTIVES ON SPACES FOR LEARNING
AND LITERACY AFTER SCHOOL

Over the last 10 years, there has been a renaissance of after-school programs in the United States, designed to fill the gap between school turning out and parents returning home, motivated by reports that designate after-school hours as at-risk time (cf. Halpern, 2002, 2003). Federal support for such programs has recently been reduced or withdrawn, yet the need for after-school programs outstrips their availability, and they remain noticeable players in today's educational arena (cf. National Institute on Out-of-School Time, 2003). The programs are not, however, without their detractors, because controversial evaluations have recently demonstrated the difference that after-school programs do not seem to make in children's safety and academic achievement (cf. Kane, 2004). From our experience, a key ideological struggle around after-school programs today is determining their nature—whether they will be extensions of the school day, designed only or primarily to continue or assist with academic work, or whether they will focus on something different or something additional: cultural enrichment, arts education, youth development, or other activities that are not as constrained by the enormous current pressures on schools to improve tests scores or to march lock-step to a mandated textbook or curriculum standards (cf. Hull & Schultz, 2002). The broad

salute the DUSTY staff, instructors, undergraduates, and participants who make our work together seem more like play. We thank Verda Delp, Tiffany Hooker, Mark Jury, Mira-Lisa Katz, Nora Kenney, Stacy Marple, Mark Nelson, Laura Nicodemus, Mike Rose, and Jessica Zacher for their insightful comments on and assistance with this chapter. Nora Kenney was the DUSTY instructor who taught Jamal, the child who is our case study in this chapter. We thank her for her insights about him as well as for her skill in interviewing him. She was assisted by Ananda Esteva, who worked with Jamal on the digital poem featured here, as did Pauline Pearson Hathorn. We thank them all for their excellent work with Jamal and the other DUSTY students. Finally and especially, we thank Jamal—for his creativity, his generosity of spirit, a wisdom that went beyond his years, and his willingness to share his work with us and a larger audience.

question, then, is what kind of space—materially, socially, and in terms of available symbolic resources—might we imagine for learning and relationships after-school?

Over 15 years ago, Cole (1996) began to create after school programs that were alternative spaces for learning, rather than replications of the school day. This work paralleled the increased interest in after-school programs mentioned earlier, but Cole's work was distinctive in being driven by an interest in exploring the implications of cultural-historical activity theory for reconceptualizing learning. Such explorations, Cole and his colleagues found, could take place more effectively out of school than in formal classrooms, because constraints on curricula and participant structures in the former were fewer. Thus was born a set of after-school programs and a national and international consortium of collaborators who shared Cole's theoretical assumptions.

Simply put, Cole and colleagues conceptualized after-school programs as "activity systems" that blurred boundaries between work and play, that provided a structure for participation allowing movement between expert and novice roles, and that took advantage of widely available computer technologies, such as e-mail and electronic games. Cole's conceptualization also linked the university and the community, bringing graduate students and undergraduates to the after-school program, and working collaboratively with community partners such as Boys' and Girls' clubs to establish the program. Called the 5th Dimension initially, this work later inspired a set of after-school programs affiliated with each of the eight University of California campuses (cf. Gutiérrez, Baquedano-Lopez, & Tejeda, 1999; Underwood, Welsh, Gauvain, & Duffy, 2000). This later project, UCLinks, was a direct response to the dismantling of affirmative action within the University of California in 1996. The hope was that well-designed, theoretically motivated after-school programs, such as UCLinks and the 5th Dimension, could increase the chances that children from low-income communities and beleaguered schools, especially youth of color, would aspire to and be able to attend a college or university, thereby sustaining or even increasing diversity on campuses such as UC Berkeley.

DUSTY began as a UClinks site; it thereby shares some of the important features of Cole's and his colleagues' conceptualization, in particular the linkage between university students and youth from the community; the commitment to establish a collaboration that draws on the strengths and resources of both community and university partners; and an interest in fashioning a space for learning that contrasts what is offered during the school day. In our work at DUSTY, we have viewed the linkage between the university and the local community as reciprocal border crossing and space creation—as a movement back and forth across social, geographic, economic, cultural, and semiotic divides and the creation through this movement of a new space for learning, one that turns the periphery into the center. We have been attentive to the way in which such a traversal of borders has implications for how we conceptualize DUSTY and its role in the community. As the opening to this chapter suggests, the differences in physical space and material resources that characterize the University and the West Oakland community, noticeable at every entry and exit, have pushed us to be aware of this larger community context and the ways in which that context both influences and is modestly influenced by our community technology center and after-school programs.

As a university–community collaborative that organizes undergraduate students to work, play, and create with children and youth at a community center, DUSTY (and UCLinks) is also part of a movement in higher education called *service learning* (cf. Furco & Billig, 2002). Prompted by recent federal legislation, but rooted in long-held conceptions of experiential learning such as Dewey's (1938), service learning courses aim to position students to serve their local community, as well as reflect on these experiences in the context of an academic course on a college campus. Thus, in the spirit of Dewey, such courses ideally connect the learning that students do in a formal classroom with participation and responsibility in the larger society. One especially vigorous and intellectually alive branch of service learning has developed within composition studies; teachers of writing in universities and colleges now regularly send their students to community-based organizations to assist with or perform writing activities or literacy-related tutoring (cf. Deans, 2000). As is demonstrated in this chapter, DUSTY also has as its centerpiece certain writing and literacy-related activities—in particular, multimedia, multimodal composing; our undergraduates both learn these new kinds of composing themselves and support children and youth from the community in their use of new and old literacies. Another way that service learning scholarship within composition studies resonates with our work at DUSTY is its critical consciousness about what constitutes an ethical relationship between the university and the community. Early on important concerns were expressed about the nature of service, particularly the unhappy possibility that university students could approach their community work with a kind of missionary zeal that reduced community members to objects for salvation (cf. Boyle-Baise, 2002; Herzburg, 1994; Himley, 2004; Welsh, 2002). Frank and helpful explorations of sustainability have also been a prominent thread, as faculty confront their university's disinterest in service and engage in the balancing act that allows them to link their teaching and research with service to the community (Cushman, 1999, 2002).

To be sure, most of the scholarship on service learning in composition studies has tended to focus on the university end of the collaboration. Although this should not be surprising, the effect has often been, from our point of view, to relegate the communities served to the shadows, places where adults and youth are sometimes characterized as needy and different or leading marginal lives. Flower (2002) describes typical inquiry patterns of service learning this way: "The research on service-learning is indeed preoccupied with *our* expertise; with developing pedagogical agendas, interrogating our middle-class ideologies, producing satisfying academic dichotomies and incisive critiques" (p. 184). Thus, the geography of service learning often becomes one of reconnaissance: forays to scout out a possibly unfriendly territory with the intent of returning to cover. For this reason, we have found especially compelling the service learning scholarship that is grounded in the community—projects involved in the creation and sustenance of community programs over time—and that explores the tensions and challenges of traversing and recharting community and university borders. We draw inspiration particularly from Flower and her colleagues (Flower, 2000, 2003; Long, Peck, & Baskins, 2002; Peck, Flower, & Higgins, 1995), who have worked within the settlement house tradition in Pittsburgh, Pennsylvania, to carry out long-term collaborations that blend university intellectual traditions with community interests and resources under the label of *intercultural inquiry.* Such inquiry, as Flower and her colleagues have persuasively documented, involves challenges to the habits of mind of those in the academy as it simultaneously supports literate action among community members. One of the central metaphors that they use in their work has an important spatial dimension—the dinner table, around which participants draw their chairs both literally and symbolically, to converse and engage in joint problem solving and the important process that Flower terms the *negotiation of meaning.*

Certainly a central theme of Flower, Peck, Long, and Baskins' joint work has been to enable participants to discover and enact their agency as individuals and community members, people operating within constraints of course, but actors increasingly aware of their ability to have an effect, especially through the deployment of strategic uses of language and literacy. The primary theoretical underpinning of DUSTY has likewise centered on identity formation, and especially the role of language and other semiotic systems in this process. We have written in detail about this framework elsewhere (Hull & Katz, in press), but in brief we have described how all semiotic systems—language, writing, images, music, dance—give us a means to embody and enact a sense of self in relation to others. In the words of Urciuoli (1995), "The creation of meaning is above all embedded in human relationships: people enact their selves to each other in words, movements, and other modes of actions" (p. 189). Thus, at DUSTY we have aimed to position participants to tell their important stories about self and community, and to use those moments of narrative reconstruction to reflect on past events, present activities, and future goals. Our curriculum encourages participants to construct stories that position themselves as agents, as young people and adults able to articulate and act on their own "wishes, desires, beliefs, and expectancies" (Bruner, 1994, p. 41) and as local and global community members able to remake their worlds (Freire, 1970). Further, we have provided a powerful mediational means for their storytelling (cf. Cole, 1996; Vygotsky, 1934/1986, 1978). At this particular historical moment, which is characterized by a pictorial turn (Mitchell, 1994; cf. Kress, 2003), we believe such means include the technical skills and social practices that constitute the version of multimedia composing that we refer to as *digital storytelling* (cf. Lambert, 2002). The variety of representational activities that occur at DUSTY—be they spoken word performances, written narratives, photo collections, storyboards, musical compositions, animations, or digital stories—we conceptualize as identity texts to call attention to the

primacy given at DUSTY to fostering and enacting agentive and socially responsible identities through the use of a range of semiotic systems (Leander, 2002; cf.
Leoni & Cohen, 2004).

In this chapter, we extend our theoretical lens to include ideas about space,
place, and landscape drawn from the field of cultural geography and related disciplines. Recently, interest has grown within literacy studies around such ideas
(see especially Leander, 2002; Leander & Sheehy, 2004), with researchers such as
Moje (2004) investigating how youth enact different identities according to the
different spaces they occupy, as they martial the available resources, textual and
material, that are associated with those spaces. Understanding how *space*, *place*, and
landscape (terms we illustrate later) intersect with senses of self, community, and
agency is especially pivotal in our work and, we believe, relevant to service learning programs and other educational efforts that cross borders literally and symbolically. Soja (2004), a well-known critical geographer, has written persuasively
about the spatial turn that is spreading fast among the human sciences. He argues
that, whereas the historical and the social have long been accepted as important
analytic dimensions, the spatial has been neglected. Yet he notes that, increasingly, we are coming to understand how the social, historical, and spatial are interwoven and in fact inseparable. Paraphrasing Henri Lefebvre (on whose influential
work he and many other critical geographers build), Soja observes that, "all social
relations remain abstractions until they are concretized in space" (p. xiv). It is
noteworthy that Soja and other theorists are fierce about not wanting to promote
an orthodoxy in terms of how to conceptualize spatiality. Instead, they urge that
we hold open "our critical geographical imagination" (Soja, 2004, p. 2) and resist
rigid relations among terms such as *space*, *place*, and *landscape* (Mitchell, 2002). In
this chapter, we accept Soja's and Mitchell's invitation as we attempt to use recent
theorizing on spatiality to gain a fresh vantage point on our community technology center, our activities there, and our university–community collaboration.

Thus, in this chapter, we use the terms *space*, *place*, and *landscape* to animate our
analysis of community relations and multimedia representational activities. In so
doing, we follow Mitchell's (2002) helpful presentation of these terms as a "dialec-
tical triad" (p. x). "If a place is a specific location," he writes, "a space is a 'practiced place,' a site activated by movements, actions, narratives, and signs, and a
landscape is that site encountered as image or 'sight'" (2002, p. x).[2] To illustrate,
our community technology center, located in a renovated Victorian that used to
be a convent, across the street from a church and an elementary school, in the
heart of the West Oakland neighborhood known as the "lower bottoms," is a place.
Our collective use of that place—through our curriculum and our social relationships, our pedagogy and our participants, and our vision of border crossing and

---

[2]In offering these understandings of space, place, and landscape, Mitchell helpfully combined
insights from LeFebvre (1974) on perceived, conceived, and lived space, and de Certeau (1984),
who juxtaposed place with space, which he conceptualized as "a practiced place" (p. 117).

multimedia making—turns that place into a lived space. When our participants describe and represent the community center, which they know as DUSTY, in their multimedia stories, written accounts, oral narratives, and in relation to themselves, it becomes a landscape. We especially like Mitchell's point that there is no hierarchy or chronological ordering to these terms. Although spatial activities can transform a place, a place can also, of course, afford or constrain activities in a social space. A landscape might have agency, predisposing viewers to conceptualize a place or engage in certain kinds of activities in a lived space.

In the sections that follow, we examine data collected through ethnographic methods over a period of 4 years, using some of the perspectives provided by critical geography, including Mitchell's distinctions among space, place, and landscape. Our data include photographs and other visual representations, as well as field notes, interviews, and long-term participant observation. Throughout we ask: How is the construction of identities, both individual and collective, influenced by and enacted through spatiality? Toward the end of this chapter, we consider how what we have learned might be of use to community-based and university educators and researchers in the after-school movement and in service learning efforts, especially in relation to the multimodal version of literacy that we call *digital stories*. To offer a counterpoint to the service learning literature that emphasizes university participants' experiences, we foreground here the experiences and points of view of community participants.

THE WEST OAKLAND COMMUNITY: AN ACTIVIST PAST AND AN UNCERTAIN FUTURE[3]

Once a mixed-use area of residences and industry, West Oakland, California, where DUSTY is located, slipped into economic decline with the end of World War II, when shipbuilding and defense-related industries were dramatically reduced (cf. Noguera, 1996). As its economic base declined, its European ethnic residents were replaced by African Americans migrating from the South and, more recently, by low-income Chicano/Latino and Asian/Pacific Islander families. Currently, West Oakland consists of some 7,000 households representing approximately 20,000 people. Seventy-four percent of residents are African American, 14% are Chicano/Latino, 10% are Asian/Pacific Islanders, 2% are White, and 1% are American Indians or Other. This section of the city has been designated as a Federal Enhanced Enterprise Community and is characterized by all of the symptoms of intense urban poverty and the educational inequities that accompany it. The neighborhood's income level and jobless rates, in fact, make its residents

---

[3]For a more detailed account of Oakland's history, we recommend Rhomberg (2004).

some of the most disadvantaged in the San Francisco Bay Area and, indeed, the nation. Educational statistics for West Oakland are similarly poor, with many students scoring far below state and national averages. Low academic performance is a disturbing and long-term trend. At the public elementary school located across the street from DUSTY, recent scores from the California Standards Test showed that 67% of fifth graders did not score in the proficient range in English Language Arts, and 68% did not score in the proficient range for math. At a Catholic middle school, also across the street from DUSTY, approximately 80% of students performed below grade level. The main public high school in West Oakland recently had an Academic Performance Index of 437, which places it in the state's lowest decile.[4]

Today in West Oakland, there are few signs remaining of the community's rich history, which included a bustling economy mid-century when the city's dry docks, railroad system, and factories attracted immigrants from throughout the world and African Americans from the South. Its activist culture during the 1960s played a pivotal role in the civil rights movement and the establishment of the union of Sleeping Car Porters and the Black Panther Party (Ginwright, 2004; cf. Rhomberg, 2004). Yet recovering and preserving that rich history, revitalizing the community, and empowering residents educationally and economically are the aims of many private citizens, local businesses, schools, and nonprofit agencies. Our DUSTY center for digital media and literacy, located in the heart of the community, is one small contribution to that effort. The revitalization of West Oakland is not, however, an uncontested process, and if the surface is just barely scratched, the tensions, competitions, contradictions, and struggles become visible, as we begin to illustrate next.

NEIGHBORHOOD SIGNAGE:
A WINDOW ON CONTESTED IDENTITIES

In a recent study of residential segregation between 1970 and 1990, Deskins and Bettinger (2002) came to the conclusion that, rather than decreasing during the decades after the civil rights movement, residential segregation among the underclass in the United States has increased to such an extreme that, not only were the African American poor economically and geographically displaced, they had also been made separate in terms of identities. That is, segregation in economic space seems also to have led to the emergence of separate identities. As Deskins and Bettinger explain,

---

[4]These data on schools and test scores came from the California State Department's Web site, except for the statistics on the Catholic school, which was personal communication with the school's principal.

Space . . . is an ideal means of creating and asserting racial identities. If a group is isolated in where it lives, this has a measurable effect on its economic position. But it also creates a group that is thought of as a separate community, a separate culture, a separate identity. Those relegated to exist in a society's pariah areas become pariahs themselves. . . . (p. 57)

So it is, we would suggest, in West Oakland. Although the San Francisco Bay Area is widely regarded as one of the most multicultural, multiethnic communities in the world, there are pockets of segregation and isolation, and West Oakland is one of these. This is not a neighborhood where many outsiders drive or visit or walk or shop. Indeed, there are no national chains of grocery stores or restaurants, nor are there the usual commercial establishments such as drugstores, banks, hospitals, or shops. There are liquor stores with convenience stores attached, there are schools and a small public library, there is a senior citizens' home, and there are many churches, often housed in repurposed buildings, but there are none of the mainstream businesses usually associated with day-to-day living in an urban area. It is no exaggeration to say that the vast majority of the thousands of people who live a mile or two outside of West Oakland never cross its borders. We would argue, following Deskins and Bettinger, that this kind of spatial and economic segregation can result in the construction, by people outside the community, of residents' identities as separate, different, and even deviant. Next we turn to a case of how this identity construction both occurs and is resisted through signage—billboards that organizations put up in the community and homemade signs that residents display.

On the southern outer border of West Oakland, within plain view of the major freeway that skirts it, there appeared during the summer of 2004 a billboard (see Fig. 14.1) picturing the face of a smiling brown-faced African-American boy in a checkered shirt on a black background, juxtaposed to handwriting in white childish script, as if on a chalkboard: "My dad just got out of prison. . . . " The "my dad" portion of the script was large, almost half as big as the child's image, while the remainder of the caption was much diminished although still readable. The line about prison was followed by another, this one written in orange, in conventional script, and less visible because of its reduced size: "With a job, a place to live & healthcare, he will make it." The bottom of the billboard returned to the childish, larger script with the exclamation, "Ex-prisoners are family too!" The lower right-hand corner, almost out of sight, provided a Web address for the social service agency responsible for the billboard, a group advocating for those recently released from prison. Written in orange, it linked with the previous orange script about the importance of jobs, housing, and health care. There were two other billboards in this series that appeared in West Oakland during the same time period—one picturing a Latino who welcomed his sister back from prison, and the other featuring a woman of undeterminable ethnicity (although not White) whose husband had similarly just been released.

FIGURE 14.1. Billboard seen from border of West Oakland.

Oakland then had a large number of parolees, and the billboards called attention to social services for recently released prisoners that were available, but perhaps not widely known. However, other messages were communicated with this signage, some of which were pejorative, particularly from the point of view of community members. Drawing on Kress and van Leeuwen's (1996) framework for understanding the "grammar" of visual design, and reflecting as well on recent work on ethics in visual research (e.g., Hammond, 2004), we can suggest how such multimodal compositions work as meaning systems and explain with some precision why these billboards offended many residents. By virtue of their design, according to Kress and van Leeuwen, visual representations set up relationships between those who view them and the people who are portrayed in them. For example, when individuals are depicted close up, as in a head shot, social distance is lessened and an intimate connection suggested. Further, when a person is depicted as looking directly into the viewer's eyes and is also smiling, the viewer is positioned to form a bond or an affinity. The compositional patterns of images also prompt viewers to experience them in particular ways. For example, in Western semiotics, information that appears on the left tends to be given and information on the right is new. Using this framework to conduct a brief semiotic analysis of the billboard in Fig. 14.1—with its presentation of a large head shot of a smiling child who looks directly into our eyes—it is clear that viewers are meant to feel an affinity with him, to read the image first by connecting with the child. Then the viewer can absorb the new information printed to the child's right—the perhaps startling fact that this child is smiling because his dad was just released from prison—and by virtue of concern for the child, presumably be positioned to be concerned as well for the father.

Kress and van Leeuwan's framework is considerably more comprehensive and complex than this partial use of it suggests, but even so our abbreviated analysis gives at least a sense of how to parse the design of the billboard and to understand its semiotic properties.[5] We want to go on to suggest, however, that it was this design that alienated some community members, and that their disapproval can be traced to issues of representational rights. Anthropologists have long been taken to task for presuming to represent the realities of the people they study, usually through a discursive presentation in ethnographic texts. Of late, however, these concerns have been extended to the photographic practices that are common in ethnography. The essence of these recent critiques can be found in Sontag's (1973) earlier argument that taking a photograph epitomizes taking something from someone. Hammond (2004) explains, "The authority of the photographer in choosing the subject matter, the time to photograph, the angles, focal length and so on encapsulate the essence of a traditional anthropological research approach that placed the researcher in the position of greatest control" (p. 136). Fieldworkers who employ photography are now attempting to address this power differential in various ways—for example, by being sensitive to how people want to dress, stand, or otherwise compose themselves for portraits that will later be published or otherwise used, or by giving cameras to the participants in research studies and making it possible for them to choose and compose the representations of their world (cf. Hammond, 2004; Papademas, 2004). In the case of the billboard in Fig. 14.1, a social service agency assumed the right to present to a community a picture of one of its children and to make that image and the message it carried available to the wider public, through the placement of the billboard in broad view of a major freeway bordering the community. It further assumed the right to present the child, in terms of his gaze and proximity, as an intimate, and to have the smiling child share his happiness about his parent's release from incarceration. In this urban community, the billboard's composition implies that it is normal for children to welcome their fathers home from jail—so normal, in fact, that the public should now understand that "ex-prisoners are family too."

We view this billboard series as a process of identity construction, on the part of outsiders, about West Oakland residents, and their community. In Kress and van Leeuwen's (1996) terms, a relationship is established between those who view the images and the people who are portrayed in them. Interestingly, signage is one way that the people who do not ordinarily come inside a community nonetheless can inscribe it. That the people pictured and connected with incarceration were people of color certainly was based on demographic truth. But for such billboards to be placed within and bordering on minority communities seemed to us to clear-

---

[5]We similarly recommend Scollon and Scollon's (2003) geosemiotic framework for analyzing texts, social interaction, and the material world.

ly racialize the neighborhood and its residents and associate certain ethnicities with the prison system. It was ironic that when we interviewed community members about the advertisement, no one we spoke with realized that the barely visible Web address was meant to point to additional information and possible assistance, while all were disturbed by the depiction. In contrast, the social service agency's impression was that the billboards were both appealing and effective, although the agency had done no formal research on their impact.

Creating a billboard and erecting it within the community, to be read or ignored or appropriated or transformed, is an example, we want to suggest, of the creation of *lived space,* in Mitchell's (2002) and LeFebvre's (1974) terms. A place— the corner of Goss and Wood Streets—was in this sense narrativized, given a storyline for all to read. Because the billboard pictured in Fig. 14.1 faced outward and was visible from a major freeway, its effect was also to create a landscape for outsiders to view from a distance, as is suggested by the backdrop of the photograph. Chain-link fencing, an old building, trash in the gutter, an older car on a mostly deserted street, and a billboard about a child being innocently joyful that his dad is coming home from prison: What more iconic representation of the ghetto, and the separateness of the people who live there, could one conjure?

To continue our study of signage in West Oakland, we photographed approximately 50 billboards and other signs during the summer and early fall of 2004, canvassing every street in West Oakland, and we examined our photographic archive for 2 previous years to determine whether it included photographs of signage (cf. Schwartz, 1989; Suchar, 1997; Wagner, 2004). Ten additional photos were added to the pool from the archive. Then we categorized the semantic content of the signs. We found that approximately 50% of the commercial billboards focused on social service issues: getting care for AIDS, finding funding to go to college, showing tough love to one's children. The latter billboard pictured an African-American woman, arms crossed, staring up into the camera, with a teenage African-American boy standing behind her against a red-lit sky; the caption was: "The Enforcer. She doesn't love being tough. She's tough because she loves" (see Fig. 14.2.) Our photograph of this billboard, with a liquor sign above it and the paper of the billboard visibly torn, creates an ironic landscape of life in West Oakland.

The other half of the billboards was primarily advertisements, predominantly for mobile phones and automobiles, while one billboard requested applications for potential school bus drivers. In contrast, the homemade signs were overwhelmingly driven by job-related issues, especially advertisements for services. For example, Fig. 14.3 is a photograph of a hand-lettered advertisement for plumbing repair and related services taken during the summer of 2004. In our archives, we found a similar sign, written in the same hand, but posted at a different location in the community. Given the cost of such repairs in the Bay Area and the difficulty of arranging for them, this kind of service is important in a community such as West Oakland. Another example of an economically motivated sign was created by the owner of an empty lot who could not afford to build anything there. Instead

FIGURE 14.2. "Tough Love" billboard on side of liquor store.

FIGURE 14.3. Homemade sign advertising plumbing repair.

he created a brightly colored mural on the fence encircling the lot; this mural depicted the kinds of shops and businesses he would like to put there, including a café and an African-American bookstore. Other economically oriented advertisements were less noticeable and more conventional. At a personal residence next door to DUSTY, a woman had created her own line of athletic clothing, designed and produced in her home; on the gate surrounding her yard, she had posted a notice of this thriving enterprise, along with the emblems of the credit cards that she accepted.

The other major type of homemade signage that we observed served the purpose of political and social protest. Our archives revealed several signs displayed in windows or posted on walls protesting the Iraq war, while one hand-painted sign covered an expanse of wooden fence with the words "Stop the Violence." Parts of West Oakland and East Oakland are indeed dangerous places, and too often one sees street shrines there: arrangements of candles, balloons, teddy bears, flowers, and other remembrances placed where someone was murdered.[6] In September 2004, one such shrine was erected for a 16-year-old girl the evening after she had been killed during a drive-by shooting as she stood in front of her West Oakland apartment.[7] The next day the shrine was gone. One also sees the ubiquitous acronym "RIP," for "Rest in Peace," written on walls and sidewalks (see Fig. 14.4).

Our study of signage in West Oakland showed unmistakable contrasts between outsiders' views of the community's needs and insiders' expressions of interests and desires. Billboards in this community are an interesting case of outsiders inscribing a place and creating a landscape that serves as an identity marker for the inner city, especially for outsiders' views of that community. Particularly prominent were depictions of the community as in need of social services and depictions of idealized community members with stereotypical identities and roles—the protective mother who exercises strict control over her children, for example, or the incarcerated dad who needs support to reenter the community. This signage seemed to us to sit like unwanted tattoos on the neighborhood. Yet despite its prominence in terms of color, design, and placement, and despite its identity-laden messages, the signage seemed hardly to impact the workings of the neighborhood. Many people whom we spoke with dismissed the billboards as propaganda or caricatures. Running parallel to them were residents' own public communications with each other, and we found these to be either economic in nature (advertisements for jobs, services, or desired economic opportunities), commemorative, or critical of socio-economic conditions. In many cases,

---

[6]The murder rate in Oakland, California, is the highest in the state—in 2003 there were 114 murders in the city—and most of these went unsolved (see "My Word," *Oakland Tribune*, November 30, 2002; see also Oakland's Urban Strategies Council, which is conducting research to understand murder patterns in the city: www.urbanstrategies.org/programs/csj/oakmurder-study.html).

[7]See "Hundreds Mourn," *Oakland Tribune*, October 1, 2004.

FIGURE 14.4. "Rest in Peace" messages written on a building to mark the place and commemorate the death of a teenager.

residents' signs were less visible and more ephemeral, lasting only an evening in the case of the street altar, yet they represented the community's continual inscriptions on the place of West Oakland, an active effort to impact their material circumstances, construct a space, and harness the power of public representation in their community, the power of shaping a landscape.

The mismatch between the community's interests and those of outsiders as represented through signage indexed a variety of tensions over the construction of the neighborhood. Often those tensions had a material base. There was a tug of war, for instance, over the use, ownership, and control of buildings and land. In patterns typical of gentrification, during the 1990s, newcomers had steadily purchased old and dilapidated, but once grand, Victorian homes at inflated prices that were far out of reach of old-time residents. There have also been recent major housing developments in West Oakland that feature newly constructed lofts and condominiums, some targeting low-income families or a range of income levels, but many catering primarily to middle-class buyers. One of the most controversial of these projects proposed the refurbishing of an old train station that had fallen into disrepair, but once was a major end-of-the-line stop for migrants moving westward. The train station's history also intersected with the formation of the Brotherhood of Sleeping Car Porters, the first union for African-American workers in the United States, some of whom were Oaklanders. The plan to build extensive middle-income housing adjacent to the old station, and to turn the station into a museum, was met with protests against what was termed by some as racist redevelopment (see Fig. 14.5). Residents of West Oakland expressed a desire to control the train station, as well as have the new housing priced within the income levels of the community. The frustration and anger that some community members felt found an outlet in several public forums, including a book tour by the author of the first history of the Sleeping Car Porters (Tye, 2004). One of the complaints voiced during this event, which overflowed the local library, was how the author, a White person who was not from the community, could presume to tell this important account of African-American history.

At its inception, DUSTY operated out of a West Oakland community center, the Prescott Joseph Center for Community Enhancement, itself once a grand old Victorian home that later became a convent and just a few years ago was converted to a multipurpose community center. Its three floors included parlors, offices for a range of nonprofits, conference rooms, a kitchen, and our multimedia center in the basement, and it regularly hosted art shows, community meetings, plays, film screenings, suppers, and other events. We have noticed that most adults who visit the Prescott Center are impressed with its expanse and décor—high ceilings and moldings, religious icons that reflect its linkage to the Catholic Church, its myriad rooms, and the memory it evokes of an earlier time. Children, we have found, are sometimes taken aback by the building, wondering aloud whether peo-

FIGURE 14.5. Protest rally against redevelopment in West Oakland.

ple actually lived in such a mansion and acting a little bit frightened by its size. Another striking response from groups of children on a few occasions has been to race through the center when it is open for public events, running from room to room, hiding in its many nooks and crannies until adults can find and expel them. This we see as an attempt on their part to occupy and lay claim to this space that sits in the heart of their community. Community members, we have realized, have sometimes been reluctant to enter into activities offered at the Prescott Center, perhaps having seen other organizations purported to serve the community come and go. They pass by but do not always feel interested in entering or that they are welcome in this place. Our desire over the years has been to create DUSTY as a lived space that is integrated into community life and that serves as a meeting ground and collaborative stage for West Oakland residents, people from the university, and the wider community. What we have not wanted to be, or to be viewed as, is just another social service billboard, come to name and mend a deficit.

YOUTH AND OUT-OF-SCHOOL SPACE AND TIME: ENVISIONING DUSTY

After-school programs in the United States date from the late 1800s, when the need for child labor decreased, compulsory schooling began to be the norm, and youth thereby found themselves with time on their hands during out-of-school hours. Worried that youth would get into trouble during this newly unsupervised time, educators and reformers developed playground programs that eventually expanded to include indoor activities, too, the antecedents of today's after-school programs (Halpern, 2002). Like the youth of a century ago, who took to the streets when given leisure from work and school, youth in Oakland and many urban centers are now often at loose ends, at once disengaged from school, lacking opportunities for work, and forced to do without social spaces and activities that could meaningfully fill their out-of-school hours. To illustrate, over the last few years in Oakland, a battle of sorts has erupted between urban youth on the one hand, and the police force and some residents, on the other. Young people in effect took to and claimed the streets, usually during late evening hours, by holding sideshows, or car-centered street rallies. At sideshows drivers blocked traffic, spun their cars in circles, doing donuts, while other youth gathered, looked on, and played music. Sometimes these gatherings attracted upward of 400 youth, and they quickly evoked concerns about safety, noise, and mischief.[8]

---

[8]See www.indybay.org/print.php?id=1566613 for a photograph taken at a sideshow and a brief descriptions of these gatherings. After a young person was killed in a car accident associated with one of the Oakland sideshows, the state mobilized, and a bill was passed outlawing and penalizing the gatherings.

We do not find it surprising that youth invent sideshows and engage in other transgressive activities to spatially, bodily, and symbolically display their agency, and we think that an analysis of such activity has something important to teach us about marginalized youth. Designing and controlling space is an important means of constructing youth culture; as Massey (1998) notes, "From being able to have a room of one's own (at least in richer families) to hanging out on particular corners, to clubs where only your own age group goes, the construction of spatiality can be an important element in building a social identity" (p. 128). Valentine, Skelton, and Chambers (1998) point out that, "the space of the street is often the only autonomous space that young people are able to carve out for themselves" (p. 7). One way, then, to understand sideshows and the community's response to them is to view them as young people's attempts to create spaces for themselves and, at the same time, adults' age-old attempts, not without reason, to control youth's spaces and behaviors.

We began DUSTY to provide a safe space physically and socially for children and youth during the after-school and evening hours and during summertime. As we illustrate in the next section, our programmatic work has centered on designing and offering programs for children and youth on creating digital stories, or multimedia, multimodal narratives, and digital music.[9] That is, we hoped to draw youth off the streets and into DUSTY through the appeal of media, music, and popular culture (Hull, 2003; Morrell, 2004) as we simultaneously pushed school-based definitions of *literacy* to include the visual and the performative (cf. Hull, 2003; Hull & Zacher, 2004). In addition, this focus would take us part of the distance in closing for the West Oakland community what is popularly called the *digital divide*. Although debate continues about the extent and nature of this divide that separates people who have access to empowering uses of cutting-edge information technologies from those who don't (cf. Compaine, 2001; Fairlie, 2003; Warschauer, 2004), there is no doubt that youth from communities like West Oakland routinely lack such opportunities. Thus, as a lived space for learning, we wanted to provide youth with equitable access to cutting edge technologies for communication and creative expression. As discussed earlier, through positioning youth to tell stories about self, family, and community through multiple media and modalities, we intended to help them develop senses of self as powerful, capable, and successful communicators. By bringing university students to the West Oakland community, and children to the university, and by continually widening the vistas of university students and children through literal and symbolic movement across communities, we hoped to enable the youth to take steps toward and develop sensibilities for shaping their futures.[10]

---

[9]Our discussion in this chapter is primarily about digital storytelling and its intersection with the enactment of identities in relation to spatiality. For an account of the deep connection between music-making and identity, see Hudak (1999).

[10]Although we do not describe the curriculum and pedagogy that underpin DUSTY in this chapter, a detailed account is provided in Roche-Smith (2004).

CHILDREN'S VISTAS AND VOICES

It was a rainy day in March, and most of the children who had been attending our middleschool DUSTY program had already gone home. A UC Berkeley undergraduate mentor stood outside the building with Stephen, one of the middle schoolers; the day darkened as they waited and waited longer still for Stephen's ride home to appear. Stella, the undergraduate, was worried about the 12-year-old. They had worked together on homework and a digital music program. But that day he had seemed withdrawn and had finally mentioned to Stella, speaking quietly and tearfully, that his dad had just passed away. It was later, after Stella and Stephen had stood on the curb together, watching evening settle onto the neighborhood as youth loudly congregated on the street corner and cars zoomed past with their spinners and 20-inch rims, that the young boy solemnly asked: "Do you really think kids in this neighborhood will go to college?"

The question was a poignant moment for Stella, who had been talking to the children about going to college, as was the DUSTY custom. Stephen in particular had been interested in this topic and was perhaps also inspired by a recent field trip to campus.[11] There had been other outings away from West Oakland as well, including a concert by Alicia Keys, the rhythm and blues super star, at a venue on the other side of the city, complete with an autograph signing afterward especially for DUSTY youth. Given all of this in conjunction with his dad's death, perhaps it is not surprising that Stephen might have been thinking about going places, maybe leaving the neighborhood, and hopefully attending college. Perhaps he visualized contrasts in landscape and especially sensed the constraints that one's locale could bring to bear on his and others' social futures.

There is a big scholarship on spatiality as it relates to the study of children. One tradition builds on Piaget's (1971) interest in how reasoning about the environment develops over time, including children's orientation in space and their mapping abilities (cf. Erickson, 1977; Matthews & Limb, 1999). Within geography there have been studies dating from the early 1970s on the social inequalities that

---

[11]Our undergraduate mentors write field notes about their observations and interactions at DUSTY. Here are Stella's field notes about Stephen's many questions regarding college:

Stephen said he wanted to be an author, a lawyer, or the president. I asked him why he came to the tutoring sessions and he said he wanted to because it helped him with his work. He is very motivated to learn and he said he loved learning and really wanted to go to college. He then started asking me all these questions about college like how do you get in, where do you live, how do you pay for it. I told him some people get scholarships and a lot of people take out loans. I explained to him what loans were. He listened very intently and nodded after everything I said. He said he might want to go to law school and he mentioned Harvard. He was like, "That's a really good school isn't it?" I replied, "One of the best!" He asked how to get into law school and I told him how he needed to go to college first and get good grades and then take the LSATs, and then write a personal statement. He was so interested and asked me so many questions.

result from the "built environment" (Aitken, 2001), such as unjust geographical allocations of educational resources like play spaces (Bunge & Bordessa, 1975). More recent work in geography is characterized by Aitken (2001) as "about the practices of young people, their communities, and the places and institutions that shape (and are shaped by) their lives" (p. 20). "Places are important for young people," he continued, "because these contexts play a large part in constructing and constraining dreams and practices" (p. 20).

We too have been interested in charting how place, space, and landscape, as associated with the community of West Oakland, play a role in "constructing and constraining dreams and practices" of area youth. But equally as important, throughout interventions at DUSTY, we have been committed to positioning youth, by providing access to potentially powerful representational tools and practices, to speak back to spatial constraints. Mitchell (2002) notes that, "landscape exerts a subtle power over people, eliciting a broad range of emotions and meanings that may be difficult to specify" (p. vii). Hearing Mitchell, we are well warned concerning the subtleties that accompany the articulation of identities in relation to place and landscape. Nonetheless, in the following section, we hope to demonstrate in an initial way some of the ideas and concerns that youth in our programs have expressed about their locales, as well as to suggest how our youth have seemed to enact identities in relation to space, place, and landscape through multimodalities and multimedia.

In our archives, approximately 200 digital stories have been created thus far by youth, children, and adults at DUSTY. Two- to 5-minute movies, the stories usually begin with a written script that is eventually accompanied by images, photographs, artwork, or snippets of video; a musical soundtrack; and the narrator's voice reading or performing the script. The still visuals are stitched together with an editing program through fades, dissolves, checkerboards or a myriad other transitions, thus allowing the illusion of movement. As a rough first cut at analyzing these stories, we developed a catalog of their major genres and purpose:

> Genres: Autobiographical Narratives; Poems/Raps; Social Critique/ Public Service Announcements; Reenactments or Extensions of Stories, Cartoons, and Movies; Animations; Reports; Biographies and Interviews
>
> Purposes: Offer a Tribute to Family Member(s), Friend(s); Recount/ Interpret a Pivotal Moment/Key Event; Represent Place, Space, Community; Preserve History; Create Art/Artifact; Play/Fantasize; Heal/Grieve/Reflect; Reach/Inform/Influence Wider Audience

Of course, many authors had multiple purposes, and sometimes the digital stories blurred genres, as befits their dynamic and evolving nature; these categories yet provide a broad if unrefined sense of forms and uses. Our archives revealed a number of digital stories by children, youth, and adults whose centerpiece was the representation of place, space, and community, and in what follows we examine one of these in detail. At this stage in our work, we do not make any claims about the relative frequency or stability of the categories. This is our first pass at developing an analytic system for understanding youth's representation of place, and self in relation to place, through multimedia/multimodality.[12]

STORIES OF IDENTIFICATION
AND DISTANCING

As we reviewed the stories in our archives, we realized that, from the inception of the DUSTY program, children and youth had created a remarkable number of stories that located themselves in relation to their neighborhoods. To suggest the flavor and range of these compositions, here are some examples. One 13-year-old boy, interested in paying homage to his posse, constructed a story that pictured each of his many friends and named them one by one, but he also carefully demarcated their neighborhood, taking photographs of street signs and domiciles and distinguishing West Oakland from East Oakland. He announced his home turf as the best section of the city in which to live, far superior to other neighborhoods. A younger boy wrote a story about a trip to Alaska, contrasting its weather and other features with those of Oakland. Most interesting to us, however, was his inclusion in the Oakland portion of a photo of the local children's hospital, announcing that this was the place where he had been born. He was quite taken aback and not at all persuaded when his mother, on viewing his digital story for the first time, told him that he had not been born at that particular hospital after all. A 9-year-old girl who had recently moved from another city contrasted her new home with her old one, and expressed considerable longing for a quieter, more pastoral space to live than West Oakland. This was, in fact, a theme that surfaced in other stories: the noise of the city and its lack of aesthetically appealing space. Another little girl developed her entire story around the pleasures of visiting a particular place, her auntie's house, where special privileges abounded.

Children choose to write about particular topics for many reasons, including the promptings of their teachers, the examples provided through previous students' work, their own interests and predilections, and the conventions that have developed and are typically promulgated in schools and other educational settings around what constitutes an appropriate storyline. Although we accept all of these possibilities as possible and likely contributors and influences, what we wish to explore here is the importance for many children of locating themselves in a particular space—"this is my house, I'm a person from West Oakland, I was born here"—and also of professing or sometimes examining their relationship with a

---

[12]To our knowledge, this is the first such study of this topic, either within literacy studies or cultural geography.

landscape and a locale—"I'm from East Oakland, and it is a cool place; I don't like my neighborhood because it's so noisy where I live." As Duncan and Duncan (2004) note, "people continually attempt to stabilize and establish secure identities and, more often than not, anchor them in place" (p. 30).

Identification with a particular place is surely a usual part of children's development, but we believe that this process takes on a special salience in neighborhoods like West Oakland, which are segregated economically, socially, and ethnically, and where many children and youth regularly experience their immediate environs as unsafe places, and where almost continuously they encounter representations of their communities as violent, unhealthy, and undesirable. The other part of our argument is that multimedia and multimodality constitute especially fitting vehicles for children and youth to represent their lives spatially. Digital stories are relentlessly visual; no matter what words and music fill the air, the stories proceed and direct composers' and viewers' attention through images and video. Because place and landscape can be readily captured through images, a digital story can provide an exceptional canvass for the exploration of the spatial. Finally, and this point is the most suggestive of all those we hope to make, we believe that forms of composing, such as digital storytelling, have the potential to afford children and youth the representational means to see themselves in relation to places, spaces, and landscapes in new ways.

We turn next to what strikes many viewers as an exceptionally powerful digital story about place, space, and landscape by a young author. Created by Jamal,[13] a 9-year-old boy who lived in East Oakland but attended DUSTY's summer program, the digital story is a minute and a half long and contains 17 images, each linked to the other by a lively visual transition such as "opening doors" or "cartwheels" that blend one picture into the next. Entitled "My Neighborhood," it is narrated by Jamal, while the jazz of Miles Davis—a cut from "Sketches of Spain"—sounds an exceptionally plaintive backdrop. The story is based on a well-known writing assignment about the senses: "Compose a poem in first person that reveals what you hear, see, feel, smell, and taste." In preparation for writing, the children participated in several preparatory activities, including a walk about the neighborhood adjacent to DUSTY, where they took note of what was salient to them.

Here is the final version of the text of Jamal's poem:

I hear the sirens of an ambulance speeding by.
I hear the sound of a car skidding.
I hear kids laughing at the boy who fell down.

---

[13]Jamal is a self-selected pseudonym; the names of other children and undergraduate participants have also been changed. To further protect Jamal's privacy, we have not made his digital poem available. However, to see examples of the kinds of stories children and adults at DUSTY create, please visit this Web site: www.oaklanddusty.org.

I see kids running down the street to the ice cream truck.

I see a brotha selling drugs on the street.

I see Asians walking up the street.

I feel the strong warm breeze against my face.

I feel the rough wall of my house.

I feel my shirt sticking to my back.

I smell the nasty aroma of urine.

I smell chicken from inside my house

I smell BBQ sauce.

I taste the cinnamony, sugary churro.

I taste the soft chocolate milk in my mouth.

I taste the dry air on my tongue.

I hear a car speeding by.

I know that this neighborhood is bad.

These lines, although wonderfully evocative, make up but the skeleton of Jamal's digital story; next we attempt to give a sense of its body, its visual components. To be sure, it is exceedingly difficult to describe multimodality through the vehicle of book chapter, and in any case it is analytically challenging to capture what is powerful about successful multimodal pieces. Their blending of words, images, voice, music, and motion creates meaning and an experience of meaning-making that differs from and exceeds what is possible through single or fewer modalities.[14] To begin to suggest what is distinctive about Jamal's digital multimodal composition, over and above the linguistic text of his poem, next we juxtapose the lines of the poem with a brief description of the image or images with which they are paired.[15]

    a. I hear the sound of a car skidding *(three Internet images: ambulance, car, skid marks on pavement)*

    b. I hear kids laugh at the boy who fell down *(Internet image of a group of children in a circle, laughing and looking down)*

    c. I see kids running down the street to an ice cream truck *(Internet image of an ice cream truck)*

---

[14]Some of our recent research has focused on devising a framework for analyzing multimodal digital stories (cf. Hull & Nelson, 2005).

[15]Jamal's digital story did not include the first line from his poem about hearing the sirens of ambulances. When he viewed his story and discussed it with us, he noted that this was a mistake and said he would like for that line to be included or for the picture of an ambulance to be deleted.

   d. I see a brother selling drugs on the street *(Internet image of a dark-skinned man taking money from a White man with one hand and passing him something with the other)*

   e. I see Asians walking up the street *(Internet image of a smiling family posed for the camera, father holding one daughter, mother's hand on a second daughter's shoulder)*

   f. I feel the strong warm breeze against my face *(photograph of Jamal's smiling face, cut out and superimposed on an Internet image of a beach scene with palm trees)*

   g. I feel the rough wall of my house *(same smiling photograph of Jamal, this one whole, his hand touching a wall behind him)*

   h. I feel my shirt sticking to my back *(photograph of Jamal from behind, on his porch at night, leaning over the railing and looking downward, as if at a street below; see Fig. 14.6)*

   i. I smell the nasty smell of urine *(Internet image of a bag of urine such as might be collected in a hospital)*

   j. I smell chicken from inside my house *(Internet image of a whole baked chicken, angle taken from above)*

   k. I smell B-B-Q sauce *(Internet image of a bottle of "Dr. Dan's BBQ Sauce")*

   l. I taste the cinnamony sugary churro *(upclose Internet image of fried pastry sticks)*

   m. I taste the soft chocolate milk in my mouth *(Internet image of a pint and a quart of chocolate milk)*

   n. I taste the dry air on my tongue *(same photo as for the previous line)*

   o. I hear a car speeding by *(Internet image of a "muscle" car, the same as the first image)*

   p. I know that this neighborhood is bad *(photograph of dilapidated houses juxtaposed to skyscrapers on Oakland's skyline)*

Bracketing the story was a black title screen with white writing and a list of rolling credits. The movie ended with the screen going black in splotches, as if paint were spattering onto the surface. The rolling credits screen, also white on black background, thanked the audience for watching the movie, and in a funny subversion of the usual conventions for watching movies, advised that no applause was necessary and warned viewers not to come again! Jamal signed his movie with a fictional production company, "Mad Dog Productions," named after a cartoon character from the TV show "Kim Possible," and he listed an imaginary Web site for it.

As we illustrate, the overall mood of Jamal's movie was serious. An ode on place with images that powerfully contextualized the words that Jamal spoke, and a jazz soundtrack that strongly evoked a melancholy mood, juxtaposing musical sophistication and world-weariness with a child's innocent voice, "My Neighborhood" could be seen as a young author's reflection on place in relation

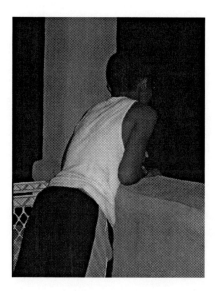

**FIGURE 14.6. Photograph
of Jamal used in his digital poem.**

to himself. There are pleasant sensations described and positive images offered to
be sure: the smell of chicken cooking in the house, children running to the ice
cream truck, the soft feel of chocolate milk in one's mouth. It is also the case that
adult viewers can see the child behind his wise piece, and this indeed adds to this
digital story's charm. For example, there is a child's aesthetic at work in selecting
energetic transitions between images, his fondness for the "bells and whistles" that
are easily produced via editing programs these days. In addition, in age-appropri-
ate fashion, Jamal matched his images to his words literally; that is, his words
indexed images instead of functioning more symbolically, to use Peirce's (1955)
typology. Nonetheless, we would argue that it is also impossible to view Jamal's
movie without recognizing a young mind in thoughtful dialogue about space,
place, and landscape, or to escape the impression that important identity work is
represented in this story.

To briefly present what we think Jamal's story signifies about spatiality in
relation to identity, we draw on our analysis of an interview with his DUSTY
instructor about Jamal, his composition process, and the other children and their
work in the program; a retrospective interview with Jamal, in which he watched,
commented on, and answered questions about "My Neighborhood" with his
instructor; conversations with his parents; and artifacts associated with Jamal's
work (including a detailed lesson plan for the poetry/senses unit and additional
poems, journal entries, and one other digital story that Jamal created during a previous DUSTY summer session).

Our first point is that, in writing his poem and selecting his images, Jamal
drew actively on his sense of what was salient about his neighborhood in terms of
both material places and lived spaces. This might be surmised by an analysis of the

story, but was confirmed through our interviews and other data. He clearly recognized that in his neighborhood could be found danger, violence, poverty, and crime, and he thought these features important to represent. For example, in commenting on his choice of a skidding car and the ambulance pictured at the opening of his story (Line a), Jamal volunteered that "almost every day I hear an ambulance." These ambulances, he said, always seemed to be going in the same direction, to the same place, to pick up people who had been fighting, been in car accidents, or overdosed. Sometimes, he mentioned, he saw people smoking dope in his neighborhood when he went outside to ride his bike with one of his family members, and once he thought he saw a drug deal taking place down the hill from his house as he stood on his porch (consequently, Line d and the Internet image of a "brotha" selling drugs).

Perhaps the most startling negative sense of place came with the line, "The nasty smell of urine," and the accompanying Internet image of a large bag of the same. Jamal giggled a little when asked how he had found that image ("I typed in *urine*) and then went on to explain more solemnly how, twice, he had smelled urine when he walked in an alleyway near his house—experiences that seemed to have made a strong impression on him given the detail he recalled about these and related discoveries. An unmistakable dimension, then, of Jamal's story is his negative contextualization of neighborhood. Lest there be any doubt about this, he chose to end his poem with what his DUSTY instructor had explained could be a sixth sense, a statement about what one knows: (Line p) "I know that this neighborhood is bad." When queried regarding this claim about his community, Jamal stated twice, with emphasis, "Some parts of it *is* bad," and mentioned the littered streets and the presence of drugs. He also identified the exact location of the photo that he had paired with this last line, a picture of dilapidated old houses in West Oakland juxtaposed to the downtown city's modern skyline. When asked what part of the city this Internet photo represented, he replied, "West Oakland and that's downtown Oakland behind it." When asked if he was sure, he replied with no hesitation, "I'm sure because I've been there before, and I've seen these buildings and these houses." In other parts of his interview, Jamal additionally revealed his knowledge of local geography, distinguishing West and East Oakland, areas within the same city that nonetheless possessed separate identities, fostering a sometimes virulent territoriality. He clarified that, although some of his images depicted West Oakland, where DUSTY is located, he intended for his poem to represent the neighborhood where he lived, East Oakland. However, he found both areas similar in containing neighborhoods that had parts that he deemed "bad."

While Jamal characterized his neighborhood and other parts of the city, he also revealed his understandings of how place intersects with racial and ethnic identity. Place and space, as many cultural geographers now note, can make a difference in terms of "how racial and ethnic identities have come to be understood, expressed, and experienced" (Berry & Henderson, 2002, p. 6). As an African-American child, and as revealed in his digital poem, Jamal had developed his own racially sensitive geography, a map, if you will, on which were charted roles, situations, and activities as they were influenced by race and ethnicity. About the famous urine photo, for example, Jamal explained that it was a "Black man" who had been urinating in the alleyway, although he confessed to not having seen him. He explained, however, that he had once seen a Black man sleeping there and that "most of them [presumably people in general or Black people in particular who sleep outside] don't have homes." Jamal was also aware of more conventional housing patterns that were racially influenced and that impacted relationships. Line e of his poem, "I see Asians walking up the street," was matched with a picture of a smiling Asian family, parents and children. In commenting on this part of his poem, Jamal observed that, although his neighborhood was mixed, "down the street from me, most people on the block is Asian." When asked whether he was friends with the Asian kids, Jamal said, no, because he had not met them yet. His three African-American friends in the neighborhood, he explained, all lived very near him, either across the street or down an alleyway.[16] This made their friendships geographically possible and desirable in an urban environment.[17]

As mentioned earlier, Jamal's digital poem contained a number of positive associations related to neighborhood—for example, a smiling Asian family walking on the street, the ice cream truck seen in the distance, the taste of Mexican pastry, and the smell of a chicken roasting inside the house. These simple, often sensory pleasures, juxtaposed to the harsher world of the neighborhood already detailed, perhaps serve to increase rather than decrease the somber feel of Jamal's poem, especially when combined with the mood set by Miles Davis' jazz. A devotee of jazz—he had many favorites, but mentioned by name John Coltraine and Miles Davis ("He is my most favorite")—Jamal selected the background music by listening to all of the cuts on the album and choosing the one he felt was most suitable: "I like the way it goes with my movie," he explained simply. However, one

---

[16]However, Jamal was not able to represent his friends as African Americans pictorially in his digital story because he could not find the images he wanted of African-American children on the Internet. Line b, "I heard kids laugh at a boy who fell down," is therefore illustrated with an Internet photo of White children laughing and gazing downward. However, Jamal reported that this part of his poem was based on his own experience of falling off his bike because of the cracks in the pavement, and his friends, who were African American, laughing at him. He had wanted these children to look like his real friends. The difficulty of finding images of African Americans through image searches on the Internet is a frequent complaint at our community technology center.

[17]We have documented many instances in which small local neighborhoods are divided geographically in ways that constrain participation in activities and the creation of relationships. For example, some parents would not allow their children to walk a small number of blocks to DUSTY, even during daylight hours, because they would thereby have to traverse borders associated with youth gangs. To give another instance, once when we sponsored a music event at another community center, an event that brought participants from the university and various neighborhood enclaves together, the man who controlled drug sales on that block stopped by to announce that this was his street, to inspect the event, and then give his blessing to the gathering.

sequence of lines and images seemed to signal a separation from the dangers and sadness of the street and the neighborhood—Lines f through h, which are based on two photos that Jamal's mom took of him at home. In Line f, he depicts the feeling of a warm breeze on his face by transplanting his smiling image to a back-drop of palm trees and ocean.[18] In Line g, we again see Jamal's face from the previous screen, but this time it is in context as he stands in front of a wall at his house, touching its rough surface with one hand. His mom took the third image from behind him to suggest the feel of his shirt sticking to his back as he stood on his porch at night, looking out and down as if to the street below (see Fig. 14.6). Jamal mentioned several times that he could see things from his porch, like drug deals or ambulances. This series of images, offered in the middle of his poem, suggested to us Jamal's protected positionality in relation to his neighborhood; that is, he could choose to observe and contemplate in safety what was happening on the streets, staying connected but also remaining apart—a terrific geographic metaphor for growing up safely and healthfully in an urban environment.

After watching his digital poem and discussing his claim and illustrations that his neighborhood was a bad place, but a bad place that also contained good things, Jamal's instructor asked him whether he would like to live elsewhere:

If you could live anywhere, where would you live? Have you seen other neighborhoods you'd rather live in than yours?

No! *(as if shocked)*

Really? But I thought you said your neighborhood's bad!

It is! *(as if bewildered)*

But you still want to live there?

Right. *(as if convinced)*

The son of two caring parents who protected him and encouraged him to study; a boy who described himself as smart, looked toward college, and imagined a career in technology (he told his instructor that he planned to be the DUSTY "technologist" when he grew up); an independent thinker and doer who could, if he needed, go against the grain (he refused to join a popular program where kids could make digital beats and rhymes because he preferred jazz to hip-hop), Jamal's ability to create an accomplished digital poem and to think productively about surrounding place, space, and landscape had many deep roots. In addition, we believe that his considerable abilities were enabled by his journey each day to DUSTY, crossing from his East Oakland neighborhood to West Oakland; by the

---

[18]When we viewed his movie with Jamal, he objected to the screen on which he had cut out his face and superimposed it on a beach scene, because he said his face did not look "real" in scale against the backdrop.

material space and resources that DUSTY offered around multimodal technologies; and by the lived space that his instructors and mentors enacted, through assignments, fieldtrips, activities, and relationships, in service of enabling youth to create and learn.

In summary, we would argue that Jamal's place-based identity in relation to Oakland neighborhoods had dimensions of both identification and distancing, and these were depicted in his multimodal digital poem with an impact that would be difficult to duplicate in a conventional linguistic text. In making his digital poem, Jamal created a landscape of West Oakland, his own complex representation of his neighborhoods, a multidimensional depiction that contrasts in its complexity the flatter, more stereotypical portraits found on neighborhood billboards. It is this representational power that is precisely what DUSTY hopes to offer its participants—the space, material and symbolic resources, relationships, and curricular direction that are needed to examine oneself in relation to present and imagined social worlds. Concluding his essay on place, space, and landscape, Mitchell (2002) wondered, "Do we make places, or do they make us?", and he acknowledged "the shifting valences of this question" (p. xii). By creating a space that positions children, youth, and adults to construct representations of landscape and place in relation to themselves, we hope to foreground and foster human agentive potential.[19]

CONCLUSION:
CONSTRUCTING HOPEFUL SPACES

We believe that service learning and after-school programs represent opportunities to help construct hopeful learning spaces for children and youth in our most neglected communities. We therefore urge a shift in the attention by those academics who are involved in this kind of work—from a focus primarily or solely on university perspectives and needs to a joint focus on sustained, long-term participation in local communities. Doing so will involve finding ways to move beyond depictions of local neighborhoods that only romanticize or demonize, toward understandings that build on historical, social, and spatial analyses—somewhat in the way Jamal does in his digital poem. On the basis of our work at DUSTY and that of others elsewhere, we further believe that a strong case can be made for crafting after-school spaces that do more than replicate the school day. In the tradition of Cole (1996), we see much to be gained from experimenting

---

[19]In this chapter, we analyzed only one kind of spatially sensitive digital story—one whose most salient dimensions were identification and distancing. Additional categories not presented here include imaginary landscapes, territoriality, interconnectedness, and diasporas, and we hope to study and write about these in our subsequent work.

with the "in-between-ness" of school time and nonschool time. As one of the children at DUSTY explained, a child who struggled deeply with the literacy requirements of schooling as well as with establishing friendships, DUSTY for him stood for something in the middle, "between school and fun," to use the words he used in his digital story. This child, especially through his relationships with undergraduate mentors, began to sort through some of his social and academic difficulties in the hybrid space of an after-school program (cf. Roche-Smith, 2004). We believe that the same has been true for many children, especially through the creation of identity texts like those that constitute the DUSTY version of digital storytelling.

A primary assumption underpinning DUSTY is the power of being able to represent—to depict one's own social reality in relation to another's, and to do so using the most current and potent mediational means. At this moment, that powerful means is multimedia and multimodality. For perhaps the first time in history, ordinary individuals can potentially wield some of communicational wizardry that used to be reserved for mass media and the elite—assuming, that is, that access is provided to material tools and supportive social practices. Regularly through DUSTY we show kids' and adults' stories on the big screen of a local theater or other public space, and we invite their friends and relatives and the wider community to view these multimodal creations and have a conversation about what they represent. At one such event, a young girl's story about the noise and litter in West Oakland attracted the interest of a city councilwoman for the neighborhood who hoped to improve it aesthetically. Youth also exchange stories with children in other locales and other countries, conducting swaps of digital media, including original beats and rhymes. Thereby we redraw the boundaries of place again, extending our sense of community to include an interconnectedness with others far removed in physical distance. Being able to communicate compellingly with words, images, sound, and movement, and being able to produce artifacts that can traverse geographical, social, and semiotic boundaries bring us close to a new definition of *literacy* (cf. Hull, 2003).

Examining children's compelling digital stories, and reflecting on the possibilities of traversing boundaries, we are apt to forget the extreme challenges that accompany attempts to sustain community and university partnerships. There is a danger, then, through chapters such as this, of creating a fictionalized, idealized landscape of after school. Thus, we look forward to examining the uphill battles that characterize our kind of work—for example, the almost constant worry regarding sustainability, the evolving relationships with local nonprofits that can prove surprisingly combative (perhaps because of an increased competition for a smaller and smaller pool of funding), the continual need to be accountable to the local community in ways that one does not always foresee or sometimes agree with, and a range of tensions inspired by the different realities of those who come from the university and those who live in the West Oakland community.

Geographer David Harvey (2000), writing as the last century closed and reflecting on the world's vast inequalities and our failures in the United States to create the kind of just society for which many yearn, nonetheless concludes, as we do, with optimism: "I believe that in this moment in our history we have something of great import to accomplish by exercising an optimism of the intellect in order to open up ways of thinking that have for too long remained foreclosed" (p. 17). He sets about theorizing the decline and revitalization of inner cities, using Baltimore as an example, and calls for a utopian imagining that would afford the design of a more equitable future. He sharply critiques the degradation of urban landscapes, and just as passionately offers a vision for what cities might become if we train ourselves to think outside existing structures and norms. The parallels between the declining inner city of Baltimore, as described by Harvey, and similar sections of Oakland, California, where we live and work, are striking, and we take heart from his encouragement to imagine alternatives. To be sure, after-school programs and service learning programs are about as marginal as organizations can be in relation to the institutions of school and university—hardly spaces from which to mount a challenge to inequalities and injustices. But we believe, and we hope we have suggested in this chapter, that it is both crucial and enlivening to choose marginality (cf. hooks, 1990) and then to create lived spaces where hopeful projects and good work are freshly imagined and kept alive. We think of DUSTY, in this way at this moment, as providing the chance to construct a space that draws on the local neighborhood, its schools, and the university community, but also transcends them, recharting our geography as we traverse it, if you will, making possible some things that are impossible in either setting alone.

EPILOGUE:
BILL SMITH AND THE CREATION
OF SPACES FOR LEARNING
Glynda A. Hull

Before I began graduate school at the University of Pittsburgh, I went to the library and read everything that I could find that had been published by the faculty in my department. On the day that classes began, I went to Bill Smith's office and introduced myself, telling him I had chosen his work to emulate and asking him to be my mentor. Looking back, I am startled that I had the chutzpah to do this, but what amazes me most now and what astounded me then was Bill's reaction. Rather than merely tolerate me or tell me to return during office hours or hold himself professorially aloof, he sat and talked and talked and talked with me. He listened, he engaged, and he revealed how much he loved his work and how much pleasure he took in being an academic. He made me think I had interesting and valuable ideas. It was enlivening. I felt a part of something important, a greater world of scholarship and colleagueship that Bill made palpable to me. At the end of our conversation, Bill cleared a table in the corner of his office high in the Cathedral of Learning, that grand gothic tower that dominates the Pittsburgh campus, and he invited me to make that space my own. I did, all throughout graduate school. Anyone who knows the symbolic value of real estate on a university campus, especially a private office, can appreciate this splendid gesture. And so began a mentorship that transformed my years as a graduate student and continues to influence in substantive ways my life as a professor. Having a desk in Bill's office was a material sign of how he created a remarkable social space for learning. The greatest joys I have had as a researcher have been collaborative ones— joint work on worthy projects with like-minded students, colleagues, and friends, work like that described in this chapter. This project, and all the ones that have come before, and the ones yet to come, I trace to the example of generosity, bigness of spirit, enthusiasm, accessibility, and intellectual curiosity that I experienced as a proud and grateful student of William L. Smith.

REFERENCES

Aitken, S. C. (2001). *Geographies of young people: The morally contested spaces of identity*. London & New York: Routledge.

Berry, K. A., & Henderson, M. (2002). Introduction: Envisioning the nexus between geography and ethnic and racial identity. In K. A. Berry & M. Henderson (Eds.), *Geographic identities of ethnic America: Race, space, and place* (pp. 1–14). Reno: University of Nevada Press.

Boyle-Baise, M. (2002). *Multicultural service learning: Educating teachers in diverse communities*. New York: Teachers College Press.

Bruner, J. (1994). The remembered self. In U. Neisser & R. Fivush (Eds.), *The remembering self: Construction and agency in self narrative* (pp. 41–54). Cambridge: Cambridge University Press.

Bunge, W. W., & Bordessa, R. (1975). *The Canadian alternative: survival, expeditions and urban change*. Geographical Monographs, No. 2. Toronto: York University.

Clark, C. T. (2002). Unfolding narratives of service learning: Reflections on teaching, literacy, and positioning in service relationships. *Journal of Adolescent and Adult Literacy, 46*(4), 288–298.

Cole, M. (1996). *Cultural psychology: A once and future discipline*. Cambridge, MA: Harvard University Press.

Cole, M. (1999). Cultural psychology: Some general principals and a concrete example. In Y. Engestrom, R. Miettinen, & R. Punamaki (Eds.), *Perspectives on activity theory* (pp. 87–106). Cambridge: Cambridge University Press.

Compaine, B. M. (Ed.). (2001). *The digital divide: Facing a crisis or creating a myth?* Cambridge, MA: MIT Press.

Cushman, E. (1999). The public intellectual, service learning, and activist research. *College English, 61*(3), 328–336.

Cushman, E. (2002). Sustainable service learning programs. *College Composition and Communication, 54*(1), 40–65.

Deans, T. (2000). *Writing partnerships: Service-learning in composition.* Urbana, IL: National Council of Teachers of English.

de Certeau, M. (1984). *The practice of everyday life.* Berkeley: University of California Press.

Deskins, D. R., Jr., & Bettinger, C. (2002). Black and white spaces in selected metropolitan areas. In K. A. Berry & M. L. Henderson (Eds.), *Geographical identities of ethnic America: Race, space, and place* (pp. 38–63). Las Vegas: University of Nevada Press.

Dewey, J. (1938). *Experience and education.* New York: Macmillan.

Duncan, J. S., & Duncan, N. G. (2004). *Landscapes of privilege: The politics of the aesthetic in an American suburb.* New York: Routledge.

Erickson, E. H. (1977). *Toys and reasons.* New York: Norton.

Fairlie, R. W. (2003, November). *Is there a digital divide? Ethnic and racial differences in access to technology and possible explanations.* Final report to the University of California, Latino Policy Institute and California Policy Research Center.

Flower, L. (2002). Intercultural inquiry and the transformation of service. *College English, 65*(2), 181–201.

Flower, L. (2003). Talking across difference: Intercultural rhetoric and the search for situated knowledge. *College Composition and Communication, 55*(1), 38–68.

Freire, P. (1970). *Pedagogy of the oppressed.* New York: Continuum.

Furco, A., & Billig, S. H. (Eds.). (2002). *Service-learning: The essence of the pedagogy.* Greenwich, CT: Information Age Publishing.

Ginwright, S. A. (2004). *Black in school: Afrocentric reform, urban youth, and the promise of hip-hop culture.* New York: Teachers College Press.

Gutiérrez, K., Baquedano-Lopez, P., & Tejeda, C. (1999). Rethinking diversity: Hybridity and hybrid language practices in the third space. *Mind, Culture, & Activity: An International Journal, 6*(4), 286–303.

Halpern, R. (2002). A different kind of child development institution: The history of after-school programs for low-income children. *Teachers College Record, 104*(2), 178–211.

Halpern, R. (2003). *Making play work: The promise of after-school programs for low-income children.* New York: Teachers College.

Hammond, J. D. (2004). Photography and ambivalence. *Visual Studies, 19*(2), 135–144.

Harvey, D. (2000). *Spaces of hope.* Berkeley: University of California Press.

Herzberg, B. (1994). Community service and critical thinking. *College Composition and Communication, 45*(3), 307–319.

Himley, M. (2004). Facing (up to) "the stranger" in community service learning. *College Composition and Communication, 55*(3), 416–438.

hooks, b. (1990). *Yearning.* Boston: South End Press.

Hudak, G. (1999). The "sound" identity: Music-making and schooling. In C. McCarthy, G. Hudak, S. Miklaucic, & P. Saukko (Eds.), *Sound identities: Popular music and the cultural politics of education* (pp. 447–474). New York: Peter Lang.

Hull, G. A. (2003). Youth culture and digital media: New literacies for new times. *Research in the Teaching of English, 38*(2), 229–233.

Hull, G. A., & Katz, M.-L. (in press). Crafting an agentive self: Case studies on digital storytelling. *Research in the Teaching of English.*

Hull, G. A., & Nelson, M. (2005). Locating the semiotic power of multimodality. *Written Communication, 22*(2), 224–262.

Hull, G., & Schultz, K. (Eds.). (2002). *School's out! Bridging out-of-school literacies with classroom practice.* New York: Teachers College Press.

Hull, G., & Zacher, J. (2004, Winter/Spring). What is after-school worth? Developing literacies and identities out-of-school. *Voices in Urban Education, 3,* 36–44.

Kane, T. J. (2004). *The impact of after-school programs: Interpreting the results of four recent evaluations.* William T. Grant Foundation Working Paper.

Kress, G. (2003). *Literacy in the new media age.* London: Routledge.

Kress, G., & van Leeuwen, T. (1996). *Reading images: The grammar of visual design.* London: Routledge.

Lambert, J. (2002). *Digital storytelling: Capturing lives, creating community.* Berkeley: Digital Diner Press.

Leander, K. M. (2002). Locating Latanya: The situated production of identity artifacts in classroom interaction. *Research in the Teaching of English, 37,* 198–250.

Leander, K. M., & Sheehy, M. (Eds.). (2004). *Spatializing literacy research and practice.* New York: Peter Lang.

Lefebvre, H. (1974). *The production of space* (D. Nicholson-Smith, Trans.). Malden, MA: Blackwell.

Leoni, L., & Cohen, S. (2004, September 18). *Identity texts: Bringing students' culture to the fore of literacy.* Paper presented at the International Conference on Cultural Diversity and Language Education, University of Hawaii at Manoa.

Long, E., Peck, W. C., & Baskins, J. A. (2002). "Struggle": A literate practice supporting life-project planning. In G. Hull & K. Schultz (Eds.), *School's out! Bridging out-of-school literacies with classroom practice* (pp. 131–161). New York: Teachers College Press.

Massey, D. (1998). The spatial construction of youth cultures. In T. Skelton & G. Valentine (Eds.), *Cool places: Geographies of youth cultures* (pp. 121–129). London: Routledge.

Matthews, H., & Limb, M. (1999). Defining an agenda for the geography of children: Review and prospect. *Progress in Human Geography, 23*(1), 61–90.

Mitchell, W. J. T. (1994). *Picture theory: Essays on verbal and visual representation.* Chicago: University of Chicago Press.

Mitchell, W. J. T. (2002). Space, place, and landscape. In W. J. T. Mitchell (Ed.), *Landscape and power* (2nd ed., pp. vii–xii). Chicago: University of Chicago Press.

Moje, E. B. (2004). Powerful spaces: Tracing the out-of-school literacy spaces of Latino/a youth. In K. M. Leander & M. Sheehy (Eds.), *Spatializing literacy research and practice* (pp. 15–38). New York: Peter Lang.

Morrell, E. (2004). *Linking literacy and popular culture.* Norwood, MA: Christopher-Gordon Publishers.

National Institute on Out-of-School Time. (2003). *Making the case: A fact sheet on children and youth in out-of-school-time.* Wellesley, MA: Center for Research on Women, Wellesley College.

Noguera, P. (1996). Confronting the urban in urban school reform. *The Urban Review, 28*(1), 1–19.

Papademas, D. (Ed.). (2004). *Ethics in visual research* [Special section]. *Visual Studies, 19*(2).

Peck, W. C., Flower, L., & Higgins, L. (1995). Community literacy. *College Composition and Communication, 46,* 199–222.

Peirce, C. S. (1955). Logic as semiotic: The theory of signs. In J. Buchler (Ed.), *Philosophical writings of Peirce* (pp. 98–119). New York: Dover.

Piaget, J. (1971). *Structuralism.* New York: Basic Books.

Rhomberg, C. (2004). *No there there: Race, class, and political community in Oakland.* Berkeley: University of California Press.

Roche-Smith, J. (2004). *Crossing frontiers and discovering paths: Young adolescents in a digital storytelling program.* Unpublished doctoral dissertation, University of California, Berkeley.

Schwartz, D. (1989). Visual ethnography: Using photography in qualitative research. *Qualitative Sociology, 12*(2), 119–153.

Scollon, R., & Scollon, S. W. (2003). *Discourses in place: Language in the material world.* London: Routledge.

Soja, E. W. (2004). Preface. In K. M. Leander & M. Sheehy (Eds.), *Spatializing literacy research and practice* (pp. ix–xv). New York: Peter Lang.

Soja, E. W. (1996). *Thirdspace: Journeys to Los Angeles and other real- and imagined-places.* Malden, MA: Blackwell.

Sontag, S. (1973). *On photography.* New York: Farrar, Straus & Giroux.

Suchar, C. S. (1997). Grounding visual sociology research in shooting scripts. *Qualitative Sociology, 20*(1), 33–55.

Tye, L. (2004). *Rising from the rails: Pullman porters and the making of the black middle class.* New York: Henry Holt.

Underwood, C., Welsh, M., Gauvain, M., & Duffy, S. (2000). Learning at the edges: Challenges to the sustainability of service-learning in higher education. *Journal of Language and Leaning Across the Disciplines, 4*(3), 7–26.

Urciuoli, B. (1995). The indexical structure of visibility. In B. Farnell (Ed.), *Human action signs in cultural context: The visible and the invisible in movement and dance* (pp. 189–215). Metuchen, NJ, & London: Scarecrow.

Valentine, G., Skelton, T., & Chambers, D. (1998). Cool places: An introduction to youth cultures. In T. Skelton & G. Valentine (Eds.), *Cool places: Geographies of youth cultures* (pp. 1-32). London: Routledge.

Vygotsky, L. (1934/1986). *Thought and language.* Cambridge, MA: Cambridge University Press.

Vygotsky, L. (1978). *Mind in society: The development of higher psychological processes.* Cambridge, MA: Harvard University Press.

Wagner, J. (2004). Constructing credible images: Documentary studies, social research, and visual research. *American Behavioral Scientist, 47*(12), 1477–1506.

Warschauer, M. (2004). *Technology and social inclusion: Rethinking the digital divide.* Cambridge, MA: MIT Press.

Welsh, N. (2002). "And now that I know them": Composing mutuality in a service learning course. *College Composition and Communication, 54*(2), 243–263.

15

CROSSING OVER

The Move From Education to Composition

Russel K. Durst

This chapter examines the career path that a number of composition specialists have followed: earning a doctorate in education, then crossing disciplinary boundaries by taking a faculty position in a college English department or free-standing writing program and pursuing a career in composition. In the chapter, I discuss my own development as an education-inflected composition scholar, a move influenced by Bill Smith's advice and mentorship, which led to my doctoral work in literacy in a school of education and my subsequent career as a composition specialist in a college English department.

In addition to discussing my own experience, I investigate more broadly how scholars with backgrounds in educational studies have contributed to the field of composition. This large, distinguished, and diverse group of scholars includes, in addition to many of the contributors to this volume, Arthur Applebee, Richard Braddock, Lillian Bridwell, James Britton, Charles Cooper, Janet Emig, Keith Gilyard, Joseph Harris, George Hillocks, James Kinneavy, Lucille McCarthy, James Moffett, Tom Newkirk, Lee Odell, Gordon Pradl, Mike Rose, Cindy Selfe, and others. These figures have contributed to the development of composition studies, in my view, primarily in the following ways: (a) by legitimizing the classroom, student, and teacher as sites for inquiry; (b) by introducing influential theoretical frameworks to the field of literacy studies; and (c) by developing and employing productive research methodologies, particularly but not exclusively varieties of empirical research. I discuss the contributions of education-trained scholars within the overall context of composition studies' embrace of literary-oriented textual study, criticism, and theory; and I examine composition's long-standing and powerful humanistic resistance to empiricism and the influence of educational studies more generally. The chapter concludes with an attempt to go beyond this disciplinary conflict by suggesting that—lingering hostility and problems notwithstanding—the field of composition studies has actually benefited in important ways from the tension produced by this combination of empiricism and opposition to empirical study.

My own work in composition has been substantially influenced by my graduate study in education. In 1980, while finishing a master's degree in linguistics and a certificate in teaching English as a second language (ESL) at the University of Pittsburgh, I began tutoring in Pitt's Writing Workshop. Bill Smith directed the workshop, and most days he would stroll in during my late afternoon hours, sometimes wearing a big cowboy hat. Lean, with thinning hair and long sideburns, Bill talked fast, with a hint of a Texas twang, and could be counted on occasionally to say provocative things. Once, he watched me for a while as I tutored, and we debriefed afterward. I remember nothing of what he said about my tutoring— I'm not sure we even discussed it—but I recall his mentioning that, at a previous institution, he and a colleague regularly observed each other's teaching. However, they did not just observe; they also took an active role in the other's classes. Bill said he once entered his friend's class, jumped up on a table, did a brief dance in front of the puzzled students, and then nonchalantly sat down to see how his friend would handle the disruption. I do not know for certain whether this incident really happened—Bill has always struck me as a deeply responsible person and not quite as outrageous as he sometimes makes himself out to be. But I love the image, true or not, of Bill Smith dancing on a table before a group of bewildered college students, then sitting down with a sly grin and waiting to see what would happen.

My plan back in 1980 was to complete the linguistics master's degree and then get a doctorate in English, specializing in composition, and become a composition person. I knew from my undergraduate experience that I wanted to spend my life researching, writing, and talking to people about what I was researching and writing; in short, I wanted to become a professor. My undergraduate experience had taught me that much. But I did not want to become a theoretical linguist or a literary scholar, the two possibilities most open to me, because these pursuits seemed too ivory tower and narrowly focused for my taste. At the time, I knew little about composition except that it was an exciting, growing, and socially conscious young discipline—Donald Murray's (1968) process pedagogy, Ken Macrorie's (1970) emphasis on real writing that cut through the jargon and cliché, and Mina Shaughnessy's (1977) ground-breaking work with open admissions students gave the field a progressive political cachet—and I thought I might want to be part of it.

The field of composition studies was academic, intellectual, and new, but it was also something more. In contrast to other disciplines, composition seemed to be about empowering disenfranchised students, helping them develop a voice, celebrating and examining those voices, and providing access to the academy. Although I had no real experience in composition yet, a background like mine—in language study and literary analysis—seemed appropriate for a field that focused on students' written communication. Although I had never taken (and never would take) a class from Bill Smith or even been a student in his department, he quickly became an unofficial mentor to me, as he was to so many others. Uncertain of my next step after the master's, I asked him about doctoral programs, and he gave me a lecture. He told me that, in composition, one applied not to a school, but to a person. The idea was to work with and learn from a leading researcher in the field, almost in an apprenticeship, and then go on to establish one's own career: I believe Bill also used the analogy of the stud farm. We both agreed I shouldn't stay at Pittsburgh, where I had done my bachelor's and was completing my master's degree.

Bill listed 10 or 15 names, few of which I recognized. He rank ordered them informally according to their research expertise and told me to write to these individuals. Initially, I was surprised to find that a number of these people were in departments of education rather than English. The composition people whose work I knew best at that time—Coles, Elbow, Macrorie, Murray, Shaughnessy—all resided in English departments. But Bill said that education was where much of the important research went on and where doctoral students were receiving the best preparation for faculty positions in English composition. He insisted I would not have a problem getting a composition job in an English department with a doctorate in education. Although he had not made this move, receiving his PhD in English with Kellogg Hunt at Florida State, he had taught in a school of education at Boston University, and his finest doctoral student there, Nancy Sommers, had moved smoothly into a college English department.

One of the top people on Bill's list, and not just alphabetically, was Arthur Applebee at Stanford University's School of Education. According to Bill, Applebee, though just in his mid-30s, a student of James Britton at the University of London, and the son of a distinguished American professor of English education, was doing the most interesting and, with several large federal grants, the most generously funded empirical research on writing in the country. An early book by Applebee, *The Child's Concept of Story: Ages Two to Seventeen* (1978), based on his doctoral dissertation, was a groundbreaking study of children's narrative knowledge and ability. Still, I had concerns. Frankly, I hadn't considered the possibility of going to graduate school in education as a way of becoming a composition specialist; this was a new idea for me, and I worried about the academic rigor of schools of education. Most of my professors turned up their noses at the mention of such places. However, Stanford was Stanford, and a little research on my part showed that its education school had an extremely strong reputation—not just in the United States, but worldwide. Plus I remembered what Bill Smith had said about the importance of working with a distinguished adviser. Arthur quickly replied to my inquiry, scrawling a note on the bottom of the letter I had sent, saying that he could use a research assistant with my background in discourse analysis to work on his large-scale study of high school writing, and the next thing I knew I was working toward my PhD in literacy with Arthur Applebee. The Applebee graduate students included some secondary English teachers who wanted to become professors of English education as well as others who, like me, were preparing to be composition specialists in a college English department. We all took more or less the same curriculum, with seminars in literacy research, language, linguistics, and response to literature, as well as classes in quantitative and qualitative research methods, and courses in educational theory and practice. I actually took five graduate classes in statistical analysis and research design, fairly typical for the time, and even my literacy related courses (except for one taught along strictly ethnographic lines by Shirley Brice Heath) involved a fair amount of quantitative analysis. But in general my course work was really not my main concern as a graduate student. Rather, I spent most of my time and energy working, often 7 days a week, as a research assistant on Arthur Applebee and Judith Langer's large-scale projects. First, I took part in the massive National Study of Writing in the Secondary School (Applebee, 1981, 1984), followed by a study involving several high schools, numerous teachers, and hundreds of students, examining the effects of different kinds of writing on student learning in the content areas (Langer & Applebee, 1987). I generally completed my course work in what spare time I had. By my second year, I was training and supervising new research assistants and developing my own program of inquiry within the Applebee and Langer framework. By my fourth and final year, I had managed several publications and conference presentations and was completing my dissertation, an empirical study of the cognitive and linguistic dimensions of analytic and summary writing, a vintage early-1980's research topic in composition. That year I also taught in Stanford's first-year composition program in order to try out what I had learned as a researcher and to make sure I would have enough teaching experience for a tenure-track position in an English department. But primarily I spent my years at Stanford learning to be a writing researcher.

The *stud farm* approach laid out by Bill Smith worked out quite well for me. After 4 years at Stanford, I completed my PhD and moved on to a job at the University of Hawaii in the English department. There, in 1987, I published the first piece of my dissertation in *Research in the Teaching of English*, the English journal that was and still is most receptive to quantitative inquiry about composition. Two years later, I moved to the University of Cincinnati's English department to direct the Writing Center, and I have been here since, publishing research on writing in a range of journals and books, while serving stints as director of composition and department head and holding offices in the National Council of

Teachers of English (NCTE) and the National Conference on Research in Language and Literacy (NCRLL).

During my two job searches in the 1980s, I had the feeling that some English departments chose not to consider me for positions because of my education school background and quantitatively oriented research, although I did not really know for sure. But judging from my interviews and subsequent job offers, a fair number of other schools showed few such qualms. I had an excellent experience in my doctoral program, intellectually rich, challenging, and full of opportunities for growth and recognition; on completion, I was able to achieve my goal of crossing back over from education to English. Yet as I prepared to start my career, one of my graduate school professors, a well-known literacy scholar, surprised me by expressing satisfaction that I would not be teaching in a department of education because, according to this professor, faculty in such programs tended not to respect one another. Although I never really got to find out how accurate that assessment was, I did soon realize that, as a composition professor in an English department, some of my colleagues had questions about me. Even within the field of composition, I have found that my education background and empirical research orientation place me within a minority that is at times marginalized by the majority, trained in departments of English, whose orientation is more humanistic and literary.

In my early years as a composition specialist, I continued to publish quantitative and cognitive or psycholinguistically oriented studies in *RTE* and elsewhere. These pieces included, among other works, a 1989 article on metacognitive monitoring processes in students' academic writing and a 1990 piece on primary trait assessment of persuasive writing (Durst, Laine, Schultz, & Vilter, 1990), both in the journal *Written Communication*. However, dating from early in the 1980's, people within the field of composition were beginning to react sharply against such empirical research. Critiques by more humanistically inclined scholars protested against the prominence of methods seemingly so at odds with the types of textual study typical of English departments. To take a prominent example, in a 1987 *College Composition and Communication* article entitled "Finding a Comfortable Identity," the published version of his address as Chair of the Conference on College Composition and Communication (CCCC), no less an eminence than William Irmscher of the University of Washington throws down the gauntlet. He suggests, referring to cognitive and experimental research in composition, that, "After one struggles through the prose and the statistics and the diagrams, one discovers that the investigator has complicated the familiar and obfuscated the obvious." Such inquiry, Irmscher continues, "lacks rigorous thought" (p. 83). He is slightly more accepting of studies by such researchers as Dixie Goswami, Donald Graves, and Lee Odell, who, as he put it, "take a larger view . . . shifting the emphasis to the social setting, advocating ethnographic approaches" (p. 84). But Irmscher concludes by employing a distinction first made by Kenneth Burke, urging composition scholars to see writing as *dramatistic*, involving symbolic action, performance, and rhetoric, as opposed to *scientistic*. "We need to reassert the humanistic nature of our own discipline." He cites a shared "common ground in the English department with critics, textualists, historiographers, bibliographers, linguists, novelists, and poet" (p. 85).

Such attacks began appearing with more frequency in composition publications and presentations from a variety of influential figures, and perhaps not surprisingly—given the increasing prevalence of such sentiment, the number of experimental and/or cognitive pieces appearing in print declined. In 1988, I wrote a largely favorable review in *CCC* of a 1987 book including mainly experimental studies, edited by Ann Matsuhashi (1987), entitled *Writing in Real Time: Modeling Production Processes.* I decided to begin the review by acknowledging an earlier critique of this sort of work, Berthoff's (1984) description of composing process studies as "dreary reports by psycholinguists." Arguing that even watching a sheepdog at work sheds more light on the nature of composition than examining process research, Berthoff, never one to mince words, asserts that all one needs to know about composing could be found in the humanistic tradition.

The Matsuhashi book seems to me, as I look back, a kind of swan song for experimental inquiry in composition. Editor Matsuhashi was a recognized name in composition at that point for her early cognitive analyses of revision in the composing process, and had been a student of Charles Cooper from the education program at SUNY Buffalo. However, after releasing this book, Matsuhashi practically ceased to publish in the field and seemed to disappear almost entirely until resurfacing recently as a writing center director and author of some work in this area of composition. Her mentor Cooper was best known at the time for publishing, with Lee Odell, two important, quantitatively oriented collections of essays on composition from NCTE entitled *Evaluating Writing: Describing, Measuring, Judging* (1977) and *Research on Composing: Points of Departure* (1979). These works reflect empirical traditions of analysis and assessment much influenced by work in education, where both men did their graduate work and spent their early years as professors. However, Cooper moved to the English department at UC San Diego and by the mid-1980s largely abandoned empirical research. With Rise Axelrod, a former student from UC San Diego, he authored *The St. Martin's Guide for Writing*, one of the most successful textbooks ever published in college composition, currently in its seventh printing (Axelrod & Cooper, 2004).

As for myself, not wishing to swim upstream, feeling intrigued by the possibility of new methods of inquiry, and finding other research questions and approaches to interest me, I decided to re-tool as a qualitative researcher using ethnographic methods. After immersing myself in these methods for several years of preparation and then carrying out the study that resulted in the book, *Collision Course: Conflict, Negotiation, and Learning in College Composition* (Durst, 1999), qualitative analysis has remained my modus operandi. Thus, while not abandoning empirical research, I did go along with the social turn in composition and ceased doing the increasingly censured work that involved experimental or quantitative analysis, in the process shifting to an approach that generated far less controversy and more acceptance in the field of composition.

It is worth pointing out that not all empirically driven work in composition comes out of school of education traditions. For example, probably the most influential empirical research strand in composition from the 1980s was the distinguished composing process work of Flower and Hayes (1981, 1984). Their studies typically employ analysis of think-aloud protocols to compare different aspects of the writing processes of expert and novice writers. This research springs from a tradition of inquiry established by Nobel Prize winning cognitive psychologist and economist Herbert Simon and his Carnegie Mellon University (CMU) colleague, Allen Newell. Their theoretical approach and studies examining expert and novice chess players, mathematicians, and physicists are discussed in the groundbreaking 1972 book *Human Problem Solving* (Newell & Simon). Psychologist Dick Hayes, working in the tradition established by his senior colleagues Newell and Simon, began to collaborate with beginning CMU English professor Linda Flower, applying protocol analytic techniques to questions of novice student writing versus expert writing. Flower had been trained in literary analysis at Rutgers but was initially hired to teach business and technical writing at CMU, where she ended up becoming a major figure in composition studies with her cognitive process work. Besides Hayes' and Flower's influential cognitive work, a generation of their graduate students carried on their tradition, including, for example, Davida Charney, Cheryl Geisler, Stuart Greene, and Ann Penrose, all of whom carried out formal case study inquiry in which they gave writers particular tasks and then analyzed the data for different aspects of their writing processes, written products, thinking, and learning. All of these scholars eventually expanded their focus to consider the contexts surrounding students' writing.

Enormously important in shifting attention in composition research and pedagogy to questions of process, partly for this reason the work of Flower and Hayes came under intense criticism from humanistically minded composition scholars almost from its inception in the early 1980s. One of the first and most influential of these negative critiques came from Patricia Bizzell, a composition scholar and English professor trained in literary critical approaches and a vocal opponent of scientific methods in composition. Ironically, Bizzell had also been a literature doctoral student in Rutgers University's English department just slightly later than Linda Flower (as had distinguished compositionist David Bartholomae as well). In a 1982 article in the journal *Pre/Text* discussing Flower and Hayes' (1981) cognitively oriented research and Flower's (1981) textbook, *Problem-Solving Strategies for Writers*, Bizzell argues that the composing process model put forth by the researchers is seriously flawed as both a research and teaching tool because it ignores the larger cultural context influencing writers' decisions and assumes that all writers, despite their disparate backgrounds, interests, and approaches, are choosing from essentially the same set of strategies. Here Bizzell strikes one of the earliest blows from the humanistic side of the field in the battle against empirically grounded work in composition. This work and similar ones critical of empirical research and/or promoting more traditional textual and critical scholarship have subsequently been much cited by other humanistic opponents of empiricism in composition studies.

In what has been termed the *social turn* in composition studies, thinking about the nature of writing was moving from an emphasis on the individual writer's exigencies to a broader examination of cultural and situational factors affecting the production and reception of written language. By the late 1980s, after many such critiques, Hayes had largely abandoned research on composing and gone back to the discipline of cognitive psychology, although he has recently also been working in the area of writing assessment. Flower, staying in composition, moved away from an emphasis on cognition to advocate a more naturalistic approach to inquiry in which cultural contexts would feature prominently. Flower's ongoing work in composition employs just such a cultural focus, as she has over the past decade studied and helped develop community literacy centers in which urban minority youth have the opportunity to talk, read, and write about issues central to their lives. Later in this chapter, I consider the reasons for and consequences of this hostility toward empirical research and toward education-trained composition scholars, but first I examine the overall contributions of these scholars to the field.

Questions of influence include a large element of speculation because, in the final analysis, it is impossible to know for certain where an idea or approach came from and exactly why it developed the way it did. The best one can do is present a case for a particular kind of influence by providing the strongest evidence possible. Accordingly, I would like to argue, based on my own experience and analysis, that people who entered the field of composition having done their graduate work in education have significantly influenced the field in some particular ways. Specifically, composition specialists trained in education have influenced the field of composition by helping to legitimize the classroom, student, and teacher as sites of inquiry; by constructing productive theoretical frameworks for conceptualizing the nature of literacy as well as its teaching and learning; and by developing popular and revealing empirical research methods, quantitative in the earlier days of modern composition studies, and, more recently, qualitative approaches. I discuss each of these broader contributions in turn.

In the tradition of English studies, the literary text and archive have served as the primary sites of inquiry. The classroom has historically not functioned as an appropriate setting in which to carry out research, student texts have not carried the prestige of published literary work, and teachers' ideas and approaches have not attracted serious scholarly interest from literature specialists. Despite a recent interest in theorizing pedagogy, particularly its politics, as seen in the fashionable new journal *Pedagogy*, published in Duke University's English department, and even in the pages of the quintessential literary journal *PMLA*, the field of literature for the most part still eschews analysis of classroom work.

Since around the early 1970s, however, the modern field of composition studies has challenged these orthodoxies, and from the start education-trained scholars have been at the forefront of this work. Influential early composition figures such as Britton (1970; see also Britton et al., 1975) and Kinneavy (1971), education professors at the Universities of London and Texas, respectively, focused intensively and in distinctive ways on the functions and audiences of written texts, particularly student texts. Britton and his colleagues' functions and audiences of writing and Kinneavy's aims of discourse, while referencing classical rhetoric, provided scholars in the emerging field of composition with new and innovative ways of talking about and categorizing texts—ways that went beyond the persuasive focus of early rhetoric or the static modes of discourse popularized in 18th- and 19th-century rhetoric. Their work had a powerful impact on an incipient field, shifting many scholars' attention to the student text as an object of inquiry.

In addition, both Britton and Kinneavy used their studies to argue for a broader definition of *student writing*, going beyond such standbys as the traditional "English theme" and the research paper to include more literary, real-world, and expressive or personal writing, as well as a greater range of audiences for student work, beyond what Britton referred to as the "teacher as examiner." Further, each of them mentored doctoral students who went on to become important figures in their own right in composition. Arthur Applebee (my own mentor) was Britton's student, while Tom Newkirk and Cindy Selfe were two of Kinneavy's successful doctoral students. Moreover, these second-generation figures have since produced their own doctoral graduates who have gone on to be recognized figures in composition and who share this interest in studying teachers and students.

Similarly, in the late 1960s, Janet Emig, in her dissertation at Harvard's Graduate School of Education, ignited interest in examining students' writing processes with her own detailed case study of Lynn and other high school writers. The dissertation was published in shortened form in 1972 in the NCTE research monograph series and was widely referenced by scholars at all instructional levels. Emig spent the bulk of her career as a professor of education at Rutgers University. Schools of education produced other researchers in the following years who focused on specific aspects of composing, such as Matsuhashi (1981) and Bridwell (1980), who examined revision, and Freedman (1987), who investigated teachers' written responses as well as student–teacher conferences and, more recently, directed the National Center for the Study of Writing, located at the University of California at Berkeley. Freedman's (1994) recent work is international in scope, making cross-cultural comparisons of high school student writing in the United States and Great Britain.

This cross-cultural, international focus has a long history in composition studies. Although working independently in the United States and England, respectively, Janet Emig had in common with James Britton a highly critical stance toward the traditional secondary English composition curriculum, arguing, and using their data to back them up, that too often school writing assignments were overly rigid, scripted, and artificial, stifling students' creativity and hindering their full development as writers and as people. Although the late 1970s and early 1980s work of Flower and Hayes, as mentioned, came from college English and psychology departments at CMU, it was Emig's ground-breaking study that initially generated the strong interest in student writing processes, creating a sympathetic and excited response for the later work when it appeared and helping to establish composition studies as an academic area in its own right.

The writing classroom as a site of inquiry has been enriched by work from a variety of research traditions, quantitative and qualitative alike. On the quantitative side, early on Richard Braddock, with collaborators Richard Lloyd-Jones and Lowell Schoer, all of the University of Iowa, published in 1963 the first comprehensive analysis of empirical research on writing. Braddock and Schoer were from education, whereas Lloyd-Jones was in the Iowa English department. They highlighted what they viewed as the highest quality studies and attempted to assess the most productive approaches for teaching students to write. However, the authors found they were hindered by the poor quality of the vast majority of studies they examined, even those they deemed as the best that existed. Braddock, Lloyd-Jones, and Schoer are perhaps best known today for likening the state of writing research in the early 1960s to that of alchemy, and for calling for more rigorous, controlled research.

A follow-up meta-analytic study by Hillocks (1984) almost 20 years later found similar systemic problems with most of the research that had been done in the intervening years. However, Hillocks employed a complex statistical procedure to sift through nearly 2,000, mainly flawed studies, finding that the most effective way of teaching writing employed what he called an *environmental* approach, with clear goals, teacher-designed activities, and a specific focus on what students were expected to learn how to do. For example, effective units focused on topics like the definition, persuasive writing, and the fable. This approach, most closely associated with Hillocks and students working in his tradition, fared better than what Hillocks termed the *natural process* approach, more closely associated with Peter Elbow, Donald Murray, and the National Writing Project, or an approach in which teachers emphasized grammar instruction and the traditional modes of discourse. Students in a natural process classroom chose their own topics and genres in which to compose and received little in the way of teacherly direction.

Among the earliest published work discussing qualitative research in composition and English education was University of Georgia education professor Ken Kantor and two colleagues' article for the journal *Research in the Teaching of English* in 1981 (Kantor, Kirby, & Goetz). Their article marked the start of an emphasis on classroom ethnography that continues in literacy studies up to the present. McCarthy's (1987) influential qualitative study "Stranger in Strange Lands," published in *RTE*, is an early ethnographic examination of writing across the curriculum.

McCarthy, a student of Linda Brodkey in education at the University of Pennsylvania, looked qualitatively in her dissertation at the disparate environments in which a first-year college student was expected to write in English, biology, and history classes, finding that faculty in different fields were under the mistaken impression that writing assignments, and their underlying assumptions, were much more comparable across disciplines than they proved to be. Her study and others that followed challenged common assumptions among composition specialists about preparing students for the variety of writing tasks that awaited them. McCarthy has gone on to collaborate with philosophy professor Steve Fishman in a series of book-length qualitative studies of classroom interaction, writing, and learning at the college level, studies that incorporate the progressive pedagogical theories of philosopher of education John Dewey to investigate questions of classroom discourse and democracy (Fishman & McCarthy, 1998, 2000). As a whole, such research has become an integral piece of the knowledge base for composition studies. Studies in this tradition are frequently cited and, although over the years maligned by critics such as Berthoff, Bizzell, and Irmscher for being reductive and unrevealing, particularly the quantitative studies, this work forms part of the fabric of our field.

In addition to spotlighting and legitimizing the student, teacher, and classroom as sites for inquiry, composition scholars with backgrounds in education also strengthened the field by introducing powerful theoretical frameworks for understanding the teaching and learning of written language, particularly its unique role as a tool for intellectual development and critical thought. Such work helped strengthen composition's academic and intellectual vitality and credibility by inextricably linking writing with learning and thinking. This work provided compositionists with a more substantive justification of the field's importance; we could no longer be said simply to be teaching formulaic writing formats or fixing students' grammar and punctuation problems. The work also leads to a curricular focus on writing activities intended not only to create certain types of text, but also to engage students in complex thinking and learning.

In a foundational work, Britton's (1970) grandly synthetic book, *Language and Learning,* drew on an impressive range of ideas, including the findings of Russian psychologists Alexander Luria and Lev Vygotsky, the pedagogy of American psychologist Jerome Bruner, the theories of philosophers Ernst Cassirer and Susanne Langer, the hypotheses of linguist Edward Sapir, and the criticism of F. R. Leavis. Britton, a professor of English education at the University of London, deployed this array of scholarship to advance the argument that it is through language use, particularly in informal, intimate settings, that we make sense of the world. We do so through language use, Britton argued, by categorizing what we see and hear, coming to grips with new experience, questioning, forming insights, and eventually reaching new levels of understanding. The classroom, for Britton, was the place where this development could take place under the watchful eye of a supportive, sympathetic, and not too directive teacher, who would create a comfortable classroom environment where students' natural curiosity and verbal interactions of many types would allow growth to flourish.

Shedding some of Britton's arguably utopian elements, Emig drew on many of the same theorists in her 1977 essay "Writing as a Mode of Learning," published in *CCC.* Emig narrowed her focus from language in general to written language, suggesting that writing, particularly analytic writing, offered students powerful opportunities, even more powerful than those offered by spoken language, for thinking through and understanding complex issues. Emig argued for a greater emphasis on writing, especially writing intended to foster critical thinking, in the curriculum for English and other subjects at all levels of instruction. Besides greatly influencing the incipient writing across the curriculum movement, the theories developed by Britton and Emig remain a key part of composition studies' founding purpose and self-justification.

Composition scholars with education backgrounds also influenced the field by introducing powerful methods of empirical inquiry. I have already described the empirical approaches of such seminal figures as James Britton, Janet Emig, and George Hillocks in investigating student writing and classroom approaches. Another key example of influence from education comes in the area of writing assessment. Such assessment may be employed for scholarly purposes or for more programmatic reasons such as placement and exit testing; whichever the intent, writing assessment methods used in composition are rooted in empirical research traditions imported from the field of education. Approaches to large-scale written language testing were systematically introduced to the young field of composition studies in ETS testing specialist Paul Diederich's *Measuring Growth in English*, published by NCTE in 1974. Diederich described in detail a method he called *holistic scoring*. He explained how to organize and carry out a large assessment of student writing under timed conditions, and his approach is still prevalent in writing programs today.

A few years later, Cooper and Odell's (1977) edited volume from NCTE, entitled *Evaluating Writing: Describing, Measuring, Judging*, built on the foundation established by Diederich. The editors and their contributors presented a detailed follow-up discussion of holistic scoring (Cooper), as well as an examination of syntactic maturity (Hunt) and an introduction to a method called *primary trait scoring* (Lloyd-Jones). These three writing assessment methods have since been employed in a myriad of studies, both scholarly and programmatic, of students' written language. To cite just one instance, Walvoord and McCarthy's (1990) book, *Thinking and Writing in College: A Naturalistic Study of Students in Four Disciplines*, employs a primary trait analysis of student texts to examine college student writing in business, history, psychology, and biology classes. In addition, the authors utilize other research methods with roots in education studies, such as Emig's think-aloud protocols and an analysis of the influence of teacher comments on students' revising patterns based on work by Sperling and Freedman (1987). Works such as these, steeped in empirical traditions mainly imported from schools of education, spread the study of written composition beyond the borders of English departments to examine the teaching and learning of written language across disciplines.

Thus, as the discipline of composition studies continues to evolve, the influence of education-inflected work remains prominent. But at the same time, so does the tradition of opposition to this influence within a field dominated by more humanistically oriented scholars. For example, a recent essay collection by Olson (2000), entitled *Rhetoric and Composition as Intellectual Work*, argues for the vitality of our field as a rigorous academic discipline with a variety of theoretically sophisticated scholarly traditions and with close connections to other humanities disciplines. Featuring chapters by such leading scholars as Sharon Crowley, Susan Jarratt, Thomas Kent, Susan Miller, John Trimbur, Victor Vitanza, Lynn Worsham, and others, the collection includes sections on disciplinary concerns, historical inquiry, ideological inquiry, philosophical inquiry, and new areas of interest such as body studies and technology. Editor Olson must surely have intended to represent rhetoric and composition in the best and most comprehensive light possible. However, in a *CCC* review, Joseph Harris, a distinguished compositionist as well as a graduate of Gordon Pradl's literacy doctoral program in Education at NYU, complains that Olson's book excludes much important work in composition. Instead Harris wants to define the field much more broadly. He argues that,

> People working in composition include not only critics and historians but also ethnographers, linguists, educational researchers, teacher developers, journalists, and creative writers—who are trained not only in graduate programs in English but also in education, linguistics, rhetoric, ESL, psychology, and communications. Their research takes place not only in archives and libraries but also in classrooms, literacy centers, workplaces, and communities. (pp. 173-174)

As a composition scholar who at times finds his empirical approach marginalized, but who is nonetheless fully committed to working in the field, I have largely come to terms with this situation and have learned to deal with the frustration that occasionally results. In my view, composition colleagues who exclude or devalue my sort of work on a general disciplinary principle illustrate Kenneth Burke's insight that a way of seeing is also a way of not seeing. Grounded in their humanistic traditions, such scholars simply do not understand, or will not acknowledge, the value of a different approach to the subject they hold dear. Paradoxically, I have a friend and colleague who is a well-respected literacy scholar in a school of education. Yet she claims that her work, grounded in critical literacy and postmodernism, has recently become both too literary and too theoretical for the mainstream in her field. She now finds she is unable to publish in educational journals and must seek out alternative venues for publication. The same narrow orientation that we empiricists chafe under in composition studies therefore would seem to exist in her field as well. Except that, in her case, the situation is reversed, with more humanistic approaches marginalized rather than valorized. Thus, I strongly suspect that what we in composition tend to see as a problem specific to our discipline may be far more widespread and is perhaps even endemic in academia.

In composition studies, people have suffered because of this exclusionary attitude, and the field as a whole has also suffered due to the loss of contributions from empirically minded compositionists whose backgrounds are in education. For example, some respected researchers no longer attend the CCCC or publish in composition journals, and our field is surely the worse for such defections. At worst, this exclusion strikes me as an attempt at what I would call a methodological cleansing of the field by those who, like Irmscher and Bizzell cited earlier, believe that nonhumanistic scholarship has little or no place in composition studies.

Yet despite these sorts of conflicts, the loss of some working scholars, and the occasional experience of marginalization, education-inflected composition scholarship continues to find its way into print and at times even prominence, contributing much to the field. Indeed, in my experience, although hostility does exist, many composition scholars value such work, particularly qualitative inquiry, when it is done well, regardless of whether they are steeped in its traditions. To cite a personal example, when I did the research and writing that resulted in my 1999 book, *Collision Course: Conflict, Negotiation, and Learning in College Composition*, a qualitative study of first-year college writing students and teachers, I was always aware that the book would be evaluated mainly by people who did not share my background in educational studies, nor my assumptions and methods. I approached this project with a strong and careful determination that my research should reflect well not only on me personally, but also on empirical study in composition generally, and that the work should make a genuine contribution to the wider field. I felt that many in composition had written theoretically or programmatically about employing politically radical teaching approaches in classes consisting of a largely conservative student body. Yet no one had bothered to examine actual students and teachers engaged in such work or investigate in a systematic way the conflicts that arose and the learning that developed. In my view, this work was needed, and most of the composition scholars who subsequently reviewed the book favorably, discussed it in their own work, or used it in their graduate courses were not empiricists.

While acknowledging that individuals pursuing empirical work have been slighted, I would argue that composition studies has in some ways actually benefited from the strain caused by this combination of empirical approaches mainly imported from education and humanistic skepticism or even hostility toward empirical study. Partly because we know that our work will be closely scrutinized by scholars indifferent or opposed to our methods, empiricists in composition strive to reach the very highest standard. Thus it is no surprise to me that scholars whose work reflects their backgrounds in education so frequently occupy leadership roles in the field of composition, as the list of distinguished names with which I began this chapter strongly suggests. We have unique contributions to make, not the least of which is our ability to study in systematic fashion the complex intersection of theory and praxis as it plays out in our classrooms.

REFERENCES

Applebee, A. N. (1978). *The child's concept of story: Ages two to seventeen.* Chicago: University of Chicago Press.

Applebee, A. N. (1981). *Writing in the secondary school: English and the content areas* (NCTE Research Report No. 21). Urbana, IL: National Council of Teachers of English.

Applebee, A. N. (1984). *Contexts for learning to write: Studies of secondary school instruction.* Norwood, NJ: Ablex.

Axelrod, R., & Cooper, C. (2004). *The St. Martin's guide to writing.* Boston: Bedford/St. Martin's.

Berthoff, A. E. (1984). Response to Richard Gebhardt, "Writing processes, revision, and rhetorical problems: A note on three recent articles." *College Composition and Communication, 35,* 95.

Bizzell, P. (1982). Cognition, convention, and certainty: What we need to know about writing. *Pre/Text, 3,* 213–243.

Braddock, R., Lloyd-Jones, R., & Schoer, L. (1963). *Research in written composition.* Urbana, IL: National Council of Teachers of English.

Bridwell, L. (1980). Revising strategies in twelfth grade students transactional writing. *Research in the Teaching of English, 14,* 197–222.

Britton, J. N. (1970). *Language and learning.* London: Penguin Press.

Britton, J. N., Burgess, T., Martin, N., McLeod, A., & Rosen, H. (1975). *The development of writing abilities.* London: Macmillan.

Cooper, C. R., & Odell, L. (Eds.). (1977). *Evaluating writing: Describing, measuring, judging.* Urbana, IL: National Council of Teachers of English.

Cooper, C. R., & Odell, L. (Eds.). (1979). *Research on composing: Points of departure.* Urbana, IL: National Council of Teachers of English.

Diederich, P. B. (1974). *Measuring growth in English.* Urbana, IL: National Council of Teachers of English.

Durst, R.K. (1987). Cognitive and linguistic demands of analytic writing. *Research in the Teaching of English, 21,* 347–376.

Durst, R. K. (1988). [Review of the book *Writing in real time: Modeling production processes*]. *College Composition and Communication, 39,* 247–249.

Durst, R.K. (1989). Monitoring processes in analytic and summary writing. *Written Communication, 6,* 340–363.

Durst, R. K. (1999). *Collision course: Conflict, negotiation, and learning in college composition.* Urbana, IL: National Council of Teachers of English.

Durst, R. K., Laine, C., Schultz, L. M., & Vilter, W. (1990). Appealing texts: The persuasive writing of high school students. *Written Communication, 7,* 232–255.

Emig, J. (1972). *The composing processes of twelfth graders.* Urbana, IL: National Council of Teachers of English.

Emig, J. (1977). Writing as a mode of learning. *College Composition and Communication, 29,* 122–127.

Fishman, S. M., & McCarthy, L. (1998). *John Dewey and the challenge of classroom practice.* New York: Teachers College Press.

Fishman, S. M., & McCarthy, L. (2000). *Unplayed tapes: A personal history of collaborative teacher research.* New York: Teachers College Press.

Flower, L. (1981). *Problem-solving strategies for writers.* New York: Harcourt, Brace, Jovanovich.

Flower, L., & Hayes, J. R. (1981). A cognitive process theory of writing. *College Composition and Communication, 32,* 365–387.

Flower, L., & Hayes, J. R. (1984). Images, plans, and prose: The representation of meaning in writing. *Written Communication, 1,* 120–160.

Freedman, S. W. (1987). *Response to student writing* (NCTE Research Report No. 23). Urbana, IL: National Council of Teachers of English.

Freedman, S. W. (1994). *Exchanging writing, exchanging cultures: Lessons in school reform from the United States and Great Britain.* Cambridge, MA: Harvard University Press.

Harris, J. (2003). Review of the book *Rhetoric and composition as intellectual work. College Composition and Communication, 55,* 172–175.

Hillocks, G. (1984). *Research on written composition: New directions for teaching.* Urbana, IL: National Conference on Research in English.

Irmscher, W. F. (1987). Finding a comfortable identity. *College Composition and Communication, 38,* 81–87.

Kantor, K. J., Kirby, D. R., & Goetz, J. P. (1981). Research in context: Ethnographic studies in English education. *Research in the Teaching of English, 15,* 293–309.

Kinneavy, J. L. (1971). *A theory of discourse: The aims of discourse.* New York: Norton.

Langer, J. A., & Applebee, A. N. (1987). *How writing shapes thinking. A study of teaching and learning* (NCTE Research Report No. 22). Urbana, IL: National Council of Teachers of English.

Macrorie, K. (1970). *Uptaught.* Rochelle Park, NJ: Hayden.

Matsuhashi, A. (1981). Pausing and planning: The tempo of written discourse production. *Research in the Teaching of English, 15,* 113–134.

Matsuhashi, A. (1987). *Writing in real time: Modeling production processes.* Norwood, NJ: Ablex.

McCarthy, L. P. (1987). A stranger in strange lands: A college student writing across the curriculum. *Research in the Teaching of English, 21,* 233–265.

Murray, D. (1968). *A writer teaches writing.* Boston: Houghton-Mifflin.

Newell, A., & Simon, H.A. (1972). *Human problem solving.* Englewood Cliffs, NJ: Prentice-Hall.

Olson, G. A. (Ed.). (2002). *Rhetoric and composition as intellectual work.* Carbondale: Southern Illinois University Press.

Shaughnessy, M. P. (1977). *Errors and expectations: A guide for the teacher of basic writing.* New York: Oxford University Press.

Sperling, M., & Freedman, S. W. (1987). A good girl writes like a good girl: Written response to student writing. *Written Communication, 9,* 343–369.

Walvoord, B. E., & McCarthy, L. P. (1990). *Thinking and writing in college. A naturalistic study of students in four disciplines.* Urbana, IL: National Council of Teachers of English.

16

ACCREDITATION, STANDARDS, AND NCTE

Shaping a Profession

Stephen M. Koziol, Jr.

A basic issue facing the National Council of Teachers of English (NCTE) as well as a number of other subject matter or specialty professional associations (SPAs) is determining what kind of role they can or should play in the credentialing of teachers. We are in a period in which there are an array of reforms in certification requirements and in the accreditation of teacher preparation programs taking place. State Departments of Education are establishing or reforming program requirements and setting new standards, especially in subject matter areas, reading, attention to diverse learners, and technology. For over 50 years, the National Council for the Accreditation of Teacher Education (NCATE) has been the national body for the accreditation of teacher education programs, and for the last 15 years it has worked in partnership with SPAs, including NCTE, to integrate into national accreditation specialty area reports responsive to the standards and review processes set by each SPA. NCATE has recently initiated a set of reforms in the accreditation process that include limiting the number of standards that a SPA can identify as the basis for accreditation and standardizing formats across SPAs for reporting how candidates demonstrate proficiencies in subject matter knowledge and pedagogical content and skills, and in affecting p-12 student learning (Wise,

2003). In addition, they want SPA reports to conform to common formats, Web-based reporting and reviewing, restrictions on the length and character of institutional reports in subject areas, and greater reliance on common sources of evidence such as Praxis I and Praxis II results; NCATE also intends to control the selection and training of reviewers, including those who review SPA reports.

These may or may not be sensible directions that meet the expectations and have the endorsement of the NCTE membership. Without question, however, they will influence the character of the accreditation process and the substance of teacher preparation programs. What is important is that NCTE give serious consideration to the role it seeks to play in teacher certification/teacher accreditation and take appropriate action. There are choices. Remaining in affiliation with NCATE and struggling/hoping to retain a degree of professional independence is one choice. It is also the case that, although a majority of institutions are members of NCATE, a substantial number, including many Research 1 institutions, are not, and at least some have become affiliated with an alternative accreditation system, the Teacher Education Accreditation Council (TEAC), which has recently been recognized and nationally approved as an accrediting body. Does affiliation with TEAC fit better with NCTE priorities? Or, it may also be time for NCTE and other SPAs to assert their own direct responsibility for program accreditation in their respective areas, a move that would be consistent with what exists in most other professions. It is an important time for the organization to make crucial decisions.

To what extent will or should NCTE take control of at least primary responsibility for identifying what English teachers should know and be able to do and how that knowledge and skill are determined to qualify for recognition as "ready to teach" English. In support of a response to that question, I begin with some background information on the nature of accreditation and governance in teacher education broadly and on the more recent role that NCTE has played in those processes. I also provide some history on NCTE's articulation of guidelines and standards for English teacher preparation and raise some policy issues that I believe to be problematic for the profession. I then make some general observations about the role of NCTE in professional credentialing and offer recommendations on policy actions that I believe would establish a more proactive role for NCTE.

TEACHER ACCREDITATION AND NCTE

Formal accreditation of teacher education programs is still a relatively young enterprise. One especially readable text that provides detailed information on the early days and development of the policies and procedures in teacher certification and the accreditation of teacher education is Cushman's (1977) *The Governance of Teacher Education.* Although the accreditation of programs for teacher education and the certification of teachers are integrally linked, certification or licensure and accreditation or program approval are not the same thing. Certification is what the individual receives as the indicator of having met specified requirements and being ready to take on a set of professional responsibilities. Accreditation is granted by some governing authority (e.g., state, federal government, professional association) to a unit to recognize that the unit has met at an appropriate level a set of standards or expectations for a program in the field.

In the 19th century, before formal certification policies came into being, determining that an individual was fit to teach was for the most part a local responsibility. Local members of the community, often constituted as school boards, were responsible for seeking out and hiring teachers for community schools or, in the latter part of the century, in reviewing the candidates recommended by the school administrator. Included in this review was usually some determination of the individual's "moral fitness to teach" (i.e., information affirming the proper moral character of the individual) and a determination that the individual had the knowledge to teach. *Knowledge* in that case was a set of specific and detailed facts that the local board had determined to be indicative of the factual knowledge that the teacher should know and transmit to students. We must remember, at that time, in the absence of extensive textbooks and when there was limited access to information resources, the teacher was the principal source of the knowledge that students obtained, and transmitting that knowledge in what we would consider didactic ways was the expected pedagogy in teaching.

Formal teacher preparation was rare, and it was typical for a teacher to be hired with little more than evidence of completion of the grade level that the teacher was going to be expected to teach. During the second half of the century, pedagogical institutes modeled after the *ecole normale* movement in France grew and began to provide practical training in pedagogy, sometimes as part of a high school education (for elementary teachers) or as a post-secondary school year (for secondary teachers) or as summer institutes. At the same time, some universities began to have faculty from traditional academic disciplines offer special courses in historical, philosophical, and psychological foundations in education—a move that eventually led first to departments of education and eventually to more broadly conceived colleges of education. With population growth, the growth in the size and number of communities, increasing industrialization and the demand for a more educated populace, and increasing social and geographic mobility among citizens in the second half of the century, the demands on a local school board to know whether a person to be hired as a teacher was fit to teach and had an appropriate or sufficient knowledge became overwhelming, prompting a move first to county-based testing of teachers and by the end of the century to a state responsibility to credential a person as fit to teach. State Departments of Education, which had earlier been established in original and new states to guide the development of state-wide policies on issues in basic K–12 schools, became the agencies charged with establishing and enforcing policies on initial teacher certification.

The coincidental emergence of attention to the preparation of teachers, especially secondary teachers, in the colleges and universities, the growth of normal schools from regional academies to 1- and then 2- and then 4-year colleges (and eventually to comprehensive universities), and the need for a state bureaucracy to manage an easily administered but defensible system for teacher certification led to a natural synergy—a system of teacher certification based primarily on documentation of completion of degree credits and eventually particular courses and experiences. Requirements for teacher certification became framed around a set of college courses, and to a limited extent, school-based experiences, and evidence of completion of those selected courses and certain training experiences became a proxy for any direct assessment of the individual. Colleges within states articulated what their programs would require to meet state requirements for a certificate area; accreditation meant that these programs were reviewed and approved by the state as fulfilling the state's curriculum requirements—hence the term *program approval.*

In the post-WWII period, concerns over the quality of teachers and quality in the programs or institutions that prepared teachers prompted a variety of groups—SPAs like NCTE, the National Education Association (NEA), the National Association of State Directors of Teacher Education and Certification (NASDTEC), the National School Boards Association (NSBA), the Council of Chief State School Officers (CCSSO), and the Association of Normal Schools which eventually became the American Association of Colleges for Teacher Education (AACTE)—to come together. The National Council for the Accreditation of Teacher Education (NCATE) was formed in 1952 by these various organizations as the entity that would formally carry out the accrediting functions for institutions seeking recognition as approved teacher preparation institutions for beginning teachers. From its inception, there were some general policy understandings about the role of NCATE:

(a) participation was voluntary,
(b) standards would be set by NCATE,
(c) the costs for accreditation were an institutional responsibility,
(d) reciprocity agreements between states would rely on NCATE accreditation,
(e) NCATE accreditation would provide a basis for the transfer and evaluation of credits from one institution to another, both within and across states.

NCATE's primary responsibility was to document that (a) institutions had curriculum requirements in place that met broad professional guidelines and, as appropriate, the guidelines of relevant associations (SPAs), and (b) the professional unit had the resources and experiences in place that minimally met the state and NCATE's requirements for professional preparation. Much was made of detailed documentation (official documents about requirements, course syllabi, faculty vitae, library and technology resources, etc.) and site visits by visiting teams to verify that the courses, resources, and policies claimed were in place. In most states, this resulted in a dual set of processes; the state-based program approval process and the NCATE-based institutional accreditation process. By the late 1970s, critics questioned the necessity for this duplication of effort and whether any substantive reviews were actually being made, especially in relation to the ever-increasing expense of the visits and data showing that few institutions ever were denied accreditation. Moreover, there was increasing public dismay at what appeared to be ill-prepared teachers in the schools, exemplified in *A Nation At Risk* (National Commission on Excellence in Education, 1983) and A *Nation Prepared* (Carnegie Forum on Education and the Economy, 1986), national reports, and the Holmes Group's (1986) *Tomorrow's Teachers.*

In the 1980s, NCATE was in trouble—it was unable to demonstrate that its largely input documentation system led to any substantive decisions about the status of participating institutions and it faced disaffection from institutions concerned about having large NCATE costs as well as costs associated with separate state program approval reviews. Moreover, there was a lack of evidence showing that NCATE accreditation made a difference in whether a teacher graduating from a program was hired or retained or that graduates of NCATE-accredited institutions were better prepared than those from institutions that were not NCATE accredited. Finally, there was growing emphasis on the teachers' subject matter knowledge as a measure of quality and too little in the then-NCATE standards or process that supported an assessment of that quality.

NCATE leadership in the 1980s began to take a series of steps to turn that situation around. They solicited the cooperation of the SPAs such as NCTE to participate more fully in the review of academic and specialized professional requirements in teacher certification programs, which led to the separate Phase 1 specialty area review process and the direct participation of SPAs, including NCTE, in the formal accreditation process. This participation by the national professional academic organization was key to the reestablishment of NCATE's academic credibility. It was also a significant occasion for the SPAs in that it brought them formally into the national accreditation process. In NCTE, the Conference on English Education (CEE) took on responsibility for developing an organization-based folio review process for institutions with secondary English certification programs who were seeking NCATE accreditation. NCTE Guidelines for the English Teacher Preparation were translated into Program Standards, program reviewers (higher education English and English education faculty and practicing teachers) were identified and trained in special sessions at NCTE national meetings to carry out the reviews, and an infrastructure within CEE and NCTE was set up to manage the review process. Although it was not essential that an institution pass every SPA review, the SPA reviews were taken seriously by most institutions with a range of positive consequences. There was renewed attention within the profession to topics, designs, and practices in teacher education, which further informed the review process and led to multiple revisions of the standards and criteria. NCTE guidelines and standards were more clearly the reference point for individual state revisions of state-based standards for English teacher preparation. There was increased emphasis on content-specific pedagogy in professional preparation programs and attention to the kind of articulation among academic, education, and field-based studies and experiences that was consonant with major reform agendas.

During the 1990s, NCATE began negotiations with a number of state departments of education that led to a set of agreements for a linked accreditation process and with ETS regarding connections between NCATE accreditation and performance on ETS tests for teacher certification. NCATE's reforms in the general institutional review process centered on shifting from what was primarily an input determination model to one that required documentation of learning, first within the programs by requiring evidence that candidates had the knowledge (i.e., through formal test data and other forms of independent documentation) and second by requiring evidence of successful performance of teaching tasks, rather than just a documentation that candidates had experiences. NCATE now requires participating institutions to provide additional documentation or at least a plan for how it will gather evidence showing not just that completing candidates had acquired desired professional knowledge and skills, but that they were also having positive effects on their students' achievement.

What is important to note in the last decade is that, although NCATE has grown significantly in stature and authority, there has been a weakening in the role that the SPAs play in determining what or how prospective teachers in that area are determined to have met SPA-based standards. When NCATE first began using the SPAs directly in the accreditation process, those organizations, including NCTE, had clear authority over the content and shape of their standards, of the documentation that institutions provided, and of the review process, including the training and orientation of reviewers. What is questionable today is whether the specialty organizations including NCTE have retained that independence and authority.

GUIDELINES AND STANDARDS

The first official set of Guidelines for English Teacher Preparation were published by NCTE in 1967. These emerged following the nationally focused attention on curriculum and teacher preparation that was part of the broader focus on education reform in the post-Sputnik era. A detailed account of the curriculum changes in English education up to and through this period is available in Applebee's (1974) *Tradition and Reform in the Teaching of English: A History,* and a thorough historical review of the attention to English teacher preparation issues may be found in Grommon's (1968) *English Journal* article. Because the authors of the *Guidelines for the Preparation of Teachers of English* (National Council of Teachers of English, 1967) express their indebtedness to two studies conducted earlier in the 1960s, I too want to focus on them to set the context for the first NCTE guidelines.

The 1963 NCTE-produced study, *The Education of Teachers of English for American Schools and Colleges* (ETEASC), reports a thorough investigation of many aspects of English teacher preparation—from information on the variable credits required in English and education by different institutions and in different states to different perspectives in local, institution, and state requirements about what minimum studies and experiences were needed for certification. The report provides information about sample programs, both traditional and innovative, and about differences in policies regarding decision making and governance. Findings show that requirements differed such that candidates in some programs or states could be eligible for certification in secondary English with as few as 12 undifferentiated credits in English, whereas in well-defined programs, candidates were required to complete from 48 to 60 credits. Studies across states showed that fewer than half of the teachers teaching English as their major assignment had either majors or minors in English in their college studies. Also common across most programs and state requirements was the relatively small number of credits required in professional studies, including student teaching (15–24 credits), with little attention to English teaching curriculum and pedagogy specifically.

One of the recommendations by the authors of ETEASC was their endorsement for establishing a minimum of 30 to 36 credits as the basis for an English major for teacher certification with a program structure to include the following:

English Language:
Courses in the history and structure of the language, including attention to modern English grammars and to usage, lexicography, and related studies

Composition:
Courses in basic and advanced composition

Literature:
A balanced program leading to the understanding and appreciation of both aesthetic and human values in literature, including some work in each of the following areas: surveys of English, American, world, and contemporary literature; types of literature; Shakespeare; literary criticism; literature written for adolescents

Related Subjects:
Courses and activities in speech, dramatics, and journalism
Courses in psychology of learning and adolescence

Methods of Teaching:

A program which, in addition to methods of teaching literature, includes attention to the teaching of reading, composition, language, critical and creative thinking.

Methods of providing for individual differences, motivating students and planning and organizing classwork while maintaining control and discipline, and evaluating students' performances.

(National Council for the Accreditation of Teachers Education 1963, pp. 186–187)

These recommendations became the template for the NCTE Guidelines, reflecting an emphasis on subject matter content knowledge while acknowledging the importance of both subject specific and general pedagogy. The ETEASC authors elaborate about the relationship between subject matter preparation and preparation for teaching in ways that certainly foreshadow the persistent tension between academic and professional studies and experiences and underscore current concerns over the large attrition rate among beginning teachers:

> Responses from beginning teachers should particularly remind colleges not to minimize the importance of their preparing teacher to face the practical, often nagging, problems arising almost daily. However superior a candidate's preparation in literature may be, if he cannot solve, for example, the fundamental problem of how to control his classes, he may never have a chance to give them the benefits of his sensibilities and his extensive knowledge, understanding, and appreciation of literature. If he cannot solve these problems in human relations and in planning and doing his teaching, he may soon be lost to teaching. (p. 188)

In another section of their study, the authors identify some of what they believe to be the standards of preparation to teach English that would be developed through their recommended course of study. Here are some examples from the areas of language study:

Language Study:
1. A fundamental knowledge of the historical development and present character of the English language: phonology, morphology, syntax, vocabulary, the relations of language and society
2. A specialized knowledge of the English language which is appropriate to the teacher's particular field of interest and responsibility.
3. An informed command of the arts of language—rhetoric and logic; ability to speak and write language which is not only unified, coherent, and correct but also responsible, appropriate to the situation, and stylistically effective.

(pp. 181–182)

The second report used as a basis for the initial set of NCTE Guidelines was *Freedom and Discipline in English* (1965) published by the College Entrance Examination Board. Although most clearly focused in articulating a highly academic orientation to the study of literature, language, and composition in the schools, the report also makes specific recommendation regarding the certification requirements for secondary English teachers:

> *Recommendation 1.* That certification to teach secondary school English be based on evidence of credible work, at the minimum, of the following kinds:
> * Formal study of the history and structure of the English language
> * Study in rhetoric and composition above the level of the freshman course
> * Work in critical theory and practice with attention to bibliography and library resources
> * At least one course in speech and oral interpretation of literature
> * Two semester courses in American literature
> * Four semester courses in English literature, of which one should be the study of a single writer (preferably Shakespeare) in depth, and of which others should represent approaches not exclusively historical
> * At least one course in English social and cultural history
> * Enough study of one foreign language to guarantee reading facility
>
> (pp. 10–11)

The report also makes recommendations for professional studies, including at least one course in the methodology of the subject and at least one semester of full-time practice teaching under close and competent supervision.

In drawing on these two studies in the preparation of the 1967 Guidelines, the authors made several important decisions. First, they chose to articulate guidelines for elementary teachers with respect to their preparation in English in addition to guidelines for secondary teachers. Second, although they chose not to specify a specific number of credits or courses per topic, they did recommend minimum credits for study in the subject field overall (at least 15 hours of studies in English above the freshman level for elementary teachers and at least 36 hours above the freshman level in English studies for secondary teachers). Third, they recommended that both elementary and secondary teachers engage in preparation programs that provided for a fifth year of study, with a special attention to graduate studies in English and English education in the fifth year for the secondary teachers. Support for 5-year or fifth-year models for elementary and secondary teacher certification is absent from subsequent versions of the NCTE Guidelines, although it resurfaced 20 years later among the strong recommendations for reform in teacher education from the Holmes Group (1986).

The authors also note two basic assumptions that underlie their recommendations, both of which have persisted as themes in subsequent NCTE Guidelines:

First, to teach the content of his subject effectively, the teacher not only must
know the varied subject matter of English but also must understand how to
communicate his knowledge and appreciation to his students; second, his
preparation for teaching English should be based upon and supplemented by
a background in the liberal arts and sciences, including psychology. (p. 2)

As the first set of NCTE Guidelines, the 1967 document provided an important template in both language and content. Recommendations were organized in
support of six broad guidelines addressing: the personal qualities of successful
ELA teachers, program structure for elementary and secondary ELA teachers,
studies in literature, studies in communication skills and language and rhetoric,
understanding of child and adolescent development, and studies in English and
reading methods, including supervised teaching. The 1967 Guidelines drew
directly from the 1963 ETEASC report for both content and language in the elaboration of standards. The standards for literature are especially revealing of how
the group/profession thought about literature knowledge and understanding at
the time.

Guideline III

A. His undergraduate program should have prepared him to read for
his own enjoyment, gain insight into himself and the work around
him, and understand and appreciate how writers order experience.

1. He should have developed a strong commitment to literature as
an experience to be enjoyed both in and out of school classes.
2. He should have developed the habit of reading beyond classroom necessity so that he can bring to his teaching a wide experience with literature and with the means for stimulating his
students' creative responses and reactions to literary works.

B. He should have studied literature systematically.

1. He should know a wide range of significant works of literature
recognized as classic and, in addition, examples of other well-
written discourse.
2. He should have studied such major literary genres as drama,
poetry, fiction, and the essay.
3. He should be able to relate contemporary writing to the traditions from which it grows.
4. He should have studied important writers and writings of
English and American literature both to extend his knowledge
of literary history and convention and to develop his critical
skill.

5. He should have studied represented works from literatures other than English and American.
6. He should have studied in depth some major authors (such as Shakespeare) and at least one literary period.

Items C, D, and E on the list go on to explicate detail relative to literary criticism and the tools of scholarly analysis, the knowledge of a wide body of children's literature (elementary) and literature for adolescents (secondary), and a variety of practices and strategies for teaching literature to students, including oral reading, oral interpretation, choral reading, and dramatic activities of all kinds. The connecting of expectations about specific areas of content knowledge in and about literature with specific pedagogy supportive of active engagement with literature is typical of the way these guidelines integrate content and subject matter-specific pedagogy in other areas and is consistent with their basic assumptions.

The 1976 NCTE Guidelines differ from the 1967 version in a number of respects. First, the title is different—now called *A Statement on the Preparation of Teachers of English and the Language Arts*— and it is written in a more narrative style. It is also noteworthy that, although the title references both the preparation for teachers of English and language arts, the distinction made between elementary and secondary preparation introduced in the 1967 Guidelines no longer appears as a major distinction; the reference throughout the document is to teachers of English and the content and topics are oriented for secondary teachers. Second, there is no mention of fifth-year or 5-year programs for teacher preparation; the matter is simply not addressed, even as an issue for discussion in the final section of the document.

However, there are a number of substantive and presentational differences that reflect the changes that had taken place generally in education and in the profession during the preceding decade. Most striking is that, in line with shifts in the profession away from the tripod Literature, Language, and Composition base for the curriculum, knowledge statements are presented more seamlessly, without the category headings, although the specifics still seem to break down by topics in language, composing, and literature. Instead of guidelines, qualifications are presented in terms of Knowledge, Abilities, and Attitudes, an arrangement much more consistent with the movement toward performance or competency-based certification of teachers and for increased accountability. The authors express their concern over how to prepare teachers for a climate in which there are adversarial relationships brought about by teachers' concerns over requirements to *demonstrate* their effectiveness as teachers to administrators and elected officials—concerns that are echoed today as we struggle with the same issues. The statement also provides a separate section on "Experiences for Prospective Teachers That Will Help Them Develop the Necessary Qualifications," which speaks most directly to the teacher preparation programs and what the authors believe are helpful experiences for preservice teachers. Under the qualifications statements is much more explicit language than in the 1967 Guidelines, which address a sensitivity to issues in socio-cultural diversity, a response and process orientation to content, and an attention to topics in popular cultural and media.

The final section of the 1976 Statement presents a series of issues for discussion in the planning of programs for preparing teachers of English. A number of these raise major issues that might have become focal points for research and inquiry among scholars in NCTE. One issue raised deals with the developmental nature of acquiring teaching expertise. A second issue addresses uncertainty about the kinds of knowledge, skills, and attitudes that are more fruitfully developed as part of inservice education, rather than in preservice studies. Questions are also raised about how levels of proficiency for identified knowledge and abilities are determined, the role of tests in determining a candidate's worthiness for certification, and the extent to which programs should be preparing candidates for special circumstances and contexts; these are important and vital questions that continue to be important today. Unfortunately, there is little indication that those questions shaped or influenced an active agenda on the part of the professional organization.

The 1986 Guidelines (National Council of Teachers of English, 1986) make few distinctions between elementary and secondary preparation. There are some references to both elementary and secondary prospective teachers and an explanation that elementary language arts teachers "must be especially familiar with children's literature, whereas secondary English teachers must be widely read in literature for adolescents," and separate annotations under some of the topics in the qualifications section that identify differences between elementary and secondary teacher expectations. The format, however, does not make for an easy picturing of the differences. This version as its predecessor presents teacher qualifications under three broad headings: Knowledge, Pedagogy (instead of abilities), and Attitudes. This version also provides considerably more detail and elaboration under statements, which is helpful in developing a fuller understanding of what the authors intend under such headings as knowledge of "how students develop in understanding and using language," "major developments in language history," and "how people use language and visual images to influence the thinking and actions of others." Although there are some word changes in the subheadings of the different sections under qualifications, they generally follow the topic headings that were present in the 1976 version.

In the "Experiences in Preparing Effective Teachers of English Language Arts" section, which parallels a similar section in the 1976 version, the authors are more forceful, with more *must's*, and *should's*, and *need to's* in the explanations. Much more is made in 1986 of the role of faculty modeling effective instruction than in previous versions, and considerable emphasis is placed on the role of cooperating teachers in the teacher preparation process. Throughout the document, there are more statements to the effect that "research on . . ." or "research supports" a particular knowledge or ability for an individual or feature of a program, although as in previous documents there is no listing of that research nor did NCTE issue related documents that presented the supporting research in relation to recommendations in the guidelines.

The 1996 edition (National Council of Teachers of English, 1996) keeps the title as *Guidelines for the Preparation of Teachers of English Language Arts*, and the authors note that they do not make sharp distinctions between expectations for elementary and secondary teachers because they see the essential elements as applicable to both groups. This edition includes a number of sections that were not present in earlier documents—a statement of underlying principles; a connections chart showing the interrelationship among knowledge, skills, and attitudes; a discussion of how the Guidelines were related to other NCTE standards projects; a brief discussion of characteristics of effective teacher preparation programs that includes comments on the NCTE–NCATE relationship and school–university collaboration; a section on the effective transition to teaching; a presentation of 10 principles for inservice education; and an appendix that includes a personal view from a beginning teacher.

The Guidelines are organized in a way similar to that of the 1986 version, with sections on content knowledge, pedagogical skills, and attitudes. On the whole, there is less explanation and elaboration of the identified understandings or abilities than in the previous edition. The authors are explicit in noting that they did not intend to set any particular levels of attainment for attitude, knowledge, or skill elements, preferring instead to leave that task to "the individual teacher education programs and the professionals who act in them," a decision that has significant policy implications in the context of current debates about common national standards of performance. Like the previous sets of Guidelines, this version avoids trying to set forth the requirements of a model English teacher preparation program, although they are much more detailed and clear than authors in previous editions about the "characteristics" of effective teacher-preparation programs for English language arts.

The authors of the 1996 Guidelines emphasize that they are presenting a "set of dispositions, knowledge, and pedagogical knowledge and skills for the beginning teacher," although they also set forth some broad principles for the career teacher in the section on inservice education. However, these principles focus on structural elements such as time, collaboration, school–community partnerships, administrative support, and the like, rather than on delineating continuing areas of knowledge, dispositions, or skills that might be the focal point for learning by the experienced teacher. The section on continuing issues, which revives a section in the 1976 edition but is not present in the 1986 edition, introduces seven broad issues in educational reform.

As discussed in the first section of this chapter, the move to involve SPAs such as NCTE directly in the accreditation review process created an unprecedented opportunity for NCTE to impact the substance and structure of teacher preparation programs nationally. That opportunity took the Guidelines beyond being documents that provided advisory recommendations to English educators for what they could or should be doing in the teacher preparation programs to being the template for a set of standards that would be used to identify whether pro-grams were recommended or not recommended for national accreditation. In 1987, a set of draft standards statements, drawn from the major elements and top-ics identified in the 1986 Guidelines document under Knowledge, Pedagogy, and Attitudes sections of the Qualification for Teachers of English Language Arts and program features drawn from the experiences part of the Guidelines, were presented by NCTE and endorsed by NCATE as the NCTE/NCATE Professional Standards for the Initial Preparation of Secondary English Language Arts Teachers, Grades 7–12. It is important to note the specification of the stan-dards was for secondary teachers with no indication of related standards for English language arts preparation for elementary teachers, an omission that remains unaddressed.

The Guidelines put forth an ambitious set of detailed statements about what secondary English teachers should know and their abilities and skills both with the content and with pedagogy. They also set forth what are largely reasonable and appropriate expectations for program experiences and policies, especially with respect to expectations about field experiences. The NCTE/NCATE Standards are faithful in content and intent to the published Guidelines.

As noted earlier, NCTE leaders actively recruited English and English edu-cation faculty and secondary school practitioners to serve on a voluntary basis as reviewers and over a 10-year period prepared a cadre of reviewers and team lead-ers that implemented a multiple-person review of programs processed through initial submission and, where necessary, the review of rejoinders and resubmis-sions. The NCTE/NCATE Matrix, which listed each standard and created space for programs to provide information about the courses and experiences in their programs that addressed that standard, was gradually refined over the first decade, although issues of its being cumbersome to use simply could not be avoided. Because the Guidelines were rich in detail about what English teachers should know and be able to do and the Standards statements attempted to be faithful to that detail, the level of specificity of the standards and the sheer number of them made completing the folio for NCTE/NCATE a laborious process. Getting good and consistent documentation in the form of syllabi, copies of handbooks, insti-tutional catalogs, and information about faculty was a persistent problem, but one that was gradually being worked out as the NCTE/NCATE folio reviewers and leadership team refined directions and review procedures.

In the 1996 edition of the Guidelines, the authors' discussion of the NCTE–NCATE connection noted that, in the opinion of reviewers who had par-ticipated over the first 8 years of the arrangement, the process was leading to sig-nificant revisions in programs nationally in curriculum, policy, and resources in the English education program. They reported that there was tangible evidence that programs, which had been turned down as not being in compliance with stan-dards and expectations, later provided evidence in rejoinders of substantive changes in policies and procedures, the design and redesign of required courses, and the offering of new or extended laboratory and clinical experiences at the prestudent teaching level. In particular, "folio reviewers reported that courses addressing adolescent literature, multicultural literature, literature by women, nonprint media study, and composition methods—all areas emphasized both in the 1986 Guidelines and now in the 1996 Guidelines—were far more likely to be required of prospective teachers of the English language arts than they were in the mid-1980's" (p. 42). This is not a trivial impact, and NCTE's participation in the national accreditation review process in that way deserves to be acknowledged as a positive influence on the profession. I want to emphasize, however, that the standards and criteria being used to make determinations of satisfactory compliance or noncompliance were those developed by NCTE, not NCATE.

Over the past several years, the context for NCTE/NCATE accreditation reviews has changed. In response to demands from NCATE, the format for standards in the review process has changed. In the most recent draft, standards are delineated with three criterion levels—Not Acceptable, Acceptable, and Target. For each standard, there has been a clear shift as well from the requirement that institutions demonstrate that they provide candidates with the types of experiences in the program appropriate for the standard to the requirement that they have information on representative performance tasks per standard, have appropriate articulated rubrics and criteria, and have appropriate benchmark/gateway performances with aggregated candidate data keyed to specific NCTE/NCATE standards. The shift from an experience documentation to a performance assessment with articulated criteria for success represents a significant change in the substance and process of program review. It is not clear whether that change is supported or even known by the NCTE membership. As noted in the discussion of accreditation, recent communications from NCATE directing changes in the number of standards to be listed and insisting on a common format for standards and reports across SPAs mark a still further shift in control—of the standards and of the program review process—from NCTE to NCATE. The question at hand is how NCTE leadership and membership will respond to these new directives and what that means for the role of the professional organization in determining the qualifications of entering candidates and how they are identified.

OBSERVATIONS AND RECOMMENDATIONS

Observation 1: Advanced Standards

A recurrent theme in the guidelines/statement over the 40 years is an awareness of differences between what a preservice teacher should or can realistically learn and what might be expected of accomplished experienced teachers. With each succeeding edition of the documents, there are stronger statements indicating a recognition that learning to teach is a continuing process and that preservice teachers can not be expected to learn all they need to learn during the pre-service years. Yet the documents say remarkably little about what those differences are, and the lists of expectations for areas of knowledge, skills, and attitudes for preservice teachers get longer each decade. Moreover, these are only expectations that are English education specific (i.e., without taking into account the related increases in coursework to meet other state or national accreditation-based mandates).

Over 30 years ago, long-time NCTE leader J. N. Hook and colleagues in the Illinois State-Wide Curriculum Study Center in the Preparation of Secondary School English Teachers (ISCPET) proposed in *What Every English Teacher Should Know* (1970) a set of perspectives on minimal, good, and superior qualifications for English teachers in five areas: language, literature, written composition, oral composition, and the teaching of English. As indicated in the Preface, the text was intended as a resource for: (a) preservice students as a vehicle to understand what was expected of them, why certain courses were required, and what electives they might choose to take to meet professional needs; and (b) for experienced teachers as a vehicle to understand areas of greatest continuing need in postgraduate studies. An example taken from the section on written composition shows ISCPET's attempt at representing different levels of knowledge and skill development:

Minimal:

Ability to recognize such characteristics of good writing as substantial and relevant content; organization; clarity; appropriateness of tone; and accuracy in mechanics and usage.

A basic understanding of the processes of composing writings of various types.

Ability to analyze and communicate to students the specific strengths and weaknesses of their writing.

Ability to produce writing with at least a modicum of the characteristics noted earlier.

Good:

A well-developed ability to recognize such characteristics of good writing as substantial and relevant content; organization; clarity; appropriateness of tone; and accuracy in mechanics and usage.

Perception of the complexities in the processes of composing writings of various types.

Ability to analyze in detail the strengths and weaknesses in the writing of students and to communicate the analyses effectively.

Proficiency in producing writing with at least considerable strength in the characteristics noted earlier.

Superior:

In addition to good competencies, a detailed knowledge of theories and history of rhetoric and of the development of English prose.

Perception of the subtleties as well as the complexities in the processes of composing writings of various types.

Ability to give highly perceptive analyses of the strengths and weaknesses in the writings of students, to communicate this exactly, and to motivate students toward greater and greater strengths.

Proficiency in producing writing of genuine power; ability and willingness to write for publication.

Although we may not agree with the specifics or scope of the competencies identified or with the designation of competencies to level, the effort here is an admirable prototype for the delineation of a developmental model for standards and expectations in the teaching of English, unfortunately a prototype that was not built on by NCTE. It was not until the work of the National Board for Professional Teaching Standards some 20 years later that there was discernable effort to identify standards for accomplished teachers of English and develop an assessment system to identify accomplished teachers. Although NCTE has been a supporter of the work of the National Board, it is not clear that NBPTS perspectives on what constitutes a vision of accomplished practice in the teaching of English and an NCTE vision of that practice are the same thing.

Recommendation 1

Reiterating in guidelines that teacher development is a career-long process and encouraging English teachers to continue their professional growth across their careers are worthy, but insufficient. NCTE needs to develop clear descriptions of its expectations for what an accomplished English teacher should know and be able to do because such a set of guidelines would articulate a clear vision by the professional organization for the profession and establish a frame of reference for preservice and inservice programs in teacher education, which is currently lacking.

Observation 2: Scope of Guidelines and Standards

The journey through the four sets of NCTE Guidelines for the preparation of English Language Arts teachers shows how much the scope has expanded over 40 years. Some of that reflects increases in the degree of specificity in the Guidelines (and related NCTE/NCATE Standards), and some represents the addition of content expectations, especially in areas related to media, popular culture, and literature by and about diverse cultural groups. Other increases come in the areas of professional attitudes and pedagogical abilities, especially with respect to attitudes regarding working in diverse contexts and with diverse learners, depth in reflection and self-study, and knowledge and understanding in the role and uses of technology and multiple assessments in teaching. I should note that these do not take into account the parallel increases in general and professional standards that programs must respond to because of state or NCATE requirements. Although framers of the Guidelines were clear in indicating that they did not want to set specific criterion levels for knowledge on specific standards, that is not the case in the contemporary milieu and current NCTE/NCATE Standards are required by NCATE to include indications of unacceptable, acceptable, and target levels of knowledge. The latter has had the impact of adding still further to the sets of expectations that we identify as necessary and appropriate for candidates who are completing a preservice program without taking into account the full range of candidates' studies and requirements and the time they have to complete them.

Recommendation 2

In the 1967 Guidelines, the authors were straightforward and well ahead of their time in making clear that they believed that candidates need at least 5 years of study to meet basic qualifications for initial certification as they had portrayed them. NCTE needs to revisit the scope of its current standards for beginning teachers for desirability and feasibility and be clear and realistic about the scope and level of knowledge and skills that are appropriate for beginning teachers within 4-year programs and if necessary, and appropriate, make clear the differences in expectation that reflect the distinctions between 4- and 5-year or fifth-year preparation programs. In addition, efforts should be made to describe relevant relationships between beginning, experienced and accomplished teachers of English.

Observation 3: Validation of Guidelines and Standards

Each of the four existing sets of Guidelines/Standards were validated using the professional consensus model, although the scope and rigor of the processes used to verify that consensus are unclear. The initial set of standards produced in 1967 was most clear in drawing on two studies of English curriculum and English teacher education as a basis for the recommendations, but later editions had no such clear anchors for the recommendations being made. There is much distrust of professional opinions unsubstantiated through some form of scientific research. Taken together, these lead to serious questions about the potency of NCTE Guidelines/Standards as a basis for a profession-based foundation for certification and program accreditation.

Recommendation 3

NCTE should make an organizational commitment to provide a set of documents to accompany the new set of Guidelines that articulate what we know of the research base to support our recommended standards, and it should commit to an ongoing series of studies that examine relationships among articulated standards, evidence that candidates have met those standards, and evidence of their effectiveness as teachers using both teacher performance assessment and information about student achievement. There is a prototype for the kind of organization–higher education institution–schools–government partnership that would be needed in the extensive work of the ISCPET studies in Illinois in the late 1960s. These studies, sponsored by a federal grant and involving NCTE, English department and Education faculty from some 20 higher education institutions in Illinois, and a host of participating secondary English teachers and schools, address a wide range of topics relevant to English teacher preparation, including studies of teaching practice, supervision of student teachers, different models of program design, and the knowledge and skill assessment for teachers of English. NCTE needs to revisit these studies as a first step toward developing an agenda for a similar set of studies today.

Observation 4: Licensure Assessment

In the absence of any formal testing initiatives from NCTE in relation to articulated guidelines/standards for English teachers seeking certification or licensure as teachers, states and ETS developed formal assessments for beginning teachers. These tests have been used by the majority of states for four decades as a separate measure and complement to the process of program approval to determine eligibility for certification within individual states. NCTE has largely taken a hands-off stance on test development (ignoring the ISCPET work) for either beginning or experienced teachers of English. Although there have been periodic studies or reports of the alignment of these externally developed tests with NCTE standards (see e.g., reviews of ETS's National Teacher Examination Tests in English [Koziol, 1976a, 1976b] and most recently in an unfortunately unpublished and not widely distributed NCTE [2000] report on ETS's Praxis II Tests for Teachers of English Language Arts), which have been very critical of these external tests, little has been done by the organization proactively to mobilize the membership to demand better or responsive tests or to provide alternatives for consideration by the states and higher education institutions.

Recommendation 4

NCTE should initiate its own development of assessments for preservice English teacher licensure and work with the states to have that assessment adopted as the basis for certification. If the externally developed tests fail to be responsive to the organization's standards and there is a substantive basis for those standards, the organization should seize the opportunity and build its own set of assessments for content and pedagogical knowledge in English language arts for prospective teachers. In doing so, I would also urge NCTE to work closely with its state affiliates, especially in identifying special adaptations that may need to be in place to meet particular requirements in individual states, but also to establish the capacity for state-based administration and scoring of tests using the existing state-based membership. In addition to the ISCPET prototypes, there is impressive work in the state of Connecticut in the design of classroom-based performance assessments of English teachers' practices and understanding of practice that might serve as a model for the organization's own initiative.

Observation 5: Scope of Programs

Although Guidelines documents continue to refer to elementary and secondary level preparation, the NCTE/NCATE Standards are clearly identified as intended for teachers in Grades 7 to 12. There is also a set of standards for middle-school English language arts teachers, apparently approved by NCTE in 1997, although a separate set of NCTE guidelines has not yet been developed. It is not clear overall which organization—NCTE, IRA, or some other—is responsible for identifying clear standards for elementary language arts, for all elementary teachers, and for those elementary teachers identifying language arts as a specialization.

Recommendation 5

Having a strong and clear impact on the nature and quality of language arts preparation for elementary teachers is important for the profession, and NCTE should take the initiative to either develop those standards alone or in cooperation with other relevant professional associations.

Underlying my observations and recommendation is my belief that a strong professional organization has the major role in determining the knowledge, skill, and disposition standards for those seeking entry into the profession. That role includes going beyond simply creating a set of guidelines or standards and making them available. It means providing information on the rationale and supporting research evidence for those standards and of the criterion levels of performance that meet the profession's minimum expectations. It means identifying the design features of programs appropriate for preparing candidates to meet those standards and the supporting research evidence for those features. It means guiding the design of the assessment systems that will be used to determine who is licensed as a professional and working in partnership with the states to implement those assessment systems. It means taking responsibility alone or with partner organizations for setting the expectations for all members of the profession, including elementary as well as secondary teachers and for experienced and accomplished teachers. It means being willing to articulate clear codes of professional knowledge and practice and engaging in the study and documentation to support those codes of professional knowledge and practice. It is time for NCTE to shape the profession.

REFERENCES

Applebee, A. N. (1974). *Tradition and reform in the teaching of English: A history.* Urbana, IL: National Council of Teachers of English.

Carnegie Forum on Education and the Economy. (1986). *A nation prepared: Teachers for the 21st century. The report of the Task Force on teaching as a profession.* New York: Author.

College Entrance Examination Board. (1965). *Freedom and discipline in English: Report of the Commission on English.* New York: Author.

Cushman, M. L. (1977). *The governance of teacher education.* Berkeley, CA: McCutchan.

Grommon, A. (1968). A history of the preparation of teachers of English. *English Journal, 57*(4), 484–527.

Holmes Group. (1986). *Tomorrow's teachers.* East Lansing, MI: Author.

Hook, J. N., Jacobs, P. H., & Crisp, R. D. 1970). *What every English teacher should know.* Urbana, IL. National Council of Teachers of English.

Koziol, S. M., Jr. (1976a). Some observations on the National Teacher Examination on English language and literature. *English Education, 7*(1), 37–39.

Koziol, S. M., Jr. (1976b). Competency assessment and English teacher preparation; *English Education, 7*(1), 26–28.

National Commission on Excellence in Education. (1983). *A nation at risk.* Washington, DC: U.S. Government Printing Office.

National Council of Teachers of English. (1963). *The education of teachers of English for American schools and colleges.* Urbana, IL: Author.

National Council of Teachers of English. (1967). *Guidelines for the preparation of teachers of English.* Urbana, IL: Authur.

National Council of Teachers of English. (1976). *A statement on the preparation of teachers of English and the language arts.* Urbana, IL: Author.

National Council of Teachers of English. (1986). *Guidelines for the preparation of teachers of English Language Arts.* Urbana, IL: Author.

National Council of Teachers of English. (1996) *Guidelines for the preparation of teachers of English language arts.* Urbana, IL: Author.

National Council of Teachers of English. (2000). *Assessment of standards for preparing teachers of English language arts.* Unpublished final report. Urbana, IL: Author.

National Council of Teachers of English. (2003). *NCTE/NCATE standards for initial preparation of secondary English language arts Grades 7–12.* Urbana, IL: Author.

Wise, A. (2003). *First report from the task force on program review.* Washington, DC.: National Council for the Accreditation of Teacher Education.

POSTSCRIPT

Bill Smith has had a major influence on the profession—to some extent through his own writing and research, but even more so because of his influence on his colleagues and over two generations of students. Bill and I go back to NCTE research meetings in the early 1970s, when we were both relatively young researchers in language development. Although our research and career paths went in different directions, we have remained friends and colleagues. I could not have been more pleased when Bill accepted a position with the University of Pittsburgh English department in the mid-1970s. I already knew of the quality of his thinking and his open, interactive style; I knew that he would be an asset to any work we were doing in English education. I did not anticipate how important he would become to me as a colleague and friend. I think back now to so many things—our collaborative efforts to develop a writing tutorial experience for English education undergraduates that served both Writing Workshop and English teacher preparation needs; his wonderful piece on overt cues versus sentence-combining practice to elicit complex syntax in undergraduates' writing; his critical, demanding, yet supportive approach with graduate students, whether they were in English or in education, and how he shaped the way they thought and reasoned about their work; about his forays into technology use and my wonder at his building his own computer; at the New Year's Eves that he and I and Sue and Scott spent together with good food, fine wine, card games, and storming the Dark Tower; and at his sharp wit and willingness to play with ideas and people that caused consternation to some but was a delight for most of us, including my children as they were growing up. Bill helped all of us, colleagues and students, see and re-see things from different perspectives; he helped us all question what appeared to be obvious, whether it was in our research or in the way we thought about curriculum and policies for students. May he continue to do so for many years to come.

17

EVIDENCE-BASED EDUCATION POLICIES

Beyond the Yellow Brick Road

Lucretia E. (Penny) Pence

Linda Jordan Platt

Any creation, primary or secondary, with any vitality to it, can "really" be a dozen mutually exclusive things at once, before breakfast.

—Ursula K. LeGuin (1992)

And Oz didn't give nothin' to the Tin Man that he didn't already have. . . .

—Dewey Bunnell (1974)

At the beginning of the 21st century, the federal government responded to a perceived crisis in education by an increased demand for rigor and for educational programs and services grounded in scientific research. For example, the No Child Left Behind (NCLB) Act (U. S. Congress, 2002) states, "Federal dollars will be spent on effective, research based programs and practices," and the Education Sciences Reform Act of 2002 holds research to "standards of scientifically valid research" (p. 3). The 2002–2007 strategic plan of the U.S. Department of Education (2002) has goals to encourage the use of "scientifically based methods in federal education programs" and to "transform education into an evidence based field" (pp. 14–15). The future of educational research, and literacy research in particular, turns on the definitions of *scientific* and *evidence* that are both explicit and implied in these laws and policies. In this chapter, we interrogate the definitions of these and other important terms, and we critique the research climate they create using *The Wizard of Oz* as an allegory for our current situation.

The *Wizard of Oz* has enthralled multiple generations over the decades since the publication of the book by L. Frank Baum in 1900 and the production of the movie by Warner Brothers in 1939 (Langley et al., 1939).[1] The story has been interpreted and reinterpreted in numerous ways—as a parable on Populism (Littlefield, 1968), an American myth that emerged from our collective unconscious (Johnson, 2000), a fairy tale (Algeo, 1986), a lesson on childhood (Ebert, 2003), and a treatise on Zen (Green, 1998). It is in this tradition that we turn to this story as a lens on the current relationship between research and practice in education. We use *The Wizard of Oz* because one of us remembers that it was a favorite of Bill Smith's[2] and because we believe it can offer guidance for literacy researchers at all levels when interpreted allegorically.

We write from two different professional positions. Linda Jordan is an associate professor in the English department of a small, Catholic liberal arts college in Pennsylvania. She is director of composition and has been instrumental in establishing its English language arts teacher licensure program within the English department. Penny Pence is associate professor in the department of Language, Literacy, and Sociocultural Studies at the University of New Mexico. She teaches English language arts methods and graduate courses in the teaching of writing and literature in a well-established licensure program situated in a large College of Education. But, like Dorothy, Scarecrow, Tin Man, and Lion, we became lifelong friends and colleagues when Bill Smith, much like Glinda the Good Witch,[3] brought us together as graduate students to work in teacher assessment—a site where research, practice, and theory are conjoined. We write this chapter not only from our separate positions, but also grounded in our shared experiences as graduate students at the University of Pittsburgh and in honor of our mentor, Bill Smith.[4]

---

[1]All quotations from *The Wizard of Oz* are taken from this script.

[2]Because only Penny remembers this, we questioned the accuracy of this statement. But we decided to proceed with the tale as our guide because Bill taught us that so long as we did a good job, it wouldn't matter if it had anything to do with him anyway.

[3]Our apologies to Bill for the gender-bending, but after hours of conversation over lunch and late into the night, we decided that his mentoring was like Glinda's. He set us on the path, let us face our own demons, but was always there to help us learn to trust our own intuition, knowledge, and ability.

[4]Bill Smith had a profound impact on both of our careers. Penny took courses from him, ran a million ideas for a dissertation past him, and modeled her identity as a professor after him. Linda taught in the composition program, tutored at the Writing Center, scored thousands of placement and exit exams, and was Bill's research assistant. She has carried on his tradition of bringing teachers together around student work, seeking not only answers, but more questions.

GLINDA: IT'S ALWAYS BEST
TO START AT THE BEGINNING

The *Wizard of Oz* begins with Dorothy Gale, a young Kansas girl, being swept away to a distant land. In our allegorical reading, Dorothy is "Miss Everyman" (Littlefield, 1968) or, in this context, "Ms. Everyeducator." She is spirited and hopeful with aspirations for the future, but she is in a crisis of social injustice. Her dog, Toto, has been taken away by the rich and powerful Miss Gulch. Like Dorothy, we, as educators and researchers, are faced with a crisis in education, as President George W. Bush (2002) articulates in his introduction to *No Child Left Behind*:

> We have a genuine national crisis. More and more, we are divided into two nations. One that reads, and one that doesn't. One that dreams, and one that doesn't . . . we have fallen short in meeting our goals for educational excellence. The academic achievement gap between rich and poor, Anglo and minority is not only wide, but in some cases is growing wider still. (p. 1)

When Dorothy runs away to retrieve Toto, to right the wrong, a cyclone sweeps her away. She is caught in the swirl of polarities surrounding the problem. As educational researchers, we, too, are caught in a swirl of polarities—quantitative versus qualitative paradigms, evidence versus perception, hard versus soft science, teacher or researcher, policy or autonomy.

DOROTHY: TOTO, I HAVE A FEELING
WE'RE NOT IN KANSAS ANYMORE

Dorothy ends up in the "Munchkin City in the County of the Land of Oz." We are plopped down in the county of "Evidence-Based Education Policies" (Slavin, 2002) in the land of Scientific Research. It is a land that is "on the brink of a scientific revolution that has the potential to profoundly transform policy, practice, and research" (p. 15). It is a land that possesses an unquestioning belief in science, as if caught "in a time warp, in a period when many naively believed science was 'objective' and outside relations of power—when we actually believed that science would save us and set us free" (St. Pierre, 2002, p. 26). Slavin (2002) recounts its history. This land was founded when the 1998 Congress appropriated funds to adopt "proven, comprehensive reform models" (p. 15). The definition of *proven* used in the legislation was defined "in terms of experimental-control comparisons on standards-based measures" (p. 15). This emphasis on establishing programs "with rigorous evidence of effectiveness" (p. 15) led to the elementary and Secondary Education Act (ESEA). Otherwise known as No Child Left Behind (NCLB; U.S. Congress, 2001), the act, he claims, "took the idea of scientifically based practice to an even higher level" (p. 15) by insisting on "scientifically based research" (p. 15) with "rigorous, systematic, and objective procedures to obtain valid knowledge" (p. 15). He argues that such policy is necessary because little has changed in education, and what little change there has been is the result of fad or fashion ("think hemlines" [p. 16], he says). He further distinguishes between programs based on scientific research and rigorously evaluated programs. He values rigorously evaluated programs and judges programs that are only *based* on scientific research to be of questionable quality because "any program can find some research that supports the principles it incorporates" (p. 18) and because "a program based on scientific research does not mean that it is in fact effective" (p. 18). However, replicable programs that are experimentally or quasi-experimentally evaluated will drag education "kicking and screaming, into the 20th century at the beginning of the 21st century" (p. 16).

The people in the Land of Scientific Research are under a school failure spell, and they blame the school-teaching profession for social inequity, leaving the Lullaby League and the Lollipop Guild devoid of responsibility. The people look to a "great and wonderful" Wizard for the answers to their problems. This Wizard is "very good, but very mysterious"; his psychometric perambulations and statistical inferences are beyond the understanding of most of the populace. But they look to him because they want "to hear about hard evidence, they want impartiality, and they want decisions to rest on reasonable, rigorous, and scientific deliberation" (NRC, 2002, p. 12). In "Scientific Culture and Educational Research," Feuer, Towne, and Shavelson (2002) laud the American people for "(again) manifesting their faith in science as a force for improved public policy. Amid the cacophony of reform proposals and the relentless barrage of data on every aspect of schools, decision makers at all levels are clearly thirsting for the rational and disciplined evidence provided by science" (p. 4).

This thirst arises out of a climate of fear, much like that created by the Wicked Witch in Oz. Testing corporations expose exactly who is failing, and based on standardized test scores, states are mandated to "develop a system of sanctions and rewards to hold districts and schools accountable for improving academic achievement" (Bush, 2002, p. 3). In other words, current policy is based on the idea that schools are not doing well because they are not afraid enough. They need a threat to help them achieve. Schools that fail to make "adequate yearly progress for disadvantaged students will first receive assistance, and then come under corrective action if they still fail to make progress" (Bush, 2002, p. 3). The state and federal Winged Monkeys will swoop down on a school if it does not meet the expectations of the government. It is not, however, that the intentions of governmental regulation are evil. Rather, it is grounded in larger cultural assumptions about the usefulness of punishment as a deterrent to wrongdoing and the responsibility of those in power to meet out that punishment.

GLINDA: FOLLOW THE YELLOW BRICK ROAD

Running through the land of Oz is the Yellow Brick Road. In Littlefield's (1968) analysis, he characterizes the Yellow Brick Road as the gold standard, and Baum's original use of magical *silver* shoes (as opposed to the ruby slippers that appeared in the movie) is a symbol of the Populist argument—that adding silver to the gold standard would improve the plight of the common man. We, too, could draw a similar conclusion about the Yellow Brick Road as the gold standard for educational research. Panels of national experts have been convened to address the question of what constitutes quality research in education. An AERA Forum Report even mentions that members of a 1999 Brookings Institute began with the assumptions that, "The 'gold standard' for high quality research involves randomized field trials, so successful in medical research" (AERA, 1999). Such thinking keeps us looking for the magic pill that will cure what ails our children, rather than understanding education as a political act (Freire & Macedo, 1987) or a caring relationship (Noddings, 1992).

In this climate, the U.S. Congress charged the National Research Council (NRC) with reviewing and synthesizing "recent literature on the science and practice of scientific inquiry in education" and considering "how the federal government can best foster and support it" (National Research Council, 2002, p. 1). In their report, the NRC, in what we imagine to be a well-meaning attempt at being inclusive, includes all research as scientific by claiming that "scientific inquiry is the same in all fields" (p. 1). The report did not say that there are valid kinds of research other than scientific; rather it tries to include all research under the purview of science. The National Research Center is caught in a lexical inconsistency. On the one hand, they seem to intend the more general meaning of *science* as "a department of systematized knowledge as an object of study," but their findings evoke the more specific definition of "knowledge or a system of knowledge covering general truths or the operation of general laws *especially as obtained and tested through scientific method*" (Merriam-Webster, 2005-2006; italics added). Several times, they claim that, "The design of a study does not make the study scientific," and they mention ethnography and descriptive studies as lying within the "boundaries for the design of scientific education research" (p. 6). However, in a later article, the authors of the NRC report state:

> The bottom line is that experimentation has been shown to be feasible in education and related fields (e.g., Bogatz & Ball, 1972; Fuchs, Fuchs, & Dazdan, 1999; see also Boruch DeMoya, & Snyder in press; Orr, 1999; Murray, 1998) and is still the single best methodological route to ferreting out systematic relations between *actions and outcomes.* (Feuer et al., 2002, p. 7; italics added)

Their more methodological definition of *science* is also evident in their "six guiding principles that underlie all scientific inquiry" (p. 2) and are consistent with the National Reading Panel's (2000) report that established hypothesis testing, experimental, and quasi-experimental methods as the gold standard in reading research.

Other research traditions are clearly marginalized by the council's language. Policy derived from these definitions narrows the focus of educational research to one set of rules for gathering, analyzing, and interpreting evidence, one ideal for scholarship, one truth, one answer. Given this way of thinking, some of the greatest and influential scholarly works in composition, literacy, and English education are not valued. Works following the traditions of ethnography (like Heath's [1983] *Ways With Words* or Rose's [1989] *Lives on the Boundary*), social criticism (like Mayher's [1989] *Uncommon Sense* or Bartholomae's [1985] "Inventing the University"), theoretical inquiry into teaching and learning (like Rosenblatt's [1938] *Literature as Exploration* or Hartwell's [1985] "Grammar, Grammars, and the Teaching of Grammar"), or descriptive studies (like Flower & Hayes' [1981] and Graves' [1975] early studies of writing processes and Shaughnessy's [1977] *Errors and Expectations*) are left on the experimental or quasi-experimental cutting room floor.

> SCARECROW: Of course, people do . . . go both ways.
>
> DOROTHY: Are you doing that on purpose, or can't you make up your mind?

Ms. Everyeducator sets out on the Yellow Brick Road, strong in her belief that science will bring her home. However, she arrives at a crossroads, where she develops some doubt about the way to go. Looking for direction, she meets Scarecrow. When using the story as an allegory on Populism, Littlefield (1968) interpreted Scarecrow as representing farmers, who seem "muddleheaded" in the face of decisions about the gold standard, but who are actually very intelligent. He offers Dorothy inconclusive advice about which way to go—she can go either way. He is, however, "not feeling at all well." He considers it "very tedious being stuck up here all day long with a pole up your back." With his instruction, she helps him down, and he turns out to be an intelligent companion, offering sound advice in tricky situations. But because he cannot scare away crows and because his head is stuffed with straw, he believes he is brainless. In our allegorical interpretation, Scarecrow represents the intellect of teaching, the specialized reasoning associated with the profession (Shulman, 1987). In the experimental paradigm, teachers' ideas and abilities are undervalued, something to be controlled when designing a study. Education is reduced to an input–output formula; actions result in outcomes. There is no need for teachers to think. The underlying assumption is that the problem of educating our children will be solved if we can just get teachers to do the right things, the things we know that "work." If we can find the right combination of tricks of the trade, all students will be able to read and write equally well—as judged by standardized measures. Such assumptions create a culture that represents teachers as straw people, responsible for guiding our children, but not intelligent enough to design curriculum, know what to say, or make valid evaluations of student learning.

> TIN MAN: . . . and right in the middle of a chop, I . . . I rusted solid. And I've been that way ever since.
>
> DOROTHY: Well, you're perfect now.
>
> TIN MAN: . . . . Perfect? Oh—bang on my chest if you think I'm perfect. Go ahead—bang on it!
>
> DOROTHY: Oh—!
>
> SCARECROW: Beautiful! What an echo!
>
> TIN MAN: It's empty. The tinsmith forgot to give me a heart.

Littlefield (1968) interprets the Tin Woodman as a symbol of the American worker, dominated by the magic of the Witch of the East, the East being a controlling government in Washington, devoted to the gold standard:

> Once an independent and hard working human being, the Woodman found that each time he swung his axe it chopped off a different part of his body. Knowing no other trade he "worked harder than ever," for luckily in Oz tin-smiths can repair such things. Soon the Woodman was all tin (p. 59). In this way Eastern witchcraft dehumanized a simple laborer so that the faster and better he worked the more quickly he became a kind of machine. (p. 4).

Similarly, when influential educational researchers embrace a scientist perspective (Pellegrino & Goldmen, 2002), they are making Tin Men out of themselves. They are not focusing on the complex relationships among teachers and their students, but rather on the quest for the ideal method. When education is defined this way, educational research focuses on observing and measuring results from carefully prescribed actions. The quest for method belies the human experience of learning and replaces it with packaged programs and prepared scripts (see Meyer, 2003 for an excellent case study of the effects of a reading program on a teacher). We are put in the position of constantly striving to prove what works, rather than engaging in inquiry into how and why people learn. The reward and sanction policy of NCLB transforms researchers into mechanical entities working hard at their own destruction and rusting in the deluge of policies pouring down on them. Research becomes synonymous with assessment, and political accountability (Miles & Lee, 2002) takes precedence over content or consequential validity.

> LION: Would ... would it do any good if I roared?
>
> SCARECROW: Who at?
>
> LION: I don't know.

For Littlefield, Lion represents William Jennings Bryant, a man who, although he tried hard, failed to gain support of Eastern Labor in his quest to move away from the gold standard. In our interpretation, the Lion represents the courage needed by educators who participate in qualitative, practitioner, interpretive, and critical research paradigms. These paradigms have been marginalized by the criteria for scientific that align primarily with the scientific method. Despite the claim that scientific inquiry informs policy, policy determines what kind of research is funded and validated. Criteria for funding research are mandated by researchers from one particular community, rather than arising from diverse communities of researchers that, despite the Feuer et al. (2002) claims, already exist and continue to evolve.

In his historical exploration of the "relationship between educational research and practice," Reese (1999, p. 2) explains that the science of education did not begin until the early 20th century. Underfunded and conducted mainly by amateurs, early research relied primarily on survey data to guide policymaking. Schools imitated scientific management in business to become "increasingly consolidated, standardized, removed from lay control, and professionalized" (p. 2). He reviews numerous historical accounts in search of nonideologically driven, replicable, and generalizable research with direct ties to practice. His search yields little, and he explains that the complexities of teaching make controlled experimental research difficult, if not impossible, especially in light of low government funding. He cites Clifford's (1973) account to characterize the relationship up to the 1960s:

> most historians traditionally wrote about the history of ideas, not school practices. How could one make useful claims about the impact of research on teaching? The problems were daunting. Given the existence of the most decentralized system of mass education in the Western world, researchers of American classrooms, for example, had understandable difficulty knowing what was typical, which subject was informed by what specific piece (if any) of research, or whether or not teachers taught as they were taught more than as some researchers desired. Did teachers, superintendents, and educators working in the schools read much research, think about its implications, and try to act upon it? (p. 12)

Implicit in this analysis is a criticism of the field of educational research for focusing mainly on ideas rather than hard data. This criticism is based on the assumptions that (a) research is supposed to guide practice, (b) standardization makes research into effective practices easier, and (c) it is the job of school personnel to read and learn from research. To remedy this schism and unequal power structure, the notion of teachers as researchers emerged in the 1980s, but hundreds of valuable studies conducted by teachers well versed in theory and research have been counted as unscientific. They are neither mentioned in the NRC report nor acknowledged in Snow's (2001) AERA presidential address, when she states that "currently available procedures for systematizing personal knowledge and analysis of personal knowledge into publicly accessible knowledge are inadequate" (p. 4).

What counts as valid research in education remains fundamental to our identity as educators (Feuer et al., 2002) and influences educational policies that frame classroom life. We are on an epistemological journey, far from home. This journey requires that we reflect on "how people know that they know, including assumptions about the nature of knowledge and 'reality,' and the process of coming to know" (Sleeter, 2001, p. 209). Inquiry into questions of the nature of reality, knowledge, and the knower, coupled with visions for the future of society, are just as important as large-scale investigations into a particular technique or program. Rather than constantly finding our field well behind "fields such as medicine, agriculture, transportation, and technology" (Slavin, 2002, p. 15), we would argue that the attention paid to ideas and personal knowledge is not a flaw in educational research, but a feature of a complex and constantly evolving epistemology. The act of teaching and learning is not a simple case of accurate input yielding desired output. Educators need to have the courage to speak out, to acknowledge the uniqueness of our field.

THE WIZARD: PAY NO ATTENTION
TO THE MAN BEHIND THE SCREEN

The "myth of rationality" (Ogawa et al., 2003, p. 172) has a hold on our educational system. Federal and state governments mandate that K-12 curriculum and teacher education courses be based on scientific research and grounded in standards. Aligning standards, pedagogy, and outcomes is desired (Slavin, 2002) and fair. Students have the right to know what is expected, to have opportunity to achieve those expectations, and to be assessed on what they have had the opportunity to learn. However, standards are neither objective nor scientific as implied by current standardized testing. Standards are derived socially, relationally, through consensus of educators and other stakeholders, not by careful analysis of patterns in student work, reliance on research findings, or even as a means of testing one learning theory over another. Standards are widely shared beliefs (Pence, 1998) that, even by Slavin's (2002) admission, "are open for interpretation." Standards represent a collective vision of our culture, our children, and our future, no more, no less, and, as such, are useful for reflective inquiry into our educational system. However, they do not represent what students will need to know and be able to do for all times and in all situations. They are our best guess at what people need to know and be able to do at a particular time and place. Definitions of literacy and descriptions of what literate people do have evolved throughout our history (Myers, 1996) and will continue to do so. The search for what works will never cease because our worldview is constantly changing, and what works is determined by society's values, not by some predetermined truth.

In addition, overvaluing experimental and quasi-experimental design does not necessarily ensure that all "interventions or approaches in education that have a demonstrated beneficial causal relationship to important student outcomes." Even the What Works Clearinghouse (2004), a Web site devoted to cataloguing results of educational experiments, recognizes that none of the interventions tested is applicable to all populations of students in all situations. We cannot control enough variables in any experimental study to make it any more worthwhile or generalizable to widely varying contexts than strong ethnographies. Standards-based curriculum approaches can be scientifically evaluated, but they are no guarantee of educational success and can actually lead to narrowing of curriculum and deskilling of teachers when applied without an overarching philosophy (Ogawa et al., 2003). A teacher's theoretical perspective affects what they say and do in the classroom (Grossman & Shulman, 1994). Hence, a teaching technique can vary according to how an individual teacher incorporates it into his or her instructional repertoire. For example, Marshall, Smagorinsky, and Smith (1995) found that two teachers can enact classroom discussions in diametrically opposed ways, with vastly different student learning, and still call them discussions. In other words, the teacher's ideas that frame instruction influence how techniques are used. In addition to the teachers involved in implementing a teaching technique, we also have to take into account the students who comprise the classroom and school culture—how their ages and where they live; their economic, ethnic, racial, age, home backgrounds; cognitive and social styles; their community belief systems; and the context of the classroom and school affect their interpretation and use of any educational activity. Teaching is not implementation of technique, but the creation of a culture and should be studied as such.

> DOROTHY: Oh, will you help me?
>
> GLINDA: You don't need to be helped any longer. You've always had the power to go back to Kansas.
>
> SCARECROW: Then why didn't you tell her before?
>
> GLINDA: Because she wouldn't have believed me. She had to learn it for herself.

It is overly simplistic to expect a one-to-one correlation between research and practice when perhaps the greatest gift of educational research is that it allows us to position ourselves in relationship to others and to better understand the structures in which we operate. Just as successful readers monitor their comprehension and their belief of what a text means (NRP, 2000), successful educators and researchers monitor their own thinking and act on it. Even the scientifically rigorous NRP reports that teachers need to be flexible in their strategies (NRP, 2000), and so, we would argue, do researchers. No one method is capable of transforming literacy, especially when notions of literacy are constantly evolving (Myers, 1996). Maybe it is not in our adoption of specific techniques, but in the exploration of our own assumptions, not placing value in the arrival, but in the journey—returning to where we began as smarter, more courageous, and compassionate.

Finally, educators cannot rely on traditional tried-and-true nor scientifically proven methods because we need to keep up with a constantly evolving society. People change based on our individual and collective vision of the kind of life we desire for ourselves and for those about whom we care. Even physics, the hardest of all sciences, is showing us the folly of objective truth when it demonstrates that research outcomes are affected by the intention of the researcher. We can not rely solely on scientific research to guide our policy and practice, and evidence can be interpreted in a myriad of ways. What should guide us is a well-reasoned, reflective, and living imagination. The ultimate value of all kinds of research, scientific or otherwise, is not, like the Wizard of Oz, its power over us, but its ability to hold up a mirror to our own beliefs and their consequences.

DOROTHY: "O . . . WHAT AM I GOING TO DO?"

Bill Smith is probably the best example of an educator and researcher who acknowledges the limits and worth of differing research paradigms. Through our relationship with him, we learned to value both personal insight and systematic inquiry; to understand the interpretive nature of quantitative inquiry and the rigor of ethnography; to trust our instincts while constantly interrogating them in light of hard data; to be strong in our beliefs, but open to change. He taught us how to not be "namby pamby graduate students" and to live with integrity in a world of conflicting agendas. Linda relates a story that illustrates these qualities:

> Bill Smith's assessment program for the composition program was both efficient and elegant, particularly in the care with which he developed, piloted, scheduled and distributed prompts for the end-of-term exam for sections of Basic Writing. A few weeks before the end of my first term teaching Basic Writing, several of us teachers opened our assessment packets and discovered that the reading for the exam was horribly familiar: we had assigned it to our students as part of their sequence of instruction. We hadn't even finished the course and already we were big-time screw-ups. And we were convinced that Bill was going to kill us.

What was a disaster in our eyes, however, was something altogether different for Bill: "This will give us a chance to run a little study to see if it makes a difference if students have read the passage before the exam." (It didn't.) For Bill, the everyday challenges of the classroom produced questions to answer things to compare, opportunities to learn.

Bill was indeed our Glinda the Good Witch. He set us on the path, gave us the tools we needed, and allowed us to discover their power. Educational researchers can learn from his example that our future can lie beyond the Yellow Brick Road (John & Taupin, 1973).

REFERENCES

AERA. (1999, September,). Education research and education policy: From conclusions to conundrum. *Forum Report. ER&P Archives.* Retrieved August 1, 2003, from http://www.aera.net/gov/archive/r1299-03.htm

Algeo, J. (1986, May 16–18). Oz and Kansas: A theosophical quest. In, R.A. Thompson & S. Gannon (Eds.), *Proceedings of the 13th annual conference of the Children's Literature Association,* University of Missouri–Kansas City (pp. 135–139). Retrieved August 1, 2003, from http://www.theosophical.org/theosophy/oz/ozandkansas/index.html

Bartholomae, D. (1985). Inventing the university. In M. Rose (Ed.), *When a student can't write* (pp. 134–165). New York: Guilford.

Baum, L. F. (1930/1999). *The wizard of Oz.* New York: Aladdin Paperbacks/Simon & Schuster.

Bunnell, D. (1974). Tin Man. Recorded by America on the album *Holiday.* Produced by Gearge Martin. Warner Bros., Los Angeles, CA.

Bush, G. W. (2002). *No child left behind.* Retrieved August 1, 2003, from http://www.rethinkingschools.org/special_reports/bushplan/index.shtml

Clifford, G. J. (1973). A history of the impact of research on teaching. In R. M. W. Travers (Ed.), *Second handbook of research on teaching* (pp. 1-46). Chicago, IL: Rand McNally.

Ebert, R. (2003). *The wizard of Oz.* Retrieved August 1, 2003, from http://www.suntimes.com/ebert/greatmovies/oz.html

Feuer, M. J., Towne, L., & Shavelson, R. J. (2002). Scientific culture and educational research. *Educational Researcher, 31*(8), 4–14.

Flower, L., & Hayes, J. R. (1981). A cognitive process theory of writing. *College Composition and Communication, 32*(4), 365-387.

Freire, P., & Macedo, D. (1987). *Literacy: Reading the word and the world.* South Hadley, MA: Bergin & Garvey.

Graves, D. H. (1975). An examination of the writing processes of seven year old children, 9(3), 227-241.

Green, J. (1998). *The zen of Oz.* Los Angeles: Renaissance Books.

Grossman, P. L., & Shulman, L. S. (1994). Knowing, believing and the teaching of English. In T. Shanahan (Ed.), *Teachers thinking, teachers knowing* (pp. 3–22). Urbana, IL: NCTE.

Hartwell, P. (1985). Grammar, grammars, and the teaching of grammar. *College English*, 47(2), 105–127.

Heath, S. B. (1983). *Ways with words: Language, life and work in communities and classrooms.* Cambridge, England: Cambridge University Press.

John, E., & Taupin, B. (1973). *Goodbye yellow brick road.* Los Angeles, CA: Island Records. Available at www.islandrecords.com

Johnson, A. (2000). *The spirituality of Oz: The meaning of the movie.* Retrieved August 1, 2003, from http://theosophical.org/theosophy/oz/spiritoz/index.html

Langley, N., Ryerson, F., & Woolf, E. A. (1939). *Wizard of Oz.* Retrieved August 1, 2003. from http://www.geocities.com/classicmoviescripts/script/wizardofoz_script.txt

LeGuin, U. K. (1992). Dreams must explain themselves. In S. Wood (Ed.), *The language of the night: Essays on fantasy and science fiction* (pp. 47-56). New York: Harper Collins.

Littlefield, H. M. (1968). *The wizard of Oz: Parable on populism.* Retrieved August 1, 2003, from http://www.amphigory.com/oz/htm

Marshall, J. D., Smagorinsky, P., & Smith, M. W. (1995). *The language of interpretation: Patterns of discourse in discussions of literature* (NCTE Research Report No. 27). Urbana, IL: NCTE.

Mayher, J. (1989). *Uncommon sense: Theoretical practice in language education.* New York: Heinemann/Bonyton/Cook.

Merriam-Webster Dictionary. (2005-2006). Retrieved August 1, 2003, from www.m-w.com

Meyer, R. J. (2003). *Captives of the script: Killing us softly with phonics.* Retrieved August 1, 2003, from http://www.rethinkingschools.org/special_reports/bushplan/capt174.shtml

Miles, C. A., & Lee, C. (2002, April 1–5). *In search of soundness in teacher testing: Beyond political validity.* Paper presented at the annual meeting of the American Educational Research Association, New Orleans, LA.

Myers, M. (1996). *Changing our minds: Negotiating English and literacy.* Urbana, IL: NCTE.

National Reading Panel. (2000). *Report of the National Reading Panel: Teaching children to read.* Washington, DC: National Institutes of Health.

National Research Council. (2002). Scientific research in education. In R. J. Shavelson & L. Towne (Eds.), *Committee on scientific principles for education research.* Washington, DC: National Academy Press. Retrieved August 1, 2003, from www.nap.edu.

Noddings, N. (1992). *The challenge to care in schools: An alternative approach to education* (Contemporary Educational Thought). New York: Teachers College Press.

Ogawa, R. T., Sandholtz, J. H., Martinez-Flores, M., & Scribner, S. P. (2003). The substantive and symbolic consequences of a district's standards-based curriculum. *American Educational Research Journal, 40*(1), 147–176.

Pelligrino, J. W., & Goldman, S. R. (2002). Be careful what you wish for—you may get it: Educational research in the spotlight. *Educational Researcher, 31*(8), 15–17.

Pence, L. E. P. (1998). Saying so will (not) make it so: Theoretical perspective in standards setting. *English in Australia, 122,* 56–69.

Reese, W. J. (1999). What history teaches about the impact of educational research on practice. In A. Iran-Nejad, & P. D. Pearson (Eds.), *Review of research in education* (pp. 1–19). Washington, DC: AERA.

Rose, M. (1989). *Lives on the boundary: The struggle and achievements of America's underprepared.* New York: Penguin.

Rosenblatt, L. (1938). *Literature as exploration.* New York: Modern Language Association.

Shaughnessy, M. (1977). *Errors and expectations: A guide for the teacher of basic writing.* New York: Oxford University Press.

Shulman, L. S. (1987). Knowledge and teaching: Foundations of the new reform. *Harvard Educational Review, 57*(1), 1–21.

Slavin, R. (2002). Evidence-based education policies: transforming educational practice and research. *Educational Researcher, 31*(7), 15–21. Retrieved August 1, 2003, from http://www.aera.net/

Sleeter, C. E. (2001). Epistemological diversity in research on preservice teacher preparation for historically underserved children. In W. G. Secada (Ed.), *Review of research in education* (pp. 209–225). Washington, DC: AERA.

Snow, C. E. (2001). Knowing what we know: Children, teachers, researchers. *Educational Researcher, 30*(7), 3–9.

St. Pierre, E. A. (2002). "Science" rejects postmodernism. *Educational Researcher, 31*(8), 25–27.

U.S. Congress. (2001). The No Child Left Behind Act of 2001. Washington, DC: Author.

U.S. Department of Education. (2002). *Strategic Plan 2002-2007.* Washington, DC. Retrieved August 1, 2003, from http://www.ed.gov/about/reports/strat/plan2002-7/plan/pdf

U.S. Department of Education's Institute of Education Sciences. What Works Clearinghouse. Accessed August 4, 2004, from http://www.what works.ed.gov

AFTERWORD

Some Thoughts on Successful Mentoring of Future Researchers

William L. Smith

My basic tenet has always been that my job as a professor is fourfold: (a) conduct research that leads to better research questions—and maybe even an answer, (b) teach courses in my area of expertise, (c) do outreach beyond the academy, and, most important, (d) replace me with much better professors.

The authors of this book fit item 4 perfectly, so I have some reason to think I have done my job. (I am writing this on the eve of my retirement, so I am allowed to be a bit vain.) This book affords me a free shot at giving advice on nourishing that better breed of professors. Here is my current list of what I consider to be the "thou shalts"—my Latest Decalogue.

I   Select really good people to mentor. (I cannot call anyone a mentee. Sounds like toothpaste.) Note that people is plural. Have several so that you will always have veterans and rookies. The veterans will teach the rookies as much as you will. Besides, at conferences, they

can root for each other. I well remember the loneliness—and ter-
ror—of my first presentation.

II   Have your own research line of inquiry. Young researchers need to
see your history (the context of your research) because, one hopes,
they will someday have their own.

III   Require all rookies to read all of your publications, chronologically. History is an excellent teacher and makes us humble (My gawd,
did I really write that back then?!).

IV   Do research every day. Although I think there is nothing more satisfying or invigorating than conducting research, I also know full
well that it is a grind, and your gang needs to see and taste that
grind. Rookies often think that all our research gets published (turn
the crank, out comes an article). They do not realize that we publish our infrequent successes, not our much more frequent failures
(can you imagine the size of our journals if we also published the
bombs?!).

V   Have everybody work on a group project, from conception to publication. Have rookies work on your latest project. Make certain
that all get authorial credit as due.

VI   Never lie. Tell them the real truth about their research, their
designs, their methods, their writing and presentations, about
research in general, about grants, grantsmanship and reviewers of
grants, about journals and how reviewers really read and decide,
and about being a faculty member—including what it takes to get
tenure (assuming tenure will still be around) and what it takes to
have a good life in the academy.

VII   At conferences, be sure to introduce your gang to everyone. Future
positions often come from such meetings, and it is a wonderful way
to grow.

VIII   Require all to write at least one article for publication or one conference presentation (I always preferred doing both) each year. Co-
authoring should be required. The days of single authoring are
happily gone. We have always done it; we just did not give our colleagues (specifically the graduate students) credit. It does not matter whether the pieces are accepted. Just doing it teaches the
process.

IX   Have the gang read the articles you are reviewing. Have them write
reviews and then discuss them. Same for grants you are reviewing.
This is excellent practice, and nothing prepares one better for publication and grant-getting. Whenever possible, get them on committees that do reviews (e.g., for presentations at conferences).

X   Have good "gang" parties at your place. It helps cement lasting
friendships.

Consider that the abstract. Here is the narrative.

I believe the hardest part of getting really good graduate students and becoming someone worthy of mentoring colleagues is preparing yourself to be open in order to gladly teach and gladly learn. Early on, I found it difficult—and embarrassing—to take the hard look at myself. What am I good at? What not? What do I rely on others for? What do they rely on me for? (Or more precisely stated: What do I allow them to rely on me for?) What am I willing to share?

Finding the answers to these questions is, of course, a life-long iterative process. The data changed as I matured, as the students pushed harder on my abilities. So the conclusions, the decalogue, also changed. Discerning and attracting those really good students become easier across time. I was very fortunate because I began my career at Georgia during the Veal–O'Donnell years (early 1970s). Ramon and Roy allowed me to be a "sorta-co-chair" on dissertations before they let me be a real co-chair. This allowed me to see them in action, and I learned much from their kindly critiques of me. I wish we could institutionalize this approach. All new faculty members should be mentored in this way. Chairing a dissertation is not the same as being a member of the committee, yet the leap is usually from member to chair. We need to develop the new faculty by having them co-chair first, until there is good evidence that they can be the mentor that major professors should be. Side note: I find it odd that comp programs quite typically require all doctoral students to take a course (or two) on how to teach freshman comp, but no courses—no training—on how to be a mentor of graduate students.

I first met most of the people I would mentor when they were students in my courses. I quite purposefully use those courses to find students I want to mentor. The characteristics I look for are (a) being prepared, (b) willing to listen—really listen—to fellow students, (c) willing to ask questions, especially questioning other students, and (d) willing to take risks and to be wrong. Conducting research requires that one be ready to do that research. This may sound obvious, but my years of reviewing articles and grants have shown me that one of the primary reasons for rejection was that the author/investigator was not ready to do the research. It was not uncommon to see a great idea (one I would have wished I thought of) in the hands of someone who could not handle it. So coming to class prepared is a marker of someone who will always be prepared. The students who listen to each other are showing two characteristics I greatly value: respect for others' views, and a desire to learn from everyone. Being a good researcher means that you will take from others as well as give to them. Being a good researcher also means giving credit to those from whom you have learned, not just those you quote. It is not possible to do collaborative research and not be a good listener. I would also note that one distinguishing trait of all good mentors is that they listen carefully. They listen more than they talk. I would like to know whether this can be taught or whether it just comes with the package. My gut tells me that there is a critical period beyond which it is not teachable. I have met few "older" faculty who are willing to make this kind of change.

Research requires questions, preferably good questions. Learning to distinguish the good questions from the less good takes time, a long time. In any class, one can spot the student who can ask the cogent, probing question. Not a question meant to belittle or embarrass, nor one to strut one's knowledge, but one which shows true interest, one that often shows one's ignorance. Students who only ask questions of the professor (certainly when I am that professor) are missing much, even most, of the knowledge and intelligence in the class. Being willing to show one's ignorance, being willing to learn from everyone, is essential to being a productive member of a research team.

Finally, and most important, Item d: being willing to take risks and be wrong. Research is a risk-taking enterprise. We all have spent a year or more on a project that did not pan out. That is not wasted time if we learn from it. The very act of submitting an article or grant is risk taking. One's reputation (and one's ego) is on the line. Researchers have to be made of sterner stuff to survive and thrive. Most students do not wish to take risks in a course. But those that do show incredible potential. Another side note: There is another common characteristic across all the students I have successfully mentored. They treat me as a colleague from the get-go. I am one of them. Not different. They remove the professor/mentor–student barrier. I can allow that to happen, I can create an atmosphere to foster it, but I have no way to make it happen. Only the students can do that. This characteristic is much harder to spot in a class unless the class develops its own organism. That has happened only a few times in courses I have taught. But when it happened, learning happened. Those are the courses one never forgets. Many of authors of this book were in those courses.

It should go without saying that mentoring is a two-way street. Unless the minds meet, mentoring as I know it cannot happen. Thus, students need to know how to pick the professors they can work with. This can be difficult because we in composition programs typically do not have a model that allows students, during their first year, to work with each faculty member. They meet us only in courses, and they do not have a how-to book for picking us. It has been my experience that most students apply to and select a university or program, not a professor. In the few cases where that was not true, a professor had a hand in helping the student select where she or he was going for the next degree. In most cases, the students do not visit the campus and "interview" the faculty and students before making their selection. Therefore, we have to be more proactive in helping them have a successful, productive time during their graduate work. I think we could increase the chances that the mentoring relationship would take root if we were to provide more systematic exposure to the faculty and to each faculty member's graduate students. I know for certain that students could quickly determine whom they could not work with.

When I talk about mentoring, I am usually asked about failure, mine and the students'. I honestly do not have an answer. We all think we have failed in some ways. Certainly, I believe I could have done a better job with some students. But only those students can explain my failure, and few have returned to say, "You blew it." I do not think the students ever really blew it. The failures, I believe, were not of people, but of timing. We were not right for each other at that particular time. Our brains did not mesh, or the student did not fit in with the gang. In some ways, the other students are more demanding and more frightening than I. Being around the authors of this book requires someone special. Not all graduate students can tolerate sitting on that high-tension wire. I cannot stress enough the importance of having a group (the gang). Each will have her or his own research, so the group members will, by being together, all learn from each other. Invariably, some will be better at methodology, some better at analysis, and so on. Thus, the collaboration evolves, as does learning answers to the "look at myself" questions posed earlier. I can attest that the authors of this book (and others not represented) all began their careers about 10 miles ahead of where I began mine.

The gang is best served when those students have varied backgrounds and interests. While at Pitt, I had the pleasure of working with students from different departments and from Carnegie Mellon (and the pure joy of working with those faculty members). I believe that all of my students gained much from being around this diversity of thought, of method, of program ethos. Composition, as a discipline, is rapidly maturing, but its future maturation depends on how much it learns and adapts from other disciplines and ways of thinking. The great strides in all fields have come from cross-fertilization, which is why so many disciplines are hyphenated. One way we can help that maturation is to ensure that the students we mentor have multiple opportunities to work with (or just be around) a diversity of colleagues. It is not enough to have one member of a dissertation committee come from a different department. We have to have our students meet that diversity from the beginning of their graduate careers. Fortunately, there are now technologies that help foster that cross-group encounter (e.g., e-mail, video-conferencing, desktop sharing software, and streaming video). There is no longer a good reason to not have my students at my university have regular meetings with yours at your university. Indeed, were I starting out today, I would be contacting you to help me teach my courses by using IP videoconferencing. How wonderful to have students at two (or more) universities being taught by more than one faculty member, especially when those faculty members have different views.

My colleagues, especially those who have different views, have certainly shaped and reshaped my research line of inquiry. But my graduate students have had a strong hand in that shaping and reshaping. What began with looking at syntax in developing writers morphed eventually into studying placement testing partially because I matured, but also because my students and colleagues led me to new ideas and new questions. If I did not have those students and colleagues, I would not have gone down those paths. That evolution of a line of inquiry is typical of all productive researchers, so having students read my history gives them, as all reading of history does, a glimpse of their future. Side note: One of the best assignments for a graduate course is to have each student pick a researcher and read, chronologically, all that the person has written. They really get to know that person. Conducting research, I have come to realize, may be in many ways natural, but it is also difficult. Like a muscle, it requires daily training. A major part of being a mentor is being a model. If research is a normal part of my day, my students will take note, and it will more likely become part of their days. They will also learn that researchers have to also do the hard parts, the stuff that is not fun. For me, analyzing data was fun and designing a study a real joy, but writing the articles was a bore and a pain (which is why I dearly loved working with those great writers with whom I co-authored). Again, this shows students that knowing one's strengths and weaknesses leads to productive collaboration. The best model I have found for learning to collaborate—and to give up territory—is to require work on group projects. The new students typically do not have projects well formulated, so have them and everyone else work on the "next project in the sequence." This gives them a chance to learn by doing, by apprenticing. Some of my fond memories are of the rookies suddenly understanding something and of their coming to realize that they too could make valuable contributions. But the fondest memories have to be of the responses those students had to seeing their names as authors. Being a part of the group made that even more special. In the bad old days when I debuted, co-authorship was rare. Although I felt incredible elation at seeing my name in print for the first time, the elation would have been greater had I shared it with a co-author. Collaboration requires honesty, and such honestly has to be modeled by the mentor at all times. It really does not help to tell someone that "X is fine" when it is not. Case in point. A student recently came to see me. He was obviously distraught. He had submitted a proposal for a session at a conference. He had given that proposal to a faculty member and was told that it was just fine. *Fine* was not one of the words on the rejection. Had that faculty member told him the truth—that his text was not well written and that his conclusions did not really come from the data presented—the pain would have been far less. Rejection from a professor can never be as great as rejection from reviewers. The student had great fears that those reviewers would remember him and never accept anything he would write in the future. Fortunately, he believed me when I told him that reviewers are human and thus have limited memory spans. The sad part of this story is that that student will never trust that professor again. Because of confidentiality, I cannot tell that professor how badly he blew it.

Shakespeare wrote, "Let me not to the marriage of true minds admit impediments." That pretty well says it all. Not telling the bald truth to the people you are mentoring, although it may hurt, admits those impediments and dissolves the marriage. The same, of course, has to be true when students or colleagues read your drafts. Some of the most productive criticism I have received has come from graduate students and colleagues, not from reviewers. This is also part of the modeling. I can produce some not so stellar text.

I am partial to having students give sessions or poster presentations at conferences. This is an excellent ways to fly a draft of an article. I suspect that more people attend a presentation than read the article in a journal (I have always wanted to do that study). Getting to talk with the very people whose articles you have recently read allows one to get a much deeper understanding. Print is much more limiting than dialogue. I remember introducing one graduate student to Richard Lloyd-Jones (a near deity), who proceeded to make that student feel like an esteemed colleague. What a joy that was to watch. Moral: Remember to do the same for others' students. In fact, I suggest arranging such meetings. Lunch or dinner with "the biggies in the field" is also productive. Many of us will remember some hours-long dinners in New Orleans at LaRuths. The restaurant is gone, but not the memories. I also recall a conference in Pittsburgh where we "owned" a table in a bar for about 3 days. We must have designed a dozen studies on the butcher paper on the table. I remember copying notes onto napkins. I wish I had kept them. Such informal sessions are basically how the Ramon Veal Research Seminar started.

Almost every student who has worked with me has on at least one occasion come to my office to complain about what he or she considered to be a terrible piece in a journal. My response has been, "That's why you should send your stuff to journals." It has always struck me as odd that we ask graduate students to write "papers" for courses, papers that are submitted only to us. What we should do is have them write the first drafts of articles that will be submitted to journals or presentations to be submitted to conferences. The feedback from the reviewers is far more potent than our mere scribbling. If I give a student an A on a paper, it means little. But if that paper is good enough for an A, it should be good enough to submit. If it is submitted and accepted, then there is a new entry in the student's CV, and that is real currency when job hunting. If nothing else, we should make deals with each other to read each other's students' papers. Your comments will mean more to them than mine, and you will get to "meet" my brilliant students (people you should hire or co-author with).

I did some research for courses I teach to graduate students in Physiology and Pharmacology and in Medical Informatics. I analyzed issues of highly rated journals, looking at three factors: citations of articles written by the members of the journal's editorial board, number of articles published in the journal by the members of the journal's editorial board, and how many of those articles were revised (many journals cite the submission and revision dates). It should not be surprising that those who review are more likely to be published and cited and to have quite different revision patterns. Of course I have no way of knowing how many times they had articles rejected, and I admit that reviewers are more senior researchers. But the evidence from that research, to me, clearly states what should be obvious: If you learn to read critically—as all reviewers must—there is a transfer to your writing. I would maintain that reviewing may be the best way to learn to write. If one reads only the published stuff, there is less to learn than if one reads the full range from "outright reject" to "publish as is." Reading the full range helps decrease the feeling—one I remember well from my early years—that "I can't compete with that." You learn what makes reviewers accept and reject. You learn to think like the reviewer. One of the truths that is too often not told is that one has to write for the reviewers because nothing that has been rejected by them gets to be read by the journal's audience. The whole point—the only point—of writing an article is to get it in print (same for a presentation at a conference). So, the more one knows about the real audience—those reviewers—the better the chance of getting accepted. I remember a long discussion I had with Arthur Applebee and Judith Langer when they edited *Research in the Teaching of English* (*RTE*; I was a reviewer) about the journal's (and my) acceptance percent. *RTE* did not have a high hit ratio, a concern for some, but we agreed that that was exactly how it should be. Reviewers should be filters. But reviewers should also write really good commentary on articles they reject or require to be revised. The ability to distinguish what has to be rejected from what can be revised or accepted is critical to reviewing. Distinguishing quality and then learning to write appropriate, helpful reviews is critical to learning how to write the acceptable stuff. Thus, to me it just makes sense to have my students read and write reviews of articles I am reviewing, and to share those reviews with each other. They can then review each others' (and my) texts more productively. My stated purpose is to replace me with better faculty, faculty who will be the next generation of reviewers. Thus, reading what I am reviewing and doing formal reviews of each other's works is a necessary part of the training. Of course, the same applies to grants.

I noted earlier that one should get one's students on review committees. The importance of this came home again to me recently when I helped get a student on the panel that reviews the graduate student pieces submitted for a conference. The student was reluctant (Who am I to do that?), but found it to be a compelling learning experience, one that showed her that she knew much more than she thought. She said it also changed the way she would write her next conference proposal. The transfer was complete. Finally, my real credo. If it is not fun, I really do not want to do it. I love teaching. I love doing research. I really love seeing those I have mentored become the new, better breed. But I also really loved all the great parties we had. Make sure you have great parties also.

To all of you who wrote this book and to all the rest of my graduate students, I am forever grateful to you for making me far better than I ever could have become without you.

CURRICULUM VITAE

William L. Smith

EDUCATION

1969   Ph.D., The Florida State University
       English Linguistics
       Dissertation: The effect of syntax on reading

1967   Summer Institute in Linguistics, University of Michigan

1967   M.A., The Florida State University
       English Linguistics

1965   M.A., North Texas State University
       English Literature
       Thesis: The development of the concept of the image of the city
       in the critical works of Charles Williams

1962   B.A., North Texas State University
       Business Administration and English

PROFESSIONAL EXPERIENCE

1997–2000	Associate Director, Center for Women's Health, Oregon Health & Science University
1995–present	Director, Educational Communications, Oregon Health & Science University
1994–present	Professor, Oregon Health & Science University
1992–1994	Chair, College Writing Board, University of Pittsburgh
1992–1994	Director, Composition Program, University of Pittsburgh
1991–1992	Associate Director, Composition Program, University of Pittsburgh
1991–1992	Director of Basic Writing, Composition Program, University of Pittsburgh
1984–1994	Director of Testing, University of Pittsburgh
1982–1994	Director, Computers in Composition, University of Pittsburgh
1979–1994	Professor, Department of English, University of Pittsburgh
1979–1992	Director, University of Pittsburgh Writing Workshop
1978–1979	Lecturer, Department of English, Framingham State College
1974–1979	Associate Professor, Reading and Language Education Department, Boston University
1969–1974	Assistant Professor, Language Education Department and Linguistics Faculty, University of Georgia
1969–1971	Research Associate, University of Georgia Research and Development Center, University of Georgia
1966–1969	NDEA Fellow, Department of English, The Florida State University
1964–1966	Instructor, English Department, Sul Ross State College

PUBLICATIONS

Book Chapters

Assessing the adequacy of holistically scoring essays as a writing placement technique. In M. Williamson and B. Huot (Eds), *Validating Holistic Scoring for Writing Assessment: Theoretical and Empirical Foundations.* Hampton Press. 1993.

The importance of teacher knowledge in college composition placement testing. In J.R. Hayes et al. (Eds), *Reading Empirical Research Studies: The Rhetoric of Research*, Lawrence Erlbaum. 1992.

Reading and understanding hypothesis testing research. In R. Brause & J. Mayher (Eds), *Search and Re-Search: What the Inquiring Teacher Needs to Know.* London: Falmer Press. 1991. Pp. 63-90.

Differential effects of sentence-combining on college students who use particular structures with high and low frequencies. In D. Daiker, A. Kerek, & M. Morenburg (Eds), *Sentence Combining: Toward a Rhetorical Perspective.* Carbondale, IL: Southern Illinois Press, 1985. With G.A. Hull.

Error correction and computing. In J.L. Collins & E.A. Sommers (Eds), *Writing On-Line: Using Computers in the Teaching of Writing.* New York: Boynton/Cook, 1985. Pp. 89-101. With G.A. Hull.

Articles

Research

Computers in the basic writing classroom part I: A taxonomy of uses for computers in teaching basic writing. *Research and Teaching in Developmental Education,* 1990, 7, 65-73. With M. Williamson & P. Pence

CONFER: Using computers to expand conferencing capacity in the composition classroom. *Pennsylvania English,* 1990, 15, 1, 5-24.

Editing strategies and error correction in basic writing. *Written Communication,* 1987, 4, 139-154. With D. McCutchen & G. A. Hull.

Some effects of varying the structure of a topic on college students' writing. *Written Communication,* 1985, 2, 73-89. With G.A. Hull, R.E. Land, M.T. Moore, C. Ball, D.E. Dunham, L.S. Hickey, & C.W. Ruzich.

Direct and indirect measurement of effects of specific instruction: Evidence from sentence combining. *Research in the Teaching of English,* 1983, 17, 285-289. With G.A. Hull.

Interrupting visual feedback in writing. *Perceptual and Motor Skills,* 1983, 57, 963-978. With G.A. Hull.

The effects of covert and overt cues on written syntax. *Research in the Teaching of English,* 1980, 14, 19-38. With W.C. Combs.

Adjusting syntactic structures to varied levels of audience. *Journal of Experimental Education,* 1978, 46, 4, 29-34. With M.B. Swan.

Increasing ninth grade students' awareness of syntactic structures through direct instruction. *Research in the Teaching of English,* 1975, 9, 257-262. With R.C. O'Donnell.

Modifying teachers' attitudes toward speakers of divergent dialects through in-service training. *Journal of Negro Education,* 1974, 43, 82-91. With W.H. Agee.

Syntactic recoding of passages written at three levels of complexity. *Journal of Experimental Education,* 1974, 43, 66-72.

Syntactic recoding of passages written at three levels of complexity. *Studies in Language Education,* 1973, Report No. 5.

The controlled instrument procedure for studying the effect of syntactic sophistication in reading: The second study. *Journal of Reading Behavior*, 1973, 5, 242-252.

Use of an instructional module to heighten awareness of syntactic structure. *Studies in Language Education*, 1973, Report No. 3. With R.C. O'Donnell.

The effects of transformed syntactic structures on reading. In *Language, Reading, and the Communication Process*, Carl Braun (Ed.), International Reading Association, Newark, DE, 1971, Pp. 52-62.

Pedagogical

Using a college writing workshop in training future English teachers. *English Education*, 1984, 16, 76-82.

Prologue. *English Education*, 1983, 15, 3-4.

Readers speak out: Results of a survey of *English Education* readers. *English Education*, 1982, 14, 131-141. With R. Rattigan.

Language awareness and reading comprehension. In G.S. Pinnell (Ed.), *Discovering Language with Children*. Urbana, IL: National Council of Teachers of English, 1981.

The potential and problems of sentence-combining. *English Journal*, 1981, 70, 6, 79-81.

Teaching real English in the vocational schools. *Focus*, 1979, 5, 3, 30-32.

Some recent research on written composition. *Notes and News*, February, 1979, 6-9.

The cloze procedure as applied to reading. *Buros' Mental Measurements*, 1978.

Close encounter of an old kind: Authoritarianism. *English Journal*, 1978, 67, 9, 10-11.

Needed research on the language development of school age children. National Council of Teachers of English, 1977.

The University of Georgia teacher education program in English. *English Education*, 1976, 7, 4, 218-235. With W.G. Ellis et al.

College foreign language study: What students and faculty say about it. *Studies in Language Education*, 1975, Report No. 11. With T.B. Kalivoda.

An historical explanation for pejorative usage. *Ohio English Bulletin*, 1973, 14, 1, 7-9.

Syntactic control in writing: better comprehension. *Journal of Reading*, 1972, 15, 5, 355-358. With G.E. Mason.

Technical Reports

Analysis of the differences in the syntactic structures used by James Kilpatrick in his oral and written discourse. Boston University, 1977.

Adjusting syntactic structures to varied levels of audience. Consortium for Basic Research in English, 1976, Report No. 4. With M.B. Swan.

An evaluation of the SCRATCH program: A study in syntactic complexity. Boston University Advisory Commission on Research, Project No. GRS-463-SOE, 1976. With M.B. Swan.

Syntactic discrepancies in tests of oral reading. Boston University, 1975.

Oral reading rate and the syntactic level of reading passages. University of Georgia, 1974. With G.E. Mason.

Characteristics of syntax used by junior high school students when rewriting controlled stimulus passages written at varied levels of syntactic complexity. University of Georgia Research and Development Center, 1972.

Comparison of syntax and morphology used by first grade students with and without preschool experience. University of Georgia Research and Development Center, 1970.

Comparison of syntactic complexity and global rating scores of early elementary school children, using two modes of writing. University of Georgia Research and Development Center, 1970.

The influence of sentential coordination on reading comprehension of passages written at low levels of syntactic complexity. University of Georgia Research and Development Center, 1969.

The influence of single and multiple relativization on reading comprehension of passages written at varied levels of syntactic complexity. University of Georgia Research and Development Center, 1969.

The development of reading comprehension passages controlled for vocabulary yet written at multiple levels of syntactic complexity. University of Georgia Research and Development Center, 1969.

Reviews

Review of *Teaching Fundamental English Today. English Journal*, 1978, 67, 5, 80-89. With S.E. Didriksen.

Review of *Clues to Reading Progress. Journal of Reading*, 1973, 16, 488-497. With P.A. Brown.

Books

Class Size and English in the Secondary School, Urbana, IL: ERIC Clearinghouse on Reading and Communication Skills and the National Council of Teachers of English, 1986. With the members of the NCTE Task Force on Class Size and Workload in Secondary English Instruction.

Editor of *Reflections*, by C. McAdoo and D. McAdoo. Manteo, NC: Island Press. 1976.

Test and Measurement Texts

Each of the following is a set of six books for grades 7-12. Only the general title
is give for each set. (N=Book Number)

Chapter and Unit Tests: Book N of THE ENGLISH BOOK: A COMPLETE COURSE.
Chicago, IL: Science Research Associates, 1983. With S. Koziol.

Whole Book Tests: Book N of THE ENGLISH BOOK: A COMPLETE COURSE.
Chicago, IL: Science Research Associates, 1983. With S. Koziol.

Instructor's Manual: Book N of THE ENGLISH BOOK: A COMPLETE COURSE.
Chicago, IL: Science Research Associates, 1983. With S. Koziol.

GRANTS

National Council of Teachers of English Research Foundation, Symposium on
research on the effects of class size in high school English classes, 1985-1986.

National Council of Teachers of English Research Foundation, Short-term and
long-term reliability of college essay placement scores, 1985.

Ford Foundation, Using cognitive research and computer technology to improve
writing in low performing college students, University of Pittsburgh, 1983-1986.

National Council of Teachers of English Research Foundation, The effects of
instruction in single sentence-combining strategies and of overt cues on syntactic choices in college students' writing, 1981.

University of Pittsburgh Central Development Fund, Contrastive analysis of
voice, error, and syntax in essays written by basic and general writers, 1980.

University of Pittsburgh Faculty of Arts and Sciences, Analysis of data gathered
in three research projects conducted during 1979-1980, 1980.

Boston University Graduate School Research Grant, An evaluation of the
SCRATCH Program: A study of syntactic complexity, 1975.

United States Office of Education, Workshop in training teachers to teach students with divergent dialects, University of Georgia, 1972. With W.H. Agee.

NDEA, Institute in Linguistics, Sul Ross State College, 1965.

PROFESSIONAL ACTIVITIES

Editorships

1997-1998   Editor, Special Issue of *Assessing Writing* on Validity

1993-present   Editorial Board, *Assessing Writing*

1985-2000   Editorial Board, *Written Communication*

1983-1988	Editor, *Newsletter*, publication of the American Educational Research Association Special Interest Group on Writing
1983	Guest Editor, *English Education*, Vol. 15, No. 1
1979-1984	Consulting Editor, *Journal of Research and Development in Education*

Reviewer for Journals

2002-present	*Journal of Writing Assessment*
1993-present	*Assessing Writing*
1992	*Journal for Research in Mathematics Education*
1992	*American Educational Research Journal*
1987-present	*College Composition and Communication*
1985-present	*Written Communication*
1976-1978	*Language Arts*
1975-present	*Research in the Teaching of English*

Committees

National Organizations

1993-1996	Chair, Trustees, Research Foundation, National Council of Teachers of English
1991-1996	Trustee, Research Foundation, National Council of Teachers of English
1987-1997	Conference on College Communication and Communication Standing Committee for ERIC/RCS Evaluation
1974-1994	Member, Standing Committee on Research, National Council of Teachers of English
1990-1991	President, American Educational Research Association, Special Interest Group on Writing
1988-1989	Conference Program Co-Chair, American Educational Research Association Special Interest Group on Writing
1987-1988	Conference Program Co-Chair, American Educational Research Association Special Interest Group on Research on Writing Skills
1985-1986	Coordinator, Symposium on Research on the Effects of Class Size on Student Achievement in High School English Classes, National Council of Teachers of English
1985-1986	Member, Program Selection Committee, American Educational Research Association Special Interest Group on Research on Writing Skills

1985-1989	Secretary and Treasurer, American Educational Research Association Special Interest Group on Research on Writing Skills
1983-1985	Chair, National Council of Teachers of English Task Force on the Effects of Class Size and Workload in Secondary English
1983-1984	Member, Nominating Committee, Conference on English Education
1982-1984	Member, Committee on Instructional Technology, National Council of Teachers of English
1978-1984	Member, Committee on Language Acquisition of Young Children, National Council of Teachers of English
1977-1984	Chair, Selection Committee, National Council of Teachers of English Promising Research Award
1976-1978	Chair, National Council of Teachers of English Institute on Research on Language Development

State and Regional Organizations

1997-present	Member, Distance Learning Steering Committee, Oregon State System of Higher Education
1994-present	Member, Inter-institutional Assessment Committee, Oregon State System of Higher Education
1994-present	Member, Inter-institutional Technology Committee, Oregon State System of Higher Education
1978-1979	Member, Task Force on Writing, New England Association of Teacher of English
1978-1979	Member, Higher Education Committee, Massachusetts Council of Teachers of English

DISSERTATIONS

Director or Co-Director

Latchaw, Joan S. *A Pedagogical Model Designed To Help Students Develop Strategies For Critical Thinking Within A Reading And Writing Context.* Department of English, University of Pittsburgh, 1991.

Hall, Mary. *A Cognitive Model For Business Writing.* English Department, University of Pittsburgh, 1990.

Ruzich, Constance M. *Investing in Writing: A Study of Negotiated Meanings of Writing in Two Graduate Business Classes.* School of Education, University of Pennsylvania, 1989.

Garrow, John R. *Assessing and Improving the Adequacy of College Composition Placement.* Department of Instruction and Learning, School of Education, University of Pittsburgh, 1989.

Aston, Jean A. *A Participant Observer Case Study Conducted in a Traditional Developmental Writing Class in an Urban Community College of High Risk Non-Traditional Women Students Who Demonstrate Apprehension about Error Production.* Department of Instruction and Learning, School of Education, University of Pittsburgh, 1987.

Odoroff, Elizabeth. *The Influence of Writers' Perceptions of Audience on Texts: A Study of the Writing Teacher as Primary and Secondary Audience.* English Department, Carnegie Mellon University, 1987.

Parlett, James. *CONFER: An ICAI System for Prewriting and Reflective Inquiry.* English Department, University of Pittsburgh, 1987.

DeBonis, Donna M. *Dissonance and Revision: The Role and Effect of Questions Asked to a Teacher and an Online Editor by Students in Grades 5, 8, and 12.* Department of Instruction and Learning, School of Education, University of Pittsburgh, 1987.

Morrow, Daniel H. *The Relationship between Feature Alternation and Error in Writing among University Freshmen Who Select Features of Black American English in Speech.* Department of Instruction and Learning, School of Education, University of Pittsburgh, 1986.

Hull, Glynda A. *The Editing Process in Writing: A Performance Study of Experts and Novices,* English Department, University of Pittsburgh, 1985.
Recipient of three awards:
    National Council of Teachers of English Promising Research Award
    American Educational Research Association Outstanding Dissertation Award for Experimental Research.
    National Academy of Education Spencer Fellowship Award.

Land, Robert E. *Effect of Varied Teacher Cues on Higher and Lower Ability Seventh and Eleventh Grade Students' Revision of their Descriptive Essays,* Department of Instruction and Learning, School of Education, University of Pittsburgh, 1984.

Moore, Michael. *The Relationship between Problem-Finding and Originality, Craftsmanship, and Aesthetic Value of the Written Product in Two Groups of Student Writers,* Department of Instruction and Learning, School of Education, University of Pittsburgh, 1983.
    Finalist: National Council of Teachers of English Promising Research Award.

Hjelmervik, Karen M. *Trends in the Written Products of General Writing, Basic Writing and Basic Reading and Writing Students across Four Points in Time,* Department of English, University of Pittsburgh, 1982.

Sommers, Nancy I. *Revision in the Composing Process: A Case Study of College Freshmen and Experienced Adult Writers,* Department of Reading and Language, School of Education, Boston University, 1978.

Recipient of the National Council of Teachers of English Promising Research Award.

Moriarty, David J. *An Investigation of the Effects of Instruction in Five Components of the Writing Process on the Quality and the Syntactic Complexity of Student Writing.* Department of Reading and Language, School of Education, Boston University, 1978.

Swan, Mary B. *The Effects of Instruction in Transformational Sentence-Combining on the Syntactic Complexity and Quality of College-Level Writing.* Department of Reading and Language, School of Education, Boston University, 1977.

Fuller, Katherine M. *An Investigation of the Relationship between Reading Achievement and Oral and Written Language of Students Enrolled in Reading and English Classes at Gainesville Junior College.* Department of Language Education, School of Education, University of Georgia, 1974.

Smith, Gary A. *Semantic Features: A Model of Lexical Development.* Department of Language Education, School of Education, University of Georgia, 1972.

Member of Committee

Bartel, Beverly. *Efficiency of Three Instructional Strategies for Identifying Importance in Expository Discourse.* School of Education, University of Pittsburgh, in progress.

Blum, Brad C. *Two Weeks in the Life of a Social Studies Teacher: A Descriptive Field Study.* School of Education, University of Pittsburgh, in progress.

Cerone, Kathleen. *A Literary Criticism of the Lead Teacher Program in Pennsylvania.* School of Education, University of Pittsburgh, in progress.

Hamilton, Rebecca L. *Chapter I Reading Instruction: Expert Reading Specialists in an Inclass Model.* School of Education, University of Pittsburgh, in progress.

Latshaw, Nancy V. *The Narrative Discourse of Seriously Emotionally Disturbed Adolescents: Dual Landscapes.* School of Education, 1993.

Goerss, Betty L. *A Study to Train Remedial Elementary Students to Become More Sensitive to Context Clues.* School of Education, University of Pittsburgh, 1993.

McMahon, Patricia L. *A Narrative Study of Three Levels Of Reflection In A College Composition Class: Portfolio Reflection, Teacher-Student Discourse, And Teacher Journal.* School of Education, University of Pittsburgh, 1993

Loxterman, Jane A. *The Effects of Coherent Text And Engagement Interventions On Students' Comprehension Of Social Studies Text.* School of Education, University of Pittsburgh, 1992.

Norris, Linda. *Developing a Repertoire for Teaching High School English: Case Studies of Preservice Teachers.* School of Education, University of Pittsburgh, 1992.

King, Caryn. *Use of Formal Literacy Tasks In One Elementary Social Studies Classroom.* School of Education, University of Pittsburgh, 1991.

Quatroche, Diana J. *Effects of Using Visual Structures for Organizing Information on Comprehension of Narrative Text.* School of Education, University of Pittsburgh, 1991.

Garfinkel, Lynn S. *The Effect of Importance Determination Training on Elementary Students' Organization of Expository Text Material.* School of Education, University of Pittsburgh, 1991.

Wallace, David. *From Intention To Text: Developing, Implementing And Judging Intentions In Writing.* English Department, Carnegie Mellon University, 1991.

Starna, Norrine. *The Influence of Gender on the Reading Process.* English Department, University of Pittsburgh, 1990.

Greene, Stuart. *Writing from Sources: Authority in Text and Task.* English Department, Carnegie Mellon University, 1990.

Rahman, Muhammad. *Some Effects of Computers on ESL Student Writing.* School of Education, University of Pittsburgh, 1990.

Ackerman, John. *Reading and Writing in the Academy: A Comparison of Two Disciplines.* English Department, Carnegie Mellon University, 1989.

Hendricks, William. *Working at Reading and Writing: Academic Literacy for Adults.* English Department, University of Pittsburgh, 1988.

Huot, Brian A. *The Validity of Holistic Scoring: A Comparison of the Talk-Aloud Protocols of Experienced and Novice Raters.* English Department, Indiana University of Pennsylvania, 1988.

Miller, Suzanne M. *Collaborative Learning in Secondary Classroom Discussions of Expository Texts.* Department of Instruction and Learning, School of Education, University of Pittsburgh, 1988.

Orbach, Linda. *A Comparison of the Pass/Fail Rates of Traditional and Nontraditional Students on an English Composition Exit Examination.* Department of Administrative and Policy Studies, School of Education, University of Pittsburgh, 1987.

DeMario, Marilyn. *Tea and Literacy: An Ethnographic Inquiry into the Social Construction of Literacy by Basic Reading and Writing Students.* English Department, University of Pittsburgh, 1987.

Givner, Christine C. *A Descriptive Analysis of the Use of Word Processing in the Development of Composition Skills of Adult Basic Education Students.* Department of Instruction and Learning, School of Education, University of Pittsburgh, 1987.

Mawritz, Kenneth. *A Comparison of Two Contract Processes in a School District in Northwestern Pennsylvania: The Communications Laboratory and Traditional Collective Bargaining,* Department of Administrative and Policy Studies, School of Education, University of Pittsburgh, 1986.

McCutchen, Deborah. *Sources of Developmental Differences in Children's Writing: Knowledge of Topic and Knowledge of Discourse and Linguistic Form.* Department of Psychology, University of Pittsburgh, 1985.

Baiocco, Sharon A. *An Analysis of the Contexts for Writing and the Predrafting Composing Processes of Eight Students Enrolled in a First-year College English Course.* Department of Learning and Instruction, SUNY-Buffalo, 1985.

Williams, Sloane E. II. *The Effectiveness of the Clause Analysis Technique as a Predictor of Assessed Quality of Freshman Writing.* School of Education, The Catholic University of America, 1985.

Menasche, Lionel. *Discourse Mode, Enabling Metaphors, and Styles of Closure in the Composing Process: Two Case Studies Based on Interruption Interviews.* Department of Instruction and Learning, School of Education, University of Pittsburgh, 1984.

Burns, Patricia E. *The Accuracy of Teacher Self-Reports: Word and Language Study Practices in High School English Classes.* Department of Language Communications, School of Education, University of Pittsburgh, 1984.

Shelly, Lynn B. *The Writer and the Text: Deconstruction and the Teaching of Composition.* Department of English, University of Pittsburgh, 1984.

Wall, Susan. *Freshman Students and Revision: The Results from a Survey and Case Studies.* English Department, University of Pittsburgh, 1982.
> Finalist: National Council of Teachers of English Promising Research Award.

Corr, Mary A. *Effectiveness of a Written Cueing Summary in Increasing Reading Rate and Retrieval Speed.* Department of Language Communications, School of Education, University of Pittsburgh, 1981.

Piazza, Carolyn. *Teacher Training in the Writing Process and Its Effects on Student Writing Performance.* Department of Instruction and Learning, School of Education, University of Pittsburgh, 1981.

Kubilius, Ausra. *A Developmental Investigation into Low Ability and High Ability Readers' Comprehension of Intrasentential Ellipsis (Deletion) in Written Discourse.* Department of Reading and Language, School of Education, Boston University, 1979.

O'Brien, Marjorie M. *The Role and Responsibilities of the Heads of the English Departments in Massachusetts Public High Schools.* Department of Reading and Language, School of Education, Boston University, 1977.

Prochilo, Michael I. *Contemporary Semantic Studies: The Development of a Model Syllabus for the Preparation of Teachers.* Department of Reading and Language, School of Education, Boston University, 1975.

Ward, Daniel C. *The Relationship between Rated Quality and Selected Syntactic Variables in Written Compositions of Second, Fourth, and Sixth Graders.* Department of Language Education, School of Education, University of Georgia, 1974.

Lange, Jarrett F. *The Effect of Continuous and Discontinuous Enrollment on Varied Achievement Tests in Elementary and Intermediate German.* Department of Language Education, School of Education, University of Georgia, 1973.

Fetscher, Margaret E. *The Speech of Atlanta School Children: A Phonological Study.* Department of Language Education, School of Education, University of Georgia, 1971.

Midkiff, Ronald G. *Relativization in Transformational-Generative Grammar: A Model of Language Development.* Department of Language Education, School of Education, University of Georgia, 1971.

NOTES ON CONTRIBUTORS

Julie Aungst completed her Bachelors of Arts degree in English Literature, as well as her Master's of Arts degree in Teaching, at the University of Pittsburgh. She then went on to teach middle-school English for 3 years in the state of Washington for the Kent School District. Next, she taught high school English for 5 years for the Mercer Island School District. Currently she teaches English literature at The Grange School, a private British school in Santiago, Chile.

Diana Bajzek is the Associate Director of the Office of Technology for Education at Carnegie Mellon University. Ms. Bajzek brings more than 30 years of experience building technology solutions and providing technology consulting and training to educators all over North America. She has been involved in developing multimedia databases, learning management systems, and other educational technology systems.

Russel K. Durst is Professor of English at the University of Cincinnati. He has served as President of the National Conference on Research in Language and Literacy, Chair of the NCTE Standing Committee on Research, and editorial board member for the journals *College Composition and Communication*, *Language and Learning Across the Disciplines*, and *Writing Program Administration*. His essays on composition have appeared in numerous journals and edited collections. His books include *You Are Here: Readings on Higher Education for College Writers, Collision Course: Conflict, Negotiation, and Learning in College Composition;* and, co-edited with George Newell, *Exploring Texts: The Role of Discussion and Writing in the Teaching and Learning of Literature.*

Anthony Edgington is an Assistant Professor at the University of Toledo. He has published in *Teaching English in the Two Year College* and the *Journal of Teaching Writing,* along with select book chapters. His published work focuses on the areas of teacher response, mainstreaming, and using reflective writing in advanced composition and business writing courses.

Stuart Green is associate professor of English, Frank O'Malley Chair of the University Writing Program at Notre Dame, and a Fellow of the Institute for Educational Initiatives. His expertise is in the area of rhetorical theory, writing in the disciplines, and literacy. He is the lead author of a textbook on written argument, *From Inquiry and Argument,* and co-editor of *Making Race Visible: The Role of Literacy Research in Cultural Understanding* and *Teaching Academic Literacy.* He is chair of both the NCTE Assembly on Research and the NCTE Commission on Composition.

John R. Hayes is Professor of Psychology at Carnegie Mellon University. His research concerns cognitive and interpersonal factors in writing.

Vicki Hester currently teaches undergraduates courses at Texas Tech University. She earned a BA in journalism and an MA in American Literature. Her doctorate in rhetoric and composition is from the University of Louisville, where she studied writing assessment with an emphasis on the connections between large-scale assessments and classroom communities. Her research and teaching interests include assessment, writing technologies, composition theory and pedagogy, rhetoric, and discourse analysis.

Glynda A. Hull is Professor of Language, Literacy and Culture in the Graduate School of Education at the University of California, Berkeley. Editor with Katherine Schultz of *Schools Out! Bridging Out-of-School Literacies with Classroom Practice,* and author with James Paul Gee and Colin Lankshear of *The New Work Order,* her research has focused on writing, adult literacy, technology, and community-based education. Recently at UC Berkeley she received the campus' Distinguished Teaching Award. With Michael James, she co-founded Digital Underground Storytelling for You(th), a community technology center in Oakland, CA.

Brian Huot is Writing Coordinator and Professor of English at Kent State University. Over the past two decades, his work has focused on writing assessment and the administration of writing programs. Besides numerous articles and book chapters, he has authored *(Re)Articulating Writing Assessment for Teaching and Learning* and co-edited several collections, including *Validating Holistic Scoring* and *Assessing Writing Across the Curriculum*. He currently edits the *Journal of Writing Assessment*.

Michael Angelo James is a former environmental scientist for the Port of Oakland in Oakland, CA. His interests include script writing and urban comedy, serving urban youth in after-school settings, and the politics and pragmatics of creating and sustaining nonprofits. He is currently the Director of DUSTY, Digital Underground Storytelling for You(th), a community technology center that he co-founded with Glynda Hull. For this work, James and Hull recently received the University of California, Berkeley's Outstanding University–Community Partnership Award.

Dan Kirby began his teaching career as a high school English teacher, then as a high school counselor and assistant principal. After earning his doctorate in English education from the University of Colorado at Boulder, he went on to teach and be both department chair and associate dean at various universities, including the University of Georgia, the University of Arizona, and, most recently, the University of Colorado at Denver. An active professional, he has presented and published widely. His books include *Mind Matters: Teaching for Thinking* and *Inside Out: Strategies for Teaching Writing*. His most recent book is *New Directions in Teaching Writing: Memoir*.

Dawn Latta Kirby began her teaching career in 1974 as a high school English teacher and department chair, teaching students at all levels, from Special Education to Advanced Placement English classes. She received her doctorate in 1985 in English education from the University of Georgia. She has taught in several states, including Arizona, Florida, Georgia, Texas, and now Colorado. She is currently a Professor of English and English Education at Kennesaw State University, where she teaches writing and English methods courses. In addition to journal articles, she has co-authored two books with her husband, Dan Kirby: *Inside Out: Strategies for Teaching Writing* (3rd ed., 2004) and *New Directions in Teaching Writing: Memoir*.

Stephen M. Koziol, Jr. taught English in the Rochester area before going on for his doctorate at Stanford University. At the University of Pittsburgh, he coordinated the English education program, served as Director of Secondary Education Programs, and then served as Chair of the Department of Instruction and Learning. At Michigan State University, he chaired the Department of Teacher Education. Since 2003, he has served as Chair of the Department of Curriculum and Instruction at the University of Maryland. In addition to his many roles with NCTE and state departments of education on teacher accreditation issues, he has been a consultant on English teaching and English teacher learning and assessment with NAEP, ETS, INTASC, and NBPTS, and from 1994 to 1997, he was co-director of two projects in Bosnia-Herzegovina. His research and scholarship have focused on issues of teacher development and teacher assessment, program design, and the use of informal drama as active learning pedagogy in the classroom.

Joan Latchaw, an associate professor, is the graduate chair of the MA program in English at the University of Nebraska–Omaha. She specializes in composition and rhetoric, teaching courses in contemporary rhetorical theory, composition studies, ethnic literature, and first-year writing. Publications include a co-edited collection, *The Dialogic Classroom: Teachers Integrating Computer Technology, Pedagogy, and Research*, with Jeffrey Galin, as well as book chapters and articles. Her most recent scholarship focuses on computer-mediated communications. Other interests include interdisciplinary teaching and poetry writing.

Bob Land received his PhD in Language Communications from the University of Pittsburgh in 1984. Currently, he is Professor of Curriculum and Instruction at the Charter College of Education, where he directs the Reading/Language Arts Clinic, co-directs the Cal State LA Writing Project, and teaches courses in diagnosing and correcting reading difficulties and in secondary English methods. Bob has extensive experience as a high school reading specialist and English teacher, a university writing program administrator, and program evaluation researcher. His recent publications have focused on the failure of scripted reading programs to improve urban children's reading abilities. Bob can be contacted at rland@cal-statela.edu.

Susan Lawrence is a graduate student in the rhetoric program at Carnegie Mellon University.

Suzanne Miller is an Associate Professor of English education in the Graduate School of Education at the University at Buffalo, where she teaches master's and doctoral courses on language and literacy, the teaching of English, sociocultural theories of learning, and qualitative research methods. Prior to this, she taught secondary-school English for 18 years and provided curriculum and staff-development workshops for teachers. Dr. Miller's research focuses on the influence of transformative literacy teaching, curricula, and programs on student learning and school change.

J. Bradley Minnick is an Assistant Professor of English education in the English department at the University of Arkansas at Little Rock, where he teaches courses such as Grammar, Composition, and Literature. He earned his BA in English Literature, and his MEd and PhD in English and Communications Education from the University of Pittsburgh. He has presented in various venues, including

NCTE and the Holmes Group, and has written articles on problem-based learning, evaluation and assessment instruments for preservice teachers, and English teaching laboratories, as well as modules on drama and journal writing for Bosnian educators. He enjoys writing short stories and working with children in community drama for educational purposes.

Michael Moore is a Professor in the College of Education at Georgia Southern University, where he teaches courses in literacy and English education. Michael is also the editor of *English Education,* an NCTE journal. He is former Director of the Literature Commission for NCTE. His research interests include literature, literacy, and problem finding as it relates to creativity, which was the subject of his dissertation. Michael studied with Bill at the University of Pittsburgh in the early 1980s and Bill directed his dissertation.

Pamela Moss is a Professor at the University of Michigan, School of Education. She received her PhD in educational measurement from the University of Pittsburgh in 1988. Her areas of specialization are at the intersections of educational measurement, validity theory, and interpretive social science. She is co-editor of the journal, *Measurement: Interdisciplinary Research and Perspectives.*

Michael Neal is an Assistant Professor of English at Clemson University, where he currently directs the First-Year Composition Program. His research includes a study of first-year composition programs across the country, ways that new teachers understand and construct authority in the classroom, multimedia composition, and connections between writing assessments and technologies. Neal teaches a variety of writing courses, including undergraduate first-year composition and technical writing, as well as graduate courses in composition theory and professional communication.

Peggy O'Neill is an Associate Professor in the Department of Writing at Loyola College in Maryland, where she teaches writing courses and directs the first-year composition program. Her published research includes articles and book chapters on writing assessment theory and practice, composition pedagogy, and writing program administration. She has co-edited two collections, *Field of Dreams: Independent Writing Programs and the Future of Composition Studies* and *Practice in Context: Situating the Work of Writing Teachers.* She continues to be inspired by Bill's enthusiasm for learning and his witty e-mails.

Amy J. Orr is Assistant Professor of Sociology, Department of Sociology and Anthropology, at Linfield College in McMinnville, Oregon. Her main fields of interest are education, race and ethnicity, gender, social policy, and quantitative methods. She currently conducts research on educational inequalities, with particular interest in the effect of wealth on achievement and the retention of minority students.

Lucretia E. (Penny) Pence is Associate Professor in the Department of Language, Literacy, and Sociocultural Studies at the University of New Mexico in Albuquerque, New Mexico. Every time she works with graduate students, she tries to live up to the model of the professoriate that Bill Smith lives. In addition, she has also grown to truly appreciate the concept of *tweener* in her work in teacher assessment.

Linda Jordan Platt is associate professor of English at La Roche College in Pittsburgh, Pennsylvania. She uses everything that Bill Smith taught her about writing and assessment every day in her work as a teacher of freshmen composition, Director of College Writing, and teacher educator. She especially values what Bill taught her about how the fields of English and education inform and enrich one another.

Connie Ruzich is a Professor of Education and Communications at Robert Morris University. She earned a PhD in Writing at the University of Pennsylvania and a master's in Literature with a concentration in Composition and Rhetoric at the University of Pittsburgh. Although not originally from Pittsburgh (she speaks with a western New York accent), she currently lives in the Pittsburgh area and has become fascinated with jumbo, jaggers, and yinzers. Her research examines the various ways in which language use and practices shape identities, from White students' resistance when studying multicultural literature to Starbucks' use of the language of love in their corporate advertising.

Nancy Sommers is Sosland Director of Writing at Harvard, where she directs the Expository Writing Program and the Harvard Writing Project. Her most recent research is a longitudinal study, the Harvard Study of Undergraduate Writing.

Erwin R. Steinberg is Professor of English and Rhetoric at Carnegie Mellon University. His teaching and research concern writing in composition courses, business, industry, and government, as well as how meaning is derived from and assigned to novels of the early 20th century.

David L. Wallace is Professor of Rhetoric and Composition in the Department of English at the University of Central Florida, where he coordinates the Texts & Technology PhD Program. He is author of *Mutuality in the Rhetoric and Composition Classroom* with Helen Rothschild Ewald, and he has written numerous articles for such journals as *College English, College Composition and Communication, Research in the Teaching of English, JAC,* and *The Journal of Educational Psychology.* His current research interests include applying postmodern, feminist, and queer theory to pedagogy; creating alternative rhetorics; and developing a pedagogy of the personal using hybrid genres. He can no longer keep up with his 18-year-old students when he runs at the university track.

AUTHOR INDEX

SUBJECT INDEX

Lightning Source UK Ltd.
Milton Keynes UK
UKOW02f1557020815

256190UK00001B/69/P